READ FOR YOUR LIFE

two successful efforts to help people read
and an annotated list
of the books that made them want to

by

JULIA REED PALMER

The Scarecrow Press, Inc.
Metuchen, N.J.   1974

Library of Congress Cataloging in Publication Data

Palmer, Julia Reed.
  Read for your life.

  1. Socially handicapped children, Books for--
Bibliography. 2. Socially handicapped, Books for the
--Bibliography. 3. Libraries and the socially
handicapped. 4. Socially handicapped children--
Education--Reading. 5. Socially handicapped--Educa-
tion--Reading. I. Title.
Z1039.S55P35   374'.012   73-14695
ISBN 0-8108-0654-1

TO MY HUSBAND

without whose help and patience
there would have been no Buttercup
and no book

the author with part of her literary circle

ACKNOWLEDGMENTS

I am grateful to so many people in connection with the programs described in "The School Volunteer Story" and "The Buttercup Story," and for help with this book and the booklist, that I could fill another book with the names of those who have contributed in one way or another.

I wish especially to thank the late Clara Blitzer and Mrs. Mary Fisk for the opportunity to become a New York City School Volunteer. I want to thank Mrs. Faith Knapp and Mrs. Constance Pike and the many other volunteers from whom I have learned so much about how to help people to enjoy reading. Mrs. Ethel Price, of the School Volunteer staff has been invaluable in her suggestions of titles and her reports from programs all over the city as to the success or failure of a given title. Mrs. Gertrude Conroy, publicity director, helped to write the section on the New York City School Volunteer Program and all the staff have played a part in enabling me to give Book Fairs and stage book exhibitions.

Of course, I also learned a great deal from many of the teachers with whom I was associated. Among many others, I shall always be very grateful to the late Margaret Douglas, Miss Georgia Washington, Mrs. Rita Chelimsky and Mrs. Mildred Vreeland.

As far as "Buttercup" is concerned, I wish especially to thank Mr. John Humphry, who first had faith that such a project had potential, the Chase Bank Foundation, and the Trustees of the Bookmobile Service Trust: Mr. Philip Adam, Assistant to the Director, Brooklyn Public Library; Mrs. Louise Bolling, Chairman, School Board No. 16; Miss Pamela Brinton, Proprietor, Brinton Book Service; Mr. Milton Byam, Director of the District of Columbia Library system; Mr. Kenneth Duchac, Director of the Brooklyn Public Library; Mr. John Franz, Director of the National Book Committee; Mr. Humphry, Assistant Commissioner of Education of the State of New York; Mr. Paul Kerrigan,

Trustee, Brooklyn Public Library; the late Frank Kissane, Vice President, Chase Manhattan Bank; Mrs. Robert Knapp, Trustee, Public Education Association, and Chairman of its Community Relations Committee; Mrs. Thelma Robinson, Executive Committee, School Volunteers, School District No. 16; and Mr. Evan Thomas, Vice President, W. W. Norton Publishers, Inc.

I also wish to pay tribute to the wonderful staff we have had on the Bookmobile: Mrs. Audrey Farmer, Mrs. Lillian Butler, Mrs. Ernestine Robinson, Mr. Charles Jones, Mr. Harold Moore, and Mrs. Evelyn Felix. The four successive able librarians who worked for the project--Mrs. Sarah Koerner, Mrs. Judith MacGowen, Mrs. Gertrude Williams, and Miss Jean Ellen Coleman--all made enormous contributions both to the success of the project and also to the booklist and the list of materials. Mrs. Felix also contributed new and useful titles. Finally, I wish to thank our special volunteer, Mrs. Jane Weld, who came twice a week during the winter of 1967/68 to fill in wherever she was needed, on the Bookmobile or in the office. She won the hearts of both the staff and our public. I am truly grateful for the quality of help that both projects consistently received.

TABLE OF CONTENTS

WE REAL COOL

We real cool.   We
Left school.   We

Lurk late.   We
Strike straight.   We

Sing sin.   We
Thin gin.   We

Jazz June.   We
Die soon.

GWENDOLYN BROOKS

YOUTH

We have tomorrow
Bright before us
Like a flame.

Yesterday
A night-gone thing,
A sun-down name.

And dawn-today
Broad arch above the road we came.

We march!

LANGSTON HUGHES

Part I

"REAL COOL" OR A BRIGHT FUTURE?

This book presents to countless Americans a simple but vital opportunity--one which can enrich their lives if they wish to take advantage of it. Very simply, it shows how one person can make an important contribution to the solution of one of our key problems--the problem of a widespread lack of reading ability.

Few people reflect on the fact that one of the reasons for this country's strength and power is that it led the world, and still does so, in the revolutionary step of making learning and knowledge available to everyone who wants them. Even less do they reflect on the fact that in this rich and literate land, over 18,500,000* Americans above the age of sixteen are for practical purposes illiterate: they cannot read and understand documents as important to them as job applications; and if the questions are read to them and explained, they do not have a vocabulary with which they can answer them.

This means that our extensive system of education frequently does not deal effectively with the most basic of all educational tools.

A staggering proportion of our poor and illiterate remain so even after "completing" their compulsory education, or if they drop out, usually because of a failure in reading. It must seem evident that a person who cannot read or write is virtually locked out of the means to deal effectively with life, and so we have ignorance and despair,

---

*This figure comes from a survey dated September 1970, conducted for the National Reading Council by Louis Harris & Associates, Inc. Readers will find the survey which explores the range of illiteracy by geographic, income and other data, very interesting.

drugs and crime, and an ever increasing welfare problem.

Fortunately from many points of view, illiteracy is one of the few problems that an individual can help to solve. In today's complicated world, one is apt to feel that an individual has no power to affect important public problems. But here is one field where that is not so. Anyone who can read and write can teach others to do so, and herewith are presented two examples of how it can be done and how rich and rewarding the experience can be.

THE SCHOOL VOLUNTEER STORY

How One Individual Can Help

Fifteen years ago, my husband said to me, "In four or five years the children will be growing up and leaving home and you will have time on your hands. Better start thinking about what will fill their place." At first, as I still wrestled with galoshes and homework, the thought of leisure time seemed both improbable and desirable. Eventually I realized that that point of view would last about a week after the last child left for school or college, and that a transitional or part-time job while the children were still around would make me a better mother and, hopefully, a more interesting wife. As a citizen, also, it was clear that a part of my future lay in some form of public service; so I started cutting out clippings from newspapers describing various opportunities. Tentatively, I established two conditions which I considered important: I would not commute a long distance--there was need everywhere; why waste valuable time in travelling? And I would not take a job having to do with children, but seek adult company.

In spite of my established criteria, a series of circumstances which I need not describe led me in January 1958 to take a forty-minute bus ride to help in a newly-opened public school in Harlem as a School Volunteer. It proved from the very first day to be a job which was rewarding beyond measure.

To be a School Volunteer offers infinite variety, all the responsibility (and sometimes a little more) that one is ready for, endless scope for individual initiative and creativity, and a sense of solid accomplishment. Among the jobs I was handed or volunteered for in the first two or three months were 1) helping to catalog the new library books (I was shown how), 2) supervising in the lunchroom, 3) reading aloud to a group of handicapped children at lunchtime, 4) lecturing on Mexico to 6th graders whose curriculum required them to study Mexico and who had never been as far from

13

home as Central Park and, 5) helping with reading on a
one-to-one basis.

This last assignment, most important of all, is the
one through which you can, quite literally, "save a soul."
To take a child who is failing in reading or even falling
well behind, and by your faith, experience and friendship
turn him from an almost certain dropout to a person for
whom many doors are open and whose self-respect is
restored, is a never-ending miracle.

Let me describe to you a sample day of an individual
School Volunteer who can give five hours twice a week.
Mrs. James arrives at 9:30 at school and checks through
her notebook to refresh her recollection of what she did with
each of her children in her last session. She lines up the
materials she wants to use, including some she has brought.
At 9:40, in comes Sam, a cheerful obstreperous third grader
with quick wit and lots of bounce but a very limited vocabulary
and almost no reading skills. He has chosen a beautiful
book The Little Island because it has a cat in it and he likes
cats. However, it is also about the ocean and beaches and
although Sam lives on the island of Manhattan, he has never
seen the ocean nor a beach. Mrs. James has brought a
shoe box full of sand with shells in it and she and Sam feel
the sand and discuss the shells. She has also brought some
pictures of Coney Island showing boys like Sam playing
there. Sam is fascinated and quite unconsciously is learning
a great many new words which will help him to read his
book. They discuss the fish store around the corner from
the school and the fact that fishes live in the ocean. (Most
ghetto city children have no idea of where the food they eat
comes from and since food is a universal interest, a discussion of its source can lead to natural history, geography,
economics and other interesting areas.)

Sam now dictates a halting story about his cat and
how she likes fish and milk to Mrs. James, who writes it
down, and then Sam tries with some success to read it
back to her. They practice one or two hard words, play a
short game and Sam departs. The forty-minute session has
flown for both Sam and his volunteer who barely has time
to make a few notes in her book before José slides into
the chair.

José arrived only two months ago from Puerto Rico.
He speaks some English but he is very shy and seems

almost in a state of cultural shock.   Mrs. James has to
listen carefully to hear his whispered responses.   However,
José is enchanted when he spots the sand and shells and
bursts into a description--mainly in Spanish--of the beach
where he used to swim in Puerto Rico.   Seizing on his
interest, Mrs. James produces a picture dictionary and together she and José look up the English equivalents of the
words José is using.   José loves to draw and he is making
an alphabet book which will be his own personal picture
dictionary of the words he has learned.   Then, they tackle
Go, Dog, Go.   José smiles at the comical pictures and is
triumphant at having mastered the first few pages.   He is
reading a book, just like every one else and when he reads
Go for the fourth time, he says it in a firm voice loud
enough for every one to hear.

        After José departs, all the volunteers produce sand-
wiches, water is heated on a hot plate and instant tea and
coffee produced from a cupboard.   Mrs. James enjoys these
lunch sessions since the other volunteers and she can compare notes.   Some of her best schemes for motivating her
children have come from these discussions.   There are six
other volunteers, two retired accountants, a free lance
photographer, two housewives and a practical nurse who
loves children and who works a 4 to midnight shift.   The
chairman, also a volunteer, asks hopefully if any one has a
pupil who is ready to graduate from the program.   The
principal has a waiting list of sixty pupils and some of them
need help badly.   Mrs. James mentions Mickey, her next
pupil, hesitantly since he now reads on grade level and is
much relieved that the chairman doesn't feel he should yet
be graduated since Mrs. James hates the thought of parting
from him.

        When Mrs. James and Mickey first met in October,
his nine-year-old face looked old and sullen.   His hair was
unkempt and his face was filthy.   So were his hands and
wrists which were easy to see since he had long since out-
grown the ragged sweat shirt he had on.   His teacher's note
explained that Mickey was being given a last chance before
suspension--he was already known to the police, he was a
ringleader of all the problem children in the class and he
either acted up or day-dreamed.   Now Mickey bursts into
the room, his clean face eagerly searching out Mrs. James.
His hair is combed and he looks his world in the eye although his clothes are not much better than they were in
October.

How does it happen that Mrs. James has wrought a seeming miracle with Mickey? The School Volunteers are not miracle workers like Annie Sullivan. It is the magic of the one-to-one relationship--of having a child like Mickey discover that someone is his friend and cares enough about him to work with him. The interest and deep concern of the adult volunteer makes learning a shared joy instead of a lonely struggle. The volunteer is often the only grown-up with whom the child has ever had a close, personal, sympathetic relationship. Unfortunately, teachers must deal with whole classes and parents with whole families. Only the volunteer has time to nourish the timid ego and the thin self-image.

Secondly, the School Volunteer does not have to deal with curriculums nor use dull and inappropriate materials. The volunteer can tailor the materials she wants to the individual child's interests and skills. The results do, in fact, seem like a miracle. A child who has no future and is despairing becomes instead a child who can read and who therefore can go on with his education and eventually become a self-respecting, self-supporting citizen.

Mrs. James' last pupil, Mary is new to her. Until this week, Mrs. James had been helping Sally, a slow, withdrawn child who had given up hope of succeeding and who sat quietly in despairing incomprehension in the classroom waiting for school hours to be over to come alive again. With infinite pains, Mrs. James had succeeded in getting Sally to try once more to learn to read and had felt only the week before that Sally was making progress. Now came the blunt word that Sally and her family had moved to Brooklyn. The door that had been opened a crack for Sally had slammed shut again and the odds were that she would spend the rest of her school years a despairing prisoner. With effort, Mrs. James shuts Sally out of her mind and greets Mary with cheerfulness which is not reciprocated. Mary proves to be an overdeveloped sixth grader. Her teacher's slip says she is twelve years old but from her looks, she could easily pass for fourteen or even sixteen. She is sullen and self conscious as she sits at the table and nervously twists her hands. In answer to Mrs. James' questions, she says she isn't interested in anything, hates school and will drop out as soon as it is legal. She is wearing a very fancy blouse and elaborate earrings, however, and these provide a clue to her interests. She admits that she likes clothes and jewelry and wishes she could buy

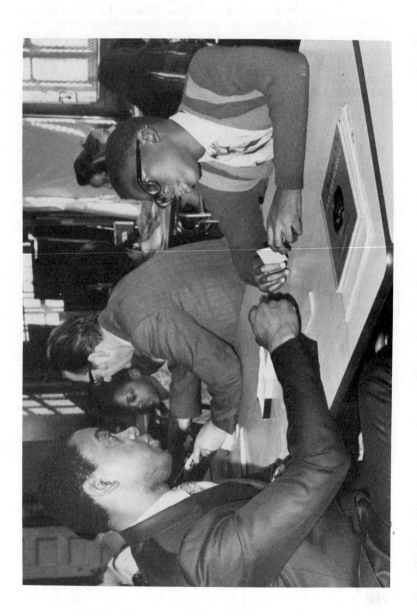

more. What she has on were a Christmas present from her
stepfather and she can't wear them every day. Instead of
reading a book with her (a tactic which Mary expects and is
all set to resist), Mrs. James discusses the new fashions
and also baby-sitting as a means of earning money for
clothes. She tells Mary she will bring a baby sitting guide
and a fashion magazine for their next session. They wind
up playing a game which tells Mrs. James a lot about
Mary's reading abilities and which interests Mary against
her will. As Mrs. James writes up her notes after Mary
departs, she feels quite hopeful about Mary.

Of course, a great many people do not have ten hours
a week available to give to helping others especially during
school hours. For people who work from nine to five there
are many tutorial programs which run during the evening
and on week-ends in churches, synagogues, settlement houses
and community centers. These tutorial programs offer the
same opportunities as the School Volunteer programs. If
there are none in your community, why not start one?

The New York City School Volunteer Program accepts
volunteers who can only give as little as three hours once a
week, though most give more. These people come from all
facets of the community, all ethnic and economic backgrounds
and all age groups. Among them are artists and actors, librarians and nurses, firemen and policemen, editors and
educators, career girls and housewives, college students and
retired professors. Husbands and wives tutor in the same
schools, brothers and sisters join the program together.

These volunteers carry on four different programs.
One group, the Reading Help Volunteers, tutors children in
reading at all age levels from kindergarten through high
school mainly on a one-to-one basis. Another group, the
Conversational English Volunteers, take children who cannot
speak any English and teach small groups of them an English
vocabulary of about 600 words. Their training is a crash
program that enables a non-English speaking child in a few
short weeks to start understanding and functioning in the
classroom instead of staring in unhappy incomprehension at
the wall.

Another group, the Early Childhood Volunteers, assist a teacher in the classroom in kindergarten or the early
grades. They relieve the teacher's burden of trying to give
individual attention to between twenty-five and thirty children

at a time and provide a useful pair of hands, a perceptive skill and a warm heart for both pupils and overburdened teachers.   The fourth group is called the Enrichment Group of Volunteers.   These are people who want to share a special talent.   They may tutor in math, teach sculpture, inspire and criticize creative writing, play the piano or whatever.   In every case, they bring an extra dimension to the children with whom they come in contact.

The New York City School Volunteer Program began as an experiment, the joint product of a civic minded woman with imagination (Mrs. Clara Blitzer) and a school administrator with flexibility and courage (Miss Florence Beaumont). About seventeen years ago, at P. S. 191 in Manhattan, a small group of twenty volunteers began helping out in the classrooms and performing all manner of tasks including putting on boots, escorting children to assemblies and trying to sandwich reading and conversation into the gaps.   The project was sponsored by the Public Education Association with the help of a Ford Foundation grant.   It became an official activity of the New York City Board of Education in 1962.

The types of services offered over the years have changed radically.   Many of their early duties have been taken over by the paraprofessionals*--often parents of children in the school--who not only guard the door, supervise the lunchroom, assist in the library and so forth but also provide a vital liaison between the school and the community. Meanwhile, it had become obvious that the great majority of teachers felt frustrated by their lack of time to do much for pupils in their classes who were well below the level of the class in reading or who could not speak English or who presented other special problems.   As a result, the volunteers found themselves more and more helping individual children with reading or with English.   Out of the experiences of these early volunteers, many of whom are still with the program, has come a training course which equips a new volunteer to start off with confidence in the field of his or her choice.

---

*A paraprofessional is a person (generally drawn from the community in which the work is being done) who is paid to assist a professional person but who does not have the degree or education of the professional.

Today, the New York City School Volunteer Program enrolls more than 2100 volunteers who serve 180 city schools spread throughout the five Boroughs. In 1972, the School Volunteer Program helped more than 13,000 children and its members donated over 130,000 hours of service.

The need for volunteers is unlimited. Thousands of children are waiting for this individual assistance. More than 200 principals of public schools in New York City have requested volunteer units of twenty persons or more and every principal who already has a School Volunteer Program asks to have it enlarged. New York City alone could use thousands. A golden opportunity is waiting for any individual who wants to help. Be a School Volunteer and learn how rich are the rewards of helping the many able children who are trapped in an air tight cage by the inability to read. *

---

*See the Appendix to Part I for information on how to join existing School Volunteer Programs or to start one in areas where there are none. There are now School Volunteer Programs in over three hundred cities.

THE BUTTERCUP STORY

Introduction

In the spring of 1967, I sat in a basement office in Bedford-Stuyvesant working to create a pilot model of library service, a novel kind of bookmobile. My clerk, Audrey Farmer, a member of the community and much interested in the project, listened quietly as she heard me describing over the phone my dream vehicle. "It's going to be eye-catching yellow," I told Mr. Rosenschweig of the Hertz Corporation which was supplying the truck. "<u>Not</u> Hertz yellow, <u>not</u> garbage truck yellow--a <u>beautiful</u> buttercup yellow with colorful posters all around the bottom."

When, on July 5, 1967, the dream came true and the project was opened with fanfare by Mayor Lindsay and others, Mrs. Farmer announced to all and sundry: "Wow! 'Buttercup' has finally been launched!" and from then on, the truck, was "Buttercup" to all the staff and many of her patrons. "Buttercup" died of old age on September 10, 1969 and was succeeded by three new bookmobiles, operated on the same lines as Buttercup and sponsored by the Central Brooklyn Model Cities Program. As of January 1, 1973, they were performing a highly useful, popular and necessary function in the community but, under the new federal philosophy, the whole program will shortly be terminated.

I had hoped, and still do, that Buttercup would spawn a whole fleet of Buttercups wherever people need help in reading and need the happiness as well as information that books can bring. Meanwhile, here is the Buttercup story and the list of the materials she carried.

The Story

In August 1966 my husband and I were on a ferry bound for an island off the coast of Maine. It was a day of high winds and lashing rain and the only other vehicle on

22

the ferry was the State of Maine Bookmobile. It was a
handsome, in fact luxurious, vehicle--though not very large--
and it was staffed by a driver and a librarian, both Mainiacs
as they proudly described themselves and both clearly very
happy in their work.   The trip to the island took almost 45
minutes in the course of which I had a chance to look around
the Bookmobile--glance at the books and talk to the staff.   I
remarked that perhaps not too many islanders would venture
forth on such a day but the librarian said with confidence
that weather made little difference to her trade.   "We can
only get here once every two weeks and they count on us"
was how she put it.

        Indeed, as we reached the wharf, a hundred or so
people of every age were standing there, in wet weather
gear mainly, although there were a few summer folk who
carried umbrellas and were having a struggle with the wind.
We lingered a few moments to watch the operation and noted
that the people there were returning books for friends as
well as themselves and all greeted the staff with gratitude
and enthusiasm.   We were much impressed and drove off
discussing what we had seen.   Yet in the back of my mind,
I kept thinking of the children I had been helping in New
York as a School Volunteer.   They were much further removed from the mainstream of American life than the children on Swan's Island.

        The Swan's Island children were part of a com-
munity and knew it.   The children on Amsterdam Avenue were not part of a community.   They lived in fear
and often had no idea whom to trust.   The children on
Swan's Island were part of the world of nature.   They
knew trees, rocks, wild flowers and birds and animals.
The gulls and the seals and the fogs and the sunsets
were all part of their lives and at an early age many
were already contributing to the family income by growing vegetables or helping on lobster boats or going clam-
ming.

        In New York I was encountering children of the same
age, who lived three blocks from rivers they had never seen
or four blocks from a park (Central) they had heard of but
didn't dare to enter.   I was helping children with reading
who had never seen a tree--who had no idea of what a frog
or a river or a hill was like and whose knowledge of animals
was confined to cats, dogs, and rats, or a school trip to the
zoo.   Yet these children had a real hunger for books that

meant something to them; folk tales like the story of the
"Hare and the Tortoise" or "Jack the Giant Killer." No
matter where you live, you will encounter people who are
like the hare and the tortoise. No matter who you are, you
are delighted to see the underdog win against great odds.
Surely these children needed a bookmobile even more than
did the children of Swan's Island.

Why couldn't they get these books from the public library or a school library? I had already discovered that
the areas in which the children lived were such that they
could not safely venture far from home. Many and many of
the books on my list testify to the fact that inner city children are living in a jungle and that if they venture beyond
safe limits (perhaps three blocks) they will be beaten up.
Few, if any, of the parents of the children with whom I was
working had ever been exposed to a public library or to
books. Most of them worked or had many younger children
and were neither able to take the children to a library nor
understood the importance of doing so.

The year before I had taken the Puerto Rican parents
of some of the children I was helping to the nearest public
library, a fifteen-minute walk through a dangerous neighborhood. When we got there, they literally shook with fright
at the strange situation, the high-ceilinged and silent rooms
and the unfamiliar forms to be filled out. The library staff
tried to welcome them but the gulf seemed to be unbridgeable.
They didn't go back.

How about the public school libraries? In New York
City, the public school libraries have been constantly up-
graded so that now the majority of schools have excellent
ones. However, books cannot circulate to the home where
there is time for reading until there is $5 worth of books
per pupil. Incredibly enough, when a new school opens, it
is allotted the same annual amount of money for books as
every other school in the system with the result that it is
three years on the average before it will have a circulating
library. If, as frequently happens, the school population
has increased so that the school has to go on double session,
it may be five years before the desired ratio is established.
There are even some schools which are now on triple session and have never been able to send books home with their
pupils. [This was true in 1970. In 1972-73, under the
school decentralization plan, the situation varies from district
to district since the local school board sets its own policy. With

the heavy emphasis on reading in the poorer neighborhoods, more books are being made available in some of the areas we served.]

Besides, the climate in many school libraries is still one to discourage all but the most enterprising and motivated children from enjoying books. Only last year, I coaxed a reluctant reader to the school library to look for a book about World War II. We found one he could read, liked the looks of and took it to be checked out, whereupon the librarian snatched it from him saying "You're not up to World War II yet, your class is still on American history." Over my protests, she handed him Johnny Tremaine, an excellent book but not what he wanted and far beyond his reading ability. He wouldn't go back again. [Some young librarians are entering the system who are dedicated to helping all children to read and who live in the areas where they work and therefore relate to the children they are helping. They create a learning climate. But there are still a great many librarians like the one in this story and incredibly enough, there is no workable mechanism for removing incompetent librarians and teachers no matter how desperate parents and children become.]

I wanted these children and their parents to have access to the kind of books that would be meaningful for them in an atmosphere that made them feel welcome and respected.

By coincidence, shortly after we returned to New York, I had a call from a friend of my daughter's who worked for a foundation and who had patiently listened to me enthusing about the School Volunteers. "We're looking for something in 'Poverty'," she said, "for about $30,000. Have you got any ideas?" I outlined my bookmobile idea and she was most enthusiastic so, urged on by the vision of $30,000 waiting in books and bookmobile for the children of Central Harlem, I made an appointment with the upper echelon of the New York Public Library. The lady who greeted me was very polite and also very able. She gently explained that $30,000 would barely buy a bookmobile and books and would leave nothing for operating expense.

I walked home in a belligerent mood and after conferring with my foundation friend once more, called Hertz truck rental. Mr. Sam Schwartz listened to my plea and said Hertz would be delighted to rent me a truck, converted by them to a bookmobile--for $5,000 a year on a two-year

lease. Back I went to the Public Library and also to the
library division of the Board of Education. Both groups said
that while they would never turn down a gift, they could not
approve of my project since they had so much better ones
of their own. After all, I was not a professional and consequently understood neither the needs of those to be served
nor the facilities that (with enough money) could be made
available.

        While I was at the Board of Education, I witnessed
an incident that stiffened my back. A new school, a so-
called "model school," had just been opened in Queens. It
contained many innovative ideas--classrooms in the round,
movable walls to create flexibility in the sizes of groups
and so forth--and was consequently getting a great deal of
newspaper coverage. The person with whom I was talking
was obliged to excuse herself to answer an urgent phone
call from the New York Times. When she came back, she
apologized for the interruption and said indignantly to her
subordinate, "Imagine! Anyone should know that it takes at
least three years to acquisition a school library!" The
school was being opened with fanfare as the model of what
a school should be and yet it had no books! It was clear
that she and I were not communicating--in fact, she dis-
missed me cheerfully saying, "I know the New York Public
Library will turn you down" and she was absolutely right.

        At this juncture, I was ready to call it quits and go
back to my school work but other School Volunteers and
several of the parents and staff with whom I had been working in Harlem said, "Look, we need this so. You can't give
up so easily, please keep trying." A friend secured me an
introduction to the director of the Brooklyn Public Library
and I went and told my story to him. To my joy, he said,
"We'll back you to the hilt. We know there is a large public
we want to reach whom we are not reaching. We are prepared to do anything that we feel will help us to reach that
public. It is important for the country to get people reading
and educating themselves and, furthermore, we cannot expect a public to whom the library means nothing to vote
funds for its support."

        This was the start of a happy association with the
Brooklyn Public Library. The library people have been as
helpful and flexible an organization as any one who loves
people and books could ever hope for. With this backing
and with the help of the library, my husband and I drew up

a budget and wrote a prospectus for the project and applied for a grant from the Chase-Manhattan Bank Foundation. In December we learned that it had been approved and in January we actually received the money.

The first step was to create a board of trustees and advisers and I quite naturally turned to the people and organizations who had encouraged me to go ahead with the idea. From the library, Mr. Humphry and his Deputy Director Mr. Milton Byam agreed to serve. Mrs. Robert Knapp represented the Public Education Association and Mrs. Thelma Robinson, a long-time resident of Bedford-Stuyvesant, the New York City School Volunteer Program. Miss Pamela Brinton, an unusually imaginative and perceptive book seller joined the board as did Mr. Paul Kerrigan, an interested library trustee who is deeply involved in helping Brooklyn. Mr. Evan Thomas, the publisher, was an invaluable friend and the Chase was represented by a very patient, conscientious and helpful gentleman, Mr. Frank Kissane. Mr. Lansing Hammond of the Commonwealth Fund and my husband completed the group.

For almost a month with the help of the trustees, I interviewed prospective staff. I was looking for a man or woman from the community who could both drive the vehicle and administer the operation. I was looking for a part-time librarian to handle book selection with me and to supervise. Eventually I was lucky enough to find an excellent librarian, Sarah Koerner, and an outstanding administrator, Lillian Butler, the wife of a minister in the area.

Mrs. Koerner, Miss Brinton and I made out my list of titles (based in large part on their exhaustive knowledge of children's literature and our school volunteer experience), and Mr. Thomas undertook the monumental task of writing every publisher whose books were on my list and asking for a first set of books free to get the project underway. I am deeply grateful for the fact that almost every publisher responded favorably.

At the suggestion of the School Volunteers and the Brooklyn Public Library, I had done some research which established that both School District 16 (Bushwick-Bedford-Stuyvesant) and School District 19 (East New York) were fertile areas for a project like mine and, in both, the School Volunteers and the library had community links which would help to ensure community acceptance. I put the choice to

the Brooklyn trustees, Mr. Humphry, Mr. Byam, and Mrs.
Robinson, and with some anguish--the need was so urgent in
both neighborhoods--they selected District 16.

District 16 was an area of great need which lay
roughly two-thirds in Bedford-Stuyvesant and one-third in
Bushwick.   It borders on Brownsville.   The population in
Bedford-Stuyvesant is predominantly black.   In Bushwick, in
the section we served there are about fifty per cent white
people (mainly older) and a large concentration of Puerto
Ricans, mainly non-English speaking.   We also discovered
a large group of non-English speaking Italians and were later
to encounter many French and Spanish-speaking immigrants
from the Caribbean area.   The following year quite a sizable
group (as it affected the schools in the area) of Rumanian
speaking refugees appeared from an area taken over by Yugo-
slavia after World War II.

Mrs. Louise Bolling, a long time Bedford-Stuyvesant
resident and chairman of the District 16 School Board, joined
our board of trustees.   With her help and advice and with
suggestions from the staff of the school district, I was able
to lay out a tentative schedule of service.   With Mrs. Butler
and Mrs. Koerner, I visited the schools and churches and
housing projects in our area.   I was able also to speak to a
meeting of the heads of all the parents' associations in the
District and the project received publicity in the newsletters
of the Bushwick Community Council, the Central Brooklyn
Coordinating Council, and the Youth-In-Action newspaper.

Unquestionably all this work was a help in getting us
started and providing us right away with people who needed
and wanted books.   And yet, in an area such as this, communication is the most difficult problem of all.   We were to
learn not to be surprised to go into a storefront branch of
the Community Council to tell them of our services and to
find that they were enthusiastic, that they had never heard
of us, and that the newsletter about us was posted on their
bulletin board!   We would find women sitting in front of one
of our posters in a community center who were eager for
our services but had never noticed the poster.   We would
have children from across the street discover us only after
two months of our being at the same stop each week.   Life
in a ghetto area is such that, to survive, an inhabitant learns
to tune out a great many sights and sounds, even smells.
This selective response is necessary to survival but it can
be deadening.   It is also one of the causes of reading

problems for it hinders observation very directly.   Additionally, it makes communication, except by word of mouth,
very difficult.

Meanwhile, the Hertz Company and I were struggling
with the details of turning an 18-foot truck into a warm,
cozy, but unusual kind of bookmobile.   It was a first for
both of us and we had many interesting experiences.   I
wanted to be quite sure a woman could drive such a truck
comfortably and managed to stall it in the middle of 10th
Avenue and 34th Street, a moment neither the Hertz man
nor I shall ever forget.

The Brooklyn Public Library generously gave me a
corner of the basement of the Saratoga Reading Center, a
branch of the library in Bushwick.   The Chase Bank waved
a magic wand and turned the corner into an office lined with
bookshelves and complete with wall-to-wall carpeting.   Suddenly, it was the middle of June.   The publishers, led by
Mr. Thomas had been most generous and either given or
sold at a large discount, from ten to twenty copies of each
of my titles, and the books were pouring in.   My tiny staff
(Mrs. Koerner, Mrs. Butler, Mrs. Farmer--a part-time
clerk who lived near the office--and a rather surly neighborhood Youth Corps boy) and I confronted the fact that we had
roughly 10,000 books and 500 dry-mounted prints to process
in ten working days.   Then we had to arrange and load the
truck which had not yet arrived.

We were having a grand and well publicized opening
of our service with Mayor Lindsay, Mr. George Champion,
Chairman of the Chase Bank, and other dignitaries as
speakers so that we just had to be ready.   It seemed impossible but Mrs. Farmer and her block association wrought
magic.   A constant stream of black and white and old and
young showed up at our door.   Often they had no idea what
they had come for or were expected to do but would say
"Audrey Farmer said I had to help and here I am."   It was
an exciting experience to see the enthusiasm of our diverse
volunteers.

Finally on July 2nd, the truck arrived, a beautiful
buttercup yellow, just as specified, with a lovely wall-to-
wall red carpet generously donated by R. H. Macy.   We
loaded (it seemed incredible) 10,000 books on that day and
the next in the back yard of the library.   A local painter
meanwhile painted on our key, the symbol of the door of

opportunity that reading would unlock and several beautiful
signs "The Bushwick-Bedford-Stuyvesant Traveling Library."

The grand opening came on July 5th.   None of us had
any idea what to expect.   The Chase had put posters around.
Would any one come or nobody? I, at least, did not yet
understand how empty life was for most children on a summer day in a ghetto in Brooklyn.   We were mobbed by a
polite, confused and appreciative group, many of whom confused the idea of books with the free Good Humors given out
by the bank, and quite genuinely (we later learned) thought
that the books also were a free gift.   With the help of a
good many volunteers, we served over 300 people and gave
out over 300 books, only about 100 of which we ever saw
again.

July 5th was heady stuff;   reporters, bands and publicity.   As Mrs. Farmer put it: " 'Buttercup' was launched. "
On July 6th, we crept out timidly on our appointed rounds and
were happy to find that we met a warm response.   The truck
itself was blatant enough and unusual enough so that many
children, at least, who are more alive and less harried than
adults, did notice us.   Not only was the color eye-catching,
but we had panels along both sides which were filled with
colorful posters.   One rear door was wide open enabling a
passerby to see the interior and so was the front door.
Over the front door was a sign of welcome in English and
Spanish and we stationed at least one of the staff on the
sidewalk to lure people on.

Children, of course, were the first to clamber aboard
and, since we were new, there was a considerable amount of
confusion.   Many of our clientele had never before encountered the library concept and were incredulous when we explained that the books were free.   Some children returned
each week for two or three weeks without registering before
they would believe there wasn't a catch.   Others had to get
permission from their parents and it came slowly.   "My
father says, 'don't never give your name and address to nobody'," confided one little girl and it took two weeks of eye-
ing Curious George before she gathered strength to make him
understand that here it was worth taking a chance and registering.   Many teenagers came aboard and wanted to buy our
books.   "How can I tell where I'll be next week?" said one.
"Here, sell me this (Diamonds are Forever) and neither one
of us will have to worry. " We held our ground.   We were
a library--although we were willing to sell such reference

books as dictionaries, atlases, cook books, Dr. Spock and
books on judo and karate.

That summer only the judo and karate books sold.
But people borrowed books. We had a growing trade. In
the first twelve months approximately 26,000 books were
borrowed and almost a thousand people a week were using
us. [We operated seven weeks in the summer, often serving
over 1,000 people per week, and 36 weeks during the re-
mainder of the year when the number of people using us
averaged around 500 a week (in bitterly cold or rainy weather
our circulation sank).]

Obviously, to take care of so many people we had to
add to our staff. We had an administrator (first, Mrs. Butler and later, Mrs. Felix); a clerk, Mrs. Robinson; a
driver, Mr. Jones, who was also a general factotum and a
specialist in our art prints; and a new and enthusiastic
Neighborhood Youth Corps boy, Harold Moore. All either
lived in the area or knew it well and had friends and relatives
who lived there. Harold was an ambitious high school dropout who liked reading. Mrs. Robinson and Mrs. Felix had
school-age children and cared deeply about helping children.
Mr. Jones had grown up in Bedford-Stuyvesant and had
grandchildren in the area. The staff felt at home with the
clientele and vice versa. [There seems to be no good word
to describe the people who borrow books and pictures from
a library or bookmobile. "Patrons" seems the antithesis of
the kind of people served. Neither "clientele" nor "customers" is accurate but I use them in default of anything
better.]

Mrs. Farmer still gave yeoman service part-time in
the office and as a lunch hour substitute on Buttercup. She
worked for us for pay in the day time. Then on many an
evening, as a volunteer publicist, she would go and speak to
Parents' Associations and community groups about what we
were trying to accomplish. We had three criteria in picking
our staff (except for the librarian): they must be familiar
with the area (preferably living in it), they must want to
read (nothing to do with educational level), and they must
want to help people. These were not standard library criteria but they were clearly our needs and created a warm
and welcoming atmosphere.

Another difference from standard library practice was
the kind of material we carried--only 800 titles at any one

time but between ten and twenty of each title.   The titles
had been picked based on School Volunteer experience and
were intended to appeal to a wide age range but a low reading level.   The books were arranged with the covers showing, as they are in stationery or paperback stores, and were
arranged by category with no segregation as to age groups.
This meant that, for example, in the mystery section there
was a hot mystery with integrated characters on second-grade
reading level at floor level and the reading and interest level rose
to the ceiling where one could find Chester Himes, James Bond
and Sherlock Holmes.   The advantage lay in the fact that a
high school dropout who was interested in sports, could pick
a fourth-grade book on football with no questions asked, a
grandmother could borrow Bible Stories on a third-grade
reading level, and a twelve-year-old could take out The
Autobiography of Malcolm X.   Additionally, the fact that
most of our books were paperbacks made them attractive to
a wide age range.   Many of our most popular biographies
(Martin Luther King: Peaceful Warrior, Jackie Robinson,
etc.) had originally come out in hardcover format clearly
intended for the juvenile market.   In paperback form they
were indistinguishable from books intended for the adult
market and yet the fact that they were on a fifth-grade reading level made them rewarding for people who were not ac-
customed to reading.

        People of all ages invariably chose paperbacks over
our few hardcover books.   Perhaps unconsciously they related paperbacks to one of the few pleasant experiences they
had had with the written word--comics (whereas hardcover
books were associated with school struggles and failure).
Even more important, the people who used Buttercup were
often so beset economically, that they were fearful.   They
asked us "What happens if I or my child borrows a book and
Something Happens?"   I use capitals deliberately because
that is how it seemed to them.   Something over which they
had little or no control Happened and they were in trouble.
If they were going to be in trouble and they were afraid they
were, better to borrow a paperback and limit their liability.
A third difference was the fact that all the staff were asked
to read our books and to be prepared to recommend titles to
our clientele.   Getting to know our stock and being able to
recommend a book from the personal experience of enjoyment
made a great deal of difference and created an instant relationship with the people who came aboard that is entirely
different from any I have ever seen in a library.   Every
customer was a potential friend and the atmosphere was

relaxed and easy with wisecracks or other remarks flying
back and forth except when the pace was very great as when
we had a surge of customers all at once.   Many lonely people came first for the friendliness and then later came to
value the books.   Many children came first for the sense of
importance it gave them to be able to have a <u>choice</u> (something that they had perhaps rarely experienced) and to have
an adult ask what they wanted and what they were interested
in and had they enjoyed the book?   It was fun and exciting to
see a child so inarticulate he could barely stammer "sports"
or "mysteries" or "I want a funny book" when first asked
his choice and six weeks later walk in boldly and greet the
staff and comment on the book he was returning.

Another important factor in the success of Buttercup
and, I am sure, one of the main reasons for its high rate
of return (ninety per cent of our books came back), was the
fact that we had a system whereby (although we had a library
card for each customer) no one could ever lose his library
card--we kept them all.   We also had no fines for lateness.
If a family catastrophe happened and a child was sent to live
with relatives for a while, when he returned weeks later, he
was given a warm welcome and no questions asked.   As a
result, people could afford to return books which were long
overdue.   However, we issued only one book to a customer.
If people who were not very used to reading, read a book a
week, we felt (and so did they) that they had done well.   If
they were real readers--three or four books a week--they
belonged in the public library.

Another innovation compared to most bookmobiles was
the fact that we carried well-made dry mounted prints which
we loaned to adults.   The purpose of this was not only to
bring pleasure to people in drab surroundings but also to encourage observation on the part of the children and especially
to encourage family conversation.   Too many children hear
little at home from their overburdened parents except com-
mands such as, "Git up, git to bed, quit that racket, etc. "
Such a child comes to school so inarticulate that he cannot
say a sentence and, of course, speaking and a vocabulary
are the first key to reading.   We carried a viewer with
thirty slides of our prints mounted on the back wall of the
truck.   That way, a customer could point and say I want
number twenty-five and one of the staff, usually Mr. Jones
since he took special pride in the pictures, would fetch the
print from a container mounted over the wheel hub.   We
gave the borrower a hanger (a heavy paper sticky on both

sides) that would support the print and in no way damage the
wall it was hung on--an important factor for those who lived
in projects.   The picture idea was only modestly successful.
Many people were too fearful.   All too often, I would hear a
mother say, "Oh, that's too beautiful.   I'm afraid my children would hurt it. "   "Lady, if I saved a lot of money, isn't
there any way I could buy it off you?"   I had had very little
idea of what would be popular and had tried to produce great
variety and lots of color.   Our most popular prints were a
magnificent Rubens, "Portrait of a Negro"; an El Greco,
"Virgin and Angels"; and a Botticelli, "Virgin and Child. "
Van Gogh's "Sunflowers" was the best liked still life and a
Dufy, "Landscape of the Riviera" (which reminded the islanders of home since it resembled a Caribbean scene), was
borrowed quite often.   Later, I happened across three prints
by Tretchikoff.   They were pictures of African women, two
of them quite dramatic and all three very beautiful.   These
prints were so much liked the borrowers refused to return
them.   One woman who conscientiously returned her own and
her childrens' books each week absolutely refused to give up
her picture and we found that if we insisted on getting back
these prints, all we did was lose a friend and customer.
These prints, by a living artist, were very expensive ($9.50
dry-mounted), but the prints that were, so to speak, in the
public domain were much cheaper ($1 apiece if bought in
quantity) and I imagine that a store which carried such prints
in an area like this could sell a great many at a fair profit.
Although I do not feel my art venture worked out as I had
planned, I learned from it and it was clear that the interest
in art and the love of art was intense.   If a foundation could
reproduce prints of Ezra Jack Keats' book illustrations and
Tom Feelings' "Madonna and Child" (to give just two examples) at a reasonable price, people would flock to buy
them and it would really affect the lives of many children.
I have seen a withdrawn and apathetic child come alive when
he saw the bright colors of "Snowy Day. "   I have seen the
excitement of a little girl when she realized Feelings' Madonna was "Black! just like me. "

     Selling reference books was another innovation that
was only modestly successful.   The problem was that the
material which people needed didn't exist.   We had quite a
few young women come aboard (especially near our Health
Center stops) and say "The doctor wants me to get a book
on how to take care of the baby. "   I would produce Dr. Spock
and the mother would say, "Oh yes, that's the name he said,
I'll buy it. "   I would insist that she look it over for a while

before I took her money and in most cases the sale would
fall through. It was clear that she didn't understand half
the words and that the reading level was way beyond her.
Equally in demand and equally non-existent were easy-to-
read but practical cookbooks. Both adults and girls as young
as twelve were really desperate for such a book. In my
school volunteer work I had often encountered sixth graders
who were doing the marketing and cooking for younger siblings with no idea of what to buy nor how to cook. I persuaded an experienced volunteer and excellent cook to write
a book on a third- or fourth-grade reading level which was
not only a cook book but also a buying and nutrition guide.
We have yet to find a publisher for it since they all contend
that those who need it can't afford to buy it.

    A market is there for low reading-level, high interest-
level books of all kinds but especially "how-to" books since
the urge for self-improvement is very great. In addition,
there is a real demand for popular books such as what we
called "movie books," Ian Fleming, Dr. Dolittle and especially movie books that have to do with black people such as
"To Sir with Love" and "In the Heat of the Night." This
would be equally true with the other ethnic groups, resulting
from, for example, movies to do with Puerto Ricans, Haitians, Cubans, etc. There is also a strong demand among
adults and older adolescents for books on Negro history and
biography.

    As our clientele grew so satisfactorily through the
spring of 1968, we faced again the problem that we would
need additional staff in the summer months ahead. Actually,
we were short staffed all year round for two reasons.
First, our one small staff fulfilled all library functions:
book selection, book ordering and processing, creation of
publicity, distribution of publicity, record keeping, house
keeping, correspondence and actual operation of the bookmobile. In a standard library situation, many of these
functions are performed centrally, leaving the branch or
bookmobile free to concentrate on operations. Second, while
the educational level of the staff was an asset in relating to
our public, it was a liability in the length of time it took
for any clerical work and in the struggle for accuracy and
completeness in record keeping. We had learned the preceding summer that we had to have staff for crowd control
and for publicity. Also, I was anxious to institute a story-
telling program and that too would require additional staff.

We had noticed the preceding summer that several
students of junior high school age had spontaneously leapt
aboard Buttercup and helped out when they saw the need and
the crowds were great. They had been able and enthusiastic
assistants and had attracted others of their age to us. With
this memory in mind, I outlined a project called grandly,
"The Future Librarians of America." I would recruit
(through the school librarians) junior high students from five
schools in our area who would help us as volunteers after
school during the spring. The best of these we would hire
to work for us part-time during the summer months. Using
the geographical layout of our schedule, I picked a Monday
school, Tuesday school, etc., so that my volunteers need
only help one afternoon each week and need only walk a
block or two from school to meet us.

I asked the Chase for $3000 to fund the project and
they very generously backed me up and gave it to me.   I
then talked to the librarians with varying success. Two
thought the children wouldn't consider volunteering although
they might be interested in a pay job in the summer, two
thought the project was excellent but didn't seem to know
their students very well partly because they didn't live in
the area and partly because both schools were having acute
problems of their own. The fifth librarian lived in the area,
knew her children well and was enthusiastic. Her pupils became eighty per cent of the future librarians. The remaining twenty per cent we picked up from among our clientele.
So the spring experience, which I had hoped would be a
training ground and winnowing ground, was only semi-successful.

Summer was another story. Our ten Future Librarians, five boys and five girls, were so enthusiastic that they
proved a catalyst to the staff and the community. Despite
the fact that they were often pelted with pebbles by young
hoodlums on roofs, set upon by neighborhood toughs, and
forced by some inconsiderate summer school teachers to
deal with disruptive children whom the teachers preferred
to ignore, they voluntarily came to Buttercup on their days
off to help out wherever needed, much to the surprise and
delight of the staff since they had been hired to work for
20 hours a week only. The Spanish-speaking youngsters
were especially helpful in telling stories in Spanish and in
interpreting our services to those parents who were shy and
hesitant. All the youngsters enjoyed making posters and
other material for publicity and some were very creative in

decorating Buttercup. Their biggest thrill came on payday
when the whole staff rode in Buttercup to the Bedford branch
of Chase to cash their checks. Three of them opened savings accounts and all set aside money for school clothes.

     The Future Librarians learned to perform all the
tasks there were in connection with the project: processing,
making out library cards, issuing and receiving books and
pictures and preparing and placing publicity material. However, their most exciting job was story-telling. We would
send them out in groups of two in a two-block radius from
our stop. Wherever there was a group of children, they
would offer to tell a story and would then offer to bring the
children back to Buttercup so they could borrow the book
from which the story came. It would usually end up by their
returning like the Pied Piper with a trail of children behind
them, but not always. As one girl described one of her experiences in her daily report, "I ask a little girl if she
wanted me to read her a story and a lady came out and
said: Leave my girl alone and get awawy from here!--and
I ran. "

     It is interesting to realize that many library systems
feel it is necessary for a person to have a college education
to be story tellers. These children, fourteen and fifteen,
came from the neighborhood and attended the local schools.
All were from minority groups and most were from severely
deprived homes, often with no father in the household. About
half were quite far behind educationally. Yet all turned in a
good responsible job, all proved to be good story tellers,
and all were quick and inventive and imaginative. All gained
clerical skills (as one girl put it, "I learned how to filed in
strick alphabetical order. I think it will help me when I
become a secretary in the future.") and the requirement that
all should be prepared to recommend books to Buttercup's
patrons really got them reading and discussing books. All
of them improved their reading as a result. It was fun, too,
to hear how strongly they felt on the subject of reading for
"little kids," as they put it, and to hear their ideas on how
kids should be brought up. All in all, they were a great
help and inspiration and a joy to have around.

     In the summer of 1968, a very able librarian, Mrs.
Gertrude Williams, took my place as administrator on a
temporary basis to give me a vacation and also to assess
our personnel situation and organization. Mrs. Williams
recommended that we have a full-time librarian in order to

free me for money raising (the Chase grant would run out
at Christmas time) and to achieve an organization that could
be handed over to a different funding and operating agency.

We were looking forward to some form of community
control and also to the hope of enlarging the scope of the
project. We both knew that there was a need for many more
Buttercups. Since this required a shift in personnel, we
closed down for what we hoped would be a short while. After
a few weeks of search, I hired Miss Jean Coleman as librar-
ian-administrator. Miss Coleman had grown up in the area
we were serving and many older poeple in the district still
remembered her father who had been a very much respected
clergyman. She had been a children's librarian for several
years with the Brooklyn Public Library (who recommended
her highly) and was looking for a more challenging job.

In the fall of 1967, we operated throughout the teachers' strike. Many of the schools in our district stayed
open, manned by a skeleton staff aided by dedicated parents.
Where schools were closed, the children whom we had served
in summer were waiting hopefully for us. We felt we were
even more needed than usual. The strike was bad for the
education of the elementary school children but it was a di-
saster for the older children.

In many middle-class areas, many children were tutored
and parents got together and organized school substitutes,
trips to museums, historic places, etc. The children in
our area were lost and underfoot and grew very discouraged.
Several very able ones whom we knew through Buttercup and
who had high hopes of getting into competitive high schools
gave up on this and did poorly on the Regents exams the
following spring.

In the fall of 1968, the teachers had again gone out
on strike and our area was in a particular turmoil. Our office was not far from the Ocean Hill-Brownsville area and
I shall not soon forget the day when I absentmindedly drove
past Junior High School #271 and found myself in a narrow street
with a couple of hundred parents on one sidewalk shouting
and waving clenched fists and a line of police on the other
side guarding the doors of the school like statutes. In addition, however, to the well publicized violence in that area,
other areas were suffering also. In one of the junior high
schools where we had many friends and borrowers, the assistant principal (a woman) opened the school and after three

days of operation, the physical education teacher, a man,
walked into her office and struck her a blow that broke her
jaw.   Since the principal was out on strike, the school
closed again.

        Much as I knew we were needed on the streets, I
didn't quite dare to reopen and went on hoping first from
day to day, then from week to week, that the strike would
end.   So many of the teachers who had gone out on strike
the year before had seen for themselves what that strike had
done to the childrens' education that I couldn't believe they
would again so damage the lives of the children entrusted to
their care.   I was wrong.   Many of them were genuinely
frightened at what they took to be an all out attack on their
job security.   Others were truly prejudiced against minority
groups and welcomed an open fight.   It was heartrending for
the children.   The Future Librarians, all of whom were
locked out of school, hung around our office like lost souls.
We couldn't give them work since were weren't functioning but
we did at least keep them reading.   It was December before
the schools and we at last reopened.   The scars and damage
to the children will last for years.

        Meanwhile, I delegated the daily administration of
Buttercup to Miss Coleman and my husband and I started to
learn about fund raising in New York.   We had been told by
some city officials that the city had a great respect for our
operation and hoped to be able to fund it and to add more
bookmobiles through the Model Cities money that the federal
government would soon supply.   Therefore, all we needed to
do was to raise enough money for a few months' operations
and all would be well.   Luckily my husband had had experience with bureaucratic red tape and immediately doubled in
his mind the few months we would have to carry it by our-
selves.   Even he, however, far underestimated the sea of
red tape in which Buttercup would become embogged.

        It took until 1970 to get a signed city contract--and
this for a project which the community wanted and had done
everything in its power to implement, a project approved by
the federal government and for which federal funds were
available.   No wonder people ask if cities are any longer
governable!

        I am very glad that I didn't know all I now know in
October of 1968, as my husband and I started our fund raising.   We first drew up a tentative prospectus and tried it

out on our trustees and a few professional money raisers.
The verdict was that our material was good but too long, so
we edited drastically, added a few pictures and had a number of copies printed. No matter how inexpensively done,
printing costs money, and I was terrified that our dwindling
bank balance would soon be exhausted but you have to spend
money to raise money as I soon learned.

Among other things we learned that winter was that
foundation staffs are very overworked; that they frequently
do not bother to answer their mail; that very, very few
of the people in charge of handing out vast sums of money
for projects in the inner city had ever spent any time in deprived areas personally and had any real contact with the
kind of people they were supposed to be helping. In fact,
many did not want to have anything to do with such people
and of all the many people we met who expressed interest in
our project, not one took advantage of an offer to be driven
out by me at any time they chose to see Buttercup in operation. We learned that foundations virtually never (luckily
not quite unanimously never) give money to keep a good
operation going. Their priority is to start something new.
Several foundations told us cheerfully that, if we had not
already proved our idea successful, they would have been
glad to fund us but now, of course, what we were asking for
was "operating money" and that no self-respecting foundation
would consider except on a project originally funded by the
same foundation. We also learned that except in rare instances it was not what your project was, but who you knew,
that counted. I suppose it has always been that way and that
the intrinsic worth of an idea has never been the governing
factor in its gaining support but somehow I had hoped that in
America doors were open to ideas rather than to people and
it was a disillusioning experience to learn otherwise.

Fortunately, some very fine people and foundations
came to our rescue and we were able to raise enough money
($60,000) to keep operating through Labor Day, 1969 (this
was before the city contract in 1970). We also received a
new grant for a second Future Librarians program for the
summer of 1969 which enabled us to hire twelve Future Librarians and a paraprofessional.

At the same time that we were working on money
raising, we were also seeking ways to turn the operation
over to community control in which we were and are firm
believers. A subcommittee of the trustees was appointed to

explore various possibilities and organizations which might
be equipped to take over administrative responsibility for the
project.   Among the ideas we considered was the feasibility
of creating a local community board of trustees, of handing
the administrative responsibility to the local school board of
District 16, and of handing the administrative responsibility
to the Central Brooklyn Model Cities Committee if they
wanted it and could fund us.

In the end, the latter alternative proved the most
feasible and in September 1969 the Central Brooklyn Model
Cities Committee assumed responsibility for Buttercup and
later added two additional bookmobiles like her for Brownsville and East New York.   Buttercup was started in an effort
to make books available and pleasurable to people of all ages
who did not yet know the rewards of reading.   Let us hope
that the U.S. Department of Education's Right to Read cam-
paign will have such support from governmental as well as
private funding agencies that by 1980, no more Buttercups
will be needed, libraries will be doing a land office business
and there will be good book stores proliferating in all the
cities in the country.   Until that happy day, though, I hope
that many more Buttercups will wend their ways through city
streets to bring the joy of reading to people who don't have
many joys in their lives and to open doors of hope and opportunity to children who are trapped in places like the
streets of Brownsville.

LIBRARY TECHNIQUES IN DISADVANTAGED AREAS

At a time and in an area where the schools were failing in many instances to produce literate self-supporting citizens,* Buttercup was reaching non-readers of every age and
inducing them to read on a regular and continuing basis.
This was exciting and worthwhile for the individual involved
but it was only half the story. One of my hopes in starting
the bookmobile had been that I looked forward to graduating
our borrowers and getting them started at the nearest public
library. With the limitations of space and the number of
titles we carried, the day was bound to arrive when a faith-
ful borrower would get on and say "Oh! dear, I've read
everything you've got that interests me. " At that point, we
tried to transfer their interest and loyalty to the public library but we were only semi-successful even with the more
self-confident individuals and we got nowhere with timid people or people who were embarrassed by their reading level
or their lack of facility in English--in other words with the
majority of our clientele.

To induce these people to go to their local library
regularly required more personnel than we had for follow-up
and liaison with public library personnel, but most of all it
required changes in the public library. The Brooklyn Public
Library, (and many others, I am sure) recognized this fact.

The principles which enabled "Buttercup" to be accepted and supported by the community could well be of help

---

*The drop out rate was extremely high in our area. One
undoubted reason was that the mean reading score in grade
9 in our school district was 7.2 (p. 16 Summary of Citywide
Reading Test Results for 1968-69, Office of Educational Research, Board of Education). The situation was worse in
1971 and 1972--in large part due to the strikes of 1967 and
1968. Not only was the children's education drastically inter-
rupted (2-1/2 weeks in 1967, 8 weeks in 1968) but the spirit
and morale of the schools was very badly damaged and violence of every kind entered the lives of many schools.

in similar areas. We were welcomed in parts of Brownsville and Bedford-Stuyvesant from which other organizations
had had to withdraw. We were welcomed in our area at a
time when the local branch library had had to close due to
vandalism and hostility on the part of a group of teenagers
in the area.

The Brooklyn Public Library has had superb and unusually creative leadership for the past six years and has
initiated many innovative projects. Mr. John Frantz, who
succeeded Mr. Humphry, started many new and exciting experiments especially in the use of volunteers. In addition
he was a tower of strength to Buttercup's staff whether the
difficulty was lack of money, lack of space, red tape or you
name it. His successor, Mr. Kenneth Duchac is carrying
on in the same tradition. However, in the effort to change
to meet changing needs, the Brooklyn Public Library has
been hampered by established library practices, by outmoded
buildings and by lack of money.

I like to imagine that I have a magic wand which I
can wave and which will produce overnight the kind of libraries that Buttercup's clientele would run to. If I had my
magic wand, I would create a series of storefront libraries
in shopping areas such as 125th Street in Harlem, Myrtle
Avenue and Broadway and Nostrand Avenue in Brooklyn, etc.
These libraries would have clean plate glass windows with
paperback books, games and records on display just as mer-
chants do who need to sell to make a living. The libraries
would be so well lit that any passerby could see past the
display to what was actually taking place in the library. Too
many potential library patrons are scared off by nineteenth-
century architecture, signs for silence, and most of all, fear
of the unknown.

What, in fact, would be taking place in such a library?
Here is an ideal list of activities which a neighborhood library should cover. Obviously, space and financial limitations will dictate how much of the list can be carried out.
A narrow storefront, limited to the ground floor and with not
much money for staff could accomplish not much more than
the Bookmobile. With more space and money, more could
be done. If only one library with all the facilities listed
could be put into operation, then people in the various communities could be taken to see it in action, to talk to the
patrons and to decide for themselves a priority list of library
facilities. Too often it is said that people are apathetic

when the trouble is that they are being asked to involve themselves in a world they do not understand and have never seen.

When I _talked_ about the Bookmobile, no one cared;
when people in the community saw it in action, they were
willing to fight to keep it. If community people can visit a
successful operation and make their own choices as to what
they most want, right away it will become their library and
a helpful one.

Here is my list, not in any order of priority: _rele-
vant books_ on every reading and interest level easily available
for loan and in the best possible format, usually paperback.
Then, the same books, but for sale. Also, records for loan
and for sale.

Short-term (three hours or less) baby-sitting available
for pre-school children. The object of the baby-sitting would
be twofold. First, and most important, would be to expose
the pre-school child to the kind of toy middle-class children
are given as a matter of course--toys which teach finger dex-
terity, recognition, creativity and broaden horizons. In addition, the children would be read to, would listen to records
and would be sung to. Such a program could be run by a
group of paraprofessionals including students under the direc-
tion of an early childhood specialist. When a mother came
to call for her child, she would be urged to borrow books
and records for herself and the child. The second object
would be to give the mother some free time. Pediatricians
are unanimous in saying that time off makes for better
parenthood and many mothers never get a moment away from
their children. Additionally, if there were enough space,
there could be group discussions of mutual problems and opportunities such as: child care, career opportunities, adult
education, etc.

Book and game clubs after school and on week-ends
for elementary, junior high and high school children. Anyone who has worked with children in an underprivileged area
is struck by the almost total absence of games. Hopscotch,
jump rope (for girls), King of the Castle and Cops and Rob-
bers about sum up the list. One reason the School Volunteers
found Go Fish so useful was the fact that the children were
thrilled at playing a card game. Most of them (at _all_ ages
including high school) had never played a card game, a board
game (Parcheesi, Monopoly, etc.), or a pencil and paper
game (tick-tack-toe, hangman, categories, etc.) in their

lives. The right games can teach children reading, writing
and arithmetic, including logic and the new math (Columbia
Teachers College is developing a whole series of games
which they consider to be one of the best methods for teaching math on the elementary level), and do it painlessly and
in a way that eliminates defeatism and overcomes despair.
A child who was certified as knowing how to play a game
(such as Go Fish) would be allowed to borrow it for a limited
time just as if it were a book.   This would multiply the effect of the game many times--involving siblings, parents, and
other adult relatives in the household.   The book and game
clubs could be run by junior and senior high school-age children assisted by paraprofessionals under the supervision of
a really top-notch professional, either librarian, guidance
counsellor or teacher who enjoyed young people and liked
games.   (See the "Notes on Games" at the end of this chapter.)

        A senior citizens' area filled with large print material
relevant to their needs and interests with one or two cubicles
where Talking Books could be played and also borrowed for
playing at home.   In New York State, persons who are certified by an oculist as blind (this does not mean the total
blindness a layman would expect) are eligible to receive a
free gramophone and Talking Books, records which cover a
whole gamut of subjects from literature to vocational training.
Needless to say few of those on welfare or in underprivileged
areas know of the opportunity or avail themselves of it.   This
is why a demonstration area is needed.

        To continue my priority list of facilities: a quiet area
where homework could be done with a helpful adult to supervise and assist when invited to.

        An area where tutoring could be done on a one-to-one
basis.   It has been now established that junior and senior
high school students who tutor younger children benefit as
much in their reading levels as do their tutees.   Many junior
high students are keen to volunteer for this work.   In addition, adults could volunteer in the evening and on week-ends.

        A back yard where children could read outdoors in
peace and senior citizens could play checkers or dominoes
in peace.

        A public information center where the patron could
count on finding information on vital current happenings--

elections, hearings, public meetings, training opportunities, health opportunities (the free chest X-ray mobile will be here next Wednesday), etc. The center should not only carry free material but also be a place where those who have a service to offer can count on getting publicity. Church fairs, school fairs, museum contests, cooperative nursery schools and the like would advertise here and poster contests could well be held to whet interest in the various events.

An area where films and film strips can be shown. This last is not so essential since almost every community has many areas where this can be done, i. e., community centers in public housing projects, churches and church houses, school assembly rooms and gymnasiums etc. A library system which goes to these areas and shows films has an opportunity to acquaint people with the services it offers under the most favorable circumstances. Often, books from which the films are taken or on similar subjects can be brought with the film for loaning and eventual return to the library, thereby introducing the borrower to the library. However, under the compartmentalized system with which many libraries are operated, this is not done as often as it could be.

One of the most essential elements in merchandising books whether in a teaching, a library or a commercial situation, is to have personnel who enjoy reading and have read and enjoyed the books they are trying to interest people in borrowing or buying. What car salesman would try to sell a car about which he knew nothing? How many vacuum cleaners would a salesman sell who had never tried the model he was peddling? Yet, the majority of teachers and librarians I encounter have never read the books they are urging on a reluctant clientele. The books are on an approved list and therefore, should be good is the general attitude. Even in an underprivileged area, there are many people who love books and the recommendation of one woman to another--"I loved this book, I couldn't put it down"-- carries real weight.

Additionally, companies spend a lot of money making market surveys. Too many teachers and librarians live outside the areas where they work and spend only their working hours there. They take courses in "The Culturally Deprived Child" but they never trouble to get to know the individual "culturally deprived child" as a human being nor stay long enough in the child's milieu to feel at home there and to

speak and understand the child's language.   As always, people are the key and the personnel who run the ideal library
will make or break the operation.

One of the obstacles libraries in the inner cities have
been encountering is vandalism and terrorism on the part of
bands of teenagers who sweep in and terrorize librarians,
clerks and patrons or who systematically smash the windows
and desecrate the buildings and grounds.   A library which
the community feels is their library instead of part of the
"establishment" and which is manned mainly by the community (junior and senior high school students, and paraprofessionals and, where possible, local professionals) is not
so likely to encounter this problem.

A library that is filling a real need will be in demand
seven days a week and in the evenings also.   Evenings do
present a real security problem as the streets grow less and
less safe but a library on a main, well-lit thoroughfare has
more potential security than a library in a residential area
set back from the street.

In addition to the opportunities in the libraries to buy
books, as many other outlets for books and records as possible should be found.   Junior Achievement helps middle-
class children to create and run their own business. Wouldn't
it be possible for high school students, with training, to run
paperback book stores in the schools and community centers
and learn about business as well as providing needed distribution of books?   Of course, sales of paperbacks in stationery stores, drug stores, etc. would also be welcomed.   At
present, in many ghetto areas of New York, it costs $. 70
in carfare to go where a book can be bought, and back.

My experience has convinced me that the so-called
culturally deprived have a deep and unmet hunger for books.
It has also convinced me that the cry for relevance has not
yet been heard and the importance of the material needed not
yet appreciated.   When I went to work as a School Volunteer
in Harlem in January 1957 I was asked to help some children
in the fourth grade who were having reading difficulties.
There were no materials available except a standard fourth-
grade reader so I started bringing my own children's books
from home.   Soon a trail of children were following me--
"Gee, Teach, can I have a book like that?   How do I get a
book like that?" and so forth.   Investigation taught me a
great deal.

First, I learned that, although P. S. 129 was a new
and handsome school and a so-called "Special Service" school
which meant that the school received extra money and special
professional help, there was no librarian nor any staff to
process the books that were being ordered for the library.
No one thought it odd or upsetting that it would be a minimum
of two to three years before library books could circulate
even to the classroom, much less to the home. This was
simply standard Board of Education procedure. In fact, I
later worked in several elementary schools whose libraries
mainly consisted of books donated by parents, and unless the
libraries were manned by parent volunteers, the books were
unavailable to students. In a middle class setting, this system might be tolerable. In areas where seventy-five per
cent of the families own not one book, it helps to account
for the reading level of New York City school children.

Secondly, I learned that a teacher was supposed to
teach reading from a reader. This was true in all grades,
kindergarten through sixth. The reader had been picked by
the Central Board and there was one reader for each grade.
Thus there were six fourth-grade classes consisting roughly
of twenty-two to thirty children each. In the class where I
was helping there were twenty-seven children--eight or nine
of them were illiterate, the majority read two years below
grade, and six or seven read on grade or above. The reader
suited the reading level of only a small minority of pupils
and even where the reading level was right, the material in
it was totally irrelevant to the children in that school since
all the stories were about middle-class white children in
either a suburban or a small town setting. At that time
(1957) there were no multi-ethnic readers and the number of
multi-ethnic trade books for children could be counted on the
fingers of one hand so schools did not have much choice.
In 1967, ten years later, in the majority of schools in
Bedford-Stuyvesant where the overwhelming majority of students are black, none of the schools the Bookmobile was
serving were using the Bank Street readers (a really top-
notch multi-ethnic reader) and the materials in the classroom
were almost as irrelevant as they were in 1957. The library
situation was much improved due to the flood of excellent
multi-ethnic books inspired by the prospect of federal money.

Next, I explored the opportunity in the area to buy
books. It did not exist and still doesn't. Scholastic Book
Services runs a splendid book club service to which an increasing number of teachers now subscribe but except for

this service, which in 1957 was not well known, book buying
is impossible in most ghetto areas. Inexpensive books, such
as the Grosset and Dunlap Easy-to-Read Wonder Books, the
Tempo Books and the Golden Books are simply not for sale
in these areas and the publishers apparently do not care.

This seems a short-sighted view to take. People can
scarcely become readers and later, book buyers, unless attractive materials are available. Not only would the country
benefit if all the population were functionally literate, the
publishers would benefit directly. The market is clearly
there, as the producers of hit records can attest. Recreation is a necessity, especially for those whose work is dull
and whose homes and lives are dreary. People on home
relief or minimal incomes somehow afford television, cheap
gramophones and transistor radios. The right book at the
right price would sell and sell even faster than records since
it would represent not only recreation but also a hope for
the future. People in the ghetto are determined to get a
good education for their children. Adolescents in these
areas (those who have not given up hope as many of them
have) are determined to better themselves. You don't meet
many hippies in Harlem. There is a real hunger for self-
improvement.

In order to explore the market for books, I investigated book fairs and found that most schools in this kind of
area had never had a book fair. Those that did, looked on
it not as an opportunity to get books into the childrens' homes
but as a money raising gimmick for the Parents' Association
--similar to, but not usually as successful as a cake sale.
As a rule, a professional book fair operator was engaged.
He was told the grades the school covered and given a suggested list of prices. He then produced a group of books on
consignment (usually grouped by price, not by subject or
reading level), the books were spread out in the library with
a bored paraprofessional (who knew nothing about the books)
in charge, and the children were turned loose class by class.
Even with this dreary background, an astonishing number of
books were sold.

In a school in Brooklyn where I was working, I found
a sympathetic assistant principal who agreed to let me run a
book fair along different lines. The school had never had a
book fair. With the exception of the president, who was a
Belgian, the Parents' Association consisted of Puerto Ricans,
several of them non-English speaking and none of them with

more than a grade-school education. Sixty-five per cent of
the pupils were from families with incomes so low they were
entitled to free lunch and forty-eight percent of the pupils
were learning English as a second language. With books
from a list similar to the "Annotated Book List" in Part II
and with the proper advance publicity for pupils, parents and
teachers, we sold 1150 books to a student body of 1000 at
cost. The following year, we raised the price of the books
to what retailers were charging and sold 1400 books. Parents who had been begrudging about spending $. 50 the year
before, now urged their children to buy more books. The
whole family had enjoyed the books and felt the purchase
was worthwhile. I had a similar experience running book
fairs in other schools.

Let's make books as readily available as drugs seem
to be and see if education does not result.

Notes on Games

Games are the best key for an older child who has
given up hope of learning to read. The School Volunteers
have probably taught more children to read by playing Go
Fish than in any other way. A game that resembles gin
rummy, Go Fish is played by assembling a trick of cards
all of which have the same beginning sound such as baby,
bat, bear, etc. Each card has the word top and bottom and
the picture of the object in the middle. By the end of two
or three games, the student not only has learned the letter
b and its sound, but has come unconsciously to recognize
the word and when he sees "bat" on a piece of paper, can
read it easily. He has learned to read without knowing it,
and, surprised by success, has the confidence to go on.
Another valuable game is Vowel Dominoes, where the domino
is placed by the sound of the vowel--block next to rock and
so forth.

"Go Fish," Vol. I (initial consonants) and Vol. II
(blends tr - str - th - etc.) and "Vowel Dominoes" are ob-
tainable from Remedial Education Press, 2138 Bancroft
Place, N. W. , Washington, D. C. 20008. The cost for each
is under $5 and each one can teach hundreds of children to
read while giving hours of fun.

Anagrams and boxes of letters (lower case ones are
much the better if you can get them) can be used in

dozens of ways to reinforce phonics or play games with.
Two paper and pencil games that are popular and educational
are Hangman and Categories. In Hangman, the volunteer
prints the alphabet at the top of the page and then silently
picks a phrase such as "a stitch in time saves nine. " At
the bottom of the page he prints:

| - | ------ | -- | ---- | ----- | ---- |

and in the middle, he draws a gallows: ⌐⌐ . The student
suggests letters to fill in the blanks. If the letter is in the
chosen phrase, it is filled in, if not, the head is drawn on
the gallows; the next bad guess adds the neck, the next, one
arm, and so on: the aim is to get the phrase before the entire body goes on the gallows. Then the student picks a
phrase and so on. This game got many students to understand the importance and use of vowels and in the meanwhile
produced shouts of laughter and triumph.

In Categories, volunteer and student together choose
three or four subjects such as Animals, Baseball players,
Hit tunes, etc. (it is important here either to find common
ground, or somehow to balance the subjects. If the student
is poor on authors, pick also a subject like hit tunes, where
the volunteer is not at home so that the contest will not be
uneven.) Then choose a word such as h o m e and try to
find a name in each category for each letter of the word.
The player with the most names wins.

	H	O	M	E
Animals	hyena	ox	mole	elephant
Baseball Player				
Hit Tunes				

This was another very popular game that helped to give the
student fluency in thinking and writing.

Some of the best games are invented by volunteers to
fit a particular situation. One volunteer, working with a boy
who was crazy about football, drew a football field, cut a
football out of paper and, in drilling on phonics, a success

meant yards gained, a brilliant answer meant a first down
and a real blooper lost him the ball. The idea could be
adapted to many other sports. After all, the name of the
game is making reading relevant. Any device or material
that relates to a student's interest will make him want to
read and having fun while learning seems to make the learning stick.

SPECIFIC SUGGESTIONS FOR HELPING

The suggestion has already been made that any individual who has the time can become a School Volunteer or a tutor in the evenings and on week-ends. It has also been suggested that if there are no programs near where the reader lives, that he get together a group of interested citizens and start one. Business men have a special stake in the literacy of their community. The functional illiterates are many of them very intelligent. They represent a pool of talent which is going to waste at a time when many skills are in short supply. Everywhere I go, I hear people saying what a need there is for good clerical help. Really good secretaries are always in demand.

Even in times of unemployment, there is a great shortage of doctors. One of the boys or girls a reader tutors can well grow up to be a Charles Drew or a Daniel Williams [see Annotated List items 1378 and 1498]. Always there is a shortage of people with creative imagination. Perhaps the reader can start a child on the road to success who will become another Benjamin Banneker or a George Washington Carver [see 1348 and 1395]. Always there is a shortage of peacemakers and never has the world needed them more than now. Two of our Nobel laureates in the field of peace are black: Ralph Bunche and Martin Luther King [see 1516 and 1482]. Indians, Mexican-Americans, and Puerto Ricans have been so downtrodden that their leaders are only beginning to emerge. Herman Badillo, Cesar Chavez [see 1487], Vita De Luria and others are leading the way. Our country cannot afford to lose the leadership potential which surely exists among the poverty-stricken American young people who are locked in by illiteracy [see 1508].

In New York City, many businesses have reached the conclusion that they cannot ignore a problem as pressing as this one. Not only are they contributing money but employees. Dozens of men and women who volunteer to do so are released by their employers on company time to tutor in nearby schools one morning a week.

An additional and important dividend to School Volunteer programs is the opportunity to discover what is actually
going on in the schools of your community. Almost everywhere in the country, school problems are making headlines
of one kind or another. People are worried and justly so
about teachers' strikes, violence and drugs in the junior and
senior high schools and steeply rising school taxes. They
hear violently partisan remarks about sex education in the
schools and various new (or old) educational theories, every
one of which is either going to cure all educational ills or
will "keep Johnny from learning to read." A citizen who is
actually in the schools or, through a tutorial program, is
actually getting to know a considerable number of students
and their problems is beginning to learn the facts of our
current situation. No problem can be solved without knowledge.

Not everyone can start a bookmobile but every citizen
can learn the facts about his local library and can begin to
influence library policy. Is your library open at the times
when the people who need it most can use it or is it open
at times most convenient for the staff? If it should be open
more at night and on weekends, can you get financial support
from the community for the additional staff or overtime pay
required? What are the library facilities in your town in
your most disadvantaged area? Could you raise the money
to provide a Bookmobile like Buttercup or a store front library? If you are a business, could your business earn
valued goodwill by providing the money to start such an
enterprise? What opportunities for starting a career in library service are open to paraprofessionals* of minority

---

*A paraprofessional is a person (generally drawn from the
community in which the work is being done) who is paid to
assist a professional person but who does not have the degree
or education of the professional. Paraprofessionals, usually
the parents of pupils, are widely and successfully used in
the N. Y. C. public schools.
  The staff of Buttercup (except the librarians) and the Future Librarians were paraprofessionals. Paraprofessionals
quite naturally vary in their competence but many of them are
extraordinarily intelligent and competent and in such a case
their links to the community can make them more useful to
a project than a professional without such links.

groups? How welcoming is the atmosphere? Are paperbacks
readily available in the public libraries and public school libraries since it is an established fact that poor readers prefer them? How easy or difficult is it for a poor illiterate
person (particularly a child) to get a library card? Could
your library experiment with the idea of no fines? (On
Buttercup, we demanded no identification of any kind and as-
sessed no fines. We got back ninety per cent of our books
consistently over a three-year period. However, we lent
only one book at a time and that book had to be returned to
obtain a new book.)

    What happens to the books your librarian decides to
discard because they are duplicates, outdated fiction or
damaged? Any library culls its books annually or oftener,
otherwise there would be no room for the new books everyone
is asking for. Most of the homes of the people using Buttercup and of the children being helped by the school volunteers
did not even have a newspaper. On Buttercup, when a book's
spine was beginning to go or a book's cover had been torn
off, it was put into a basket near the back door. The sign
on the basket read "Take One" and many children were
thrilled to own a book at last. They would make their own
cover for a coverless one or mend the book in some way
and bring it back proudly to show us.

    Many communities have annual book fairs using the
books discarded by the library and thereby raise money for
more books. They can also use, at these annual fairs, the
books of private citizens who are culling their own personal
libraries. The School Volunteers are often offered books by
private citizens who have heard of the program. Almost in-
variably they are on a high reading level and on subjects of
little interest to the people we are helping. These same
books sold could buy the books we need. Some communities,
for reasons I have never been able to grasp, destroy their
surplus books. What happens in your town?

    The TV programs "Sesame Street" and "Electric Com-
pany" are among the most exciting and encouraging events
that have happened in American education in years. Children
who watch the programs are really learning reading and
arithmetic readiness or, in the case of older children, really
learning to read. Furthermore, children who watch the programs are learning at an early age that it is a multi-ethnic
world and it's not the color of your skin that counts but
what's inside the skin. "Children who watch the programs"

is the operative phrase. Does your town have good reception
for "Sesame Street" and is it on at a time when the children
who need and would enjoy it can watch it? If not, why not
and what can be done about it? Does the harried mother in
a slum area who has no newspaper and doesn't go to the library know about "Electric Company" and how much it can
mean to her children? If you're gifted at poster art, if
you're in the field of publicity perhaps you can mount a cam-
paign to publicize these two programs. Contrary to mythology, not all poor families have TV sets. In some areas,
groups have arranged group viewing opportunities for such
children and their mothers in churches, synagogues and community centers.

        Learn the facts about the schools, learn the facts
about the libraries and get to know the people in disadvantaged areas.

        Several churches I know in New York City have
adopted some tenements in East Harlem. Members of the
congregations visit the buildings regularly to find out what
the tenants' problems are. Almost every member of the
visiting committees has told me that one of their greatest
rewards was getting to know the people who lived in the
buildings. "They are great people!" they exclaim in some
surprise and with real enthusiasm. "When I think of the
courage of Mary Jones and see the job she is doing with
those five children of hers!" says one. "I wish you could
meet John Smith," says another. "I know he's only an elevator operator downtown but you should see the way he draws
and he's so interesting to talk to. I really look forward each
week to our meetings." Another one says, "I used to be
frightened when I drove through the streets in summer and
saw people sitting on their stoops and a group of teenagers
lounging on a street corner. I wondered what menace was
there especially with what I heard on TV. Now I feel that
the group is not a gang. It is Johnny and Mike and José
and Calvin all looking for fun and I am looking for a place
where they can get it. A black librarian who had worked in
a library on the edge of East Harlem and later worked on
Buttercup said "I thought I knew my people. I thought I was
seeing the underprivileged. Now I realize that I was only
seeing the ones who were already started. But somehow, I
have never met children more appealing to me than these,
who need help so badly."

        I speak from experience. Some of my warmest friends

live in Bedford-Stuyvesant. Some of the most rewarding moments of my life came on "Buttercup." Many of the children
and adults I met in Brooklyn had never met a white person
as a friend or equal. (They were sometimes scared of me,
a fact I found incredible.) The white people they met were
authorities: teachers, librarians, doctors, policemen and
other city officials. Most of these people were trying hard
to be helpful but they did constitute authority. And yet, the
mothers I was trying to help and I had so many things in
common. We all worried about our children: we all wanted
them to get ahead academically and in other ways. As
wives, we all wanted to create pleasant homes for our families and ran out of ideas as to what to give our husbands
for dinner. As humans, we all longed for spring in winter
cold and for fall in summer heat. I found satisfaction in
helping people who needed help. I found richness of feeling
and openness of heart in Bedford-Stuyvesant. It's waiting
for you in your town too.

2) APPENDIX: BECOMING A SCHOOL VOLUNTEER

There are School Volunteer programs in several hundred cities and towns in the United States. To find out if
there is one in your town, telephone or write your Board of
Education. In New York City, the address and telephone
number of the School Volunteer Program is 20 West 40th St.,
New York 10018, (212) 563-5620. There are no fixed educational requirements for volunteers. The only physical requirements for volunteers are a satisfactory chest X-ray
(which can be done free at the Board of Health, 125 Worth
St., or a local health clinic) and good general mental and
physical health. School volunteers often have to climb stairs
and always work with active, often noisy children. Requirements of School Volunteer programs vary according to local
situations. If there is no program in your town, visit a
successful one near you. To find out where one is, write
National School Volunteer Program, Inc., 450 North Grand
Ave., Room G-372, Los Angeles 90054; or Volunteers in
Education, US Office of Education, ROB 3, Room 4614, 7th
and D St. SW, Washington, D.C. 20202. In addition, the
following books will be a help:

School Volunteers, by T. Margaret Jamer ($4.25).
Order this directly from Miss Jamer (112 East 70 St., New
York 10021), who was the first director of the New York
City School Volunteer Program. The book gives the basic
philosophy and history of the first six years of the Program.
It was written in 1962 and is therefore a little out of date
but is certainly worth having as a guideline on how to begin
a successful operation.

School Volunteer Reading Reference Handbook and
Basic Kit ($1.50), by Charlotte Mergantine, a manual for
volunteers in the Reading Help Programs by a former read-
ing coordinator for the program and Handbook for Reading
Volunteers in Secondary Schools (39p., $1.50), by Ethel
Price. Both should be ordered from the School Volunteer
Program, 20 West 40th St., New York 10018.

>School Volunteer Programs--How They are Organized
and Managed, ($4) by John W. Hubley; published by School
Management Institute, 6800 High St., Worthington, Ohio
43085.

If the people you want to help have a language problem,
the following book is a must: Conversational English for the
Non-English Speaking Child, by N. Phillips ($3.50). Teachers
College Press, Columbia University, New York 10027. This
is the manual for the crash program in conversational English
mentioned in "The School Volunteer Story."

Also available from the New York City program is a
black-and-white 16 mm. film (2 hours) summarizing the
12-1/2 hour training course in Reading Help developed by
the City School Volunteer program. It is useful not only for
pre-service training but for supplementary instruction or as
a refresher for experienced volunteers.

In starting any project, if an individual can get help
from an organization in supplying recruits, volunteers for
special services such as clerical work, publicity, etc., he
or she is given a real head start ... Investigate the possibility of getting help from organizations such as the local
council of churches, the local council of rabbis, a branch
(if there is one) of the National Council of Jewish Women,
of the National Council of Negro Women, of the N.A.A.C.P.,
and of the Urban League. However, even if no help is forth-
coming, remember that any individual can start something
even if it consists at first of one lone tutor and one lone
child.

I have done considerable research trying to find a
manual on tutorial programs that would correspond to the
books listed on School Volunteer Programs. My search was
unavailing. I found many tutorial programs: some very successful, some on the verge of falling apart. All seemed to
have grown by trial and error. Many of the successful ones
had used information supplied by the books above.

Two very helpful books which have many suggestions
on interesting children in reading are A Parent's Guide to
Children's Reading, by Nancy Larrick, and The Proof of the
Pudding, by Phyllis Fenner. In addition, I hope the bibliography, following, will prove useful.

BACKGROUND BIBLIOGRAPHY

    The following books are useful in depicting the school
systems that have failed to teach people to read, or in sug-
gesting new and successful trends in education or in illuminating the background of life in areas where there are many
illiterate people.

   · Airtight Cage: A Study of New York's West Side, by
Joseph P. Lyford. New York: Harper, c1966; pb
$2.25.
    A fascinating study of life in a changing city area by
a sociologist who bought a house in an urban renewal area
and found that he was not only an observer but actively and
financially involved. I used to say that this book (published
in 1966) was out of date since the people he discusses
(Mayor Wagner et al.) had left the scene. I have now con-
cluded, alas, that it is timeless. The names and faces may
change but the situation, so far, has not.

    Crisis in the Classroom: The Remaking of American
Education, by Charles E. Silberman. New York:
Random, c1970; $10; Vintage pb $1.95.
    An extraordinary survey of education in America
funded by the Carnegie Foundation, this book documents the
many current failures of the American educational system
and also the new methods which seem to be bringing a prom-
ise of success.

    Death at an Early Age: The Destruction of the Hearts
and Minds of Negro Children in the Boston Public
Schools, by Jonathan Kozol. Boston: Houghton Mifflin,
c1967; $5.95.
    Mr. Kozol tells of teaching in the Boston Public School
system and makes it abundantly clear why so many children
are lost to education by the end of third grade. I find parallels in some of my experiences. In Brooklyn, Buttercup
served one school for three years without any member of the
school faculty visiting us although we were parked at their
doorstep weekly. The principal, when I visited him, assured
me the area was hopeless; neither parents nor children were
interested in education. We could only spare this location an
hour between twelve and one and each week about a hundred
children skipped lunch in order to borrow a book. The sixth
graders (in the absence of any adult from the school) kept
order and managed crowd control in what was a dangerous

traffic area.   After two years the principal sent for me and
I raced to his office on wings of hope.   His message was
that he had complaints from teachers that our bookmobile
was blocking the exit from the teachers' parking lot and making it difficult for them to leave for lunch!

Hooked on Books: Program and Proof, by Daniel N.
Fader and Elton B. McNeil.   New York: Putnam,
c1968, $6.95;   Berkley, (c1966) pb $.75.
The exciting story of a successful new way of teaching
reading and writing to seventh graders in a midwestern reform school and a junior high school in Washington, D.C.
Mr. Fader's results are astonishing and heartwarming.   His
methods may not suit every situation but the principles behind
them do and merit study by anyone interested in getting people and books together.

How Two Gerbils, Twenty Goldfish, Two Hundred
Games, Two Thousand Books and I Taught Them How
to Read, by Steven Daniels.   Philadelphia: Westminster, c1971; $4.95;   pb $2.45.
Mr. Daniels found himself teaching in a junior high
school in Philadelphia with no prior or in-service training.
His class was bright, deprived and undisciplined, and he
failed miserably to help them.   The following year, having
had the time to work out a program, he was outstandingly
successful with a similar class.   This book is a must for
teachers of similar pupils and full of helpful lists and suggestions as well as thoroughly good reading.

I Wish I Had an Afro, by John Shearer.   New York:
Cowles, c1970; $3.95.
A photographic documentary of life in a black family
in Westchester (the richest county in the United States, I
believe).   The story is not a dramatic one--the father is in
the home and working to support the family;   there is no
tragic illness nor violence--but the cumulative effect of the
various accounts of the life led (told in succession by different members of the family), the lack of opportunity, and the
despair that crippling poverty induces is devestating.

It's Wings That Make Birds Fly: The Story of a Boy,
by Sandra Weiner.   New York: Pantheon, c1968;
$3.95.
Another photographic documentary with the text based
on tapes recorded and edited by the author-photographer.
This one tells the story of a boy in Harlem whose situation

is touching, dreary and typical until he is killed in a traffic
accident.   I have seen this and the book above on several library lists for black people.   They are the last people to be
given these books which are both authentic and depressing.
After all, the black people of Harlem and Westchester already
know what is in these books.   It's the people who are sealed
away from their life who need to read them.

Making Schools Work: Strategies for Changing Education, by Marcus Foster et al.   Philadelphia: Westminster, 1971; $5.95;   pb $2.45.
An outstanding black educator tells the methods he
used in Philadelphia to create good morale and a learning
climate in high schools that were torn racially and full of
drugs and violence.   A constructive and heartwarming book.

The Other America: Poverty in the United States,
by Michael Harrington.   Rev. ed.   New York:
Macmillan, c1970; $7.95 (orig. ed., Penguin pb,
c1962, $1.25).
This book documents, in a very understated way, the
poverty from which so many Americans are so insulated that
they don't believe it exists.   I took my mother to a book fair
in South Brooklyn and she said to me, looking at well scrubbed,
well dressed children "In my day, the poor looked poor.
If you hadn't told me how deprived these children were, I
wouldn't believe it."   The clothes came from Woolworth, the
cleanliness was sometimes deceptive and always a struggle
and many of the children were literally hungry but they didn't
look it.   This book is a real must.

Pygmalion in the Classroom: Teacher Expectation
and Pupil's Intellectual Ability, by Robert Rosenthal
and Lenore Jacobson.   New York: Holt, Rinehart,
c1968;   pb $5.
A description of an experiment which proved how important a role expectation plays in any kind of education.
Two Harvard psychologists found that rats, randomly selected,
proved brilliantly successful in intelligence tests when their
handlers had been led to believe that they were genetically
superior.   The psychologists got similar results in schools
in California and Washington when the teachers had been told
that a randomly selected group of children were, in fact,
especially bright and full of potential.   Tragically, the experiment also proved that after the sixth grade, expectation
could no longer reverse an attitude of despair and failure.

Schools Without Failure, by William Glasser. New
York: Harper & Row, c1969; $4.95.

Another innovative solution to motivating children who
feel they have no hope of success. Dr. Glasser, a psychol-
ogist, got involved with education in his work at a home for
teen-age unwed mothers, most of whom were uneducated and
illiterate. The methods which were successful with the girls
later proved to work with children of every age and large
portions of the California school system are currently using
his techniques with great success. It is noteworthy that
most of the successful educational ideas in the books in this
bibliography cost little or no money. Basically, what the
authors call for is thoughtful awareness and a new attitude
on the part of educators.

The Way It 'Sposed to Be, by James Herndon. New
York: Simon & Schuster, c1968; $4.95; Bantam
pb $.95.

The author taught a class in Harlem and learned a
great deal. He is not sure how much his pupils learned
from him but he felt that he had made a real impact on their
lives. One year was not enough, however, to repair years
of deprivation and damage and the book, which has humor,
drama and depth ends on a sad note. A very revealing book.

The Wretched of the Earth, by Frantz Fanon, with a
preface by Jean-Paul Sartre. New York: Grove,
c1961; pb $1.25.

This book, by a black psychiatrist from the island of
Martinique, is called "the hand book for the black revolution."
It is certainly read and quoted with deep emotion by thousands of black Americans and people of the third world.
Dr. Fanon was assigned to a hospital in Algeria during the
French-Algerian War and his experiences there produced
this book. His experiences and observations are about Algeria but almost everything he says could apply equally well
to the Americans and Vietnamese. This is a book which
has already influenced history and will continue to do so.

MEMO TO THE BOOKMOBILE STAFF
(The Bushwick-Bedford-Stuyvesant Travelling Library)

The aim of the Bushwick-Bedford Stuyvesant Travelling

Library and its reason for being is to provide books and
pictures for the recreation and pleasure of the people of the
neighborhood and to persuade people of every age who have
never before enjoyed reading, that there <u>are</u> books that they
can read easily on subjects they care about and that can give
them either information they want or relaxation and enjoyment.

How do we do this? We start by trying to create a
pleasant and welcoming atmosphere. The truck itself is a
gay yellow with bright posters and decorations on the outside.
If there is a community event (church fairs, school play,
etc.) that we can publicize, we are delighted to act as a
town crier and to carry posters to advertise the affair to
the neighborhood. In fact, our gifted Future Librarians often
make up the posters for community events. Over the en-
trance is <u>welcome</u> in English and Spanish, and we mean it.
On the inside, the truck has a bright red rug and flower
power decals. It has a warmth and cheer even in a snowstorm. This is the physical picture.

Now we come to people. First, the only rules we have have to do with safety. We don't allow smoking since it would be very dangerous in a small area with thousands of paperback books. We don't allow children to ride on the back of the truck in motion. Except for safety, we try to keep rules to a minimum--there's no room for studying, therefore no need for quiet; no fines for lateness, therefore a warm welcome even if a borrower has been ill or out of town for a while. We'd rather children didn't eat on the truck nor drip ice cream cones over the books but we welcome the child _first_; correct him later. To make someone a reader is more important than to protect the books.

It is important to understand that we welcome every kind of person under any circumstances. Therefore, the books also are arranged in a welcoming way--they are arranged by subject matter, not by age. We try to have a good mystery, for example, for people reading on a second-grade level as well as for James Bond addicts, and we are glad to see anyone take a book from anywhere. Our aim is _never_ to limit a book by labelling it for one or another age group and _never_ to limit a person by making him feel unwelcome or ashamed of something which is no fault of his, i. e. , the degree of his lack of education.

Just as important as the physical set-up is the staff, which has the responsibility of making every one who comes on the Bookmobile feel at home. In fact, the responsibility starts earlier than that--in good weather, we stand outside in slack moments with book marks and try to lure people on. Some of the staff have gone as volunteers to speak at PTA meetings or community groups on the importance of books and reading. The staff has the advantage of coming from the neighborhood and knowing the community. Both the clientele and the staff can feel at home with each other.

The staff, however, has the responsibility of persuading people to read and they can only do it if they honestly believe what they say. Unlike library situations, our staff is asked to recommend specific titles. You can only sell what you yourself know and like. Therefore, it is the responsibility of the staff to read widely among the titles we carry and to be able to recommend with genuine enthusiasm. This doesn't mean that a staff member who hates baseball has to read a lot of baseball books. We try to have a staff comprising a varied group of ages and tastes. A young mother on the staff who can say, "I read this to my little girl and she loved it," carries weight.

A teenager who tells another teenager about a book
that was groovy and opened a new world to him--carries
weight.   One older person who can say to another, "This is
old timey but I like the memories"--carries weight.   And
the weight means that many non-readers are acquiring reading skills at best or at least finding pleasure and recreation in
our books.

We have some special problems and opportunities.
Many of the children we deal with have been much shouted
at both at home and in school.   Because of overcrowding
they have not been treated as individuals worthy of respect.
We therefore make a special effort never to shout and to
treat each child as a special individual.   If a child comes
on in a delinquent situation--for example, with a lost or
damaged book, we make a great effort to hear the child's
explanation before we say anything.   So many of these children have such difficulty in saying anything (some, at first
cannot even give their names and addresses), that to explain
a situation in which they feel at fault is almost beyond them.
Many who have never had a book at home before are genuinely
surprised when a younger brother or sister snatches and tears
the book or spills food on it or whatever.

Many mothers in our area do not realize that the years
up to 5 are when a child learns all its habits and way of
thought.   If the mother would read to her children and to herself, it could make the whole difference to her child's school
career.   We try to get that message across.

We lean over backwards not to be authoritarian.   Our
main principle is to teach and reach by example--not by
preaching.   We have practical rules which must be met.   If
you want a new book, you must return the old.   This is self-
evident or we would run out of books.   We are prompt and
reliable as to our schedule.   Our clientele also have to learn
to be prompt and reliable if they want to use us.   The main
principle of the staff is to listen first, talk later and to have
the kind of manners we want to instill.

Last but not least in importance is our choice of books.
We try to carry books of all kinds for all ages but obviously
with the space we have we cannot please everyone.   Therefore, since our special mission is to reach people who have
not been using the public library, we do not cater to people

who ask for best sellers or who are highly sophisticated and motivated readers but who come aboard because we are <u>there</u>. We want to meet <u>needs</u> not requests for titles. We, therefore, try to carry books which <u>any</u> young child will enjoy and books for older children and teenagers which have real quality, books which a girl or boy will remember several years later. We try to carry a good line of biography and especially a good amount of history and Afro-American history.

Especially we try to carry and emphasize books which bring real pleasure to the reader. A person who reads because he feels he should, will read only two or three books a summer; a person who has come to enjoy books will keep on reading for life. He can't wait to get to the next one. That is why we let our clients (from four to eighty-four) choose what they want. If a child wants to read the same book about Curious George four weeks in a row, let him. If he's enjoying the book, he's gaining. But again, our job is to open doors, to know the books we carry and why we carry them. Many really good books are going unread on the Bookmobile because they have unfamiliar sounding titles or are on subjects that are not on TV. Read them and your clientele will want to too.

BUDGET(S) FOR BOOKMOBILE(S)

1) Summary (February 1969)

Capital expenditures run $30,000 per new bookmobile (this includes all books, records, and filmstrips, but excludes the cost of the vehicle and its preparations for use, which is covered by a lease rental of about $6,000 a year). The present bookmobile will only require $5,000 of capital expense to enlarge its office and to add audio-visual equipment.

The annual operating budget is $60,000 per bookmobile (including the item of $6,000 for lease-rental).

The annual budget for the Future Librarians program will be between $3,000 to $5,000 per unit, depending on the number of junior high school students involved in each unit.

A detailed breakdown of the budgets follows.

2) Budget per Bookmobile (Capital Expense)

Office Equipment

Book cases, desk, typewriter, ditto machine, paper cutter, etc.	$ 3,000

Bookmobile Equipment

Audio-visual equipment	$ 2,500
Generator	600
Viewer and slides	250
Heaters	400
Door	80
Rug	80
Chairs, etc.	25
Books (20,000 or more)	19,500
Records & Film strips	2,000
Pictures	1,300
total	$29,735

The above capital figures hold true for each bookmobile, regardless of the number commissioned at a time.

3) Annual Operating Budget for One Bookmobile

Administrative Expense

Salaries	$10,733.88[a]	
Accounting	250.00	
Photography and Reports	500.00	
		$11,483.88

Operating Expense

Salaries	$33,178.69[b]
Rent of vehicle	6,000.00[c]
Insurance	1,350.00[d]
Telephone	300.00
Office supplies	1,200.00
Publicity in area	500.00[e]
Office maintenance, vehicle painting	300.00

Balance Forward (Admin. Expense) $11,483.88

Operating Expense (cont.)

Consultant fees, organizational fees, travel	250.00d	
Misc., emergency reserve	800.00e	
		$43,878.69

Materials

Books, a/v (new and replacement) $ 4,800.00e

Total expenses $60,162.57

No figure has been included for rent since office space has been supplied by the Brooklyn Public Library. This budget contains no funds for the Future Librarians program (see "Summary"), which will have to be funded separately. It will cost from $3000 to $5000 per bookmobile, depending on minimum wage scales, plus administrative costs, if enough junior high school children are involved. Last year's program involved fifteen children, ten of whom became regular summer volunteers and summer employees.

Notes

a. Fifty per cent of librarian/administrator's
        salary $ 5,250.00
    Good secretary (20 hours per week)   4,000.00
    Ten per cent salary-related benefits   925.00
        Subtotal $10,175.00

    Five per cent increment after twelve
        months, following NYC practice   508.75
    Ten per cent salary-related benefits
        on increment   50.88
    Total administrative salaries $10,734.63

b. Fifty per cent of librarian/adminis-
        trator's salary $ 5,250.00
    Bookmobile Administrator   6,500.00
    Clerk/driver   6,300.00
    Senior clerk   5,200.00

Junior clerk	4,300.00
Part-time clerk (relief for lunch, etc.,	
10 hours per week)	1,040.00
Subtotal	$28,590.00
Ten per cent salary-related benefits	2,859.00
Subtotal	$31,449.00
Five per cent increment (see a above)	1,572.45
Ten per cent salary-related benefits on	
increment	157.24
Total operating salaries	$33,178.69

(It should be noted that these increments have been computed on an annual basis but will probably only apply to the fourth quarter. It should also be noted that with one exception, all salaries go to people from the area served.)

c.   The rent of the present bookmobile, a second-hand vehicle, has gone from $104.90 per month to $108 in the last year, because of a cost-of-living clause which is still in effect. New bookmobiles (to quote Hertz) will be a few dollars more a week. This includes fifty per cent of initial outfitting, plus garaging, plus maintenance including road service, plus gas and oil for 100 miles a week, a mileage so far never exceeded.

d.   This figure covers every kind of personal, automobile, and property liability to the general public, the clientele and the employees plus a burglary and floater policy on the contents of the office and bookmobile. It also includes, on the advice of the insurance broker, a fifteen per cent rise in rates in 1969.

e.   All three of these figures trouble the trustees. They appear to the trustees as being too low for a sensible operation. Their suggested minimums were $1000 for publicity in area (we want to reach people but will try to do it through volunteers), $1500 for emergency reserve and miscellaneous, $5500 for materials. The materials figure covers books (new titles and replacements for those that are worn out), records (ditto), pictures (ditto), films and film strips. We find that many paperbacks can circulate fifteen times. We do a final mending to those that have not then disintegrated and then give the book away to a customer.

4) Annual Budget for Additional Bookmobiles

To add one or two more bookmobiles to the overall operation would require, as to each, an increase of thirty per cent per year (compounded) to administration expense, but would slightly decrease the per vehicle operating expense because of common inventory, storage and processing. Hence the operating costs become, on an annual basis:

	1 vehicle	2 vehicles	3 vehicles
Administrative Expenses	$11,500	$ 14,600	$ 21,400
Operating Expenses	48,700	100,000	150,000
Total	$60,200	$114,600	$171,400

A total operating budget of $180,000 per year would leave some room for the Future Librarians program.

Note: The Central Brooklyn Model Cities Committee elected to buy new bookmobiles rather than to rent from Hertz. The results have been very poor. The original cost of each vehicle was very high and the upkeep (garage space and vehicle and generator maintenance) has also been extremely high compared to the Hertz figures. In addition, there have been so many mechanical problems with both the vehicles and their generators that the operation has been substantially damaged by lack of continuity. Customers, especially the sort we serve, become easily discouraged by nonappearance of a service especially as it is impossible to notify people in an area ahead of time that the bookmobile will not be there. This leads to diminished circulation and very much affects the morale of the staff who are eager to be out serving the public, not doing busy work in an office. The Brooklyn Public Library has had similar problems with their bookmobiles. In short, Hertz was old Mr. Reliable and cheap to boot.

A SUMMER BOOKMOBILE SCHEDULE

This is a sample summer schedule with explanations of why we felt the locations would be fruitful. Our plans were based on research, neighborhood information and past experience. If we found we were wrong, of course we

changed, but we tried to stick to our plans so people could
depend on us and almost never changed our route after the
first week of each season. [The successors to "Buttercup,"
operated by the Central Brooklyn Model Cities Committee,
are able to operate in the evenings and on weekends--an even
better time to reach people.]

MONDAY

9:30 - 11:15   Bushwick Avenue and Madison Street:
                a health center with a large playground
                next to it.
11:30 - 12:30   Grove Street and Evergreen Avenue:
                a school which had a summer school;
                this was a neighborhood we served with
                great success in winter and summer.
12:45 - 2:30   Weirfield Street between Central and Wilson
                Avenues:
                a play street near a day care center.
2:45 - 4:45   Knickerbocker Avenue at Halsey Street Park:
                a park adjoining a very successful winter
                area.

TUESDAY

1:30 - 3:00   Evergreen Avenue between Weirfield and
                Hancock Streets:
                an area near a school served with suc-
                cess winter and summer.
3:15 - 4:45   Knickerbocker and Suydan Avenues:
                an area near a lot of small stores;
                especially good.

WEDNESDAY

9:30 - 11:15   Gates Avenue between Ralph and Buffalo
                Avenues:
                a play street near a housing project
                (Albany Houses).
11:30 - 3:15   Kingston Park at Prospect Place:
                a popular park with lots of children and
                story telling opportunities.
3:30 - 4:45   Prospect Place between Schenectady and
                Troy Avenues:
                St. John's Recreation Center filled with
                summer day camps and adjoining a huge
                housing project.

THURSDAY

9:30 - 11:30	Monroe Street near Summer Avenue: another play street.
11:45 - 1:15	Putnam Avenue between Throop and Tompkins Avenues: near a day camp and Golden Age Center.
1:30 - 2:30	Tompkins Avenue and Floyd Street: near a housing project we served in winter.
2:45 - 4:45	DeKalb and Summer Avenues: between outdoor fruit and vegetable markets and a housing project.

FRIDAY

9:45 - 12:00	1600 Eastern Parkway between Prospect and Saratoga Avenues: an enormous summer day camp.
12:15 - 2:00	St. Mark's Avenue between Ralph and Howard Avenues: a very deprived neighborhood around the corner from a portable swimming pool.
2:15 - 4:45	Brevoort Houses off Patchen Avenue: a large housing project between two elementary schools, both with summer programs.

SAMPLES OF VOLUNTEERS' JOB REPORTS

The Future Librarians were highly motivated children thirteen or fourteen years of age who had come to our attention either because they had volunteered on Buttercup in the spring or had been favorably recommended by their school librarians. Many of them were intelligent (one was brilliant) and several were quite artistic. All performed their jobs well once they learned the ropes. All had "successfully" completed the eighth grade in New York City schools. Note the level of literacy in the following reports.

By JENNIE SANTIAGO.

We write to four spanish kids
+ two negros. On Irving and
gates. Then we went down
Ridgewood + Pamelo to some
italian kids then we walk on
untel we got back to Pamelo
and the bookbomile. The
books I read where I big
green things + How do the
animals get to the zoo. They
seem to like it because we
like show them the pictures
of the different animals in the
book How do the animal get
to the zoo

Report

Last Wednesday Robert and me went to
P.S. 243 And told stories.
The children All enjoyed it and went
with me Back to the Bookmobile And
Borrowed books.
They wanted me to tell them more stories
this Wednesday.
I enjoyed their company Just Like they enjoyed
my's.
                                        The End

Mypa

To Whomever it may Concern: 7/15/68
    I translated 5 stories to Spanish
for 10 Puerto Rican kids. The
stories were: Puss 'n' boots
        Donald Duck Book
        Smiley Lion Book
        The Apple Book
        The Parrot Book
The kids ranged from 3 to
9 yrs. The kids liked the
stories very much especially
Puss 'n' boots.
           Robert Castro

Dear ?
    I read a story to a 3 year
old and it turn out ok.
    But I ask a little girl to if
she wanted me to read her a story
and a lady come out and said:
Leave my girl alone and get away
from here! = and I Ran.
          Linda

Valentina

I learned how to filed
in strick alphabetical
order. I think it will
help me when I become
a secutary in the future
            Working in the
Book mobil helps me
to get along with kids
and understand what
they like or dislike.
I think that working
with the kids now that
when I get marry I will
have an idea of what
kids are like then.
            I think that the
Book mobil will be a
successful traveling library
and help the children
get a better reading habit

Part II

ANNOTATED BOOK LIST (INTRODUCTION)

A NOTE ON THE TITLES AND THEIR SOURCES

This is a list of books which are recommended as
being most likely to interest people in reading with pleasure
who have had little or no experience with books.   The list
has been compiled on the basis of three related but somewhat different experiences, and the source of the experience
has in general been noted as to each book.

The first source is the cumulative experience of the
School Volunteers (originally sponsored by the Public Education Association, but now part of the Board of Education).
Starting with about twenty volunteer, part-time helpers in
1956, the School Volunteers are now over 2000 strong.
Their experience in leading children in deprived areas to
enjoy reading and improve their reading level results from
many thousands of hours of work with thousands of children.
The day-to-day experience of finding books useful or not,
for this purpose, found its way to a central office, and this
information has been available and used.

The second source is again the cumulative experience
of two and a half year's operation of a bookmobile in the
Bushwick-Bedford-Stuyvesant area of Brooklyn, during which
over 100,000 books were loaned to over 35,000 people of
all ages.   Often more than a thousand people a week borrowed books (virtually all paperbacks) and returned over
ninety per cent of them in good condition.   Many borrowers
read four or five, and in quite a few instances over fifteen
books.   The bookmobile project, funded initially by the
Chase Manhattan Bank, has been highly successful and is
now operated by the Central Brooklyn Model Cities Program,
with three bookmobiles in action six days a week.

The third source is a personal assessment made by
me on the basis of my experience from 1957 to 1966 as a

School Volunteer, my experience in 1966-1969 in organizing and supervising the bookmobile "Buttercup," and my practice of reading virtually all books published which seem to merit consideration for the purpose at hand. These books are indicated by an asterisk, and have not yet been tested in use as have the others.

In general the list follows the Dewey Classification System. A few features of the list may surprise some librarians and teachers. First, for reasons stated in "The Buttercup Story," there is no separation of titles by age groups. Second, under fiction, the titles in Human Experience are ones which (in my judgment) have a universal quality which transcends the usual barriers. For example, Brown Girl, Brownstones [876] is about a West Indian woman who sacrifices all consideration for her husband, all thoughts of kindness or of friendship, to become a home owner. Since the book is about West Indians, I have seen it mainly displayed in black literature sections in bookstores. But the woman's ambition and the bitter generation gap it creates between her and her daughter have nothing to do with race and have occurred over and over again in history. In the minorities section (also under fiction), I have included not just ethnic or racial minorities but books about newcomers of many kinds who are also a minority until they have become assimilated.

Third, the section classified as Picture Books is quite literally that--i.e., books which would have no reason for being without their illustrations. Books frequently put into the picture book section of children's libraries, for example, Peter's Chair [760] and Curious George [983] are listed under the appropriate Dewey classification as are easy-to-read books.

Just as an adult differentiates between two kinds of books and likes one title and not another, so do children. The child who loves The Cat in the Hat [974] and Where the Wild Things Are [1018] is apt to find Little Bear [794] too cozy and young and Apt. 3 by Ezra Jack Keats [865] too slow going. And the children who like the latter often are repelled by the former.

I often take children to public libraries in New York, Philadelphia, Long Island and Maine. With the current arrangement of books in most children's libraries, it is very difficult if not impossible for pre-schoolers and poor readers

to select books in any meaningful way. In most libraries,
books are shelved with the spines showing the title and
classified as Picture Books or Easy-To-Read Books all
lumped together until you reach books on a fourth-grade
reading level. And yet it is just those reading <u>below</u> that
level that most need to be convinced of the value of books.

In Maine, one library I know has taken a very small
space--approximately 14 x 14 feet--and displays its books
with the covers showing and highly categorized: Stories
about famous people, Stories about girls, Family stories,
Sports stories, etc. There are even three different categories of animals (dogs, cats, and other animals). Even
young children and very poor readers quickly learn the categories and I hear a four year old saying, "This week I want
a story about a dog," or a slow fourth grader, "This week I
want a story about a girl who got to be famous," and in the
library they march off with eager confidence and rarely seem
disappointed. Nothing can be more discouraging than to take
home a selection thinking it is one kind of book and find
it is quite another, and yet, picking by title or appearance,
this often happens. Since the space used can display only a
part of the collections, the displays are replenished each day
from a back-up collection and the circulation is very high as
well as very satisfying both to the children and to the librarian.

A book like <u>Peter's Chair</u> can be a rewarding emotional experience for a child worried about his position in
his family. If it is treated with respect by the library and
categorized as to content, the child will also feel respected.
If it is lumped indiscriminately in Picture Books (to many
children, this means "baby" books), it is not only less likely
to be found and enjoyed but the user also to some extent
feels denigrated.

A NOTE ON THE ANNOTATIONS

It is often said that you can't tell a book by its
cover. Unfortunately, that is the way many people judge
a book and especially people who have never had a pleasurable or useful experience with the written word. Therefore,
in the "Annotated Book List" the reader will find a great

many comments dealing with format--by which is meant the
physical appearance of the book--both outside and inside.
To School Volunteers and the staff of the bookmobile, the
ideal format is one which makes a book attractive to the
largest audience possible.   This means it must be appealing
to many age groups.   In general, except for pre-school
children and those in the first three grades, the more a
book appears aimed at an older age, the more appealing it
is to several age groups.

Where they exist, both paperback and hardcover
trade editions are listed.   Since every person encountered in
these programs from grade three up preferred paperbacks to
hardcovers, the paperback edition is listed first.   An exception to this rule is shown when a program used a book which
has subsequently been issued in paperback.

Out of print books are still listed for two reasons.
First, many libraries may still own these titles and will be
glad to know that they are useful.   Second, many books go
in and out of print so fast that the titles may well be in
print again by the time this book is published.   For example,
in 1969, two very useful titles, Down the Mississippi [823]
and Cotton Comes to Harlem [1143], were out of print.   As
of February 1971, both were back in print.

Reading levels given are subjective, but follow pretty
much the standards of the Harris word list.   Where a double
reading level is given ("3-4") the book is preponderately
third-grade reading level with some fourth-grade words.
Many third graders will be able to enjoy the book with or
even without a little help.   If the book were labelled "4" it
would be missed by many potential readers.

Obviously, most of the books on the list could be
recommended for private and suburban schools.   I have only
marked certain books "P" (see code below), since I want to
call attention to them.   Too many children are growing up in
the affluent suburbs without ever encountering children of
minority groups.   Knowing little or nothing about minority
children except what they are told in Brotherhood Week or
see on television in crisis situations like the New York City
school strike, the suburban children get a very distorted
picture which is damaging for them and dangerous for the
country.   If they begin at an early age to empathize with
minority children by reading and enjoying books like Benjie
[870] and the Ezra Jack Keats books [397 and 782], we shall
all be the better for it.

Although I have tried to cover as many books as possible, the list does not pretend to be all inclusive. When I first started to help with reading in January 1957, the number of multi-ethnic books for children could be counted on the fingers of one hand and The Cat in the Hat and easy-to-read books were not yet on the market. Anyone trying to help disadvantaged children improve their reading would indeed be grateful for the flood of easy books and of multi-ethnic books which have since appeared.

However, not all of the latter are appropriate for programs for minority children. Books like Call Me Charlie by Jesse Jackson and Durango Street by F. Bonham were unanimously rejected by the bookmobile staff on the ground that while the stories they told could well be true, all they would do to a black boy would be to lower his morale and possibly to use racism as an alibi for not trying to perform. They felt vehemently about this and commented, "I'd never let my son read this" of "I wouldn't let my younger brother have this book. "

Many of the new books may well have a role to play in alerting white middle-class children to the effects of racial prejudice and economic injustice. The criterion used by the bookmobile staff and the School Volunteers is "whether a book will not only be enjoyable but also constructive or at the very least not destructive so that a child will feel at least as good, or better about his identity than he did before he read the book. " In the light of that standard, many of the books about minority children now being published seem to be for white children only.

EXPLANATION OF SYMBOLS

*   indicates a new title to which there has not yet been a reaction

B   bookmobile--indicates use on the "Bushwick-Bedford-Stuyvesant Travelling Library"

c   copyright

HS   high school

IL: interest level (in grades)

JH   junior high school (grades seven and eight)

M   multi-ethnic

OP   out of print

P   recommended for use in private and suburban schools
        to broaden their students' experience of a multi-
        ethnic world

pb   paperback

RL: reading level (in grades)

S   indicates use in the New York City School Volunteers
        program.

The information as to editions and prices was taken from
Books in Print, published by R. R. Bowker Company, 1972,
or in some cases from information supplied by the publisher.
Since prices change so rapidly, they are given simply to
indicate relative values.

A KEY TO THE ARRANGEMENT

THE BOOK LIST

0 GENERAL REFERENCE

1 The American Heritage Dictionary, edited by William
    Morris. American Heritage and Houghton Mifflin,
    c1969. $7.95
    RL: Adult   IL: JH-adult   S
This dictionary has two enormous advantages for a school
program: (1) it is up to date on scientific matters which
are moving so fast that a dictionary published ten years ago
(and it takes years to produce a new dictionary) will not
list many words (especially those concerning the environment) that are now in common use and essential, and (2) it
is heavily illustrated--a very important advantage, especially
for people who have problems with reading or the English
language. It is an adult counterpart of the Courtis-Watters
Golden Illustrated Dictionary [3].

2 The American Heritage Dictionary, abridged edition,
    edited by William Morris. American Heritage and
    Dell, 1970. pb $.75
    RL: Adult   IL: JH-adult   BS
This abridged edition of the above has the usual problem
of paperback dictionaries, small print and incompleteness.
However, it is certainly one of the best of the paperback
dictionaries and does contain useful illustrations. The
best buy in paperback dictionaries for most adults, it is
somewhat more difficult reading then number 6 below
(Scholastic Dictionary) and somewhat less expensive and
with clearer illustrations.

3 Courtis-Watters Golden Illustrated Dictionary, by Dr.
    Stuart A. Courtis and Mrs. Garnette Watters. Western,
    c1965. $3.95
    RL: 3-4   IL: K-adult   S
The School Volunteer program has had one or more of
these dictionaries in each of their programs since the in-
ception of the Reading Help Programs in 1958. For the
first few years these dictionaries were illustrated in color

and children who had started to look up a word were lured
on by the illustrations to browse and often learned a great
deal that way. It was a book that opened doors. The current edition is in black and white and is still very useful
since its definitions are in words most of our readers can
understand. However, the browsing quality has disappeared
except for good readers. Schools use a number of inter-
mediate dictionaries but we find that this, the Scholastic
Dictionary (also liberally illustrated), and the American
Heritage are the best for our purposes--i. e. , to interest
and inform people who are intelligent but not deeply book
or academically oriented.

4   My First Golden Encyclopedia, by Jane W. Watson.
      Illus. by William Dugan.   Western, c1969. $4. 95
      RL: 2-4   IL: Read aloud-5   *SMP
This first encyclopedia has lots of colorful pictures to encourage browsing and on the whole does a masterful job of
describing a child's world in clear and simple terms.   I
hope that the next edition will not treat Indians so much as
a part of the past and will give them a little more present
and possibly even a future !

5   Richard Scarry's Storybook Dictionary, by Richard
      Scarry.   Western, c1966. $3. 95
      RL: 2-3   IL: Read aloud-4, Non-readers to Adult *S
A wonderful book with interest and humor.   Each definition
tells a short story and the same animal characters appear
and reappear.   Over 2500 words are defined and there are
over 1000 pictures.   A real must for the elementary schools.

6   Scholastic Dictionary of American English, edited by
      Alvina Treut Burrows, et al.   Illus. by Allen Young.
      Scholastic, c1966.   pb $1. 65
      RL: Varied   IL: 4-adult   BS
With 898 pages of definitions and over 1000 illustrations,
this dictionary is a real bargain.   It is a very useful book
although the necessarily small print makes it difficult for
adults who would otherwise find it very helpful.

7   Tell Me Why, by Arkady Leokum.   Illus. by Cynthia
      Koehler and Alvin Koehler.   3 vols.   Grosset, 1969.
      $4. 95
      RL: 5   IL: Universal   S
Excellent reference books with short answers.   General
information books that are, in effect, beginning encyclopedias
on an older and more universal interest level than My First
Golden Encyclopedia [4].

1 PHILOSOPHY AND PSYCHOLOGY

8 About Sex and Growing Up, by Evelyn Millis Duvall. Illus.
   by Simon Frankel. Association Press, c1968.
   pb $1.50
   RL: 5-6   IL: 4-HS   *BS
This book has a very pedagogical format including a vocabulary to learn at the end of each chapter. This may put
some readers off but on the whole, the interest in the subject
matter will overcome the handicap. The book's asset is
the amount of sociological and psychological information it
includes. It makes it clear that growing up is a many
faceted process of which the physical side is only one part.

9 Ann Landers Talks to Teen-agers About Sex, by Ann
   Landers. Fawcett, Crest, c1970. pb $.60
   RL: 5   IL: 4-HS   BS
The famous columnist gives her answers to the problems
about which teen-agers have written her. This is a very
popular book which interests even poor readers.

10 The Art of Dating, by Evelyn Millis Duvall and Joy D.
   Johnson. Illus. by André Ecuyer. Association Press,
   c1968. pb $.95
   RL: 6   IL: 4-adult   BS
The repellent format of this book makes it less popular
than it should be as it is full of the kind of moral and
social guidance young people are seeking. Those who borrow it always come back to borrow other books so must
have liked it.

11 Facts of Love and Marriage for Young People, edited
   by Aron M. Krieh. Dell (Laurel), c1962. pb $.60
   RL: varied, mainly 6-7 IL: JH-adult   BS
This excellent collection of essays on all aspects of love
and marriage and parenthood has to be introduced. It has
a drab cover, fine print and quite a high reading level.
However, it also has a lot of wise advice on emotional
health and how to make a marriage work that does not
seem to be available in other books with similar titles.

12 Love and the Facts of Life, by Evelyn Millis Duvall. Illus.
    by André Ecuyer. Association Press, c1967. $4.95
    (pb $.95)
    RL: 6   IL: 4-young adult   BS
This book is a revised version of Love and the Facts of
Life for Teenagers, one of the most popular books for
young people ever published. Many beyond the teen years
can benefit by its wisdom and common sense and the new
title looks to a wider audience. Unfortunately the paperback version has exceptionally poor print.

13 Nobody Knows My Name, by James Baldwin. Dial,
    c1961. $5.95 (Dell, Laurel, pb $.60)
    RL: adult   IL: HS-adult   BM
A series of autobiographical essays in which the famous
author outlines his philosophy and the difficulties of finding
one's identity as a black American. This book is borrowed
even by those who find it difficult reading.

14 Sex: Telling It Straight, by Eric W. Johnson. Lippin-
    cott, c1970. $3.95
    RL: 4-5   IL: 4-adult   *BSM
A very important book. I cannot imagine a child, or
adolescent or young adult who would not reach for this
book and benefit by the knowledge he would gain from it.
Mr. Johnson, who impresses me as a man who truly understands children and teenagers frankly discusses all aspects
of sex in simple straightforward language with some emphasis on the aspects of sex which are most apt to worry
children. It is an honest book. He includes the slang four
letter words which are used in the street to describe sex
as well as the standard words. I consider this an asset
but some adults will be bound to object, so be prepared.

15 Teen Love, Teen Marriage, by Jules Saltman. Grosset,
    Tempo, c1960. pb $.75
    RL: 6   IL: 6-HS   BS
A series of articles by different experts which give scien-
tific information and wise advice on teen love and marriage.
A very popular book.

16 To My Son, the Teen-Age Driver, by Henry Gregor
    Felsen. Dodd, Mead, c1964. $3.50 OP (Bantam,
    Pathfinder, $.50)
    RL: 6   IL: 6-HS   BS
All boys long to drive. This excellent book by the author
of Hot Rod and Crash Club is full of thought-provoking

counsel on driving and on priorities for teenagers.   It is
popular and boys accept the advice of an expert.

17   The Wisdom of Martin Luther King--In His Own Words,
         ed. by the staff of Bill Adler Books, Inc.   Lancer,
         c1968. $. 75 OP
         RL: adult   IL: JH–adult   BMP
Excerpts from Martin Luther King's writings, speeches and
sermons arranged by subject matter, this book was much in
demand for a while after King's death.   At the moment, he
seems to be out of favor except with the older generation.

2 RELIGION

18 <u>Arch Book Series</u>.   Concordia Pub. House, 1965. $.39
    RL: 3   IL: Read aloud-adult   B
These brightly illustrated books each tell a Bible story in
rhyme.   As in all series, some titles are better than others.
All of the books, however, seem to be very popular with elementary age children even though they are in a rather out-
of-the-way spot on the bookmobile and no attempt has been
made to call special attention to them.   They must be ordered from the publisher.   See the list of publishers and
their addresses in the Appendix to Part II.   See also 33.

19 <u>Bible Stories to Read Aloud</u>, compiled by Oscar Weigle.
    Illus. by Ann Brewster.   Grosset, Read Aloud Wonder
    Book, c1962.   OP
    RL: 4   IL: 4-adult   B
Bible stories of every kind are very popular.   This inexpensive book is very well done with a colorful cover and an illustration for each story.

20 <u>Black and Free</u>, by Thomas Skinner.   Zondervan, c1968.
    $2.95   (Pyramid pb $.95)
    RL: 5   IL: 5-adult   *BSMP
Evangelical religion--i.e., fundamentalist Protestant religion--
is spreading like wildfire all over the world and especially
among young people.   This is an extraordinary story of a
young gang leader in Harlem who was converted by a gospel
radio program and who has since dedicated his life to bringing Christ into the lives of others.   Many photographs show
him at work.   Similar to <u>Run Baby, Run</u> and <u>The Cross and
the Switchblade</u>, this kind of book is a quiet best-seller.

21 <u>A Certain Small Shepherd</u>, by Rebecca Caudill.   Illus.
    by William Pène du Bois.   Holt Owlet, c1965.   pb
    $1.45
    RL: 4   IL: Read aloud-5   BS
The story of a Christmas miracle when a small mute boy
finds the courage to speak.   Books of this kind which deal
in a loving and affirmative way with a child with a handicap

are very important.   An excellent family real-aloud story
and much liked especially by girls.

22   The Creation.   Text from the Jerusalem Bible.   Illus.
        by Jo Spier.   Doubleday, c1966. $3.95
        RL: 5   IL: Read aloud-6   S
There is a real hunger for Bible stories among many underprivileged children.   This story of the Creation taken from
the Jerusalem Bible has simple language and extraordinarily
beautiful pictures.   Note the reasonable price.

23   The Cross and the Switchblade, by David Wilkerson.
        Geis, 1962. $4.95 (Pyramid, 1964, pb $.95)
        RL: 6-7   IL: JH-adult   BSMP
The extraordinary story by the fundamentalist founder of
Teen Movement, of how he became involved with young drug
addicts in Brooklyn.   This book has been a best seller,
rivalling Dr. Spock and Perry Mason, for the last ten years.
It is still attracting new readers and new converts.

24   David and Goliath, edited by Barbara S. Hazen.   Western,
        Golden Press, 1968.   OP
        RL: 4   IL: Read aloud-6   B
A well-illustrated edition of one of the most popular stories
in the world.

25   David and the Giant, by Mike McClintock.   Illus. by
        Fritz Siebel.   Harper, I Can Read, c1960. $2.50
        RL: 2-3   IL: Read aloud-4   *BS
A beautifully illustrated and excitingly told version of the
story of David and Goliath.   Very popular

26   Dove Books, by Harold Winstone et al.   Macmillan,
        1960.   6 Books, $.59 each
        RL: 3   IL: Read aloud-6   B
This excellent series of paperback Bible stories has very
colorful pictures on every page and is very popular.   The
titles are: Balaam and his Ass, Zacheus the Publican,
David, The Lamb of God, Jonas, and Jesus by the Lake.

27   Every Man Heart Lay Down, by Lorenz Graham.   Illus.
        by Coleen Browning.   Crowell, c1946, c1970. $3.75
        RL: 3-4   IL: Read aloud-adult   *BM
W. E. B. DuBois said of this story "This little poem does
not use the conventional words and phrases which by long
usage often obscure the meaning of these tales."   It is the
story of Jesus in the words of an African child and the

superb illustrations reflect African designs and culture. This
would be wonderful for any program of religious education
and also for many story-telling programs.

28 The First Christmas, by John Paris. Illus. by Harry
    Beckhoff. Random, Step-Up Book, c1970. $1.95
    RL: 3   IL: 2-JH   *BS

This account, in modern language, of the birth of Christ is
well done and reverent. It starts with Isaiah and gives the
story of the first Christmas from three points of view--
Elizabeth's, that of the son of the innkeeper, and those of
the three wise men. There is a real hunger for religious
stories among many underprivileged children and all children
love Christmas. This should be very much in demand.

29 God's Trombones: Seven Negro Sermons in Verse, by
    James Weldon Johnson. Illus. by Aaron Douglas.
    Viking, c1927. pb 1969 $1.35)
    RL: Mainly 6   IL: JH-adult   *BM
Seven poems which give the spirit and language of old time
Negro ministers' sermons. Powerful and beautiful, this book
will be very popular with older people. Striking drawings
enhance each sermon.

30 Good News for Modern Man, translated by Dr. R. G.
    Bratcher. Illus. by Annie Vallotton. American Bible
    Society, 1966. $.95
    RL: 6   IL: JH-adult   *BS
This book is subtitled, The New Testament in Today's English. First published in 1966, by 1969 it has exceeded Dr.
Spock in sales as the all-time best seller among paperbacks.
It should have special appeal for young people who are confused or repelled by the conventional Biblical language. This
simple, direct version is well done. It is illustrated by line
drawings with a universal quality. There is also a large-
print edition at the same price.

31 Hanukkah, by Norma Simon. Illus. by Symeon Shimin.
    Crowell, Holiday Book, c1966. $2.95
    RL: 3-4   IL: Read aloud-adult   B
It is a good thing for all Americans to understand the religious holidays that some Americans celebrate and through
the stories and legends associated with the holiday to learn
something of the past. This is a simple well-illustrated
story of how the first Hanukkah came to be and is well liked
if it is introduced by an adult. Otherwise it is never borrowed on the bookmobile.

32   The How and Why Wonder Book of The Old Testament,
     by Dr. Gilbert Klaperman.   Illus. by John Hull.
     Grosset, 1964.   OP
     RL: 4-5   IL: 3-JH   B
A book about the Bible that stimulates the imagination and
teaches a lot of history.   Borrowed by young good readers
and adults over sixty who are poor readers but care a lot
about the Bible.

33   Jon and the Little Lost Lamb, by Jane Latourette.   Illus.
     by Betty Wind.   Concordia, Arch Book, 1965.   pb $.39
     RL: 4-5   IL: Read aloud-4 and adults   B
This is a rhymed and imaginative version of the parable of
the lost sheep with many dramatic illustrations.   It and the
other Arch books are popular with young children, parents
and older adults, mainly older women who love the Bible
and Bible stories.

34   Joseph and the Coat of Many Colors, adapted by Lavinia
     Derwent.   Illus. by Joe Lasker.   Scholastic, 1967.
     pb $.60
     RL: 3-4   IL: 3-adult   B
A dramatic and popular Bible story.

35   More Stories from the Old Testament, adapted and illus-
     trated by Piet Worm.   Sheed, 1957. $3.50
     RL: 5   IL: 5-adult   B
A simplified edition of the Douay Bible with unusual illustrations that are like illuminations in the old manuscripts.   Easy
reading but a difficult format.   The letters are in script.
The illustrations are uniformly popular as is book number
37.

36   Run, Baby, Run, by Nicky Cruz with Jamie Buckingham.
     Pyramid, 1968. $.75
     RL: 5-6   IL: 5-adult   *BS
The story of a Puerto Rican, head of a brutal street gang,
whose life was changed by the Pentecostal movement.   He is
now a Pentecostal missionary trying to rescue boys who, like
himself, know nothing except the savage life of the streets.
An authentic account of the way things are in some places in
America and what one group is doing about it, which is already a best seller and will be much borrowed and read by
teenagers and adults.   The book enhances and amplifies The
Cross and the Switchblade [23].

37   Stories from the New Testament, adapted and illustrated

by Piet Worm.   Sheed, 1959. $3.50
RL: 5   IL: 5-adult   B
As in 35 above, the script print makes this difficult going
for poor readers.   However, it is much borrowed for the
pictures even by those who cannot read the text.

38   Stories from the Old Testament, adapted and illustrated
     by Piet Worm.   Sheed, 1956. $3.50
     RL: 5   IL: 5-adult   B

39   Strength to Love, by Martin Luther King, Jr.   Harper,
     c1963. $5.95   (Simon & Schuster, Pocket Books, pb
     $.75)
     RL: Adult   IL: Adult   B
A group of Martin Luther King's sermons published several
years ago.   It is much borrowed by older women but would
be popular with a larger group if it were up-dated and contained his last sermons.

3 SOCIOLOGY--CAREERS

40 <u>Animal Doctors: What Do They Do?</u>, by Carla Greene.
    Illus. by Leonard Kessler.   Harper, I Can Read,
    c1967. $2.50 (Scholastic pb $.60)
    RL: 3-4   IL: Read aloud-6   *BS
Any child who loves animals is interested in this account of
animal doctors and what they do. The book also reassures
children who are scared to go to the doctor that a doctor's
goal is to heal individuals. Very popular.

41 <u>Apron On, Apron Off</u>, by Helen Kay. Illus. by Yaro-
    slava. Scholastic, 1968. pb $.50
    RL: 3   IL: Read aloud-3   *BSMP
Joan and her mother take off their aprons and go downtown.
They discover how many different men wear aprons that fit
their occupations, carpenters, newsboys, bakers and printers.
A nice way of illustrating what some Daddys do.

42 <u>Arrow Book of Nurses</u>, by Mary Elting. Illus. by Chuck
    McVicker. Watts, 1951. OP (Scholastic, pb 1963 OP)
    RL: 4   IL: 3-JH   BS
A factual account of what nurses do and how to become one.
Too bad a book on this popular subject has no multi-ethnic
illustrations. It has nonetheless been very much in demand.
It is currently out of print. Hopefully, it will be reissued
with modern illustrations.

43 <u>The Baker's Children--A Visit to a Family Bakery</u>, by
    Grete Mannheim. Knopf, c1970. $3.95
    RL: 3   IL: K-6   *SMP
Everybody loves a bakery. This book shows the Fingerle
family at work making and baking bread and rolls and cakes.
The children, Linda and Michael, are real helpers. The
photographs illustrate the simple text and children will get
a clear idea of how a bakery operates. Many of them will
wish their families ran a bakery too.

44 <u>City Workers</u>, by Jeanne Rowe. Grolier, Watts, 1969.
    $3.95

RL: 2-3   IL: Read aloud-6   S
Very large print; excellent photographs of policemen, firemen, postmen, telephone repair men, etc. A good conversation piece for reading-help programs. This book may help
in lessening the hostility of minority groups toward firemen,
repairmen and other essential workers.

45   Doctors and Nurses: What Do They Do?, by Carla
        Greene. Illus. by Leonard Kessler. Harper, c1963.
        $2.50
        RL: 2-3   IL: Read aloud-5   BS
A clear and reassuring description of what doctors and nurses
do that will both reassure future patients and interest all children. It may even inspire future doctors and nurses. Let's
hope soon for multi-ethnic illustrations in this useful series.
See 40 and 53.

46   The Hat Book, by Leonard Shortall. Western Pub.,
        Golden Press Shape Book, 1965. $.29
        RL: 3   IL: Read aloud-3   BS
Many different kinds of hats illustrate many different kinds
of careers. A lot of information is packed into this short
colorful book. See 388 for comment on this series.

47   Home Economists in Action, by Nancy and Angela Mills,
        authors and illustrators. Scholastic, 1968. pb $1.00
        RL: 6-7   IL: 6-HS   BS
Thirty-five success stories of women in the varying fields
that are open to a home economics major. Very useful
career information including how to test your interests, how
to write a résumé and how to choose a college which will
give good training in this field.

48   I Want to Be ... books (e.g., ... Airplane Pilot, ...
        Baseball Player, ... Fireman, ... Policeman), by
        Carla Greene. Various illustrators. Various copy-
        rights, Children's Press. $3.00
        RL: 2   IL: 1-5   BS
The variety in this series is wide enough to meet the interest
of every child. The print is large and the books are colorful. The volumes I have seen were all issued between 1957
and 1963 but new titles have been issued at least through
1969. Probably later volumes have multi-ethnic illustrations.
This is a useful series which could be even more valuable if
the format were older since the information given interests
a child much older than grade three, the top level of interest
according to the publisher's blurb.

49 I Want to be a Ballet Dancer, by Carla Green. Illus.
    by Mary Gehr. Children's Press, 1959. $3.00
        RL: 3   IL: Read aloud-5   BS
How ballet dancers are trained, a subject that fascinates
many girls who have seen ballet on TV. A very popular
book.

50 A Job for You, by Miriam Morrison Peake. Scholastic,
    1964. pb OP
        RL: 6   IL: 6-HS   BS
An excellent and much needed manual on job-getting techniques with imaginative job suggestions.

51 Jobs in Your Future, by Miriam Lee. Illus. by Dorothy
    D'Anna. Scholastic, 1967. pb $1
        RL: 5-6   IL: 7-HS   BS
It would appear that this title is replacing number 50. If so,
there is cause for regret. Number 50 is an attractive paperback with excellent content. Number 51 is a patronizing
workbook with a mish mash of quizzes, information and
watered down short stories. Nevertheless, I list it in default of a better title because it does have some valuable information on jobs and job hunting that I have not found elsewhere.

52 Need a Lift? The American Legion Educational and
    Scholarship Program, Indianapolis 46206, 1970. $.50
        RL: Adult   IL: HS-adult   *BS
This is a valuable handbook of information about career and
educational opportunities. It is revised annually and should
be in every library. Browsing through this pamphlet would
certainly encourage and inform a teenager. It shows how
big the world of opportunity is.

53 Policemen and Firemen: What Do They Do?, by Carla
    Greene. Illus. by Leonard Kessler. Harper, I Can
    Read, 1962. $2.50
        RL: 2-3   IL: Read aloud-3   BS
Another easy-to-read book describing the careers of policemen and firemen in glowing and suspenseful terms. Only
moderately popular. Inner city children do not, as of now,
trust policemen. They also do not understand and recognize
the brave and useful function firemen perform. See Uptown
[55].

54 True Book of Policemen and Firemen, by Irene S. Miner.
    Children's Press, 1954. $3.56

RL: 2-3   IL: Read aloud-5   S
An easy-to-read text with lovely illustrations.   See comment
on 53 above.

55 Uptown, by John Steptoe.   Harper, c1970. $3.50
    RL: 3   IL: 6-adult   *BSMP
John and Dennis, his "main man," aged anywhere from eight
to twelve years old, wander around Harlem discussing what
they want to be when they grow up.   Among the careers they
discuss are those of pimps and policemen.   The latter, they
agree, is out--none of their friends would have anything to
do with them.   This book is a vivid, moving and despairing
picture of life in Harlem as it appears to be (and often is)
for boys with little or no family backing or loving adult to
depend on.   An important conversation piece with high school
students.   Good illustrations by the author.

56 We Have Tomorrow, by Arna Bontemps.   Houghton
    Mifflin, c1945. $3.95
    RL: 6   IL: 6-HS   *BSMP
This book first appeared in 1945.   It tells the story of twelve
young black Americans who were then launching themselves
on what appeared to be excellent careers.   It was re-issued
in 1960 and the author had picked well, since all the subjects
had gone on to fame and fortune.   Reading the book in 1973,
the youngsters involved will seem to today's teenagers
strangely unmilitant in the face of injustice and discrimination.
However, reading of the successful efforts of these twelve to
establish themselves should encourage other boys and girls
to choose the career they want and to pursue it in spite of
obstacles.

57 When I Grow Up, by Jean Bethell.   Illus. by Ruth Wood.
    Grosset Easy-To-Read Wonder Book, 1965. $.59
    RL: 2-3   IL: Read aloud-3   BS
A small girl imagines herself in different careers--a cow-
girl, a nurse, an airline hostess and so forth.   The picture
on the cover of a girl looking in a full-length mirror acts
like a magnet to little girls.

58 The World of Work, edited by Kay Koschnick.   New
    Readers' Press, c1969.   pb $1.25
    RL: 5   IL: 6-adult   *BSM
This splendid manual packs an extraordinary amount of information into its forty-eight pages.   It discusses how to decide
what job to apply for and how to go after it.   It gives samples of General Aptitude Test questions and job applications.

It tells how to read the employment ads and how to behave
at a job interview.   It discusses how to hold a job and jobs
for teenagers, older people and handicapped people.   It even
discusses volunteer jobs!   As indispensable booklet with many
encouraging multi-ethnic photographs of people who seem happy in the world of work.   This title is far superior to Jobs
in Your Future [51], which is along the same lines, and deserves wide distribution.

3 SOCIOLOGY--ETIQUETTE; FAMILY; HUMAN ECOLOGY

59   Boy Dates Girl, by Gay Head (pseud.).   Illus. by John
  Fernie.   Scholastic, 1955.   pb OP
  RL: 5   IL: JH-HS   BS
Slightly out of date but very popular in Brooklyn.   Questions
and answers on a subject of burning importance.

60   Come Over to My House, by Theodore Le Sieg.   Illus.
  by Richard Erdoes.   Random House Beginner, c1966.
  $2. 50
  RL: 2-3   IL: Read aloud-4   BS
A very popular book which invites the reader into every kind
of house all over the globe.   This sounds like a teaching device, but actually it is so well done that the boys and girls
with whom I have used this book have really enjoyed what is
a well-presented cornucopia of facts.   In fact, everyone of
every age cares deeply about styles of life and housing.
This easy to read book brings the fact home.

61   Cowboy Small, by Lois Lenski.   Walck, 1949. $3. 00
  RL: 2-3   IL: Read aloud-3   BS
How a cowboy lives.   Still very popular with the very young.

62   Date Talk: How to Talk to a Boy ... To a Girl, by
  R. N. Lawrence.   Illus. by Irwin Greenburg.   Scholas-
  tic, c1967.   pb $. 50
  RL: 6   IL: 6-young adult   BS
Helpful advice on the art of conversation.   No teen should
be tongue-tied after reading this.   Very popular.

63   Etiquette for Young Moderns, by Gay Head (pseud.).
  Illus. by Irwin Greenburg.   Scholastic, c1954.   pb OP
  RL: 6   IL: 6-HS   BS

This excellent guide covers letter writing and every other
social situation one can think of in connection with manners.
Inner city children often seem to be longing for guidance of
every kind and this is a very popular book.

64   The Family Nobody Wanted, by Helen Doss.   Scholastic,
       c1954. pb $.75
       RL: 6   IL: 6-adult   BSMP
The incredible true story of the minister and his wife who
adopted twelve children--the majority of them non-white from
different minority groups or different countries--and seem to
be raising a happy and memorable family.   A book of wide
appeal.

65   Felipe the Bullfighter, by Robert Vavra.   Harcourt,
       1967. $3.95
       RL: 3   IL: 3-JH   S
This beautiful book with photographs of intense color appeals
especially to children of Spanish heritage.   The story of how
Felipe practices to become a bullfighter interests girls also.

66   How to Deal with Parents and Other Problems, by Dr.
       Ernest G. Osborne.   Illus. by Susan Perl.   Grosset,
       c1962 (Tempo pb $.60)
       RL: 6   IL: 6-HS   BS
A basically sound and extraordinarily popular book (even with
non-readers) which discusses family relationships and problems.   Many children come on the bookmobile specifically to
borrow this title having heard of it from a friend.

67   The Indians Knew, by Tillie S. Pine and Joseph Levine.
       Illus. by Ezra Jack Keats.   McGraw-Hill, c1957.
       $3.95 (Scholastic, 1968, pb $.60)
       RL: 2-3   IL: Read aloud-6   BSMP
A very unusual book which combines science and social
studies.   It tells of the many interesting things which the
Indians discovered and used in their daily lives.   This is a
rather special book, not widely popular but it means a great
deal to those who do like it.   They borrow it again and
again.

68   Kai Ming, Boy of Hong-Kong, by Dominique Darbois.
       Follett, 1960. $2.97
       RL: 2-3   IL: Read aloud-5
Beautiful photographs will give a treasure house of informa-
tion to a child curious to learn how other children live.
This is also a valuable book for our increasing number of

Chinese children, many of whom come from Hong Kong.

69   Love and Sex and Growing Up, by Eric W. Johnson and
         Corinne B. Johnson, Lippincott, c1970. $3.95
         RL: 5   IL: 5-HS   *BSP
An excellent book which combines sex education with information about evolution and the beginning of families.   It discusses three different kinds of family arrangement: the
modern American, the Iroquois, and the Japanese ways.
Finally, there are also several chapters on plant and animal
reproduction.   It is intended for children from ten to twelve
years old but will interest junior high and high school children as well.   If I were a parent today, I should want to
own both this book and number 14 by the same author and
would then feel that my children were armored with knowledge
they needed to cope with today's world as far as sex information was concerned.   With today's ferment on marriage
and family relationships, I'd also be very grateful at the
ideas the different family arrangements described in the book
open up.   A fine conversation piece for School Volunteers
and possibly a life saver for some children.

70   Miguel's Mountain, by Bill Binzon.   Coward, 1968.
         $3.69
         RL: 2-3   IL: Read aloud-4   SMP
Miguel's mountain is a snow pile.   Older city children become interested in Miguel's Mountain because they recognize
the authenticity of the city scene.

71   Mother, These Are My Friends, edited by Mary A.
         Gross.   City Schools Curriculum Service, 1968.   pb
         $1.00
         RL: 2-3   IL: Read aloud-5   SMP
The wishes of city children in their own words.   The book
has a short wish on each page with space for a child to write
his own wish or draw a picture.   Very thought-provoking and
a wonderful conversation piece.   It has been very popular in
the reading help programs.

72   Papa Small, by Lois Lenski.   Walck, 1951. $3.75
         RL: 2   IL: Read aloud-2   B
How the Small family lives and what they do.   Children still
love these small books about the Smalls--as documentaries
and also as easy to read books.   It is available in other
languages.   See Book List classification 4.

73   People Are Important, by Eva Knox Evans.   Illus. by

Vana Earle. Western, Golden Press, c1951. $3.95
    RL: 4   IL: 2-6 and older non-readers   *BSMP
A unique book that introduces children to the common factors
that bind mankind--the need for food, housing, clothing and
customs and the various ways in which different peoples satisfy those needs. Children will enjoy this book since it does
not talk at them but involves the reader. It also has humor
both in the text and the illustrations. A wonderful job.

74 A Place to Live, by Jeanne Bendick. Parents' Stepping
    Stone, c1970. $3.78
    RL: 3-4   IL: Read aloud-6   BSMP
A very well-written explanation of environment and what it
means to insects, animals and children.

75 Project 1-2-3, by Eve Merriam. Illus. by Harriet
    Sherman. McGraw-Hill, c1971. $4.95
    RL: 3   IL: Read aloud-3   *BSMP
This very brightly colored book describes in words and pictures a big city housing project. Children who live in such
a project will enjoy the familiar and also learn a bit about
the mechanics of running what is a small town. Others will
be interested in such a different way of life.

76 S.O.S. Save Our Earth, by Giancarlo Massini. Illus.
    by Allessandro Pacini. With an introd. by William D.
    Ruckelshaus. Grosset, c1972.
    RL: 7   IL: 4-adult   *BSP
This imaginative book originated in Italy and has proved instantly popular with every one to whom I have showed it.
On the outside cover, floating in the ocean, is a bottle and
when the reader pulls out the message, it unfolds to proclaim
"Help! Nature is Dying!" Inside is the best and clearest
explanation I have seen of the web of life, the problems of
pollution and what we can do to help. The graphics and devices used to explain and to interest the reader are full of
humor and genius. A good teacher could make use of this
book at almost any age level and its message is vital to
everyone.

77 Who Cares? I Do, by Monro Leaf. Lippincott, c1971.
    $3.59 pb $1.95
    RL: 3   IL: Read aloud-6   *BS
Munro Leaf preaches but in a way that children enjoy because
he talks straight and draws funny pictures. In this book,
which tells children how to help keep America beautiful, there
are also many graphic photographs from interested government

agencies. A useful book, though with nothing like as much
coverage as 74 and 76. See also The Lerax [1006].

78 Who Lives Here?, by Judith Varga. Grosset Wonder
     Book, c1958. $.39
     RL: 2-3   IL: Read aloud-3   BS
With a picture and a couplet to a page, this book discusses
who lives where and packs in a good deal of information
about birds and animals. Not a must but a good inexpensive
start on ecology and much enjoyed by children.

79 Why It's a Holiday, by Ann McGovern. Illus. by Dagmar
     Wilson. Random, 1960. $1.95
     RL: 4   IL: Read aloud-JH   BS
A useful explanation of national and religious holidays that is
very much liked in reading help programs and is popular on
the bookmobile.

3 SOCIOLOGY--MINORITY GROUPS

80 Anyplace but Here, by Arna Bontemps and Jack Conroy.
     Hill & Wang American Century Series, c1945, c1966.
     pb $1.95
     RL: Adult   IL: HS-adult   BM
This is a revision of an earlier (1945) book called They
Seek a City, by the same authors, dealing with the migration
of black people from the South and what they found in the
North, Midwest and West. It is interesting but diffuse and
difficult reading. On the bookmobile it has only been borrowed by a few older people. Curiously, it has very little
in it about New York but a great deal about Chicago, Detroit
and Watts. I think it might be very popular with adults over
thirty in those cities.

81 Black Like Me, by John Howard Griffin. Houghton
     Mifflin, c1961. $4.95 (New American Library,
     Signet, pb $.75)
     RL: 6   IL: 5-adult   BSMP
An enormously motivating book. The story of a white man's
travels through the south passing as a black man, this is one
of the most popular books on the bookmobile and in the School
Volunteer program. People of all ages ask for it and cannot
lay it down.

82   The Black Muslims in America, by C. Eric Lincoln.
       Beacon Press, 1961.   pb $1.95
       RL: Adult   IL: HS-adult   BM
This account of the Black Muslim movement published in
1961 is a very full one and gives a considerable account of
the African roots of the movement and its local development
in this country.   It is well worth reading even though outdated.   See 83 below.

83   Black Nationalism, by E. U. Essein-Udom.   Dell,
       Laurel Leaf, 1962.   pb $.75
       RL: Adult   IL: HS-adult   BM
This book, published a year later than the one above, is
interesting because of the author's acquaintance and many
interviews with Elijah Muhammed.   It is also interesting because its author is a Nigerian whose nationality relieves him
from the choice of accepting or rejecting the separatist theme
of the Muslim movement.   There is a small but steady demand for it.   See 82 above.

84   The Black Panthers, by Gene Marine.   New American
       Library, Signet, c1969.   pb $.95
       RL: 6-8   IL: 6-adult   B
A very interesting and balanced account of how the Black
Panthers started, who they are and what they have done up
to early 1969.   The last chapter of this book contains one
of the most sensitive descriptions I have seen and is must
reading for all white Americans.   This book is very popular
on the bookmobile even though some of the vocabulary is difficult.   People are interested in the Panthers whether they
are for them or against them.

85   Black Skin, White Masks, by Franz Fannon.   Grove,
       c1952. $5.00   (Evergreen pb $.95)
       RL: Adult   IL: Adult   BM
This book of essays by the black Carribean psychiatrist is
in demand in spite of difficult reading.   People borrow it
and are enthusiastic about it though one suspects that it is
more skimmed and quoted than actually read.

86   Black Woman, by Harold McDougall.   Photographs by
       Chester Higgins, Jr.   McCall Books, c1970.   pb $2.95
       RL: 4   IL: All ages   *BSM
I am not sure what the significance of this book is but it will
certainly be justly popular among blacks.   It is a series of
superb photographs of beautiful black women of every age
from three years old to great-grannies accompanied by short

statements by each subject on how she feels about life. It
reinforces the "I am black and I am proud" theme and will
be a wonderful conversation piece for tutorial programs.

87 The Black Woman: An Anthology, edited by Toni Cade
     Bambara.   New American Library, Signet, c1970.
     pb $.95
     RL: Varied-mainly high IL: HS-adult   *BM
This anthology on the theme of the black woman has a few
poems and some fiction, but most of the book consists of
essays on the place of blacks in society, on the place of
women in society and, of course, the place of black women
in society.   With a striking picture of a handsome young
woman on the cover, it will certainly be borrowed on the
bookmobile but whether the interest in the subject matter will
counter the high reading level only experience will show.

88 By Any Means Necessary: Speeches, Interviews and a
     Letter by Malcolm X, edited by George Breitman.
     Merit Book, Pathfinder Press, c1970. pb $1.95
     RL: Varied   IL: HS-adult   BM
This collection of the speeches and interviews of Malcolm X's
last year are a continuation and expansion of Malcolm X
Speaks [97].   Like everything to do with him, the book
is popular, especially with young adults.

89 Chicory--Young Voices from the Black Ghetto, edited by
     Sam Cornish and Lucian W. Dixon.   Association Press,
     c1964. pb $1.75
     RL: Varied-mainly 5-6 IL: JH-adult   *BSM
Excerpts from a magazine called Chicory put out by the Library Community Action Program in Baltimore, this book is
similar to The Me Nobody Knows [98].   It contains poems,
commentary and fiction.   I like it: it gives a picture of life
in the inner city, but it has more humor and picturesque
speech than the other, which gives it a balance that adds
a great deal.   I especially liked the section entitled Street
Chatter and some of the poems.

90 The Children: Poems and Prose from Bedford-Stuyvesant,
     edited by Irving Benig.   Grove Press, c1971. pb $.95
     RL: 4   IL: 4-adult   BM
This book will interest and encourage minority group parents
everywhere who know that their children can succeed academically if given a chance.   Other inner city children will enjoy
reading it and empathize with the situations described.

91   Civil Rights and Civil Liberties, by Bernard Ludwig.
     Edited by Gerald Leinward. Washington Square Press,
     Problems of American Society Series. pb, c1968.
     $. 75
     RL: Varied-6-adult   IL: HS-adult   *BSMP
This book poses a number of questions on the first page that
will interest young people (examples: "How long is long hair?
Does a student accused of cheating have a right to a hearing?
Should accused rioters be granted due process of law and
what does that mean?") The text then describes the problems and history of the struggle for civil rights, illustrating
its points with many relevant photographs and cartoons. The
second half of the book (selected readings) gives the Constitution and Bill of Rights, the decisions in a number of vital
civil rights cases and some fascinating interviews including
one with a number of high school students involved in the
problems in Little Rock. An exciting book whose interest
will overcome any reading difficulties, this should be in
every high school and will also interest the general reader.
The format is excellent and not like a textbook.

92   The Fire Next Time, by James Baldwin. Dial, c1963.
     $3. 95   Dell, pb $. 75
     RL: 6   IL: HS-adult   BMP
This strongly written social and political commentary on being
a black man in America by a noted black writer is still borrowed by older readers.

93   Graciela: A Mexican-American Child Tells Her Story,
     with photos and editing by Joe Molnar. Watts, c1972.
     $4. 50
     RL: 4-5   IL: 4-adult   *SMP
An excellent documentary with many photographs and a simple,
straightforward text. Graciela lives in Texas but goes to
Michigan every year to pick crops. Her life has many hardships but some happy times too. A must for private and
suburban schools, this will also be very popular in areas
where Chicanos live.

94   I Am from Puerto Rico, by Peter Buckley. Simon &
     Schuster, c1971. $4. 95
     RL: 5   IL: 4-adult   *BSMP
A portrait in words and photographs of a twelve-year-old
Puerto Rican boy, Frederico Ramirez, who emigrated to
New York City when he was ten and now has gone back to
Puerto Rico to live. The book gives an interesting picture
of the problems Frederico encounters and a warm and

truthful account of his family life in Puerto Rico.   Any boy
will find this book interesting.

95 I Have a Dream: The Quotations of Martin Luther King,
    Jr., compiled and edited by Lotte Hoskins.   Grosset,
    c1968.   pb $1.00
    RL: Adult   IL: HS-adult   *BM
Quotations from the speeches and sermons of Martin Luther
King, Jr. arranged alphabetically by subject.   Dr. King still
has a strong following among middle-aged and older people
who will want to borrow this.

96 If They Come in the Morning, by Angela Y. Davis et al.
    New American Library, Signet, c1971.   pb $1.25
    RL: Adult   IL: HS-adult   *BM
Subtitled "Voices of Resistance," this book is an examination
of American justice by a group of people who call themselves
political prisoners.   The articles and essays vary in quality
but add up to a scathing indictment of the American prison
system and certainly lead one to question how well the system
of justice works for a poor member of a minority group who
is accused of a crime.   Angela Davis's case has united all
segments of the black community (the book has forewords by
Julian Bond and James Baldwin) and this book will be very
popular.

97 Malcolm X Speaks, edited by George Breitman.   Grove
    1967.   pb $.95
    RL: Adult   IL: HS-adult   BM
Malcolm X's most famous speeches.   They are well worth
reading and are very popular with adults.

98 The Me Nobody Knows: Childrens' Voices from the
    Ghetto, edited by Stephen M. Joseph.   Avon c1969.
    pb $.95
    RL: Varied, mainly 6 and below IL: 5-adult   BSMP
A fascinating and depressing group of short pieces by New
York City school children describing themselves, their environment, and their thoughts.   On a one-to-one basis this may
well inspire other children to write.   I have never seen it
borrowed by a child on the bookmobile but the School Volunteers have found it useful in their reading help programs.   It
is certainly authentic and illuminating.

99 Merit Press Series.   Pathfinder Press, 873 Broadway,
    New York, N.Y. 1003.   These publishers put out a
    series of pamphlets which have tremendous appeal

to high school students and adults.   They should not be confused with the Pathfinder imprint of Bantam Books.   Obviously, with so high a reading level the people borrowing
them were highly motivated by the subject matter.   Their
appeal might well be greater except that their size was a
very awkward one (roughly 4" x 8") which made it difficult
to display them to advantage.   The format was also so drab
that they were clearly only borrowed by those who had a
prior interest in their subject matter.   The pamphlets range
in price from $.25 to $1.   Their reading level is varied
but is mainly on the seventh grade level or higher.   Items
F, G, and I (listed below) have recently appeared as chapters
in the book, Malcolm X: The Man and His Times [1475].

(A)	Black Uprising (Newark, Detroit, 1967)	$.35
(B)	Black Nationalism and Socialism	$.50
(C)	Case for a Black Party	$.35
(D)	The Black Ghetto	$.50
(E)	How a Minority Can Change Society	$.35
(F)	Malcolm X on Afro-American History	$1.00
(G)	Malcolm X: The Man and His Ideas	$.35
(H)	Marxism and the Negro Struggle	$.65
(I)	Myths about Malcolm X	$.50
(J)	Murder in Memphis: Martin Luther King and the Future of the Black Liberation Struggle	$.25

100   Negro in the City, edited by Gerald Leinward.   Wash-
         ington Square Press.   Problems of American Society
         Series, c1968.   pb $.75
         RL: Varied-mainly 6-7 IL: 5-adult   BSMP
This useful book is an examination of the black American in
urban society.   The first part gives a brief historical background of how Afro-Americans came to be in America and
in cities.   This is followed by excerpts from the writings
of fifteen famous Afro-Americans.   There are many photographs.   This is another must for junior high and high schools
and is also of great general interest.   It is popular on the
bookmobile when it is recommended by the staff.   The title
and cover do not appeal.

101   The Negro Revolt, by Louis E. Lomax.   Harper &
         Row, c1963. $6.50 (New American Library, Signet,
         pb $.95)
         RL: Adult   IL: JH-adult   BM
Although this book is not up to date, it is still an excellent
explanation of why blacks have revolted and a well-written

account of their movement through 1962 including their hopes
for the future.   This account of the expectations aroused by
the Brown decision of 1954 and still (in 1973) not fulfilled,
as far as most black children's education is concerned, is
a moving one and troubling to the conscience of any American.

102 Nobody Knows My Name, by James Baldwin.   Dial,
        c1961. $5.95   (Dell, Delta, pb $.60)
        RL: Adult   IL: HS-adult   BMP
A series of autobiographical essays by the famous author,
this book is borrowed by adults who know his novels.   The
essays vary in reading difficulty and interest and many people can enjoy ones such as Fifth Avenue, Uptown: A Letter
from Harlem, A Fly in Buttermilk and Nobody Knows My
Name: A Letter from the South.   Others are written for a
very sophisticated audience.

103 The Other City, by Ray Vogel, et al.   David White,
        c1969.   pb $1.95
        RL: 3   IL: 5-HS   BSMP
This book has superb pictures and a minimal text by four
junior high school children from a school in Brooklyn.   Children enjoy seeing themselves and their surroundings.   Bleak
and realistic as the portrait of the neighborhood is, the book
does have some positive factors.   The children do have fun
in fact and also in the pictures.   A must for private and
suburban schools.

104 Picking Up the Gun, by Earl Anthony.   Pyramid, c1970.
        pb $.95
        RL: Adult   IL: HS-adult   *BM
A fascinating account by a young well-educated black militant
of his experiences as a Black Panther.   He joined the party
in 1967 and was expelled two years later when the party was
riven by dissent and factionalism.   This will be very popular.

105 A Piece of the Power: Four Black Mayors, by James
        Haskins.   Dial, c1972. $4.95
        RL: 7   IL: HS-adult   *BSP
An examination of the careers of four black political leaders:
Richard Hatcher, Kenneth Gibson, Carl Stokes, and Charles
Evers.   It is also a study of American politics and where
the power is.   This will be very popular in paperback on the
bookmobile and is especially pertinent to anyone who hopes
to persuade underprivileged people to work through the ballet
box.

106   Poems by Kali, by Kali Grosvenor.   Photographs by
      Joan Halifax and Robert Fletcher.   Doubleday, c1970.
      $3.50
      RL: 3-4   IL: Universal   BSMP
This little book of poems by an eight-year-old child can
hardly qualify as poetry but does give a very clear picture
of what a young bright, black New Yorker thinks about the
world.   Black children like it because they recognize themselves.   Privileged white children of corresponding age do
not understand the poems and are bothered by the misspell-
ings but high school students are interested.

107   Problems of American Society Series, edited by Gerald
      Leinward.   Washington Square Press, c1968, c1972.
      $.75 and $.95
      RL: Varied   IL: 6-adult   BSMP
This series is designed for use in urban high schools but
most of the titles I have seen have great general interest and
value for any American.   Although much of the reading level
is difficult, the interest in the subject matter is so intense
that even poor readers borrow them and get a great deal
from them.   The books usually consist of an illustrated text
posing and discussing the title problem and followed by selected readings which make the problem personal and vital.
The format is not like a textbook and the titles we have carried are popular.

108   Ronnie, by Eileen Rosenbaum.   Photographs by Gloria
      Kitt and Carmel Roth.   Parents, 1969. $3.95
      RL: 3   IL: Read aloud-4   *BSMP
The story, in simple text and photographs, of a day in the
life of a small city boy and his family.   The story is both
real and heartwarming and, for a change, cheerful.   The day
is a happy day and the joys and small sorrows are those that
belong to small boys everywhere.   Another good conversation
piece for Reading Help Programs.

109   Seize the Time: The Story of the Black Panther Party
      and Huey P. Newton, by Bobby Seale.   Random,
      c1968, 1970. $6.95   (Vintage pb $1.95)
      RL: 6   IL: 6-adult   BM
This has been one of the fastest moving titles on the bookmobile.   It is especially in demand in Panther neighborhoods,
of course, but it is also much read in other neighborhoods.
Whether people like or dislike the Panthers, they are very
much interested in them although not quite as much now
that the party seems to be splitting into factions.   This book

is long and full of street talk and profanity but the author's
sincerity and conviction come through, whether or not the
reader agrees with his ideas and conclusions.   See also The
Black Panthers [84], the last chapter of which is important
reading for every citizen.

110   Souls of Black Folk, by W. E. Burghardt DuBois.
        Dodd, Mead, c1903: additional material, c1953.
        $4.50   (Fawcett, Premier, pb $.75)
        RL: Adult   IL: HS-adult   BSMP
This extraordinary book, written in 1903, was the signal for
Afro-Americans to turn away from the pragmatic (and to
many minds subservient) policies of Booker Washington to
demands for civil rights and justice.   It is a searching into
the dilemma of being black in America, a classic which is
still highly relevant.   I have heard it quoted from by black
leaders and ministers twice in the last month.   One essay,
"The Passing of the First Born," is often reprinted and is
heartbreaking in its implications in spite of the old fashioned
and somewhat florid language.

111   Soy Chicano (I Am Mexican-American), by Bob and
        Lynne Fitch.   Photographs by the authors.   Edited by
        Paul J. Deegan.   Creative Educational Society, c1970.
        An Amicus St. Book. $4.95
        RL: 4-5   IL: 5-adult   BSMP
A thirteen-year-old Mexican-American girl describes her
family, her life and her world.   Illustrated with excellent
photographs.   This is very like Graciela [93] and equally
valuable.

112   The Sweet Flypaper of Life, by Roy de Carava and Langston
        Hughes.   Hill and Wang, c1955. $3.50 (pb $1.50)
        RL: 5-6   IL: 5-adult   BSMP
This book is a real work of art.   Originally published in 1955,
it mirrors life in Harlem as of that date (i.e., no overt militants).   It has depth and universality and beauty.   It is very
popular with adults.

113   Tell It Like It Is, by Chuck Stone.   Trident, c1968.
        (Simon & Schuster Pocket Books, 1970, pb $.95)
        RL: 6-7   IL: HS-adult   BM
This series of newspaper columns were written in 1963 and
1964 but they are just as relevant as if they had been written
last week since the issue of race prejudice is still with us.
Mr. Stone is witty, consistently interesting and sometimes
moving and this book is much in demand.

114 <u>To Die for the People: The Writings of Huey P. New-</u>
        <u>ton</u>. Random House, c1972. Vintage, pb $1.95
        RL: Adult   IL: HS-adult   *BM
Speeches, essays and excerpts from the Black Panther newspaper comprise this book. The ten Panther demands which
open the book are very reasonable but Newton's own experience of injustice and racism have so influenced him that he
is a convinced revolutionary and the book is full of Marxian
dialectics. His earnestness and sincerity and eagerness to
help his race seem very genuine and the book will certainly
move on the bookmobile.

115 <u>Train Ride</u>, by John Steptoe. Harper, c1971. $3.95
        RL: 3   IL: 6-adult   *SMP
Children sitting on a stoop in Brooklyn discuss where the
city is and where the home-going crowds work. They take a
ride to Times Square, have a dreamlike time in a penny ar-
cade and see white people who are not policemen, teachers
or librarians and go home to a beating. The author's illustrations are very colorful. The language is street language.
An accurate picture of the way many children live, think and
feel in New York City.

116 <u>Uptown</u>, by John Steptoe. Harper, c1970. $3.50
        RL: 3   IL: 6-adult   BSMP
John and Dennis, his "main man," wander around Harlem discussing what they want to be when they grow up. A vivid
picture of a section of life in Harlem as it appears (and often
is) to boys with little or no family background or rock to
stand on. Moving and despairing. An important conversation
piece with the high school age.

117 <u>The Way It Is</u>, edited by John Holland. Harcourt,
        c1969. $3.25
        RL: 4   IL: 3-adult   BSMP
Very much like <u>The Other City</u> [103] and <u>World Friends</u>;
<u>The City's Children</u> [121], this book is a fuller account of
life in a slum. Fifteen boys from a school in Brooklyn took
the pictures and wrote the text. It gives a very complete
picture of the city as I have seen it on the route of Buttercup.

118 <u>A Week in Henry's World: El Barrio</u>, by Inger McCabe.
        Macmillan, c1971. $4.50 (Collier, pb $1.36)
        RL: 3   IL: For Puerto Ricans in New
        York: Read aloud-adult. For others: 3-adult *BSMP
A documentary book which gives a picture, in photographs

with a small amount of text, of the life of a Puerto Rican
family in El Barrio (the upper east side of Manhattan). The
picture is not typical in every detail but on the whole it is a
truthful and realistic one.

119   Where Do We Go From Here: Chaos or Community?,
         by Martin Luther King, Jr.   Harper, 1967. $4.95
         (Beacon Press, pb $1.95)
         RL: Adult   IL: JH-adult   BMP
Dr. King's last book is a plea for community cooperation that
is still very relevant today.

120   Why We Can't Wait, by Martin Luther King, Jr.   New
         American Library, Signet, 1964.   pb $.75
         RL: Adult   IL: JH-adult   BM
There is a small but steady demand for all of Dr. King's
books but this is one of the less popular ones since it is
neither religious nor autobiographical nor his last book.   It
is the story of the three century struggle for equality and
why blacks feel they can no longer afford to be patient.

121   World Friends;   The City's Children, by M. M. Edwards.
         Friendship Press, 1967.   OP
         RL: 3   IL: Read aloud-5   BSMP
A wonderful picture book showing life in a city ghetto.   Black
children, like all children, like to see themselves and their
surroundings depicted and recognize this as a true picture.
Although it pulls no punches, the book also has hope and
positive factors.

122   Your Right to Welfare, by L. Marks.   Citizens' Com-
         mittee for Children of New York, Inc., and Columbia
         University's Center on Social Welfare Policy and Law.
         RL: 5-6   IL: Adult   B
One of the most popular books on the bookmobile with adults
(and staff) in the summers of 1968 and 1969 was this factual
volume which documented what people on welfare were entitled
to receive.   The book was given us free since the bookmobile
was circulating it to people who needed help.   The supply of
these books is now exhausted and the Citizens' Committee in-
forms us that it will not be reprinted.   It is listed, however,
since it is such an excellent example of a book which is in
demand because it is relevant to peoples' needs.   People who
came to the bookmobile to borrow it were led to borrow other
books later.

123   <u>ABC: An Alphabet Book</u>, by Thomas Matthiesen, photog-
        rapher.   Platt & Munk, 1966. $2.50
        RL: Read aloud picture book   IL: Pre-school-2   BS
This has gay, eye-catching, uncluttered photographs of single
objects familiar to all children.

124   <u>ABC and Counting Book</u>.   Illustrated by Mary Horton.
        Grosset Wonder Book, 1963. $.39
        RL: 2-3   IL: Pre-school and all beginning readers   BS
The alphabet, illustrated in simple colorful pictures of familiar objects, and five illustrated nursery counting rhymes
make this book an excellent buy.   It has a good format and
is well-liked.

125   <u>A Big City</u>, by Francine Grossbart.   Harper, c1966.
        $3.50
        RL: 2-3   IL: Pre-school and beginning
        readers of all ages   BS
Bright colors and good illustrations of familiar city objects
are popular with all ages.   This book, like the Ezra Jack
Keats books, has the power to make a person see the city
with new eyes.

126   <u>Curious George Learns the Alphabet</u>, by H. A. Rey.
        Houghton Mifflin, c1963. $3.50
        RL: 2-3   IL: 2-5   S
Delightful pictures illustrating a rather young text in which
humor extends the appeal beyond the beginning grades.   Helpful in teaching phonics.

127   <u>Harold's ABC</u>, by Crockett Johnson.   Harper, 1963.
        $2.50
        RL: 2-3   IL: K-3   BS
Any age can enjoy Harold and I have used this book with
junior and high school students who were shaky on the alphabet.   The objects Harold uses for each letter are familiar
yet surprising.   Young children like this one also.

3 TEACHING TOOLS--COUNTING BOOKS

128 <u>My Red Umbrella</u>, by Robert Bright. Morrow, 1959. $3.14
RL: 2   IL: Read aloud-2   *BS
This can be either a book for young children starting to read or a counting book. The little girl's red umbrella stretches to cover all kinds of different animals in ones and twos and threes and fours.

129 <u>One, Two</u>, by Annie De Caprio. Illus. by Seymour Nydorf. Grosset Early Start Series, 1965. $.69
RL: Pre-primer IL: Pre-school-2   *BS
A counting rhyme book. This is one of a useful series of books and very popular.

130 <u>One, Two, Three for Fun</u>, by Muriel Stanek. Illus. by Seymour Fleishman. Whitman, c1964. $3.25
RL: 2   IL: Read aloud-2   *BSMP
This counting book bursts with so much happy activity that children love it and learn the numbers up to five quite unconsciously. Several pages of fun for one, then two, three, etc. Integrated illustrations.

131 <u>One, Two, Three, Going to Sea</u>, by Alain. Scholastic, 1969. pb $.50
RL: 2   IL: Read aloud-3   BS
A counting book about fishermen with very funny illustrations. Children love this one.

3 TEACHING TOOLS--PLAYS

132 <u>The Bag of Fire</u>, by Fan Kissen. Houghton-Mifflin, 1964. $3.88
RL: 3-4   IL: 3-JH   S
This author has produced three very valuable books of easy plays. They are very useful in reading-help programs. Many children who shy away from books will strain to read in order to take part in a play. Other children who hate to read aloud, lose their self-consciousness. See 133 and 140.

133 <u>The Crowded House and Other Tales</u>, by Fan Kissen.

Houghton Mifflin, 1964. $3.88
RL: 3-4   IL: 2-JH   S
Folk and fairy tales made into simple entertaining plays each
with a narrator and between eight and fifteen additional parts.

134 Folk Plays for Puppets You Can Make, by Tom Tichenor.
      Abingdon, 1959. $2.50
      RL: 2-3   IL: K-6   S
How to give a puppet show and how to make puppets.   Also
a valuable collection of plays for children at a low reading
level and with good appeal.   Older slow readers need not
feel embarrassed by the reading level if they put on easy
plays for younger children.   The Three Billy Goats Gruff,
The Little Red Hen, The Princess Who Wouldn't Cry are
some of the stories included.   The line drawings which illustrate this have humor and verve.

135 From Plays into Reading, by Gerald G. Glass and
      Muriel W. Klein.   Allyn & Bacon, 1969. $2.50
      RL: 4-6   IL: 3-JH   SM
This book contains fourteen plays, many of them dramatiza-
tions of very popular books such as Pippi Longstocking and
Mr. Popper's Penguins, and some folk tales, Dick Whitting-
ton and His Cat, The Golden Touch and others.   It has one
play with historical significance, The Early Life of George
Washington Carver.   There are nice line drawings.   It is
very much liked and really gets junior high poor readers
reading.

136 Little Plays for Little People.   Selected from Humpty-
      Dumpty's Magazine, edited by Freya Littledale.   Illus.
      by Ilse-Margaret Vogel.   Parents, c1965. $3.95
      RL: 2-3   IL: K-4   *S
This will be an invaluable book for the Reading Help programs.
Many inarticulate children will speak if they are playing a
part.   The fourteen short plays in this book are mostly based
on familiar folk tales or fables such as The Lion and the
Mouse.   Children of any background will understand and relate to them.   The introduction by a founder of the famous
Paper Bag Players shows how to make simple costumes and
scenery from such everyday items as grocery bags and cray-
ons.   Note the low reading level.

137 The Old Man and the Tiger, by Alvin Tresselt.   Illus.
      by A. Aquino.   Grosset, Easy-To-Read Wonder Book,
      c1965. $.59
      RL: 2   IL: 2-5   S

A play based on the old folk tale of the mouse and the lion.
Very popular with elementary school children. Also available
in Spanish. See Book List classification 4.

138   On Stage for Teenagers, by Helen Louise Miller. Plays,
      1958. $7.95
      RL: 5-6   IL: 5-HS   S
This play collection is a mixed bag. Some of the plays
really catch the student's imagination and lure him on to
reading heights. Others are a waste of time. With careful
preparation ahead of time to suit the student or group of
students, this can be a valuable book.

139   Radio and Television Plays, edited by Lawrence H.
      Feigenbaum. Globe Book Co., c1956. OP
      RL: Varied, mainly 5-6 IL: JH-HS   S
Relatively easy plays of high interest level which are useful
for expressive reading. The tutor or teacher should select
carefully among them, however, since some are too sophisticated.

140   The Straw Fox and Other Plays, by Fan Kissen.
      Houghton Mifflin, c1964. $3.28
      RL: 3   IL: 3-JH   S
Another in this useful series of folk tales in play form.
They have wide appeal and facilitate expressive reading.

141   Thirty Plays for Classroom Reading, edited by Donald
      D. Durrell and B. Alice Crossley. Plays, c1968.
      $5.00
      RL: 3-4   IL: 3-JH   S
A wide variety of plays based on fairy tales, fables, history
and biography enables a teacher or tutor to choose a subject
suitable to the interest level of any grade or student below
the high school level.

3   TEACHING TOOLS--GENERAL

142   Best Word Book Ever, by Richard Scarry. Western
      Golden Press, c1963. $3.95
      RL: 3 IL: Read aloud-4 and older non-readers S
One of the great books of all times, children seem to be almost
physically cheered by the illustrations of a bear and his

adventures.   This is close to being a beginning dictionary and
is successful with all children from pre-schoolers to non-
English speaking high school students.

143 <u>A Boy, a Dog, and a Frog</u>, by Mercer Mayer.   Dial,
         c1967.   Scholastic, pb $.50
         RL: No text   IL: Read aloud-3   S
Funny pictures tell the story of a boy and his dog who try to
capture a frog.   A good conversation piece to help a child
learn how to tell a story.

144 <u>Brave Daniel</u>, by Leonore Klein.   Illus. by John Fischett.
         Scholastic, c1958.   pb $.50
         RL: 2-3   IL: 2-6   BS
Brave Daniel's deeds are in fact rather sophisticated plays on
words which makes this an excellent book for reading help
programs with older children.   It can be used in junior high
with slow readers.   Not very popular on the bookmobile because of its sophistication.

145 <u>Cat in the Box</u>, by Dana Michel.   Illustrated by Rosalind
         Welcher.   Grosset Easy-To-Read Wonder Book Series,
         c1963. $.69
         RL: 2   IL: Read aloud-3   BS
A little grey cat lives in a box on a chair in a house on a
street in a town in a nation in a world in space.   In fifty-
eight words, a child is oriented.   This is very useful on a
one-to-one basis in helping a child to discover where he lives
and as a start to map work.   Younger children like having it
read to them.

146 <u>Did You Ever See?</u>, by Walter Einsel.   W. R. Scott,
         1962. $3.25 (Scholastic, pb $.50)
         RL: 2-3 IL:Read aloud-4 and older non-readers   BS
This book has a thirty-five word vocabulary and is almost a
word-game rhyming book.   Excellent for a one-to-one situation, it requires an adult for the child to enjoy it.

147 <u>Do You Hear What I Hear?</u>, by Helen Borten.   Abelard-
         Schuman, c1960. $3.95
         RL: 3   IL: Read aloud-3   S
Beautiful pictures and word images awaken the child's interest
and sharpen his ear.   A book to read and discuss with a young
child.

148 <u>Do You See What I See?</u>, by Helen Borten.   Abelard-
         Schuman, c1959. $3.50

RL: Read aloud and 3   IL: Pre-school-4   S
A book of lines and shapes and colors which is a good conversation piece and useful for increasing perception in a one-
to-one situation.

149   Do You Want to See Something?, by Eve Merriam.
        Illus. by Abner Graboff.   Scholastic, c1965.   pb $.50
        RL: 2   IL: Pre-K-3   BS
Another good book for sharpening a child's perceptions.   This
and similar books are borrowed by the primary children and
well liked.   However, we are trying to persuade the mothers
of pre-school children to take them and read them aloud.

150   Everyday Reading and Writing, by Frank C. Laubach,
        Elizabeth Mooney Kirk and Robert S. Laubach.   Illus.
        by Suzanne Morrow Joynt.   Readers Press--The New
        Streamlined English Series, c1970.   pb $3.95
        RL: Varied   IL: HS-adult   S
An extremely valuable text book designed to help older functional illiterates, this book starts with street signs and helps
a student to read newspapers, fill out applications, read want
ads and other ads etc.   It has many graphics and illustrations,
including relevant excerpts from comic strips.   It also contains much excellent practical advice.   This little known publisher has other valuable material for adult illiterates.   His
catalogue is well worth getting.

151   Funny Baby, by Margaret Hillert.   Illus. by Hertha
        Depper.   Follett Just Beginning To Read Series, 1963.
        $1.25
        RL: Pre-primer   IL: Pre-K-s   S
A familiar ugly duckling tale in an attractive book that somehow seems unusual even though the vocabulary is restricted
to forty words.

152   Go, Dog, Go!, by Philip D. Eastman.   Random House
        Beginner Book, c1961. $2.50
        RL: Pre-primer   IL: Universal for anyone
        learning to read   BS
One of the great books for helping with reading.   We have
used it with high school non-readers.   Has humor.

153   The Good Bird, by Peter Wezel.   Harper, c1964.
        $3.27
        RL: Non-worded   IL: Pre-school-3   S
The story in pictures of a bird who befriends a fish, this
book may be used imaginatively for oral or written creative
writing and story-telling.

154   Hi, All You Rabbits, by Carl Memling.   Illus. by Myra
        McGee.   Parents, 1970. $3.95
        RL: 2   IL: Read aloud-2   *S
I know many city children who sing Old McDonald Had a
Farm lustily without a clue as to what a pig that goes oink
looks like or is useful for.   This gaily illustrated book is
like a picture story of McDonald's farm and would be very
useful in any program for younger children as well as any
program where children are trying to learn English.

155   Hop on Pop, by Dr. Seuss.   Random House Beginner,
        c1963. $2.50
        RL: 1-2   IL: K-4 and older non-readers   BS
An easy-to-read comical book which is basically a play on
words.   The pictures make it popular fun with phonics.

156   I Read Signs, by Tom Funk.   Illustrated by the author.
        Holiday, c1962. $3.95 (Young Readers Press, pb
        OP)
        RL: 2   IL: K-3   BS
Gay pictures draw attention to the many street signs which
surround us.   Many of the children who need reading help
are very unobservant and need to have their perception
sharpened.

157   Is This Your Dog?, by Sally Jackson.   Illus. by Dick
        Martin.   Reilly & Lee, c/o Henry Regnery, c1962.
        $4.50
        RL: Pre-primer   IL: Read aloud-2   S
For youngsters needing vocabulary reinforcement on a pre-
primer level, this book serves a needed purpose although its
illustrations are very white middle class.

158   Karen's Opposites, by Alice and Martin Provenson.
        Western Golden Press, c1963.   OP
        RL: 2-3   IL: Read aloud-4   S
A wonderful picture book which illustrates hard-to-understand
concepts.   Great for teaching antonyms.   Let's hope so useful a book will soon be back in print.

159   Magic Made Easy, by Larry Kettlekamp.   Illus. by
        William Meyerriecks.   Morrow, 1954. $3.56
        (Scholastic, c1963.   pb $.60)
        RL: 5   IL: 5-HS   BS
Easy-to-do magic tricks.   This book is very appealing to non-
readers and can be used with groups in tutorial situations.

160   Mother, These Are My Friends, edited by Mary A.
          Gross.   City Schools Curriculum Service, 1968. $1
          RL: 2-3   IL: 2-5   S
The wishes of city children in their own words.   This book
has a short wish on each page with space for a child to
write his own wish or draw a picture.   Very thought-provoking and a wonderful conversation piece.   It has been very
popular in the reading help program.

161   The Noisy Book, by Margaret Wise Brown.   Illus. by
          Leonard Weisgard.   Harper, 1939. $3.95
          RL: 3   IL: Read aloud-4   S
A little dog, his eyes temporarily bandaged, listens to familiar noises.   This book sharpens childrens' interest in hearing accurately.

162   One Fish, Two Fish, Red Fish, Blue Fish, by Dr.
          Seuss.   Random Beginner, 1960. $2.50
          RL: 1-2   IL: 1-3 and older non-readers   BS
Another very helpful, easy-to-read book in the same class
as Hop On Pop.

163.   Pop-Up Sound Alikes, edited by Albert G. Miller.
          Random, c1967. $2.50
          RL: 3   IL: 4-JH   S
Humor imprints knowledge firmly.   Older elementary and
junior high slow readers will love this book and really learn
the hilarious homonyms.

164   A Shuffle Book, by Richard Hefter and Martin Stephen
          Moskof.   Western Golden Press, 1970. $3.95
          RL: 2-3   IL: 2-6 and older non-readers   *S
A book? maybe; a game and a first rate teaching tool certainly.   Fifty-two book size brightly colored pieces of card-
board with one word or several on each side can be shuffled
and recombined to make a million different stories.   Children
really enjoy this and it prods their imaginations.

165   Spooky Magic, by Larry Kettlekamp.   Illus. by William
          Meyerriecks.   Morrow, 1955. $3.14 (Scholastic,
          pb $.50)
          RL: 5   IL: 4-7   BS
Eerie looking tricks made easy.   Books like this often catch
the interest of students who shy away from fiction.

166   Ten Apples Up on Top, by Theodore Le Sieg.   Random,
          1961.   Beginner. $2.50

RL: 2   IL: K-4   BS
Another excellent book for learning both numbers and phonics
relatively painlessly. This has the same silly illustrations
that make Go, Dog, Go [152], so popular.

167 Up and Down, by Maggie Jardine. Illus. by Richard C.
     Lewis. Grosset Early Start Series, 1965. $.59
     RL: Pre-primer IL: Read aloud-2   BS
This little book shows, in pictures and words, ten objects
which go up and come down. It has a thirteen word vocabulary and is very popular since so many children can read it.

168 What Whiskers Did, by Ruth Carroll. Scholastic, 1965.
     pb $.60
     RL: No text   IL: Pre-school-2   BS
A picture story without words of a runaway puppy's adventures. This is a wonderful conversation piece for a one-to-
one tutorial situation.

169 Word-A-Day, by Mickey Bach. Scholastic, c1960, 1963.
     pb $.50
     RL: 6-adult   IL: JH-adult   *S
If I were a high school teacher or tutor of young adults, I
would certainly keep this book next to the American Heritage
Dictionary and allow unobtrusive time for browsing. The
words in Word-A-Day are certainly difficult for many students
but the cartoons which illustrate the meaning are funny and
illuminating--see "buoyancy." I think most students would
love this book and be inspired by it to go further.

3   TEACHING TOOLS--USEFUL SERIES

        These series cover more than one classification.
Other series which confine themselves to one subject will be
found under that heading, viz. Let's Read and Find Out
Science Series will be found under classification 5, SCIENCE.

170 Bank Street Pre-Primer Series. Macmillan, various
     dates. $.60 to $1, according to title.
     RL: Pre-primer IL: Pre-school-JH   S
A very useful set of books. Even older students who are
non-readers will accept these books as a first step. City

backgrounds and multi-ethnic children are used.

171   Bank Street Readers.   Macmillan, various dates.
        $2.15 to $2.75, according to grade.
        These superb readers should be in all city schools.
They reflect city situations and have multi-ethnic stories and
illustrations.   They also seem meatier than ordinary readers.
The stories are not so saccharine and some even have an unhappy ending.   The School Volunteer program does not use
readers.   Even good ones are not as much fun to read as
other books.   We carried samples of these readers on the
bookmobile and showed them to parents to let them know what
was available.   They were uniformly enthusiastic.   At that
point none of the schools we served in Bedford-Stuyvesant,
Brownsville and Bushwick used these readers, although the
school population was definitely multi-ethnic.

172   Dolch Pleasure Reading Series, by E. W. Dolch et al.
        Garrard, various dates. $2.69
        RL: 3-5   IL: 2-HS   S
Several of this series have proved very popular in our read-
ing help programs, especially the titles on RL 3 and RL 4.
Among the most liked titles have been Andersen's Stories,
Aesop's Stories, Robinson Crusoe and Gulliver's Travels.
However, these books, while they fill a need, are a little
like a salt-free diet.   If you want to create a real appetite
for books, they should be used sparingly.

173   Doubleday Semaphore Series.   Various dates. $1.75
                                                             BS
A paperback edition of many of the Doubleday Signal Series
[see 174].   The format is excellent, the price is right and
I hope all the Signal Series titles will soon be in paperback.

174   Doubleday Signal Series.   various dates.
        RL: 4   IL: 4-6-HS and adult, depending on title   BS
An excellent series with many good titles.   Some, like Shy
Girl, the life of Eleanor Roosevelt, have been very successful with senior citizens groups.   Others like Big Band and
High School Dropout find their audience at the junior high
level.   I am very grateful for this series which is very popular and especially glad that many of the titles are now out in
paperback.   [See 173].

175   Falcon Books.   Noble & Noble, various dates.   pb
        $.75 each
        RL: Mainly 6   IL: 6-adult   BSM

A valuable series of interesting titles in an attractive format,
these books have been abridged and adapted for poor readers.
Although the language has been simplified, it is not stilted
and the flavor of the original book has been preserved. The
titles are: <u>Anne Frank: The Diary of a Young Girl</u>, <u>April
Morning</u>, <u>Call of the Wild</u>, <u>A Choice of Weapons</u>, <u>Dracula</u>,
<u>Fail-Safe</u>, <u>Go Tell It on the Mountain</u>, <u>Go Up for Glory</u>, <u>I
Always Wanted to Be Somebody</u>, <u>Karen</u>, <u>The Listening Walls</u>,
<u>Times Four</u>, <u>A Tree Grows in Brooklyn</u>, and <u>West Side
Story</u>. These books are available only to non-profit organi-
zations.

176 <u>Grosset & Dunlap Early Start Series</u>. Various dates.
     $. 59
     RL: Pre-primer   IL: Read aloud-2
This series has books on subjects of interest to young children which use only twelve to twenty-five words. As a result the books are very popular with beginning readers who
gain a real sense of accomplishment.

177 <u>Grosset & Dunlap Easy-to-Read Wonder Book Series</u>.
     RL: Primer-3 depending on title
     IL: Read aloud-HS depending on title
This is an excellent series of books. The reading level runs
from a vocabulary of fifty words in <u>The Cat in the Box</u> and
<u>I Draw a Line</u> to RL 2-3 in books like <u>The Clumsy Cowboy</u>.
The interest level is intended for pre-school and younger
elementary children but I have seen junior high and even high
school non-readers enjoy the folk tale <u>The Boy Who Fooled
the Giant</u> and the story <u>One Kitten Is Not Too Many</u>. The
price, $. 59 or $. 69, is amazingly low and the books stand
up physically very well. Some on the bookmobile have gone
out twenty-seven times and are still being borrowed. It is
important to be selective as to title as some titles (<u>Barby</u>,
for example) are very poor. Others, such as the titles mentioned above, are among the most useful and popular books
on this list, especially for those in reading help programs.

178 <u>Grosset & Dunlap Read-Aloud Wonder Book Series</u>.
     Various dates. pb $. 49
     RL: 3 and 4-5   IL: Read aloud-6   BS
These books fill a real need. Their reading level runs from
3 to 4-5. Their interest level runs from third through sixth
grade but they are especially important for the many fifth
and sixth graders we see who want to read fairy tales and
books like <u>Heidi</u> and <u>The Wizard of Oz</u> and <u>Alice in Wonder-
land</u> and are frustrated by their low reading ability. These

children are enchanted to find books they can read and come
back for more, often gradually moving up to harder books.

179   Grosset & Dunlap Tempo Series.   Various dates.   pb
        $.50 or $.60, depending on title.
        RL: 5 & 6 & 6-7   IL: 5-adult, depending on title   BS
This paperback series is mainly on a fifth- or sixth-grade
reading level though some titles are more difficult.   It is
aimed at sixth, seventh, and eighth graders but we have
found that many titles are of interest to adults.   The format
is excellent since any age from sixth grade on up feels free
to borrow these books.   Again, it is important to be selective as to title.

180   Harper I Can Read Series.   Harper & Row, various
        dates. $2.50
        RL: 2-4   IL: K-5 or 6, according to title
An excellent series of books that are very popular with elementary children.   The stories and mysteries are for young
children (see I Should Have Stayed in Bed [894]), and The
Case of the Hungry Stranger [1142], but some of the science
I Can Read and History I Can Read can be used successfully
with older non-readers through junior high school.   See
Steven and the Green Turtle [299] and The Drinking Gourd
[824], which is about the Underground Railroad.

181   Let's Go Series.   Putnam, various dates. $2.68
        RL: 3   IL: 3-5   S
This useful series covers almost every situation a child would
encounter (Post Office, Firehouse, Supermarket, Hospital,
Zoo, etc.) and some trips he would like to take.   However,
it is worth leafing through them to pick and choose.   Like
any series, they vary in quality and some are so packed with
facts that they are dull and will discourage a slow reader who
perhaps does not want to know that much about the subject.

182   Little Golden Series.   Western Golden Press, various
        dates. $.39
        RL: Mainly 3   IL: Read aloud-3   BS
Many of these books are useful if it is borne in mind that
some have a high reading level for their interest.   For
example, by the time a child can read The Little Red Hen,
he probably wouldn't want to.   It is, however, an excellent
read-aloud and a good story for a storyteller.   We carry the
titles listed below for age groups pre-school to third grade.
There are other good titles if you watch for them and some
quite poor ones.   On the whole, though, a valuable series

if you can buy just the titles you want although the books
cannot take the physical wear and tear of the Grosset Series
[176 and 177].
Five Little Firemen, Little Golden ABC, The Little Red Hen,
Little Red Riding Hood, Mother Goose, Peter Rabbit, The
Pokey Little Puppy, Snow White and the Seven Dwarfs, The
Three Bears, and The Three Little Kittens.

183 McGraw-Hill City Limits Series. Various dates.
        $1.84 each
        RL: 4-5   IL: 5-adult   *BSMP
An excellent series of original stories mainly about city situations which will interest young people very much.   Although
the reading level is low, the language seems natural (and not
colorless) and the books have plenty of action.   A welcome
series for those who want to persuade teenagers that books
have meaning for them.

184 McGraw-Hill Reading Shelf Series. Various dates.
        $1.48 and $1.60
        RL: 4-5   IL: 5-adult   *BSMP
An excellent series of well-chosen titles, both fiction and
non-fiction, abridged and adapted for easier reading.   The
adaptations have been so well done that one is not conscious
of the controlled vocabulary.   This series fills a real need
and will be extremely popular.

185 Mr. Bumba Books, by Pearl Augusta Harwood.   Illus.
        by Joseph Folger.   Lerner Publications, Inc., 1964.
        $2.95
        RL: 2-3   IL: Read aloud-3   *BSMP
A series of easy-to-read books about an artist called Mr.
Bumba and some neighbor children who are his friends.
Pleasant but not very exciting.   The ten titles are: Mr.
Bumba's New Home; Mr. Bumba Plants a Garden; Mr.
Bumba Keeps House; Mr. Bumba and the Orange Grove;
Mr. Bumba's New Job; Mr. Bumba Has a Party; Mr.
Bumba Draws a Kitten; Mr. Bumba's Four-legged Company;
Mr. Bumba Rides a Bicycle; Mr. Bumba's Tuesday Club.

186 Mrs. Moon Books, by Pearl Augusta Harwood.   Illus.
        by George Overlie.   Lerner Publications, 1967.
        $1.95
        RL: 3   IL: Read aloud-4   *BSM
This delightful series of books has ten titles.   Each is centered around Mrs. Moon, an energetic and cheerful retired
librarian who has a series of adventures with the children

who live in her building. Mrs. Moon is a most unusual retired person--she can pole vault across a brook and slide
down a rope from high up in a tree. No matter what happens she never loses her "cool." Children will love her
and teachers and librarians will like the sturdy colorful books
about her. The titles are as follows: <u>Mrs. Moon's Story
Hour</u>, <u>Mrs. Moon and Her Friends</u>, <u>Mrs. Moon's Polliwogs</u>,
<u>Mrs. Moon Goes Shopping</u>, <u>Mrs. Moon's Picnic</u>, <u>Mrs. Moon's
Harbor Trip</u>, <u>Mrs. Moon's Rescue</u>, <u>Mrs. Moon Takes a
Drive</u>, <u>Mrs. Moon and the Dark Stairs</u>, and <u>Mrs. Moon's
Cement Hat</u>.

187 <u>Random House Beginner Books</u>. Various dates. $2.50
    RL: 2-3   IL: Read aloud-4   BS
All Random House Beginner Books are very popular with
children because of their colorful illustrations and the need
they fill for books that a child can read at a very early stage
in his education. Many of them reinforce phonics in a way
that children look on as a game. After a while, the same-
ness of the style of illustration becomes boring to both children and teachers and provides a spur to more difficult books
with more variety.

188 <u>Random House Bright and Early Books</u>. Various dates.
    $2.50
    RL: Pre-primer   IL: Pre-school-2
A series of books on the pre-primer level which encourage
beginning readers by giving them a sense of accomplishment.
Some such as <u>One Fish, Two Fish</u> [162] have great imagination; others are dull but useful teaching aids.

189 <u>Random House Step-Up Books</u>. Various dates. $1.95
    each
    RL: 3-4   IL: 3-JH   BS
This is an excellent transition series between the reading
level of easy-to-read books and trade books for fourth and
fifth graders and bridges an important step in reading skills.
The print is large and well arranged on the page and there
is just the right amount of space devoted to illustrations.
As in any series, the quality varies. <u>Meet Abraham Lincoln</u>
and <u>Meet George Washington</u> are great favorites and very
well done. I disliked <u>Meet John Kennedy</u> and so did many
children. The science fact books about animals, fish and
insects are popular and the series can fill a real need provided it stays away from being either cute or patronizing.
There are times when some of the titles lean that way.
There are twenty-one titles in the series.

190   The Sesame Street Book of ... (People and Things;
        Numbers; Shapes; Puzzles; Letters). New Ameri-
        can Library, Signet, c1970, 1971. pb $.95
                                                          BSM
These books are intended to help children with reading readiness and can be used and enjoyed whether or not a child has
watched the Sesame Street program. They are full of humor
and children look on them as games. Unfortunately the binding is shoddy and the books fall apart very easily. There
is also a Sesame Street magazine with games and suggestions
for making things. Children love this.

191   Springboards.   Noble & Noble, Portal Press. $1.00
        for an envelope of 20 copies of one story.
        RL: 4,5,6   IL: 4-HS   S
Springboards is the title of a series of stories for the above
reading levels. The format of a folded paper containing
three pages of story and one page of comprehension questions
(which need not be used) is novel. The shortness of the selection, the attractive lead photograph, and the diversity of the
subject matter make these valuable additions to a library
aimed at the retarded, older reader. This resourceful publisher has even presented stories based on a strong use of
Spanish cognates to show the Spanish-speaking child how he
can develop an understanding of English words.

192   "This Is" Series.   Follett, various dates. $1.25
        RL: 3   IL: Read aloud-4   BS
This is an excellent series for broadening the horizons of
children whose lives are circumscribed by poverty. Some
titles we use are This Is a Supermarket, This Is a Department Store, This Is a Newspaper, etc. I have worked with
many children in New York City who had never encountered
supermarkets, department stores or newspapers. Note low
price.

193   True Book Series.   Children's Press. $3.75
        RL: 2-3 & 3-4   IL: 2-5   S
This series has excellent illustrations and good quality.
There are many good titles, e.g., The True Book of Policemen & Firemen, about people and places that all children
should know. If the series were reissued in a slightly older
format (Voyager or Dell Yearling) in paperback and with
multi-ethnic illustrations, it would be enormously useful.
True Book of Airports & Airplanes, by John Lewellen.
        Illus. by R. Gates RL: 2   IL: 2-5

True Book of Automobiles, by Norman V. and M. Carlisle.
    Illus. by J. Barnahl.   RL: 3   IL: 3-5
True Book of Energy, by Illa Podendorf.   RL: 2   IL: 2-6
True Book of Insects, by Illa Podendorf.   Illus. by C.
    Maltman.   RL: 2   IL: 2-JH
True Book of Magnets and Electricity, by Illa Podendorf.
    Illus. by Robert Borja.   RL: 2   IL: 2-JH
True Book of Money, by Benjamin Elkin.   Illus. by M. Gehr.
    RL: 2-3   IL: 2-JH
True Book of Moon, Sun and Stars, by John Lewellen.   Illus.
    by L. Fisher.   RL: 2   IL: 3-JH
True Book of Ships & Seaports, by Katherine Carter.
    RL: 2   IL: 2-JH
True Book of Your Body and You, by Alice Hinshaw.   Illus.
    by Frances Eckhart.   RL: 2   IL: 2-JH

194 <u>Are You My Mother?</u>, by Philip D. Eastman. Random
      House Beginner Book, c1960.
      RL: 2   IL: Read aloud-2
A highly satisfying and truly funny easy-to-read book for
younger children. This is very popular in every neighborhood. Available in Spanish: <u>Eres Tu Mi Mama?</u>, transl.
by Carlos Rivera. $3.66   B

195 <u>Arty the Smarty</u>, by Faith McNulty. Illus. by Albert
      Aquino. Grosset, c1962.
      RL: 2-3   IL: Read aloud-3
Arty the smart fish outwits his enemies in a way that cheers
and entertains young children. Available in Spanish: <u>Arturito</u>
<u>el Astuto</u>, transl. by Pura Belpré. $.69   B

196 <u>Cat in the Hat</u>, by Dr. Seuss. Random, 1957.
      RL: 2-3   IL: Read aloud-3
A story in rhyme, this is one of the very first easy-to-read
books with humor and imagination ever to be published. It
tells of a girl and a boy, confined to the house by bad
weather, who have a magic visitor, a cat who can perform
humorous wonders. This is very popular with most children
although some shy ones seem almost to be frightened by the
illustrations. In French-and-English: <u>Le Chat au Chapeau</u>,
transl. by Jean Vallier; in Spanish-and-English: <u>El Gato</u>
<u>Ensombrerado</u>, transl. by Carlos Rivera. both $3.66   B

197 <u>The Curious Cow</u>, by Esther K. Meeks. Illus. by Mel
      Pekarsly. Follett, c1960.
      RL: 2   IL: Read aloud-3   BS
A funny story of a cow whose curiosity leads her into adventures and misadventures. Available in French: <u>La Vache</u>
<u>Curieuse</u> (used on bookmobile), and in German: <u>Die Neugierige</u>
<u>Kuh.</u> both $1.38

198 <u>Fish Out of Water</u>, by Helen Palmer. Illus. by P. D.
      Eastman. Random Beginner, c1961.
      RL: 2   IL: Read aloud-3

A boy's pet fish grows until he is too big for any tank but a swimming pool.   A funny fantasy in easy-to-read form, deservedly popular.   In French-and-English: Un Poisson Hors de l'Eau, transl. by Jean Vallier; in Spanish-and-English: Un Pez Fuera del Agua, transl. by Carlos Rivera.   both $3.66 B

199   Gertie the Duck, by Nicholas P. Georgiady and Louis
       G. Romano.   Illus. by Dagmar Wilson.   Follett,
       c1959.
       RL: 2   IL: Read aloud-3   BS
Gertie the duck lays her eggs in such an awkward spot that it changes people's lives.   Not only do the babies hatch but people learn to slow down and be friendly for their sake. Small children find this a very satisfying story.   Available in Spanish: Tulita la Patita. $1.38   B

200   Gilberto and the Wind, by Marie Ets.   Viking, c1963.
       RL: 2   IL: Read aloud-3   BSM
Gilberto races the wind and uses its help to sail a boat and set soap bubbles floating high in the sky.   One of the earliest books to be published about a Spanish-American child, it has imaginative illustrations.   Available in Spanish: Gilberto y el Viento, transl. by Aurora Labistida. $3.37

201   Here Comes the Strikeout, by Leonard Kessler.   Har-
       per, c1965.
       RL: 2-3   IL: 2-6   BSM
Bobby always strikes out.   Finally he learns to practice and winds up with a triumph.   A very popular easy-to-read baseball story.   Available in Spanish: Aqui Viene el Ponchado, transl. by Pura Belpré. $2.92   B

202   Hole in the Hill, by Marion Seyton.   Illus. by Leonard
       Weisgard.   Follett, 1960.
       RL: 2   IL: Read aloud-3   BS
The pre-historic Stone family searches for a pet.   Children love the cartoon-like illustrations in this one.   Available in French: Le Trou dans la Colline, $1.38 B and in Spanish: El Hoyo del Cerro, $1.38 B

203   Hurry Up Slowpoke, by Crosby Newell.   Illus. by the
       author.   Grosset Easy-to-Read Wonder Book, c1961.
       RL: 3   IL: Read aloud and K-4   BS
This humorous story has so much appeal that it can overcome the fact that it is about a family of mice.   Normally, we never carry books about mice.   A mouse immediately reminds a ghetto child of rats and unpleasant experiences.   Fortunately,

the entertaining pictures are not very mouselike and the book
is consistently popular.   Available in Spanish: Date Prisa
Cachazudo. $.69 B

204 Let Papa Sleep, by Crosby Bonsall and Emily Reed.
        Grosset Easy-to-Read Wonder Book, c1963.
        RL: 2-3   IL: Read aloud-3   BS
A humorous easy-to-read book about life with father that is
very popular with the young.   Available in Spanish: Dejen
que Papá Duerma, transl. by Pura Belpré. $.69   B

205 Little Auto, by Lois Lenski.   Walch, 1934.
        RL: 2   IL: Read aloud-2
All about a little automobile by a popular author.   Available
in Spanish: Auto Pequeño, transl. by Sandra Streepey.
$3.50

206 Look at Your Eyes, by Paul Showers.   Illus. by Paul
        Galdone.   Let's Read and Find Out Science Series,
        c1962.
        RL: 2-3   IL: Read aloud-5   BSM
This book explains basic facts about our eyes in an interest-
ing way and with good illustrations.   Available in Spanish:
Mirate los Ojos. $4.50 B

207 Mable the Whale, by Patricia King.   Illus. by Katherine
        Evans.   Follett Beginning to Read, 1958.
        RL: 2-3   IL: Read aloud-3   BS
A suspenseful story about a whale with a sunburned fin based
on a true incident.   Available in French: Mabelle la Baleine,
and in Spanish: Elena la Ballena.   both $1.38   B

208 Mire y Apprenda Inglés, By Elena Zayas.   Dell Laurel,
        pb OP B
A very useful book in Spanish which tells how to learn English.   It has helpful illustrations.   As long as it was in
print, we sold this on the bookmobile and had many grateful
comments later from the buyers.

209 Mother Goose in French, translated by Hugh Latham.
        Illus. by Barbara Cooeny.   Crowell, c1964. $3.95 B
Lovely illustrations make this an appealing book and it is
eagerly borrowed by the many Haitians and other French-
speaking immigrants in New York.

210 Mother Goose in Spanish, transl. by Alastair Reid and
        Anthony Kerrigan.   Illus. by Barbara Cooney.

Crowell, c1968. $3.95 B
Another lovely edition of Mother Goose, this time in Spanish.
Both words and illustrations are redolent of Spain and are
much enjoyed by Puerto Ricans, Colombians and other
Spanish-speaking children in New York.

211 No Place to Play, by Paul Newmann. Illus. by David
      Lockhart. Frosset & Dunlap Easy-to-Read Wonder
      Book, c1969. $.69
      RL: 2-3   IL: Read aloud-3   BSM
Three boys who are in the way wherever they go, finally
manage to build a clubhouse out of an old crate. The story
has humor and appeals to early graders. Available in
Spanish.

212 The Old Man and the Tiger, by Alvin Tresselt. Illus.
      by A. Aquino. Grosset Easy-to-Read Wonder Book,
      c1965.
      RL: 2   IL: 2-5   S
A play based on the old folk tale of the mouse and the lion.
Very popular with elementary school children. Available in
Spanish: El Viejo y el Tigre, transl. by Pura Belpré,
$.69 B

213 Ote: A Puerto Rican Folk Tale, by Pura Belpré.
      Illus. by Paul Galdone. Pantheon, c1969. $3.95
      RL: IL: Read aloud-3   *B
The story of a near-sighted devil who steals a family's food
and how he was outwitted by the smallest child, this has
dramatic illustrations. It is a fine story for story telling
but not so appropriate for a child to read to him or herself.
In general, the age that can and wants to read fairy tales
prefers fairy princes and princesses to devils and small
children. Available in Spanish: Ote: Un Guento Folklorico
Puertorriqueño. $4.79 *B

214 Papa Small, by Lois Lenski. Walck, 1951. $3.75
      RL: 2-3   IL: Read aloud-3
Children love the Small family as shown in Lois Lenski's line
drawings and factual prose. This simple book about Papa
Small is available in Spanish-English: Papa Pequeño: Papa
Small, transl. by Maria Dolores Lado, and in French-English:
Papa Petit: Papa Small, transl. by B. Kay. both $3.50 *B

215 Straight Hair, Curly Hair, by Augusta R. Goldin. Illus.
      by Ed Emberley. Crowell, Let's Read and Find Out
      Science Series, c1966. $3.75 (Crocodile, pb $.95)

RL: 3   IL: Read aloud-5   BSM
This tells about the cross sectional shape of hair and about
its follicles. It presents experiments that require only the
reader's hair, Scotch tape, keys and some curiosity. A
good book on a subject that seems very important to young
people. Available in Spanish: Pelo Lacio, Pelo Riso.
$4. 50 *B

216 Terry and the Caterpillars, by Millicent E. Selsam.
       Illus. by Arnold Lobel. Harper & Row, I Can Read
       Series, 1962. $2. 50
       RL: 3   IL: Read aloud-4   *BSMP
A girl collects three caterpillars and learns through watching
them the cycle of a moth's life. This book will make other
children want to collect caterpillars also. It is easy to read
in every sense and even has suspense. Very well done.
Also available in Spanish.

217 Too Many Dogs, by Ramona Dupré. Illus. by Howard
       Baer. Follett, c1960. $1. 59
       RL: 2   IL: Read aloud-3   BS
A comical story with great appeal to animal lovers about two
pet dachshunds who adopt another dog and her nine puppies.
Available in French: Trop de Chiens. $1. 38 *B

218 Vaquero Pequeño: Cowboy Small, by Lois Lenski.
       Walck, c1960. $3. 50
       RL: 2   IL: Read aloud-2   *B
Cowboy Small is shown doing everything a cowboy should:
wrangling, branding, busting broncos and caring for his
horse. The simple text is in Spanish and English and the
pictures appeal to children everywhere.

219 What Do I Do?, by Norma Simon. Illus. by Joe Lasker.
       Whitman, c1969. $3. 95
       RL: 2   IL: Read aloud-3   SM
This cheerful picture book depicts a day of a Puerto Rican
child living in the city. The simple phrases he uses are in
both Spanish and English. This is an excellent book for
teaching Spanish children English or American children Spanish. It is also a valuable book for families where the mother
speaks little or no English. The translations, however, are
not literal as the book is designed for reading for pleasure,
not as a teaching text.

220 What Do I Say?, by Norma Simon. Illus. by Joe
       Lasker. Whitman, c1967.

RL: 2   IL: Read aloud-3   SM
Similar to 219, and just as useful. The many Puerto Rican
children in the School Volunteer program really enjoy these
books and love to see the familiar scenes of their own surroundings.

221. What the Moon Is Like, by Franklyn M. Branley.
     Illus. by Bobri. Crowell, Let's Read and Find Out
     Science Series, c1963. $3.75
This beautifully illustrated book came out long before we put
a man on the moon. However, it has enough general information about the moon to interest children even though it is
not up to date. Available in Spanish: Como Es la Luna?
$4.50 *B

222. What's Behind the Word?, by Sam and Beryl Epstein.
     Illus. by Laszlo Roth. Scholastic, c1964. $.60
     RL: 5-6   IL: 6-HS   BS
A first book of words and how language originated and grows.
Very thought-provoking in Reading Help programs, especially
the section on slang. The book gets the student interested in
and enjoying words instead of looking at new words as a
threat.

223. Will You Come to My Party?, by Sara Asheron. Illus.
     by Susanna Suba. Grosset Easy-to-Read Wonder Book,
     c1961. $.69
     RL: 2-3   IL: Read aloud-4
How the grey squirrel gave a party. All children like parties
and books about parties. Available in Spanish: Vendras a
Mi Fiesta? $.69 *B

224 Your Skin and Mine, by Paul Showers. Illus. by Paul
    Galdone. Crowell, Let's Read and Find Out Science
    Series, c1965. $3.75
    RL: 3   IL: Read aloud-5   BSM
The story of our skin, what it is and how it protects us.
Told with verve and imagination by a close look at three
boys: an Oriental, a Negro, and a Caucasian. Available
in Spanish: Tu Piel y la Mia. $4.50 *B

5 SCIENCE

225 <u>Adventures in Space</u>, by Sara Bulett. Illus. by Charles
      Meder. Follett, c1970. $2.36
      RL: 3   IL: 3-JH   S
Short selections on the conquering of space; easy, yet of
wide interest, especially to older boys.

226 <u>Air</u>, by John Feilen. Illus. by Joseph Rogers.
      Follett, c1965. $1.25
      RL: 4   IL: 3-HS   BS
This well illustrated book describes air and its functions in
straightforward language. It shows simple experiments that
can be done at home with ordinary household equipment.
Much of the information in it would be new and valuable to
many adults and it has been successfully used in adult literacy programs in spite of the childish format.

227 <u>All About Us</u>, by Eva Knox Evans. Illus. Frank Alois.
      Western, Golden Press, c1947, 1968. $3.95 pb $.75
      RL: 4-5   IL: 3-adult   BSMP
A popularly written yet highly informative book about the races
of man; excellent format; very popular.

228 <u>All Kinds of Babies</u>, by Millicent Selsam. Illus. by
      Symeon Shimin. Scholastic, c1967. pb $.60
      RL: 3-4   IL: 2-5   BS
The world is full of babies. This popular and beautifully illustrated beginning science book shows that only some babies
look like their parents when they are born but all look like
their parents when fully grown.

229 <u>Answers and More Answers</u>, by Mary Elting. Illus.
      Tran Mawicke. Grosset, c1961. $3.95
      RL: 4   IL: 4-adult   S
A useful browsing and reference work of science facts similar
to the Wonder Book or a beginning encyclopedia.

230 <u>The Apple and the Moth</u>, by Iela and Enzo Mari. Illus.
      by Iela Mari. Pantheon, c1970. $3.95

RL: No text   IL: Pre-school-4   *S
An unusual picture book, without words, which vividly tells
the story of the life cycle of the moth in a way that a child
will understand and find interesting.

231   Arrow Book of Answers, by Mary Elting. Illus. Tran
      Mawicke and Richard Pricet. Scholastic, 1961. pb
      $.45
      RL: 4 OP   IL: 4-adult   BS
Simply written answers to science questions, this book could
stand updating but is very popular. It has all the browsing
fascination of the Wonder Book. It has many illustrations.
I wish there were more books like this.

232   Arrow Book of Science Facts, by Mary Elting. Many
      illustrators. Scholastic, c1959. pb $.60
      RL: 4   IL: 4-adult   BS
A very popular book similar to the Arrow Book of Answers.
Both these books were drawn from Answers and More An-
swers, published in hard cover by Grosset and Dunlap.

233   Arrow Book of Science Riddles, by Rose Wyler. Illus.
      Robert Osborn. Scholastic, c1964. pb $.60
      RL: 5   IL: 4-JH   BS
All riddle books are popular and this one is no exception.
It has many humorous illustrations but is full of serious
knowledge.

234   A Baby Starts to Grow, by Paul Showers. Illus. by
      Rosalind Fry. Crowell, Let's Read and Find Out
      Series, c1969. $3.75 (pb .95)
      RL: 3   IL: 2-JH   *BSMP
A simple account of a subject of interest to all children.

235   Bees, Bugs and Beetles, by Ronald Rood. Illus. Denny
      McMains. Scholastic, c1965. pb $.50
      RL: 5   IL: 3-JH and older non-readers   *BS
This is almost an encyclopedia on the title subject. It has
good illustrations and information which relates the subject
matter covered to daily life. Very well done.

236   Before You Were a Baby, by Paul Showers and Kay
      Sperry Showers. Illus. Ingrid Fetz. Crowell, Let's
      Read and Find Out Science Series, c1968. $3.75
      RL: 3-4   IL: 2-JH   BSMP
A simple straightforward account of how babies come to be,
grow and are born that will answer childrens' questions.

Any one who has taught will know how many misconceptions
many children have on this subject and how unhappy their
ignorance can make them.   This book will do a great deal
of good.

237   A Book of Real Science, by Mae Freeman.   Illus. John
        Moodie.   Scholastic, c1966.   pb $.50
        RL: 4-5   IL: 4-JH   BS
Beginning physics in simple terms but with no condescension.
Much liked by children of many age levels.   More science
paperbacks are badly needed.

238   The Chicken and the Egg, by Iela and Enzo Mari.   Illus.
        Iela Mari.   Pantheon, c1970. $3.95
        RL: IL: Read aloud-4   *S
A beautiful picture book with no words but with illustrations
which clearly show the life cycle of the chicken in a way a
child will understand and enjoy.   An excellent conversation
piece as well as one that will impart knowledge.

239   A Crack in the Pavement, by Ruth Howell.   Photographs
        by Arline Strong.   Atheneum, c1970. $3.75
        RL: 3   IL: Read aloud-5   BSM
A simple and uncondescending text and clear photographs illustrate nature in the city.   Some subjects covered are trees,
weeds, flowers, pigeons, ants, squirrels and animal tracks.
It is well-written and would be an excellent family read-aloud
and discussion book.

240   Crowell Young Math Series.   Crowell. $3.75 (pb $.95)
        RL: 2-3   IL: 2-JH   BSMP
This excellent series makes math interesting, fun and relevant by explaining math concepts in simple language, by involving the child in do-it-yourself examples and by relating
the concepts to factors in the life of every child.   The humorous and vivid illustrations clarify and enhance the text.
This series is a winner.   The titles so far are Estimation,
Straight Lines, Parallel Lines, Weighing and Balancing, and
What is Symmetry?

241   Dinosaurs, by Jane W. Watson.   Illus. by Rudolf
        Zallinger.   Western, c1962. $3.95 (Golden Press,
        1968, pb $.75)
        RL: 5   IL: 4-adult   BS
A clear and beautifully illustrated book on a subject which
seem to fascinate children and is of growing interest to older
people now that the possibility of man's becoming obsolete

has been suggested. See 242 and 263 below for easier
books on the same subject.

242 Dinosaurs and More Dinosaurs, by M. Jean Craig.
     Illus. by George Solonevich. Four Winds, 1965.
     $4.95 (Scholastic pb $.75)
     RL: 4   IL: 2-6   BS
A straightforward description of the different kinds of dinosaurs with many monochrome illustrations. This is very
popular and is neither as difficult nor as meaty as 241.
See also 263.

243 Do You Know About Stars?, by Mae Blacker Freeman.
     Illus. George Solonevich. Random House, 1970.
     $2.95
     RL: 3   IL: Read aloud-4   *BSMP
An excellent easy-to-read book about the stars with unusually
apt illustrations.

244 Do You Know About Water?, by Mae Blacker Freeman.
     Illus. Ernest Kurth Barth. Random House, 1970.
     $2.95
     RL: 3   IL: Read aloud-4   *BSMP
There is a tremendous demand for easy-to-read science books.
This one is very clearly written and on a subject of interest
to all. Note the good price and multi-ethnic illustrations.

245 Dolphins, by Mickie Compere. Illus. Irma Wilde.
     Scholastic, 1964. pb $.50
     RL: 3   IL: Read aloud-5   BS
An excellent beginning science book with good illustrations
about a subject which is appearing increasingly on TV.

246 Egg to Chick, by Millicent E. Selsam. Illus. by
     Barbara Wolff. Harper, Science I Can Read, c1970.
     $2.50
     RL: 2-3   IL: Read aloud-4   BS
A simple account of the development of a chick from the moment the egg cell is joined by a sperm until the day when the
chick pecks its way out of the shell. The first half is illustrated with clear drawings and the second with photographs of
the baby chick. Well done and fascinating to children, especially the many city children who have never seen a hen.

247 Estimation, by Charles F. Linn. Illus. by Don Madden.
     Crowell, A Young Math Book, 1970. $3.75 (pb $.95)
     RL: 2-3   IL: 2-JH   BSMP

Math is fun with a book like this one. Interesting and amusing pictures clarify the meaning of the text on estimating and simple experiments are suggested which any child can do at home and which any child would enjoy. The book makes clear the relevance of estimation. This is a superior book.

248   Exploring Other Worlds, by Rose Wyler Ames and
         Gerald Ames. Illus. by John Polgreen and George
         Solonevich. Golden Press, c1968. pb $.75
         RL: 5   IL: 4-adult   BS
A beginning science book about astronomy which is very popular, (probably because of the colorful illustrations) even though it was published before man reached the moon.

249   First Days of The World, by Gerald and Rose Wyler
         Ames. Illus. by Leonard Weisgard. Harper & Row,
         c1958. $3.79 (Scholastic pb $.60)
         RL: 4-5   IL: 4-adult   BS
Dramatic pictures make this a popular science book. An excellent clear account of how scientists think the world began. The book also explains evolution.

250   First Men in Space, by Sara Maynard Clarke. Illus.
         by Kurt Wiese. Follett, 1970. $2.36
         RL: 3   IL: 4-adult   *S
Excellent short selections about pioneers in space starting with the early balloonists. Good illustrations and adult format make this book suitable for an exceptionally wide age range.

251   Floating and Sinking, by Franklyn M. Branley. Illus.
         by Robert Galster. Crowell, Let's Read and Find Out
         Series, c1967. $3.75
         RL: 3   IL: Read aloud-6   BSMP
This clear account of why certain things float is illustrated both in word and picture by objects familiar to all children. It is especially valuable for the many children who are learning to swim and are frightened of the water.

252   The Follett Beginning Science Series. Follett. $1.25
         RL: Mainly 3 with some scientific terms IL: 3-adult
A valuable series with many titles which convey ecological information of a kind which every citizen of Planet Earth is going to have to have if the world is to survive. Some especially important titles are: Air, Our Planet Earth, Water, Weather, Your Wonderful Body, and Your Wonderful Brain. The illustrations in this series are uniformly good.

Unfortunately, the shape of the books and the pictures of children in some of the illustrations tend to limit the series' usefulness as older students and adults assume wrongly that the content is childish. However, the books are a great buy for the money.

253 Fun with Scientific Experiments, by Mae B. and Ira M.
    Freeman. Random House, c1960. $2.50
    RL: 3   IL: 2-6   BS
Feasible experiments illustrated with large, clear photographs.
The authors have the knack of explaining scientific principles
in clear and interesting terms.

254 Golden Press Paperbacks. Western Pub., pb $.75 each
    RL: 5-6   IL: 4-adult   BS
This series of paperbacks has twelve titles which deal with
science. In every case the text and illustrations are excellent. The series is very popular and is especially useful because both the format and content are appropriate for any
age group.

255. Grandpa's Wonderful Glass, by Samuel and Beryl Ep-
    stein. Illus. by J. Elgin. Grosset & Dunlap, Easy-
    to-Read Wonder Book, 1965. $.59
    RL: 2   IL: Read aloud-3   BS
This simple story about a magnifying glass seems to be very
popular.

256 Gravity All Around, by Tillie Pine and Joseph Levine.
    McGraw-Hill, c1963. $3.50
    RL: 2-3   IL: 2-5   S
The format of this book is young although the content lends
itself to many interest levels. Once introduced by a simple
question like "Why do things fall?" the reader is caught.
Even more popular since Apollo's 10 and 11.

257 Gravity and the Astronauts, by Mae Freeman. Illus.
    by Beatrice Darwin. Scholastic, c1970. pb $.60
    RL: 3   IL: 2-JH   BS
A description in words and pictures of weightlessness and
gravity. This book is a good beginning but not as meaty as
Gravity All Around. However, the format is older which
makes it more acceptable to older children.

258 The Great Whales, by Herbert S. Zim. Illus. by James
    Gordon Irving. Scholastic, Morrow, 1951. pb $.50
    RL: 4   IL: 4-HS   *BS

An excellent account of whales and whaling with plentiful good
illustrations.   Let's hope there will still be whales when the
next generation is adult.

259   Hidden Animals, by Millicent E. Selsam.   Harper, I
         Can Read Series, c1969. $2.50
      RL: 3   IL: Read aloud-4   BS
This book will appeal to a lot of children of different ages.
A pre-schooler will enjoy trying to find the insects and animals in the photographs which illustrate the book.   Older
children will be able to read the book for themselves and
begin to understand the principle of evolution from the clear
and simple explanation.   Note the reasonable price.

260   How Animals Sleep, by Millicent E. Selsam.   Illus. by
         Ezra Jack Keats.   Scholastic, c1962.
      RL: 3   IL: Read aloud-4   BS
With text on one page and a picture opposite, this book explains how 24 different animals sleep.   It includes birds and
boys and girls and hibernation.   Very popular.

261   How the Animals Get to the Zoo, by Mary Elting.   Illus.
         by Stefan Martin.   Grosset, Easy-to-Read Wonder
         Book, 1964.   pb $.59
      RL: 2   IL: Read aloud-4   BS
A useful book for the factually minded children who say they
don't like stories, this illustrates the many ways in which
zoo animals are collected.

262   The Human Body, by Cyril Bibby and Ian T. Morrison.
         Penguin, A Puffin Picture Book, 1969. $1.25
      RL: 6   IL: 4-adult   *BS
This thirty-page picture book is packed with information about
the human body put as simply as the scientific terms used
will allow.   Virtually every New York City junior or senior
high student I encountered in Reading Help programs would
be the better for the knowledge in this book and it would be
much appreciated by many parents who came to the bookmobile.

263   In the Time of the Dinosaurs, by William Wise.   Illus.
         by L. Zacks.   Scholastic, 1971.   pb $.60
      RL: 2-3   IL: Read aloud-4   *BS
At last, an easy-to-read book about dinosaurs.   It is well
done and will lead children on to the more difficult books on
the subject of the beginnings of our planet.

264 Is Something Up There?   The Story of Flying Saucers,
     by Dale White.   Scholastic, 1970.   pb $.60
     RL: 6-7   IL: 6-adult   BS
We had many requests on the bookmobile for books about UFO.
This one is as good as any I have seen.   All are on a too difficult
reading level for the people who make the request.   Photographs.

265 Junior Science Book of Icebergs and Glaciers, by
     Patricia Lauber.   Illus. by Evelyn Urbanovich.
     Scholastic, 1961.   pb $.60
     RL: 4-5   IL: 3-JH   BS
An interesting account of icebergs and glaciers starting with
the sinking of the Titanic and switching to the reader's own
kitchen.   There is a tremendous demand for science books
on this and easier reading levels.

266 Junior Science Book of Penguins, by Patricia Lauber.
     Scholastic, c1963.   pb $.60
     RL: 4-5   IL: 3-JH   BS
A book about penguins which explains their survival through
adaptation.   Many photographs.

267 Let's Find Out About Heat--Weather and Air, by Nina
     and Herman Schneider.   Illus. by Jeanne Bendick.
     Scholastic, c1946.   pb $.60
     RL: 4   IL: 3-JH   BS
A very useful science book on subjects that affect everyone.

268 Let's Find Out About the Moon, by Martha and Charles
     Shapp.   Illus. by Yukio Tashino.   Scholastic, c1965.
     pb $.60
     RL: 3   IL: 3-JH   BS
Published in 1965 and therefore a little outdated, this book is
on so low a reading level and is so well liked it is still a
good book to carry in paperback.

269 Let's Read and Find Out Science Series.   T. Y. Crowell.
     $3.75 each
     RL: 3 and 3-4   IL: 2-JH   BS
Every day on the bookmobile, we longed to have dozens of
easy science books.   Many eager children came aboard and
said proudly "I like science," "I want a science book" and
we had so few titles to fill the bill that they soon got discouraged.   Now this series is growing rapidly and will fill
a real need.   Of the titles I have seen, the text has been
clear and well presented and the illustrations have been good.
I am especially grateful for the multi-ethnic illustrations and

for the fact that the cover has the same picture as the dust
jacket. I am very happy to see that the publisher has started
to issue many of the titles in paperback. This will make the
books much more readily available and many families will
own books they would not otherwise have seen. Before You
Were a Baby, for example, is a book which should be owned
by many, many families and, in fact, most of this series
would be of interest and help to many families where the
parents had not had the chance to get a good education.
(And sometimes even where they have!) Some useful titles
in this series are: A Drop of Blood, Before You Were a
Baby, Gravity Is a Mystery, Hear Your Heart, Look at Your
Eyes, Rockets and Satellites, What Happens to a Hamburger?
See under Book List classification 4 for more reviews of good
individual titles which are available in English, Spanish and
other languages.

270   Life Under the Sea, by Rachel Carson.   Adapted by
        Anne Terry White.   Western, Golden Paperback,
        c1958.   pb $.75
        RL: 6-7   IL: 6-adult   BS
A useful condensation of The Sea Around Us in an excellent
adult format with large print and many photographs and illustrations.

271   Mabel the Whale, by Patricia King.   Illus. by Katherine
        Evans.   Follett, 1958. $1.25
        RL: 2-3   IL: Read aloud-4   BS
A suspenseful story about a whale with a sunburned fin.   This
book is based on a true incident and children find it fascinating.

272   Magnets and How to Use Them, by Tillie S. Pine and
        Joseph Levine.   Illus. by Bernice Meyers.   Scholastic,
        1963.   pb $.75
        RL: 3-4   IL: 2-6   BS
This book contains a magnet so the reader can perform the
many easy experiments described.   A very popular science
book.

273   Mark Trail's Book of Animals, by Ed Dodd.   Scholastic,
        c1955.   pb $.60
        RL: 6   IL: 4-JH   BS
An encyclopedia of animals for zoo goers and budding artists,
this is a good conversation piece for many who cannot read.
Illustrated with pen and ink drawings.

274 Men, Microscopes and Living Things, by Katherine B.
     Shippen. Illus. by Anthony Ravielli. Viking, 1955.
     $3.50 (Grosset Tempo. pb $.60 OP)
     RL: Adult   IL: HS-adult   B
A well written series of short lives of biologists from Aris-
totle to the present. We carry a few of this kind of book for
scientifically-minded high school students and adults, although
the reading level presents a real obstacle to all but the highly
motivated. We need many more science books of high interest level-low reading level in paperback.

275 The Monkey in the Rocket, by Jean Bethell. Illus. by
     Sergio Leone. Grosset, Easy-to-Read Wonder Book,
     c1962. $.69
     RL: 2-3   IL: Read aloud-4   BS
Authentic description of training an animal for rocket travel.
An easy science story which is dated but children still enjoy
it.

276. The Moon Explorers, by Tony Simon. Illus. by Lloyd
     Birmingham. Scholastic, c1970. pb $.75
     RL: 6   IL: 5-adult   BS
The whole story of America's moon project, this book is
really up to date. In addition to the drawings which make
technical situations clear, the book is full of photographs of
Apollo 11 and the landing on the moon.

277 My Visit to the Dinosaurs, by Aliki. Crowell, 1969.
     $3.50 (pb $.75)
     RL: 2-3   IL: Read aloud-4   BS
An enchanting picture book on a very popular subject.

278 Our Planet Earth, by Philip B. Carona. Illus. by Alex
     Ebel. Follett Beginning Science Series, c1967. $1.25
     RL: 4   IL: 4-adult   BS
Thirty well-illustrated pages tell of the beginnings of our
earth and suggest easy experiments to do with erosion that
can be carried out in a backyard or vacant lot. A basic book
that leads on to more specialized titles in the same series.
Used successfully by the School Volunteer program in New
York City junior high and high schools.

279 Our Senses and How They Work, by Herbert S. Zim.
     Illus. by Herschel Wortik. Morrow, 1956. $3.75
     RL: 6-7   IL: 5-adult   BS
A book on a subject of interest to everyone. In sixty-four
pages of large print, it explains the physiology of the senses

and how they work.   The information is given in a way that
makes the reader feel he is reading about himself.   There is
a real hunger in underprivileged areas to find out more about
how the body works.   There is also a real need for education.
This book will interest a wide age group.   It would be valuable
in an adult format in paperback.

280   A Place to Live, by Jeanne Bendick.   Parents, 1970.
        $3. 47
        RL: 3-4   IL: K-4   S
Every plant and every animal including man needs a place to
live with sun and air and food and water and space.   This
book discusses environment and ecology in simple language.
It is invaluable for calling a child's attention to what goes on
in his neighborhood and for helping him to place himself in
his world.

281   Plants, Animals and Us, by Bertha Morris Parker.
        Illus. by Harry McNaught.   Western, Golden Paper-
        back, 1968.   pb $. 75
        RL: 5-6   IL: 4-adult   BS
In seventy-eight colorfully illustrated pages culled from The
Golden Book of Science, the author provides an extraordinary
amount of information on plants and animals and how they
survive and reproduce.   It is a pity that the people shown do
not include minority groups and that there is no discussion of
air and water pollution but the basic scientific facts are there
and the book gives high value for its price.

282   Prove It!, by Rose Wyler Ames and Gerald Ames.
        Illus. by Talivaldis Stubis.   Harper, 1963. $2. 50
        (Scholastic pb $. 60)
        RL: 2-3   IL: 2-6   BS
Easy to do science experiments using ordinary household
items.   An invaluable book for scientifically minded non-
readers of whom the School Volunteers and bookmobile have
many.

283   Question and Answer Book, by Mary Elting.   Illus. by
        Elizabeth Dauber.   Grosset, Easy-to-Read Wonder
        Book, c1963. $. 59
        RL: 2-3   IL: Read aloud-6   BS
The questions in this very easy to read science book are the
kind children ask and the illustrations are clear and often humorous.   It is deservedly popular.

284   Questions and Answers About Ants, by Millicent E.

Selsam. Illus. by Arabelle Wheatley. Four Winds,
1967. pb $.60 (Scholastic $.50)
RL: 3-4   IL: 2-6   BS
Ants do not seem to repel children the way cockroaches do.
In fact, the purposefulness of ants seems to fascinate most
children of elementary school age. A popular book, illustrated with excellent line drawings.

285 Rain, Hail, Sleet and Snow, by Nancy Larrick. Illus.
     by Yap. Garrard, 1961. $2.59 (Scholastic OP)
     RL: 3-4   IL: 2-JH   BS
A clear and scientific explanation of a subject which interests
everyone. Very popular and useful also with older non-
readers.

286 Rascal, by Sterling North. Dutton, 1963. $4.50
     (Avon Camelot pb $.75)
     RL: 6   IL: 6-adult   BS
This book about a boy and his pet racoon is very useful because there are animal lovers of all ages. It has been very
popular. The black and white illustrations by the author are
excellent.

287 The Real Magnet Book, by Mae Freeman. Illus. by
     Norman Bridwell. Scholastic, c1967. pb $.60
     RL: 3-4   IL: 2-6   BS
Basic facts about magnetism with fun to do experiments, this
book includes a real magnet. Very popular in the School
Volunteer program and at book fairs, it is also a popular
library book where magnets are available--i.e., near a
Woolworth's or stationery store. Some neighborhoods have
virtually no inexpensive merchandise like cheap magnets for
sale.

288 Rocks and Minerals, by Lou Williams Page. Illus. by
     George and Irma Wilde. Follett Beginning Science,
     c1962. $1.25
     RL: 3--with some scientific terms   IL: 3-HS
Almost any child enjoys collecting pebbles and rocks--even if
only from the vacant lot across the street. Any child ob-
serves the different textures of buildings and of stones and
marbles. This book gives a simple clear description of the
different kinds of rocks and minerals and what created them.
A good start on geology, the illustrations make the text very
clear.

289 S.O.S. Save Our Earth, by Giancarlo Massini. Illus.

by Allessandro Pacini. With an introduction by Wm.
D. Ruckelhaus. Grosset, c1972.
    RL: 7   IL: 4-adult   *BSP
This imaginative book originated in Italy and has proved instantly popular with every one to whom I have shown it.
On the outside cover, floating in the ocean, is a bottle and
when the reader pulls out the message, it unfolds to proclaim
"Help! Nature is Dying!" Inside is the best and clearest explanation I have seen of the web of life, the problems of pollution and what we can do to help. The graphics and devices
used to explain and to interest the reader are full of humor
and genius. A good teacher could make use of this book at
almost any age level and its message is vital to everyone.

290   Science Book of Volcanoes, by Patricia Lauber. Scho-
        lastic, 1969. pb $.60
    RL: 4-5   IL: 4-adult   *BS
The story of volcanoes--their nature and the history of
famous eruptions. This easy science book with exciting photos will be of interest to many. Children from the Caribbean are especially interested in the eruption of Mt. Pelee,
on the island of Martinique, of which many of them have
heard.

291   Science in Your Own Back Yard, by Elizabeth K.
        Cooper. Harcourt, c1958. $3.50 (Voyager pb $.65)
    RL: 5-6   IL: 5-HS   BS
This book explains in simple terms how to study scientifically
the contents of a back yard or city park. It is well written
and can open new worlds to inner city children who have access to a yard or vacant lot. It could prove equally valuable
to a country child but will usually require a knowledgeable
adult to get the children started.

292   Science Teasers, by Rose Wyler and Eva-Lee Baird.
        Illus. by Jerry Robinson. Harper & Row, c1966.
        $2.95
    RL: 4   IL: Upper elementary-HS   S
A light and amusing book which relates every day phenomena
to scientific principles. Discusses things like parlor tricks,
Indian rope tricks and Archimedes. Good illustrations and
short selections make this a very useful book.

293   The Search for Planet X, by Tony Simon. Illus. by Ed
        Malsborg. Scholastic, c1968. pb $.60
    RL: 6   IL: JH-HS   B
The exciting scientific detective work that led to the discovery

of Planet X--now known as Pluto. The space programs have
created new interest in the heavens.

294 The Silent World, by Jacques-Yves Cousteau and
       Frederic Dumas.   Harper, 1953. $7.95 (pb $.75)
       RL: 6-7   IL: 4-adult   BS
Through television, many people of all ages are fascinated
by the undersea world. A very popular book on an increasingly popular subject.

295 Snakes, by Herbert S. Zim. Illus. by James Gordon
       Irving. Scholastic, 1965.   pb $.60
       RL: 5   IL: 4-HS   BS
A factual book about snakes with excellent illustrations on
every page. Many children are interested in snakes and the
book is very popular.

296 Space and Time, by Jeanne Bendick. Watts, c1968.
       $3.95
       RL: 2-3   IL: 2-6   BSMP
An easy-to-read science book which explains basic concepts.
It is truly heart warming at last to see a book like this illustrated with integrated pictures. The book can be read in
short selections making it doubly useful in a tutorial program.

297 Space Dictionary, by Isaac Asimov. Scholastic, c1969.
       pb $.60
       RL: 3-4   IL: 3-JH   BS
A dictionary of space terms. Each term is defined in simple
language and illustrated with a photograph. Just the kind of
easy authentic science books we are all looking for. A very
good job.

298 Stars, by Isaac Asimov. Illus. by Herb Herrick. Dia-
       grams by Mike Gordon. Follett--Beginning Science
       Series, c1968. $1.25
       RL: 3-4   IL: 2-JH   BS
A clear and well illustrated science book, this is popular
even though the stars are hard to see in a city.

299 Steven and the Green Turtle, by William J. Cromie.
       Illus. by Tom Eaton. Harper & Row, I Can Read
       Series, c1970. $2.50
       RL: 2-3   IL: Read aloud-4   BS
This story of a boy in Costa Rica is both a pet story and a
scientific account of the life of the green turtle. It is very
likable. Harper's Science, I Can Read Series give so much

science information that even though the books are written in
the guise of fiction, they fall into the science classification.

300   The Story of the Atom, by Mae and Ira Freeman.
        Random House, Gateway Book, 1960. $2.95
        RL: 3-4   IL: 3-JH   BS
A valuable book by two excellent writers who have a gift for
simple explanations of complicated subjects.   The price is
right also.

301   The Story of the Ice Age, by Rose Wyler and Gerald
        Ames.   Harper & Row, 1956. $3.79 (Scholastic
        pb $.50)
        RL: 5   IL: 5-adult   BS
Lunar exploration seems also to have stimulated an interest
in the earth's history.   This well told story of the ice age
is very popular.

302   Terry and the Caterpillars, by Millicent E. Selsam.
        Illus. by Arnold Lobel.   Harper & Row, Science I
        Can Read Series, 1962. $2.50
        RL: 3   IL: Read aloud-4   *BSMP
A girl collects three caterpillars and learns through watching
them the cycle of a moth's life.   This book will make other
children want to collect caterpillars also.   It is easy-to-read
in every sense and even has suspense.   Very well done.
Also available in Spanish.   See also 216.

303   Tony's Birds, by Millicent E. Selsam.   Harper & Row,
        A Science I Can Read Book. $2.50
        RL: 2   IL: Read aloud-4   BSMP
Another in this excellent series (see 180).   This book about
birds features a black boy.   Very popular.

304   Trees, by George Sullivan.   Illus. by Norman Adams.
        Follett Beginning Science Series, c1970. $1.25
        RL: 3 (with scientific terms) IL: 3-adult   BS
Trees are not only beautiful but almost everyone uses their
products in either wood or plastic form.   This colorfully illustrated book will interest a wide age range.   It is too bad
that a book published in 1970 shows an area being sprayed with
insecticide from an airplane, a practice most scientists now
deplore.

305   True Book of Science Experiments, by Illa Podendorf.
        Illus. by Mary Salem.   Childrens Press, 1954. $3.00
        RL: 3-4   IL: 3-5   S

Easy-to-do science experiments involving concepts about air,
magnets, gravity, water, sound, heat and cold.   It has proved
very valuable in the School Volunteer program but its childish
illustrations and format will repel older readers unless it is
introduced by someone they trust.

306 Turtles, by Bertie Ann Stewart and Gordon E. Burks.
     Illus. by William Hutchinson.   Golden, c1962.   OP
     RL: 3   IL: 2-5   BS
A beginning science book with beautiful illustrations.

307 Water, by Philip B. Carona.   Illus. by Phero Thomas.
     Follett Beginning Science Series, c1966. $1.25
     RL: 3   IL: 3-adult   BS
One of the best of this series on a subject everyone is vitally
concerned with.   In simple language and relevant illustrations
it gives an extraordinary amount of scientific information.

308 The Water Book--Where It comes From and Where It
     Goes, by Sean Morrison and Ira Freeman.   Random,
     c1970. $3.50
     RL: 4   IL: Read aloud-4
The animated three-dimensional illustrations in this book are
like a portable science museum.   Children can pull the tabs
and see the water turn from ice to water to vapor as the
temperature rises.

309 Weather, by Julian May.   Illus. by Jack White.   Follett
     Beginning Science Series, c1966. $1.25
     RL: 3   IL: 3-adult   BS
An excellent book on weather full of facts and very much involving the reader.

310 Weighing and Balancing, by Jane Jonas Srivastava.
     Illus. by Aliki.   Crowell, A Young Math Book, 1970.
     $3.75 (pb $.95) Ed. by Max Beberman.
     RL: 2-3   IL: 2-6   *BSMP
A book which will interest any child, the text uses things like
see-saws and scales made from wire coat hangers to explain
the concepts of weighing and balancing.

311 The Whales Go By, by Fred Phleger.   Illus. by Paul
     Galdone.   Random House, Beginner Book, 1959.
     $2.50
     RL: 3   IL: 2-5   BS
An easy-to-read factual book about whales.   Although the
subject seems a little remote to interest city children, this

book is very much in demand.   The illustrations are colorful.

312   What Happens to a Hamburger?, by Paul Showers.
       Anne Rockwell, Illus.   Crowell, Let's Read and Find
       Out Series, 1970. $3.75
       RL: 3   IL: 2-JH   BS
This simple explanation of what happens to a hamburger after
it has been eaten will be enjoyed by any child and at the same
time the child will be assimilating a considerable amount of
scientific knowledge.   This book not only satisfies curiosity,
it also whets it and most children will take off from this book
to learn more about themselves.

313   What's Inside, by May Garelick.   Photog. by Rena
       Jakobsen.   W. R. Scott, 1955. $2.75   (Scholastic,
       1968.   pb $.60)
       RL: 2   IL: Read aloud-3   BS
A wonderful beginning science book, this is the picture story
of the hatching of an egg and what emerges.   This is a book
that will need a helpful adult to introduce since the photographs
are fascinating but not appealing as a rule to the average
child.

314   Where Does the Butterfly Go When It Rains?, by May
       M. Garelick.   Illus. by Leonard Weisgard.   Hale,
       1961. $2.88   (Scholastic, 1968.   pb $.60)
       RL: 2   IL: 2-3   BS
A picture book with stunning blue and white illustrations describing where each animal or insect goes during a rainstorm.

315   Where Does the Day Go?, by Walter M. Myers.   Illus.
       by Leo Carty.   Parents, 1969. $3.95
       RL: 2-3   IL: Read aloud-4   *SMP
Where does the day go?   Four children on a walk through
Central Park advance several theories--both ingenious and
poetic and finally learn the true answer from the father of
one of them.   A happy, relaxed story that will stimulate
ideas.

316   Why Can't I?, by Jeanne Bendick.   Scholastic, c1969.
       pb $.60
       RL: 2-3   IL: Read aloud-4
An entertaining book in which a child wonders why he can't
fly, swim like a fish, hibernate and do all the things animals
and bugs can do.   Not much logic but a lot of imagination
and information and humorous, stimulating illustrations.

317 <u>Wolfie</u>, by Janet Dai Chenery.   Illus. by Mare Simon.
     Harper and Row, Science I Can Read Book, 1969.
     $2.50
     RL: 2-3   IL: K-4   *S
This amusing story of two boys and the kid sister of one of
them centers around their struggle to feed and care for a
wolf spider.   Children love it and learn a great deal about
spiders.

318 <u>The Wonders of Seeds</u>, by Alfred Stefferud.   Illus.
     by Shirley Briggs.   Harcourt, 1956.   Voyager, pb
     $.45
     RL: 5   IL: 5-adult   BS
A fascinating book about seeds which is not much in demand
in the inner city but which means a lot to a scientifically
oriented student.   Sometimes school or park gardens interest
people in a book like this and then it really opens doors.

319 <u>Wonders of the Human Body</u>, by Anthony Ravielli.
     Viking, 1954. $3.00   (Scholastic, pb OP)
     RL: 5   IL: 4-adult   BS
A superbly illustrated straightforward account of the human
body and how it works.   This book has a fascination even
for non-readers and is one of the backbones of any reading
help program.   I have used it with great success with retarded children as well as with intellectually gifted ones.

320 <u>World of Rockets</u>, by Alexander L. Crosby.   Random,
     c1965. $1.95
     RL: 4   IL: 4-JH   BS
A clear simple explanation of the scientific facts about rockets,
illustrated with many photographs.   Can be of interest to any
child who ever tried to make a sling shot as well as those
who follow the moon shots on TV.

321 <u>You Will Go to the Moon</u>, by Mae and Ira Freeman.
     Random House, Beginner, c1959. $2.50
     RL: 2-3   IL: K-4   BS
Although events have outstripped this book, it is still reasonably authentic and tops in popularity.   Easy to read science
books are very much in demand and hard to find.

322 <u>You Will Live Under the Sea</u>, by Frederic and Marjorie
     Phleger.   Illus. by W. Brackett.   Random House Be-
     ginner, c1966. $2.50
     RL: 2   IL: 2-5   BS
A projection of facts about our newest frontier to explore.

323   <u>Your Body--Bones and Muscles</u>, by Sean Morrison and
       Ira Freeman.   Illus. by Gwen Gordon and Dave
       Chambers.   Random House, c1970. $3.50
       RL: 4   IL: Read aloud-JH & HS poor readers   *S
This is an extraordinary book for teaching biology to children.
The animated illustrations provide three dimensional models
to show how a muscle works, how one breathes, etc.   Children will be fascinated.

324   <u>Your Heart and How It Works</u>, by Herbert S. Zim.
       Illus. by Gustav Schrotter.   Morrow, c1959. $3.75
       RL: 6-7   IL: 6-adult   *BS
An excellent explanation about the heart and how it works
which would interest adults and many scientifically minded
students, especially would-be doctors.   There is a great
demand for books like this and the information in it could
save lives.   It would be very popular in paperback in an
adult format.

325   <u>Zero to Zillions: The Arrow Book of Number Magic</u>,
       by Irwin Weiss.   Illus. by Bernice Myers.   Scholastic,
       c1966.   pb $.50
       RL: IL:
A wonderful book about numbers which in the hands of a
skillful adult can convince even a child who hates arithmetic
that numbers can be fun and interesting.   It is full of tips
to help make arithmetic easier and to stretch the imagination.
It also has puzzles to solve and tricks to do.

326 Arrow Book of Project Fun, by Leonore Klein. Illus.
      by Dan Dickas. Scholastic, c1965. pb $.50
      RL: 5   IL: 2-7   BS
This book outlines a wide variety of projects and games,
none of them requiring any equipment that needs to be bought.
A good book for middle graders. Many of the projects or
games can be done alone and would be valuable to a child
confined to bed by a minor illness or accident.

327 Codes and Secret Writing, by Herbert S. Zim. Illus.
      by J. MacDonald. Morrow, c1948. $3.95 (Scho-
      lastic, pb OP)
      RL: 4-5   IL: 4-JH   BS
Popular with sixth, seventh, and eighth graders, this is also
a useful book for School Volunteers. Secret writing can
prove very motivational reading.

328 The Co-Ed Book of Charm and Beauty, edited by the
      editors of Co-Ed Magazine. Illus. by John Fernie.
      Scholastic, 1962. pb $.60
      RL: 5   IL: 5-adult   BS
This useful guide to good grooming is very popular and has
been cited by several teachers as attracting girls who never
use the school library.

329 The Co-Ed Sewing Book, by Marian Ross. Illus. by
      Elena Neri. McGraw, c1968. OP (Scholastic pb
      $.75)
      RL: 6   IL: 5-adult   BS
Not as easy to read as Measure, Cut & Sew [342], and
clearly addressed to a teenage market, nevertheless this book
is a mine of useful information. It is by a woman who has
been a fashion director for the Singer Company and is full of
practical and interesting ideas and suggestions. Girls and
women really struggle to master this one.

330 The Denise Nichols Beauty Book, illustrated by Denise
      Nichols and Carl Owens. Cornerstone Library

(distributed by Simon & Schuster) c1971.   pb $1.45
RL: 5-6   IL: 5-adult   *BS
A black actress gives sound advice on all aspects of beauty
care including diet.   The many drawings add a great deal to
the good advice.

331   Filming Works Like This, by Jeanne and Robert Ben-
        dick.   McGraw-Hill, c1970. $4.95
        RL: 5-6 with many essential technical words.
        There is a glossary.   IL: 5-adult   *BM
An excellent manual on how to start making films of every
kind.   The information it gives is reliable and well organized
and the illustrations not only illumine the text but are also
truly comic.   A good job in a field that is increasingly important and popular.

332.   Foods, by the editors of Co-Ed Magazine.   Scholastic,
        1969.   pb $.65
        RL: 5   IL: 5-adult   *BS
One of a series called Better Buymanship, this book is filled
with useful information and good advice about nutrition, costs
and consumership in the field of food buying.   It will be useful and popular although it is often impossible for people on
a marginal income to take advantage of sales, discounts for
quantity, etc.

333   Get Your Money's Worth, by Aurelia Toyer.   Holt,
        Rinehart and Winston, c1965.   pb $2.40
        RL: 3-4   IL: 6-adult   B
Lessons in the handling of money and consumership in the
form of a story.   Adam Johnson, an unemployed coal miner,
who has always lived in a company house and bought on credit at a company store in a company town, moves to the city
and learns about leases, transportation, supermarkets, etc.,
etc.   This clear and well written manual covers almost every
subject needed for living in a city including credit, insurance,
nutrition, medical care, mortgages, zoning etc.   The prices
in the book may seem, alas, out of date but the advice is up
to the minute.

334   Here's How, edited by Joanne Schreiber.   Illus. by
        James Reid.   Scholastic, 1967.   pb $.50
        RL: 6   IL: 6-HS   BS
Tips on grooming, home expertise and party-giving.   A type
of book which draws both good and poor readers.

335   How and Why Wonder Book of Machines, by Dr.   Jerome

J. Notkin and Sidney Gulkin. Illus. by George J.
Zapfo. Grosset, 1960. $1.50
RL: 4-5   IL: 4-adult   B
This book is crammed full of factual information on such
basics of the machine world as the lever, fulcrum and wheel
as well as the sources of energy used to make the machine
work.   The fine illustrations portray adults thus making the
book acceptable to any age reader.

336   How to Care for Your Dog, by Jean Bethell. Illus. by
      Norman Bridwell. Four Winds, c1964. $2.50
      (Scholastic pb $.60)
      RL: 4   IL: 2-JH   BS
An excellent guide to dog care.   Except in housing projects
where they are not allowed, dogs are very numerous in the
inner city, often for protection as well as companionship,
and dog care advice is needed and appreciated.   The humorous
illustrations make the book doubly popular.

337.   How to Write Codes and Send Secret Messages, by
       John Peterson. Illus. by Bernice Myers. Four
       Winds, c1966. $3.95 (Scholastic pb $.60)
       RL: 3   IL: 3-JH   BS
Many children are fascinated by puzzles and secrets.   This
book has started quite a few poor readers on learning how to
read well enough to make secret ink and how to code secret
messages.   This is easier to read than 327 on the same subject.

338   Just a Box?, by Goldie Taub Chernoff. Illus. by
      Margaret Hartelius. Scholastic, c1971. pb $.75
      RL: 3   IL: Pre-school-6   BS
A jewel of a book which shows how to turn various kinds of
boxes (familiar to any household) into zoos, doll houses, airplanes, castles, even useful objects like book-ends, etc.   The
explanations are clear and simple and I have used it very
successfully with four-year-olds and with sixth graders.
Older children are inspired by it to think up their own more
elaborate projects.

339   Let's Face It--The Guide to Good Grooming for Girls
      of Color, by Elsie Archer. Illus. by Harper Johnson.
      Lippincott, 1968. $4.95 (pb $1.50)
      RL: 5   IL: 5-adult   BS
This excellent book by the former fashion editor of Ebony is
not only a grooming guide, it has good advice on consumership, job interviews, health and love.   It is invaluable in

filling a long-felt need. School Volunteers have been asking
for a book like this for years.

340 Lucky-Sew-It-Yourself Book, by Camille Sokol. Illus.
      by Bill Sokol. Four Winds, 1964. $2.50 (Scholastic
      pb $.50)
      RL: 2-3   IL: 2-5   BS
This sewing manual is an excellent book for motivating reading among the many girls who have not learned to like books
but do like clothes.

341 Machines, by Edward Victor. Illus. by Mel Hunter.
      Follett, 1962. $1.25
      RL: 3-4   IL: 3-JH   BS
This book on how machines work is popular with elementary
school children. It is slightly easier to read than The How
and Why Book of Machines [335] and also younger in format
which makes the latter book more useful with older students.

342 Measure, Cut and Sew, by Johneta Starks. Holt, Rine-
      hart & Winston, c1966. $2.88
      RL: 4   IL: 6-adult   BS
This manual which covers every type of sewing and is on a
very easy reading level was carried for sale on the Bookmobile. There is great interest in sewing in underprivileged
areas and many women wanted to buy it but few had the price.
We then circulated it and had quite a few borrowers who,
however, would keep the book for the length of time it took
for their project and only returned it after repeated reminders.
Good seamstresses tell me that the advice is excellent but
the fashions in it are out-of-date. The Co-Ed Sewing Book
is only slightly more difficult to read and has a much more
attractive appearance and up-to-date fashions so we no longer
carry this title. I am told the Singer Company has a number
of pamphlets at $.29 and $.35 on such subjects as How to
Sew for Children, How to Make Drapes, etc., which would
be well worth investigating.

343 101 Things to Make for Fun or Money, by Miriam Mor-
      rison. Illus. by June Ferguson Nicol. Scholastic,
      1964. pb $.60
      RL: 5-6   IL: 5-adult   B
Handicrafts are "in" these days, financially and in other ways
as witnessed by the popularity of Aran Island sweaters and
the Freedom Co-op quilts. It has always been my dream to
see women tied down by small children gaining a measure of
independence with handicrafts. High school dropouts too could

well gain dignity and income if they had materials and merchandising outlets.   The Aran Islanders, Navahoes and Mexicans do not sell their wares because they read well.   Those
that have <u>access</u> to a good market (granted all too few) have
dignity and satisfaction in their work and at least some income.   This book is full of practical ideas and suggestions
to start people creating for their own pleasure and decor,
or, eventually with the right encouragement and backing to
start a creative group.

344   <u>Pancakes, Pancakes</u>, by Eric Carle.   Knopf, 1970.
      $4.50
      RL: 3   IL: Read aloud-4   *S
This book has such colorful illustrations that it will make
any child feel more cheerful.   It tells how a boy got pancakes
for breakfast starting with the wheat being sickled and going
through the whole process.   A good conversation piece for
many children who have no idea of the origin of the food they
eat.

345   <u>Plants to Grow Indoors</u>, by George Sullivan.   Illus. by
      Bill Barss.   Follett, c1969. $1.25
      RL: 2-3   IL: Read aloud-5   *BS
This is a wonderful book for city children who long to grow
plants.   It tells how to grow a plant from an alligator pear,
how to grow sweet potatoes, carrots and pineapples.   The
simple instructions require only inexpensive materials and it
is explained where to find them--mainly at the 5 and 10.   A
book which will bring a lot of happiness to a lot of families.

346   <u>Sewing Is Fun</u>, by Edith Paul.   Illus. by Catherine
      Scholz.   Scholastic, c1958.   pb $.60
      RL: 5   IL: 5-HS   BS
Very much in demand, this book has clear directions on how
to make dozens of pretty and useful objects.   It was first
published by the Singer Sewing Machine Company and is an
excellent sewing text though not as full as 329 or 342.

347   <u>Story of Flight</u>, by Mary Lee Settle.   Illus. by George
      Evans.   Random, 1967. $1.95
      RL: 3   IL: Read aloud-JH   *BS
A well written history of man's efforts to fly, with clear illustrations, this book carries the story through Gagarin's
space flight.   It is of interest to a wide age range.

348   <u>Taffy's Tips to Teens</u>, by Dolly Martin.   Grosset
      Tempo, 1964.   pb $.75

RL: 6-7   IL: 5-HS   BS
This useful book of good advice on shopping, etiquette, fashion, health, beauty, etc. , for teenaged girls needs updating
and integrating. However, this kind of book is so badly
needed and so much appreciated, that it is still very popular
and lures many nonreaders.

349   This is Cape Kennedy, by Miroslav Sasek. Macmillan,
         1965. $4.95
      RL: 3   IL: 3-JH   S
A beautifully illustrated explanation of the space center written with some humor. Note how wide an age range can enjoy
this book.

350   Drugs, by Barbara Milbauer and Gerald Leinwand.
      Washington Square Press, c1970.   pb $.75
      RL: Varied   IL: JH-adult   *BSP
This is a textbook in a series called Problems of American
Society.   The first section which discussed the problem and
challenge of drug abuse is very difficult reading.   However,
the second section, Selected Readings, which gives vivid accounts of actual cases of drug abuse is valuable and would
interest a great many people.   I regret the questions at the
end of each case history since they do not enhance the text
and will irritate students and the general public alike.

351   The Good Drug and the Bad Drug, by John S. Marr,
      M.D.   Illus. by Lynn Sweat.   M. Evans, c1970.
      $3.96
      RL: 4-5   IL: 3-adult   *BSMP
This is probably one of the most important books on this list
from the point of view of what it can accomplish if given the
wide distribution it deserves.   It describes in as simple
terms as possible what happens inside the body when anyone
takes either a good drug administered on the advice of a
doctor or a bad drug at the instigation of a friend or acquaintance.   Many children (and even many adults) have little or
no education on what goes on inside their bodies.   It is a
common occurrence for a child to come to school and say "I
was sick so I went to the doctor and had a needle."   The information in this book, given at an early enough age, can
be the armor to protect children from the drug habit.   I am
not so simplistic as to think that the need for an anodyne--
whether alcohol or heroin--is eliminated by the knowledge of
what harm the drug can do a person.   This book, however,
will (if properly used) eliminate the use of hard drugs out of
curiosity or on a dare, and can at least give the young the
straight information they need as to the risks they run.   I
hope this book will soon be out in paperback and will also
be in use in schools all over the country.   Every classroom
in city schools on every level (including high school) should
have a copy of this, and I am sure it would be in enormous
demand.

352   Turned On, by Dick Schaap.   New American Library,
      Signet, c1967.   pb $.75
      RL: 6   IL: 6-adult   BS
This tragic story of the death of Celeste Crenshaw of an
overdose of drugs and of her wealthy lover who is now in
jail is one of the fastest moving titles on the Bookmobile and
has a fascination for all ages.

353   What You Must Know About Drugs, by Harvey R. Green-
      berg, M. D.   Scholastic, c1970.   pb $1.25
      RL: 7   IL: 5-adult   *BSP
A well-balanced clear account of what goes on when a person
uses and abuses the various drugs now creating problems for
society.   This is a serious straightforward book with no
preaching and will be very much in demand.   Unfortunately,
the reading level is high for many who need this kind of book.

354   What You Should Know About VD and Why, by Bruce
      Webster, M. D.   Scholastic, 1967.   pb $.85
      RL: 6-7   IL: 6-adult   *BSP
The only paperback book I have seen on this important subject, this again is a straightforward scientific account with
no preaching.   It certainly will be in demand.

7 RECREATION AND THE ARTS--FINE ARTS

355 <u>Afro-American Artists, New York and Boston</u>, published
   by The Museum of the National Center of Afro-American Artists and the Museum of Fine Arts. Boston,
   1970. $4.50 plus $.50 shipping chg.
   RL: Adult   IL: 5-adult   *BSMP
This large soft cover book contains an interesting historical
survey of Afro-American art and then sixty-seven black and
white reproductions of works of art by Afro-Americans which
were on display for five weeks in 1970 at the Museum of
Fine Arts. At the end are brief biographies of the artists
represented. Much of the art is impressive. The styles
and subjects are very varied. This kind of book will be a
real inspiration to a great many young people. The liking
for and interest in art is very high in inner city schools.

356 <u>Barnes and Noble Art Series</u>. Barnes and Noble,
   various dates. $.75 each
   RL: 7   IL: Universal   BS
This is an excellent Art Series much appreciated in junior
and senior high. These books are enjoyed by children who
cannot read much of the text but do appreciate the pictures.
Each book gives a twenty-page biography of an artist and then
about sixty pages of reproductions of his works, mainly in
color. The quality of the reproductions is astonishingly good
for the price. All the old masters are represented as well
the Impressionists. Cézanne is a favorite and El Greco is
another. The students I have worked with are appalled by
Reubens' lush nudes and by Gauguin's South Sea islanders.
They are divided on modern art. Religious art seems to be
universally popular.

357 <u>Black Artists on Art</u>. Vol. I, by Samella S. Lewis and
   Ruth G. Waddy. Contemporary Crafts, c1969. $14.50
   (Ritchie pb $7.50)
   RL: Adult   IL: JH-adult   *BSMP
This is a good-sized paperback book containing photographs,
short biographies, statements and reproductions of the works
of approximately seventy-five black artists. The work

naturally varies in quality but the variety, both of styles and
media, is great. I think any black person who is interested
in art would be inspired to see what other artists of his race
are doing. The book can also be an excellent conversation
piece for a student who likes art and needs practice in speaking since the pictures and photographs really comprise the
book. The text is relatively unimportant.

358 Black Pilgrimage, by Tom Feelings. Lothrop, c1972.
       $5.95
       RL: 6   IL: Universal   *BSMP
The text of this book is described in the section on autobiography. It is included here because almost every page has
one or more drawings and there are thirty-three pages of
reproductions of this artist's pictures, eight of them in stunning color. A beautiful book.

359 How to Draw and Paint, by Henry N. Gassner. Dell,
       Laurel Leaf, 1955. pb $.75
       RL: 7   IL: 6-adult   BS
Difficult reading but we get many requests for this type of
book, and children who are interested will really work to get
the meaning. There are many illustrations of different kinds
to help the artist along.

360 I Made a Line, by Leonard Kessler. Illus. by the
       author. Grosset Easy-To-Read Wonder Book, c1962.
       $.69
       RL: 2   IL: Read aloud-3   BS
A very imaginative book which is useful with non-English
speaking children and popular with all budding artists.

361 Images of Dignity: The Drawings of Charles White.
       Ritchie, c1967. $10.00
       RL: Adult   IL: All ages   *BSMP
This superb book of the drawings of the famous black artist,
Charles White, is worth twenty books explaining that "Black
is beautiful." The pictures are indeed "Images of Dignity"
that will speak to anyone who has an appreciation of beauty.
There is a commentary by B. Horowitz which gives a brief
biography of the artist, an introduction by James Porter and
a foreword by Harry Belafonte.

362 Pencil, Pen and Brush, by Harvey Weiss. Scholastic,
       1961. pb $.75
       RL: 6   IL: 4-adult   BS
There is a great interest in art in the inner city. Many

non-readers are gifted artistically and feel they can succeed
in art if not in the academic world.   This book is carried
because of requests for books on how to draw and is much
in demand.

363   Start to Draw, by Ann Campbell.   Grolier Watts, 1968.
      $4.50
      RL: 5-6   IL: 4-JH   S
A very motivating book for upper elementary and junior high
children especially for those who draw better than they read.
There is an enormous interest in the arts.

7   RECREATION/ARTS--HUMOR (Non-Fiction)

364   Are You My Mother?, by Philip D. Eastman.   Random,
      Beginner, c1960. $2.50
      RL: 2   IL: Read aloud-3   BS
A highly satisfying and truly funny easy-to-read book for
younger children.   This is very popular in every neighborhood.

365   Arrow Book of Jokes and Riddles, illustrated by William
      Hogarth.   Scholastic, c1958.   pb $.50
      RL: 4   IL: 4-JH   BS
This has a deceiving format.   It is much borrowed by second
and third graders who can't possibly read or understand it.
It is much enjoyed by those who can read it.

366   Black Is, by Turner Brown, Jr.   Illus. by Ann Weis-
      man.   Grove, c1969. $1.25
      RL: 6   IL: JH-adult   BM
A drawing on one page is explained by a sentence on the opposite page; for example, "Black Is finally getting open oc-
cupancy at Khe Sanh."   Extremely bitter humor but very popular especially with the young.

367   Black Misery, by Langston Hughes.   Illus. by Hill &
      Wang, 1969. $2.50
      RL: 5   IL: 5-adult   BSMP
This book of illustrated sardonic sayings by the famous poet
about the black situation is one of the most popular we have
ever carried on the bookmobile.   All ages of black people
savor it.   It has more good humor in it than Black Is [366

above], but is, if anything, even more telling in its indictment of the injustices black people endure because of the
color of their skin--"Misery is when you learned on the
radio that the neighborhood you live in is a slum but you
always thought it was home!"

368   From the Back of the Bus, by Dick Gregory.   Avon
      Books, c1962.   pb $.60
      RL: 7   IL: 6-adult   BM
Humorous commentary, illustrated with photographs, about
U.S. racial relations.   This is an old book but still popular.

369   Is This You?, by Ruth Krauss and Crockett Johnson.
      Scholastic, c1955.   pb $.60
      RL: Primer   IL: Read aloud-2   BS
A great book for sharpening observation in a humorous way.
Small children laugh out loud at this one.

370   Jokes and Riddles, compiled by Jonathan Peters.   Illus.
      by David Lockhart.   Grosset, Easy-To-Read Wonder
      Book, c1963. $.69
      RL: 2-3   IL: 2-6   BS
This joke and riddle book with cartoon-like illustrations is
very popular with good readers as well as poor ones.

371   Jokes and Riddles to Read-Aloud, compiled by Oscar
      Weigle.   Illus. by Jessica Zemsky.   Grosset, Read-
      Aloud Wonder Book, 1968.   pb $.49
      RL: 4   IL: Read aloud-6   BS
Another very popular joke and riddle book with an older interest level than the above.

372   Laugh Your Head Off, edited by Helen Alpert.   Scholas-
      tic, 1969.   pb $.50
      RL: 6   IL: 6-HS   BS
Good humor for teenagers.   Illustrated with cartoons, this
kind of book attracts and helps nonreaders.

373   Luther from Inner City, by Brumsic Brandon, Jr.
      Eriksson, c1969.   pb $1.95
                                                         BS

374   Luther Tells It As It Is, by Brumsic Brandon, Jr.
      Eriksson, c1970.   pb $1.95
      RL: 4   IL: 6-adult   BS
Two marvellously funny comic books about Luther and his
friends which tell the story of life in the ghetto with wit and

humor. Should be in every school and library in the country.
Very popular.

375 More Jokes and Riddles, compiled by Jonathan Peter.
     Illus. by Albert Aquino. Grosset, Easy-To-Read
     Wonder Book, c1963. $.69
     RL: 2-3   IL: 2-6   BS
Jokes and riddles are a good lure for non-readers and are
very popular with all children.

376 Pop-Up Sound Alikes, edited by Albert G. Miller.
     Random House, c1967. $2.50
     RL: 2-3   IL: 4-JH   *S
Humor imprints knowledge firmly. Older elementary and
junior high slow readers will love this book and will really
learn and remember the hilarious homonyms.
          Eight little worms were having fun
          Sitting in the morning sun.
          They saw the early bird too late
          That hungry robin ate all eight!

377 Some Things are Scary, by Florence Parry Heide.
     Illus. by Robert Osborn. Scholastic, 1969. pb $.50
     RL: 2   IL: Read aloud-4   BS
Humorous cartoons poke fun at dark rooms, fearsome insects,
strange grown-ups and other scary objects. A therapeutic
book which tells a child that other children are also scared
and that many fears are unjustified.

7 RECREATION/ARTS--PICTURE BOOKS
(Books that would not exist if it were not for their illustrations)

378 Black, Black, Beautiful Black, by Rose Blue. Illus. by
     Emmett Wigglesworth. Grolier Watts, c1969. $3.95
     RL: 2-3   IL: Read aloud-3   BSMP
A simple story of a visit to the zoo is illustrated with handsome black and white drawings that show the beauty of many
black things without straining the point. Children will like
the ending.

379 A Boy, a Dog, and a Frog, by Mercer Mayer. Scholas-
     tic, c1967. pb $.50

RL: No Text   IL: Pre-school-3   BS
Funny pictures tell the story of a boy and his dog who try
to capture a frog. A good conversation piece to help a child
learn how to tell a story.

380 Brian Wildsmith's Circus, by Brian Wildsmith. Watts,
     c1970. $4.95
     RL: No text   IL: All ages   S
This colorful series of circus pictures is a real conversation
piece. Children are familiar with circuses at an early age
because of TV even though they may never see a live one.
This circus has many exciting things in it including ones
children can try to imitate--jugglers, tightrope walkers, and
clowns.

381 City in Summer, by Eleanor Schick. Macmillan, c1967.
     $4.50
     RL: 2-3   IL: Read aloud-3   SM
A picture book story of the city in summer and an old man
and a young boy's visit to Coney Island.

382 City in the Winter, by Eleanor Schick. Macmillan,
     c1970. $4.95
     RL: 3   IL: Read aloud-3   SM
A quiet story with warm illustrations of a boy's day at home
in a big snowstorm in the city. Appeals to city children.

383 City Rhythms, by Ann Grifalconi. Bobbs Merrill,
     c1965. $4.95
     RL: 3   IL: Read aloud-4   SMP
Jimmy's father tells him the city has a rhythm of its own
and Jimmy finally masters its beat after listening to all the
city noises. Not much action but superb pictures. This is
popular with any city child and especially so with black children who, like all children love to see themselves in picture
books.

384 The Day We Saw the Sun Come Up, by Alice E. Goudey.
     Illus. by Adrienne Adams. Scribner, c1961. $4.95
     RL: 2-3   IL: Read aloud-4   S
An excellent read-aloud book with beautiful illustrations for
younger children. It treats natural phenomena in a very
poetic way.

385 Emilio's Summer Day, by Miriam Anne Bourne. Illus.
     by Ben Shecter. Harper, c1966. $3.50
     RL: 4   IL: Read aloud-3   SM

A scorching day in Spanish Harlem is illustrated in a series
of pictures of a small boy. Like all children, inner city
children delight in reading about themselves and seeing their
home surroundings in books. This is very popular in School
Volunteer Programs and would be popular on the bookmobile
in paperback.

386 Faces, by Barbara Brenner. Photographs by George
     Ancona. Dutton, 1970. $4.95
     RL: 3   IL: Read aloud-2   *SMP
A picture book full of beautiful photographs. An excellent
springboard for conversation with a younger child.

387 Gilberto and the Wind, by Marie Hall Ets. Viking,
     c1963. Seafarer, pb $.85
     RL: 3   IL: Read aloud-3   BSMP
Gilberto races the wind and uses its help to sail a boat and
set soap bubbles floating high in the sky. One of the earliest
books to be published about a Spanish-American child, it has
imaginative illustrations. It is also available in Spanish.
See Book List classification 4.

388 Golden Shape Books, Western Golden Press. $.29
     RL: 3   IL: Read aloud-3   BS
The books in this series are shaped according to the title,
(Bears, Boats, Hats, etc.) and consist of a series of pictures with a small amount of text at the bottom of each page.
They are intended for pre-school children but on the bookmobile, they are very popular with children through the third
grade. They are full of accurate information and can be used
successfully with an older child in a one-to-one situation.

389 The Good Bird, by Peter Wezel. Harper, 1964. $3.27
     RL: No text   IL: Pre-school-3   S
The story in pictures of a bird who befriends a fish, this
may be used imaginatively for oral or written storytelling
and creative writing.

390 Harold and the Purple Crayon, by Crockett Johnson.
     Harper, 1955. $2.50 (Scholastic, pb OP)
     RL: 2-3   IL: Read aloud-4   BS
Harold uses his purple crayon to take him on exciting adventures. This imaginative book can be used with a non-reader
of any age by a tutor with insight. It is also very popular
with young children.

391 Hi, All You Rabbits, by Carl Memling. Illus. by

Myra McGee.   Parents, c1970. $3.95
    RL: 2   IL: Read aloud-2   *S
I know many city children who sing <u>Old McDonald Had a
Farm</u> lustily without a clue as to what a pig that goes oink
looks like or is useful for.   This gaily illustrated book is
like a picture story of McDonald's farm and would be very
useful in any program for younger children as well as any
program where children are trying to learn English.

392   <u>Hi Cat</u>, by Ezra Jack Keats.   Macmillan, c1970. $4.50
    RL: 2-3   IL: Read aloud-3   BSMP
Archie is friendly to a newcomer to the neighborhood, an
alley cat, who proceeds in exchange to break up Archie's
magic show.   Children love this book which is really a picture of inner city children fooling around on a city street
done by a superb artist in colors that stick in the mind as
one goes through the city.

393   <u>It's Time Now</u>, by Alvin Tresselt.   Illus. by Roger
        Duvoisin.   Lothrop, 1969. $3.95
    RL: 2-3   IL: Read aloud-3   *SMP
One of the most satisfying picture books I have seen in years,
this portrays and celebrates the seasons in the city in such
a way that every city child will feel a happy glow of recognition.

394   <u>My Five Senses</u>, by Aliki.   Crowell, c1962. $3.75
        (Pb $.95)
    RL: 2-3   IL: Pre-school-3   BS
A lovely book of drawings about the five senses.   A valuable reading-readiness tool.

395   <u>Quiet As a Butterfly</u>, by Lawrence F. Lowery.   Illus.
        by Rita Zorberg.   Western, Golden Press, 1969.
        $1.95
    RL: 3   IL: Read aloud-3   BS
A beautiful picture book which can be used not only to sharpen
children's ears but also to celebrate the joys of quiet things.
A book like this in the hands of a skilled teacher or Volunteer, can help to reassure and bring out a shy, quiet child
who is being drowned by the activists in the group.   Note the
low price.

396   <u>Shapes</u>, by Miriam Schlein.   Illus. by Sam Berman.
        Hale, 1952. $2.88
    RL: 2-3   IL: Pre-school-3   S
Pictures and word pictures of shapes.   Humorous illustrations

give information and provoke thoughtful perception.

397   The Snowy Day, by Ezra Jack Keats.   Viking, c1962.
         $3.50   (Scholastic pb $.75)
         RL: 2-3   IL: Read aloud-4   BSMP
A beautiful picture book about Peter, a small black boy, in
the city and what he does on a snowy day.   The effect of the
colorful illustrations, which illumine what is lovely in the
city, on a ghetto child cannot be described.   A magical book.

398   A Thousand Lights and Fireflies, by Alvin R. Tresselt.
         Illus. by John Moodie.   Parents, 1965. $3.95
         RL: 3   IL: Read aloud-3   BS
This extraordinarily well-illustrated picture book contrasts
the city and the country, finding beauty in both and that people are the same everywhere.

399   Wake Up City, by Alvin R. Tresselt.   Illus. by Roger
         Duvoisin.   Lothrop, 1966. $4.50
         RL: 2-3   IL: Read aloud-3   S
A lovely picture book story of what happens between dawn
and sunrise.

400   What Makes a Shadow?, by Clyde Robert Bulla.   Illus.
         by Adrienne Adams.   T. Y. Crowell, 1962. $3.75
         (Scholastic pb $.75)
         RL: 2   IL: Read aloud-3   *BS
A picture book on a subject that interests all children.   It
will sharpen the eye of beginning readers.

401   Where is Everybody?, by Remy Charlip.   Hale, c1957.
         $2.79   (Scholastic pb $.75)
         RL: 2   IL: K-3   BS
An artfully constructed picture book with simple line drawings
that create a sunny woodland scene and then a rainy one.
The book sharpens a child's vision and inspires young artists.
It is popular on the bookmobile but especially valuable in
Reading Help programs.

402   Your Face Is a Picture, by Clifford.   Illus. by Aliki.
         Seale, 1965.   OP
         RL: No text   IL: Pre-school-4   S
A magnificent book of photographs which will involve even the
shyest child in conversation.

7   RECREATION/ARTS--RIDDLE BOOKS

403   Bennett Cerf's Book of Animal Riddles, by Bennett
      Cerf.   Illus. by Ray McKie.   Random Beginner,
      c1964. $2.50
      RL: 2   IL: Read aloud-3   BS
This book has more humor than most riddle books.   All children seem to love riddles and puns--even bad ones.   Riddle
books are excellent for interesting children in words and word
games.

404   Guess What?, by Lene Hille-Brandts.   Adapted by
      Elizabeth Duckworth.   Illus. by Doris Dumler.   Chil-
      drens Press, 1968. $3.50
      RL: 3   IL: Read aloud-4   S
Fourteen riddles in rhyme with the answers illustrated on
the following page.   A little cute but children love this one
when reading it with an adult.

405   Jokes and Riddles, compiled by Jonathan Peter.   Illus.
      by David Lockhart.   Grosset & Dunlap, 1963. $.69
      RL: 2-3   IL: 3-6   BS
This joke and riddle book with cartoon-like illustrations is
very popular with good readers as well as poor ones.

406   Jokes and Riddles to Riddles to Read Aloud, compiled
      by Oscar Weigle.   Illus. by Jessica Zemsky.   Gros-
      set Read-Aloud Wonder Book, c1962.   pb $.49
      RL: 5   IL: 4-HS   BS
Play-on-words humor in both long and short riddles, jokes
and funny stories.   Another popular one.

407   Lucky Book of Riddles, by Eva Moore.   Illus. by
      Olivia H. H. Cole.   Scholastic, 1964.   pb $.35
      RL: 2   IL: Read aloud-4   BS
This tiny riddle book (about 2-1/2" x 4") gets lost on the
bookmobile due to its size but is a best seller at book fairs
and a real conversation piece for School Volunteers.

408   Plenty of Riddles, by William Wiesner.   Scholastic,
      1966.   pb $.50
      RL: 3   IL: 2-5   BS
Another tiny collection of riddles which is lost on the book-
mobile because of its size but is loved by children in the
Reading Help Program.

7 RECREATION/ARTS--SONGS

409 Lift Every Voice and Sing, by James Weldon Johnson
     and J. Rosamund Johnson.   Illus. by Mozelle Thomp-
     son.   Hawthorn, c1970. $3.95
     RL: Adult   IL: 5-adult   *SMP
A striking illustrated edition of the song that has become
known as the Negro National Anthem.   The book also has the
music in a piano arrangement with guitar chords.   Augusta
Baker, the well-known black librarian, describes the song
as "this song of faith and courage, hope and joy."

410 The Little Drummer Boy, by Ezra Jack Keats.
     Macmillan, 1968. $3.95   (Collier pb $.95)
     RL: 2-3   IL: Read aloud-4   S
A beautifully illustrated version of a popular Christmas carol
which is so rhythmical that even little children soon sing
along and learn the words.

411 New Treasury of Folk Songs, compiled and arranged by
     Tom Glazer.   Bantam, c1961.   pb $.60
     RL: Varied   IL: 6-adult   BS
Eighty pages of America's best loved songs with the melody
arranged for piano or guitar.   In a section at the end, Glazer
explains about different guitars, how to go about buying one
and also how to start playing one.   A pleasant book for a
family and a popular book for teenage would-be guitarists.

412 Old MacDonald Had a Farm, illustrated by Abner
     Graboff.   Scholastic, 1969.   pb $.50
     RL: 2   IL: Read aloud-2   BS
A colorful version of the old song with a new twist at the
end.

413 One Wide River to Cross, adapted by Barbara Emberley.
     Illus. by Barbara and Ed Emberley.   Prentice-Hall,
     1966. $3.95   (Scholastic pb $.75)
     RL: 2   IL: Read aloud-3   *BS
Imaginative treatment of the old folk song and good counting
practice as the animals board the Ark.   Striking wood cut
illustrations.

7 RECREATION/ARTS--SPORTS (Non-Fiction)

414 Amazing Baseball Teams, by Dave Wolf.   Random,
        c1970. $1.95
        RL: 6   IL: 6-adult   *BSM
The story of seven famous ball teams, one from each decade
of the twentieth century. I'm not sure how many of today's
fans will read the whole book but they'll all eat up the chapter
on the amazing Mets. Photographs. Note the nice low price.

415 The Amazing Mets, by Jerry Mitchell.   Grosset, c1966.
        $2.50 (Tempo, c1970, pb $.75)
        RL: 5-6   IL: 4-adult   BSM
All of Brooklyn wants a book about the Mets, and since the
1969 season so do all baseball fans. This book is one which
has been revised and enlarged to bring it up to date.   It is
very popular.

416 Art Arfons, Fastest Man on Wheels, by Frederic Katz.
        Adapted by Lawrence Swinburne. Illus. by Wolfgang
        Otto. McGraw-Hill, Reading Shelf Series, c1965.
        $1.48
        RL: 5   IL: 5-adult   *BS
The true story of the man who builds his own racing cars
and went 536 miles per hour on the Bonneville Salt flats.
He hopes someday to break the sound barrier.   Racing car
buffs will go for this one.

417 Baseball Hall of Fame: Stories of Champions, by
        Samuel and Beryl Epstein. Scholastic, c1965.   pb
        $.50
        RL: 3-4   IL: 4-adult   BS
A very useful collection of short biographies of baseball champions.   Short biographies are always in demand in reading
help programs and are popular with bookmobile patrons also.

418 Baseball Is a Funny Game, by Joe Garagiola.   Lippin-
        cott, 1960. $4.50 (Bantam Books, 1962, pb $.75)
        RL: 5   IL: 6-adult   BS
Baseball fans keep this circulating although it came out so
long ago.

419 Baseball Laughs, by Herman L. Masin.   Illus. by
        Harry A. Schneider and Charles Beck.   Scholastic,
        c1964.   pb $.50
        RL: 4-5   IL: 6-adult   S

Funny stories about famous players, coaches and umpires.
Popular with boys in junior high and high school and will
often interest a poor reader who, however, is an expert on
big league ball.

420   The Baseball Life of Mickey Mantle, by John Devaney.
        Scholastic, c1969.   pb $.60
        RL: 5   IL: 4-adult   BS
Though called the "baseball" life of Mickey Mantle, this book
can be of interest to non-baseball fans.   Mantle, one of the
great ball players of all times has shown great courage in
battling osteomyelitis.

421   The Baseball Life of Sandy Koufax, by George Vecsey.
        Scholastic, c1968.   pb $.60
        RL: 5   IL: 4-adult   BS
The story of another baseball player who has made an extraordinary record in spite of the crippling pain of arthritis.
Koufax has retired to become a sports announcer.   A
sports biography of wide appeal.   Photographs.

422   The Baseball Life of Willie Mays, by Lee Greene.
        Scholastic, c1970.   pb $.60
        RL: 5   IL: 5-adult   *BSMP
This book is just what its title says it is, the baseball life
of Willie Mays, but his baseball record is so extraordinary
and his character and leadership so great both in triumph
and defeat that it will interest many who are not ordinarily
baseball fans.   Photographs.

423   Baseball's Unforgettables, by Mac Davis.   Bantam
        Pathfinder, c1966.   pb $.75
        RL: 5   IL: 4-adult   BSM
The cover of this book with a color photo of Sandy Koufax
and Willie Mays in the midst of humorous pen and ink drawings of other ball players attracts many readers.   It is an
entertaining collection of true anecdotes and stories about
ball players.

424   Basketball Is My Life, by Bob Cousy (as told to Al
        Hirshberg).   Prentice-Hall, c1957, Pratt, 1963.   OP
        RL: 4   IL: 5-adult   BS
The life of the famous basketball star.   Easy and interesting
for basketball fans who like the book although Cousy is no
longer playing.

425   Better Scramble Than Lose, by Fran Tarkenton (as told

to Jack Olsen).   Scholastic, c1969.   pb $.75
    RL: 6   IL: 6-adult   *B
Strictly for football fans but of keen interest to them, especially to those teenage football players who hope to use the
sports route to fame and fortune.   Photographs.

426   The Black Athlete, by Jack Orr.   Lion Press, c1969.
     Pyramid, 1970.   pb $.95
    RL: 6   IL: 6-adult   *BSMP
A well written account of the achievements of black athletes
in America.   The book tells of their frustrations and the
problems they met but the note is a positive one and should
spur youngsters on.   Introduction by Jackie Robinson.
Photographs.

427   Black Champion--The Life and Times of Jack Johnson,
     by Finis Farr.   Fawcett, 1969.   pb $.75
    RL: 7   IL: 6-adult   *BSMP
The story of Jack Johnson, the first black man to become
boxing champion of the world.   Exciting and tragic.   Photographs.   This book is becoming more popular as Johnson's
story becomes known to this generation through plays and
stories.

428   Black Think: My Life as a Black Man and a White
     Man, by Jesse Owens and Paul G. Neimark.   Morrow,
     c1970.   OP
    RL: 6   IL: 6-adult
The story of the famous track star who won at the Olympics
over which Hitler presided.   Although some modern black
athletes feel Owens was unfairly exploited and although he
does not minimize the difficulties he encountered, he is
strongly for integration and for the way of life he feels
America offers even to a black man.

429   Bruce Tegner's Method of Self-Defense, by Bruce
     Tegner.   Bantam, pb, revised edition, c1972. $1
                                     BS
Boys will really work to read this one on a very popular subject.   We sell this for $1 on the bookmobile and it is aston-
ishing how many young boys manage to raise this rather large
sum of money.   The library tells us that their loan copies go
out and never come back.   The following books by the same
author on this subject are available: Bruce Tegner's Complete
Book of Karate, Bantam pb $1;   Bruce Tegner's Complete
Book of Judo, Bantam pb $1.   Many inner city boys and girls
are fearful of bodily injury (with reason) and even poor

readers will work to read these books all of which have many
diagrams illustrating the different holds and positions. Judo
and karate schools are also very popular for those who can
afford them.

430 Cassius Clay, by Claude Lewis. MacFadden, c1971.
       pb $.60
       RL: 5-6   IL: 6-adult   BSM
A well written biography of the black prize fighter by a well
known black newspaper commentator. Cassius Clay or
Muhammed Ali as he prefers to be called, is a fascinating
and controversial figure. His story is well worth reading
and is very popular on the bookmobile.

431 Famous Negro Athletes, by Arna Bontemps. Dodd,
       Mead, c1964. $3.50   (Apollo pb $1.95)
       RL: 6   IL: 5-adult   BSMP
It may seem redundant still to carry this book (which was
published in 1964) when so many new ones now celebrate the
black athlete individually and collectively, but I love the way
Bontemps writes and he writes of some heroes who are now
neglected. Joe Louis, Satchel Paige and Jesse Owens are
almost unknown to a new generation. Even Jackie Robinson
sometimes isn't recognized. Yet these men were trailblazers
as was this book. It was on the bookmobile when we opened
in July 1967 and very popular. Now most people pass it by
for more up-to-date paperbacks. It has just been reissued
in paperback which may renew its popularity. Photographs.

432 Go Up for Glory, by Bill Russell, as told to William F.
       McSweeny. Berkley, c1966. (Medallion pb $.60)
       RL: 6   IL: 6-adult   BSMP
The autobiography of the great basketball player. This is
also available in a Falcon edition. See Falcon Books [175].

433 The Great Auto Race & Other Stories of Men and Cars,
       edited by Ruth Christopher Carlsen and G. Robert
       Carlsen. Scholastic, 1965. pb $.50
       RL: 6   IL: 6-HS   BS
Popular collection of auto stories.

434 Great Moments in Pro Basketball, by Dave Wolf and
       Biu Bruns. Random, c1968. $1.95
       RL: 6   IL: 6-adult   *BSMP
A series of accounts of great moments in basketball which in
effect give a history of the game. An exciting book for fans
illustrated with excellent photographs. Note low price.

184   Read for Your Life

435 <u>The Greatest in Baseball</u>, by Mac Davis. Scholastic,
      1962.   pb $.50
        RL: 6   IL: 5-adult   BS
Short, factual biographies of Baseball's Hall of Famers.
Baseball buffs seem to have an endless appetite for baseball
facts.   Photographs.

436 <u>Harlem Globe Trotters</u>, by George Vecsey. Scholastic,
      1970.   pb $.75
        RL: 5   IL: 5-adult   BS
The story of the famous black basketball team.   Of interest
to a basketball fan and would-be players.   Photographs.

437 <u>How to Star in Baseball</u>, by Herman L. Masin. Photo-
      graphs by Owen Reed.   Four Winds, c1960. $2.95
      (Scholastic pb $.60)
        RL: 5   IL: 4-HS   BS
A very clear, heavily illustrated baseball manual.

438 <u>How to Star in Basketball</u>, by Herman L. Masin.
      Photographs by Leonard Kamsler.   Four Winds, c1958.
      $2.95   (Scholastic pb $.60)
        RL: 5   IL: 4-HS   BS
An excellent, heavily illustrated manual, similar to 437.

439 <u>How to Star in Football</u>, by Herman L. Masin. Illus.
      by Alan Maver.   Four Winds, c1959 and c1966.
      $2.95   (Scholastic pb $.60)
        RL: 6   IL: 6-HS   BS
A manual on how to play good football, this book is liberally
illustrated with photographs.

440 <u>I Always Wanted to Be Somebody</u>, by Althea Gibson.
      Edited by Ed Fitzgerald.   Harper, c1958.   Perennial,
      pb, 1965. $.75
        RL: 6-7   IL: 5-adult   BMP
The story of the famous tennis player from Harlem, this book
is increasingly popular as more and more people watch tennis
on TV.   Also available in an adapted and simplified version:
<u>I Always Wanted to Be Somebody</u>, by Althea Gibson, adapted
by F. Allen and Stephen M. Joseph.   Noble and Noble, Falcon
Books, c1967.   pb $.56

441 <u>I Am Third</u>, by Gale Sayers with Al Silverman. Viking,
      c1970. $6.95   (Bantam pb 1972, $1.25)
        RL: 5-6   IL: JH-adult   *BSMP
Gale Sayers, the well known pro football player, tells the

story of his life and of his friendship with Brian Piccolo, his
white football roommate who died of cancer.   It is an inspiring story of courage, determination (he started life in the
ghetto) and love.   It is already very popular.

442   Iron Man, by Billy Williams with Rick Simon.   Childrens
      Press, c1970. $3.00   (An Open Door Book, pb $.75)
      RL: 5   IL: 5-adult   *BSMP
Billy Williams grew up in poverty but with a happy united
family.   He went straight from school into pro baseball and
had a lonely time of it as the only black on the team.   He
is now well known and glad he took the road he did.   This
book will be very popular.

443   Jackie Robinson of the Brooklyn Dodgers, by Milton J.
      Shapiro.   Messner, c1966. $3.50   (Washington Square
      Press, Archway, 1967, pb $.50)
      RL: 6   IL: 5-adult   BMP
The moving story of the first black baseball player in the
white leagues.   Engrossing even to those who are not interested in baseball.   Photographs.

444. Jake Gaither, Winning Coach, by Wyatt Blassingame.
      Illustrations and photographs by Raymond Burr.
      Garrard, c1969.   (Americans All) $2.79
      RL: 4   IL: 4-HS   *BSM
The biography of Jake Gaither, the well known football coach
at Florida A and M will interest and inspire some boys while
others may find it simplistic and overly moral.   Gaither is
undoubtedly a very fine man and a very successful coach but
many young militants will feel unhappy that he has spent the
whole of his working life in a segregated world and is the
most successful coach in the National Negro Conference rather
than the truly National Small College League which should
exist.

445   Jim Ryun, Master of the Mile, by John Lake.   Random,
      c1968. $1.95
      RL: 5-6   IL: 6-adult   *BS
The story of Jim Ryun, the amazing track star.   The book
brings out to what an extent Ryun's record runs are the
product of unremitting work.   An interesting story.   Many
photographs.

446   Jim Thorpe, by T. Fall.   Illus. by J. Gretzer.
      Crowell, c1970. $3.75
      RL: 3   IL: Read aloud-JH   *BSMP

A good biography of the famous Indian athlete which will interest all would-be football players and also boys who dislike
school. See also below for a more mature biography.

447 The Jim Thorpe Story, by Gene Schoor. J. Messner,
     c1967. $3.50 (Washington Square Press, Archway,
     pb $.60)
     RL: 5   IL: 5-adult   *BMP
The subtitle of this book is "America's Greatest Athlete" and
the story of Jim Thorpe, the Indian, is in fact an extraordinary one. Will be especially popular with football fans.
Photographs.

448 Little Men in Sports, by Larry Fox. Grosset, Tempo,
     c1968. pb $.95
     RL: 6   IL: 6-adult   BSMP
The stories of twenty pint-sized athletes who became nationally famous in spite of their size. They include Juan Rod-
riguez, the 119-pound Puerto Rican who was the first of his
island to become a recognized golf star and Henry Armstrong,
the thirteenth child of a Mississippi sharecropper who became
the featherweight, lightweight and welterweight boxing champion, a triple winner.

449 Look to the Light Side, by Dave Stallworth with R.
     Conrad Stein. Childrens Press, An Open Door Book,
     c1970. $3.50 (Pb $.75)
     RL: 4-5   IL: 6-adult   *BSMP
Dave Stallworth, the basketball player for the Knicks had
everything going for him until he had a serious heart attack
and was told he could never play again. This is the story of
his extraordinary recovery and comeback, ending by his rejoining the Knicks in 1969. Especially valuable for young
people with health problems. Photographs.

450 My Ups and Downs in Baseball, by Orlando Cepeda
     with Charles Einstein. Putnam, c1968. $4.95
     RL: 5-6   IL: 6-adult   BSMP
Ninety per cent of this book will only interest baseball fans,
and fairly ardent ones at that, who want the play-by-play description of a number of famous games from a player's point
of view. However, the remaining ten per cent makes this an
important book for a lot of people. Cepeda is the first Puerto
Rican to make a major reputation in the major leagues. He
is also one of the first cripples to be voted most valuable
player in the National League. When that happened, he was
wearing a shoe that weighed twenty-two pounds. Born with

a deformed leg which has been corrected twice by surgery, Cepeda has had a physical battle to contend with as well as other difficulties but has come out on top.

451 O. J. : The Education of a Rich Rookie, by O. J. Simpson with Pete Axthelm. Macmillan, c1970. $5. 95
RL: 6   IL: 6-adult   BM
The famous black football player tells the story of his first year in pro-football. In contrast to many earlier black athletes, he seems started on a multi-money-making career which will make him solidly rich. He also, due to the attention of the media no doubt, feels that every detail of his life is worth recording, not only every detail of each game but also of each plane ride, practice session etc. However, the book will be worth buying for would-be pro-football players when it is out in paperback as it surely will be.

452. Old Bones, The Wonder Horse, by Mildren Mastin Pace. Illus. by Wesley Dennis. McGraw-Hill, c1955. $4. 95 (Scholastic, 1965, pb $. 50)
RL: 4-5   IL: 4-JH   BS
A good true story of a remarkable race horse, with black and white illustrations by an artist who is noted for his portraits of horses.

453 Pro Basketball Champions, by George Vecsey. Scholastic, c1970. pb $. 60
RL: 5-6   IL: 5-adult   BSMP
The stories of ten superstars, this book has a dramatic picture on the cover of Wilt Chamberlain scoring. It is very much in demand. Photographs.

454 Pro Football Heroes, by Steve Gelman. Scholastic, c1968. pb $. 60
RL: 5-6   IL: 5-adult   BSM
Exciting, fast-paced biographies of Jimmy Brown, Deacon Jones, Johnny Unitas and seven other superstars. Illustrated with photos, this also has a cover photo which has made it instantly popular.

455 Somebody Up There Likes Me, by Rocky Graziano with Rowland Barber. Simon and Schuster, Pocket Books, c1955. pb $. 50
RL: 6-7   IL: 6-adult   BSMP
The moving story of a boy who started out with two left feet and at least two strikes against him but who wound up both a famous prize fighter and a good citizen. Very popular with boys and adults.

456   Stand Tall: The Lew Alcinder Story, by Phil Pepe.
      Grosset, c1970. $5.95
      RL: 5   IL: 6-adult   SMP
The story of the famous basketball player told by a sports
writer who has known him since the star was thirteen and
just starting his career. For basketball fans.

457   Star Pitchers of the Major Leagues, by Bill Libby.
      Random, 1971. $1.95
      RL: 6   IL: 6-adult   BSMP
The kind of factual accounts of famous pitchers that fans and
would-be baseball stars like to read. Photographs.

458   Sugar Ray, by Sugar Ray Robinson with Dave Anderson.
      New American Library, Signet, c1969. pb $.95
      RL: 5-6   IL: 6-adult   BSM
The fascinating story of the boxer who rose from poverty to
make and squander $4,000,000. His story of how he tried
to make a comeback reminds one painfully of the prize-fighter
has-been in Requiem for a Heavyweight. A disarming book
which has been very popular.

459   Ten Great Moments in Sports, by Maury Allen. Illus.
      by Edward J. Smith. Follett, c1961. $1.77
      RL: 3   IL: 4-HS   BS
An invaluable book for older boys, this series of ten short
articles has suspense and high interest at a truly low reading
level.

460   The Tommy Davis Story, by Patrick Russell. Double-
      day, Signal, 1969. $3.50 (Doubleday, Semaphore,
      pb $1.75)
      RL: 4   IL: 4-adult   BSMP
The life of the famous baseball player, this is more for fans
than for the general public. Several setbacks make it clear
that even for a talented youngster, white or black, pro-base-
ball is not an easy ladder to fame and fortune.

461   Victory Over Myself, by Floyd Patterson and Milton
      Cross. Geis, c1962. OP (Scholastic pb 1965)
      RL: 6   IL: 5-adult   BSMP
This autobiography of the boxing champion is thought-provoking
and absorbing even to people who dislike boxing and are un-
interested in sport. It is dedicated to the Wiltwyck School
for problem boys which he feels rescued him from a hopeless
situation and gave him his start to a decent life and an honor-
able career.

462 <u>Willie Mays</u>, by Arnold Hano.   Grosset and Dunlap,
        Tempo, c1966.   pb $.75
        RL: 5   IL: 5-adult   BSM
A well-written biography of the famous ball player.   Popular
with all ages.

463 <u>Wilt Chamberlain</u>, by Kenneth Rudeen.   Illus. by Frank
        Mullins.   Crowell, c1970. $3.75
        RL: 3   IL: 2-JH   *BSMP
Wilt Chamberlain was born poor and black.   He is so tall
that most people would consider him a freak.   However, he
is also one of the best basketball players in the world.   This
account of his life has enough breadth so that non-basketball
players will enjoy it as well as those who hope to follow in
his shoes.   See 464 below for a more difficult and adult
biography.

464 <u>Wilt Chamberlain</u>, by George Sullivan.   Grosset,
        Tempo, c1966.   pb $.60
        RL: 5   IL: 5-adult   BS
An exciting biography of the famous basketball player.   See
also 463 above on an easier reading level.

465 <u>Young Olympic Champions</u>, by Steve Gelman.   Grosset,
        c1964. $3.95 (Scholastic pb $.50)
        RL: 5-6   IL: 5-adult   BSMP
Eleven biographies of Olympic champions written with suspense.   Many girls who are not interested in books are
thrilled by the story of Wilma Rudolph, the Olympic track
star.

466   Amercian Negro Poetry, edited by Arna Bontemps.
      Hill & Wang, c1963. $4.95 (American Century
      Series, pb $1.95)
      RL: Varied: mainly HS-adult   IL: 4-adult   BSMP
An excellent collection, much in demand with adults and high
school students. It contains 171 poems by fifty-five poets
covering a period of seventy years. The short biographical
sketches of the poets at the end of the book will interest
readers and add a great deal.

467   Arrow Book of Funny Poems, edited by Eleanor Clymer.
      Illus. by Doug Anderson. Scholastic, c1961. pb
      $.50
      RL: 5   IL: Varied: mainly 5-JH, but
      some poems would interest any age   BS
An excellent collection of poems, mostly humorous but many
philosophical. It has a very deceiving format. On the bookmobile, young children grab it and cannot read it.

468   Arrow Book of Poetry, edited by Ann McGovern. Illus.
      by Grisha Dotzenko. Scholastic, 1965. pb $.50
      RL: 5   IL: 4-adult   BS
A good collection with poems about the city as well as the
country, and good illustrations.

469   Ask a Daffodil, by Adele H. Seronde. Edited by H.
      Wenkart. Illustrated by the author. Wenkart, 1967.
      $3.95 (pb $1.95)
      RL: 2-3   IL: 2-3   S
Ingenious use of phonics as a teaching device incorporated in
poems of interest to city children. Excellent illustrations.

470   Bed-Stuy Beat, by Rose Blue. Illus. by Harold James.
      Grolier, Watts, 1970. $4.50
      RL: 2-3   IL: All ages   *BSMP
A swinging song, the Bed-Stuy beat is a poem of life in the
Bedford-Stuyvesant section of Brooklyn. Both the poem and
the pictures say "I'm proud to be black" but there is no

reason why white people cannot enjoy both the rhythm and the
beauty of the book and, in fact, the reader can hardly sit
still as he reads, the words swing so.

471   Best Mother Goose Ever, illustrated by Richard Scarry.
        Golden Press, 1969. $5.95
        RL: 5   IL: Read aloud-2   *BS
Children love Mr. Scarry's pictures and these fill seventy-
five per cent of the nice big pages of this book.   The pictures are also large enough so that they will be easy for a
group of children to see at a story hour.

472   Bronzeville Boys and Girls, by Gwendolyn Brooks.
        Illus. by Ronni Solbert.   Harper, c1956. $2.50
        RL: 3-4   IL: Read aloud-JH   BSMP
A very popular collection of poems for and about children by
a noted black poet.   Good pen and ink drawings.

473   Charge of the Light Brigade and Other Story Poems,
        eidted by Scholastic editors.   Scholastic, c1969.   pb
        $.60
        RL: Varied   IL: JH-adult   BS
A rich variety of story poems including such old favorites as
"Casey at the Bat" and "Abdul Abulbul Amir," this book is
full of poems which are excellent to read aloud to a group.
Once young people have heard some of these poems, they
are anxious to read the poems themselves but the book must
be started on a read-aloud basis since the language of many
of the poems makes for difficult reading.   On the bookmobile
it is borrowed because of the dramatic picture on the cover
but most borrowers find they cannot read it.

474   The City Spreads Its Wings, edited by Lee Bennett
        Hopkins.   Illus. by Moneto Barnett.   Franklin Watts,
        c1970. $4.95
        RL: 3   IL: Read aloud-5   *SMP
A portrait of city life painted by twenty-one poems in simple
language of elements of a city that any child will recognize.
The illustrations are full page and cheerful.   The book (like
the E. J. Keats' books) gives a truthful picture and yet a
positive one.

475   City Talk, compiled by Lee Bennett Hopkins.   Photo-
        graphs by Roy Arenella.   Knopf, c1970. $3.95
        RL: Varied-mainly 4   IL: 2-JH   *SMP
Forty-five pages of poetry written by city children and photographs of city children and their milieu.   The compiler, a

consultant for the Bank Street College of Education and Scholastic became intrigued by the poetry form called cinquain and went all over the country introducing it to city children. The book is made up of the poems which resulted. Some are spontaneous, some are stilted and use unnatural language and symbols. However, there are many poems here which city children would enjoy and which would enable them to see and hear city sights and sounds in a new way. The book will also, of course, encourage other children to become poets even if all the so-called poems are not poetry. I am glad to report that most of the poems in this book are cheerful!

476   Crystal Cabinet, by Horace G. and Marya Zaturenska.
        Illus. by Diana Bloomfield. Holt, Rinehart, 1962.
        $3.50
        RL: 5   IL: 5-adult   S
Poetry with wide variety for more mature students.

477   Don't Tell the Scarecrow & Other Japanese Poems, by
        Issa, Yayu & Kikaku and others. Illus. by Talivaldis
        Stubis. Four Winds, 1969. $4.50 (Scholastic, pb
        $.75)
        RL: 3   IL: 3-JH   *SB
Thirty-four brief poems, called haiku, each crystallizing a thought, feeling, or observation with dreamlike, striking full color illustrations. Haiku have been very successfully used in School Volunteer programs with older elementary and junior high students to prompt the student to write poetry on his own.

478   Don't You Turn Back--Poems by Langston Hughes, edited
        by Lee Bennett Hopkins. Illus. by Ann Grifalcone.
        Knopf, 1969. $3.95
        RL: Varied   IL: 4-adult   *BSMP
Children and young people respond deeply to the poetry of Langston Hughes. His Dreamkeeper [479] and The Panther and the Lash [504] are very popular both in School Volunteer programs and on the bookmobile. This book will be popular also and is another must for school libraries. I read so many bitter books on the polarization of America because of race, I wish every white American child could read and understand the poem in here called "As I Grew Older" and every non-white child learn and take to heart the poem "Color." Of course, Hughes also wrote many poems of deeply universal quality. He speaks to all men. Note the nice price, low for the content and illustrations.

479   Dream Keeper and Other Poems, by Langston Hughes.
      Illus. by Helen Sewall.   Knopf, 1932. $4.19
      RL: 4   IL: 4-JH   BSMP
An excellent collection of easy poems by Langston Hughes.
Very popular.

480   Favorite Poems to Read Aloud, edited by Art Krusz.
      Grosset & Dunlap Read-Aloud Wonder Book Series,
      1965.   pb $.49
A good collection of familiar poems and nonsense rhymes for
younger children.   Black and white illustrations.

481   Favorite Pop-Rock Lyrics, edited by Jerry L. Walker.
      Scholastic, c1969.   pb $.60
      RL: 4   IL: 5-young adult   BS
The lyrics to fifteen pop rock hits with an eye-catching cover
and lots of photographs.   A good introduction to poetry and
an excellent opener with a distrustful junior or senior high
school student in a Reading Help session.   See also 512 and
513.

482   Favorite Rhymes from a Rocket in My Pocket, edited
      by Carl Withers.   Illus. by William Weisner.   Scho-
      lastic, 1967.   pb $.50
      RL: 1-2   IL: Read aloud-JH   BS
Jump-rope rhymes, autograph rhymes, all kinds of rhymes
for many ages with comical pictures on every page.

483   Golden Slippers, edited by Arna Bontemps.   Illus. by
      Henrietta Bruce Sharon.   Harper & Row, 1941. $5.95
      RL: Varied   IL: 4-adults   BSMP
This anthology of poetry by black Americans first appeared in
1941 and I am sure that many black militants would reject it
out of hand.   The title page has a picture of a black man in
tattered clothing sitting on an upturned crate and strumming
a guitar.   I hope it will be made available, however, to all
American children.   The older poems are full of humor and
courage in the face of adversity and certainly every child
should know poems like "Lift Every Voice and Sing" and
"Mother to Son."   The book is labelled "for young readers"
but adults enjoy it equally.   There are brief biographies of
the poets at the end of the book.

484   Here I Am, edited by Virginia Olsen Baron.   Illus. by
      Emily Arnold McCully.   Dutton, c1969. $4.95
      (Bantam Pathfinder, pb $.75)
      RL: Varied: mainly 4-5   IL: 4-HS   BSMP

This is subtitled an anthology of poems written by young people in some of America's minority groups and it is an accurate description. This is a valuable book on two counts.
All the poems (whether real poetry or not) are excellent conversation pieces and starting points for discussion groups.
Secondly, many of them have a common bond even though
their authors come from widely differing backgrounds i. e.
Brooklyn, the Navaho reservation, Alaska and so forth. This
will surprise and interest students from the areas represented.
In addition, several of the poems strike me as really good
and should inspire would-be poets.

485   Hi Diddle Diddle--Mother Goose, pictures by Nola
        Langner. Scholastic, c1965. pb $. 60
        RL: 1-2   IL: Read aloud-3   BS
Mother Goose with comic illustrations. Every child should
learn the Mother Goose rhymes as part of the heritage of
the English language but many of the children who come on
the bookmobile or are in the School Volunteer program have
never heard of them.

486   Hold Fast to Dreams, edited by Arna Bontemps.
        Follett, 1969. $4. 95
        RL: Varied   IL: 4-adult   BSMP
Some of the older poems in this anthology will seem very
sentimental to those who enjoy LeRoi Jones. However, this
is an excellent collection of "poems old and new" to quote the
jacket, selected by a man who was himself a poet, and can
be very popular. The poems at the start of this book came
from this anthology which is not limited to black poets but
includes Burns and Wordsworth as well as many American
poets such as Frost, Lindsay, and Robinson.

487   Honey and Salt, by Carl Sandburg. Harcourt, c1963.
        $5. 50 (pb $. 50)
        RL: Varied   IL: JH-adult   BS
This collection of Sandburg's later poems seems to have a
special appeal for teenagers and young adults. It contains
quite a few love poems and his language is simple and direct.

488   I Am the Darker Brother, edited by Arnold Adoff. Illus.
        by Berry Andrews. Macmillan, c1968. $4. 95
        (Collier, pb $1. 25)
        RL: Varied   IL: JH-adult   BSMP
A superb collection of poems by black poets. More up to
date than 466, this book is popular on the bookmobile and
would be very popular in any junior or senior high school in

the hands of a teacher who loved poetry. It has brief biographies of each poet at the end of the book.

489   I Feel the Same Way, by Lilian Moore.   Illus. by
        Beatrice Darwin.   Scholastic, c1967.   pb $. 60
        RL: 3   IL: Read aloud-6   *BS
Twenty simple poems that reflect and expand a child's world.
Most of them can apply to a city child's experience.   All
children enjoy them.   Very popular.

490   I Know An Old Lady, by Rose Bonne and Alan Mills.
        Illus. by Abner Graboff.   Rand McNally, 1961. $3.95
        Scholastic, pb $. 60
        RL: 3   IL: Read aloud and K-3   BS
This rhyme about the old lady who swallowed a whole menag-
erie is popular in every area and income bracket.

491   I Like to Live in the City, by Margaret Hillert.   Illus.
        by Lillian Obligado.   Western Pub.   Little Golden
        Book, c1970. $. 39
        RL: 2-3   IL: Read aloud-4   BSMP
One of the best buys in this bibliography, this little book has
twenty-three poems and twenty-three bright (and integrated)
illustrations celebrating the good things a child can encounter
in city living.   Most of the poems describe daily experiences
and the ones about the river and the zoo and parades and the
library may inspire parents or older siblings to take children
there.   If I had my way every child in a city school in first
grade would be given this book for Christmas.

492   I See the Winds, by Kazue Mizumura.   Crowell, c1966.
        $2. 95
        RL: 3   IL: 2-5   S
A beautiful book with handsome illustrations in the Japanese
manner for free verse images known as haiku.   Can also be
used as a picture book with younger children.

493   I Think I Saw a Snail, selected by Lee Bennett Hopkins.
        Illus. by Harold James.   Crown, 1969. $3. 50
        RL: 3   IL: Read aloud-4   S
This is a book of poetry appropriate for each season whose
poems and illustrations will really speak to city children.
Many of the poems rhyme and would be fun for a child to
memorize.   It is already very popular in the New York City
School Volunteer program.

494   The Life I Live, by Lois Lenski.   Walck, 1965. $7. 50

RL: 5   IL: Read aloud-6   S
This collection of Lois Lenski's poems has many poems in
it which I have used successfully with high school students
and others that appeal to adults.   Unfortunately, the format
and illustrations are so babyish that this edition cannot be
used above fourth grade.   Let's hope it will be brought out
in paperback with, perhaps, the format and type of illustrations in Good News For Modern Man.   The price of this
hard cover has just risen to a point which really puts it out
of our market.

495 Little Brown Baby--Poems for Young People by Paul
       Lawrence Dunbar: Selections with Biographical Sketch,
       by Bertha Rodgers. Illus. by Erick Berry. Dodd,
       Mead, c1968. $3.00
       RL: Varied, but difficult   IL: Read aloud-adult BM
These lovely poems are all in dialect--a dialect still heard
all the time on the streets and in the schools of New York.
Read aloud by the right person, children love these poems;
they don't read them to themselves but are interested in the
short biography once they have heard the poems.

496 Mother, Mother, I Feel Sick, by Remy Charlip and
       Burton Supree. Illustrated by Remy Charlip. Parents,
       1966. $3.95
       RL: 3   IL: Read aloud-3   *S
This rhymed fantasy about a boy who feels sick because he
has eaten things as varied as his mother's hat, the teapot,
a bicycle, etc. will have the same fascination for children
as I Know an Old Lady.   Storytellers and children alike will
have a wonderful time with this one which has a lovely touch
of humor at the end.   This would be very popular in paperback.

497 My Box and String, by Betty Woods. Reilly & Lee,
       1963. $3.95 (Scholastic, pb $.50)
       RL: 2   IL: Read aloud-3   BS
Easy verse about a boy who learns that a playhouse is more
fun when it is shared.   Illustrated.

498 New Black Poetry, edited by Clarence Major. New
       World, 1969. $5.95 (International Pub., pb $1.95)
       RL: Varied   IL: HS-adult   BSM
A collection of poems by seventy-six young Afro-American
poets.   This poetry is mostly bitter and some of it quite difficult.   It is very definitely contemporary.

499 New Negro Poets: U.S.A., edited by Langston Hughes.
Indiana University Press, c1964. $6.95   (pb $1.95)
RL: Varied   IL: JH-adult   BSMP
This book of poetry has a short and interesting introduction
by the well-known black poet Gwendolyn Brooks and brief
biographies of each of the poets included. These should give
courage to would-be poets. I found many of the poems obscure but many others would be meaningful to a wide age
range. Many young adults coming on the bookmobile asked
for poetry by black poets and at that time we didn't have
many titles to offer. This book has many more poems and
seems to me to be a better buy than The New Black Poetry
[498]. It would not be as widely popular, however, as I Am
the Darker Brother [488].

500 The Night Before Christmas, by Clement C. Moore.
Illus. by Leonard Weisgard.   Grosset, 1954. $1.25
(pb $.39)
RL: 4   IL: Read aloud-6   BS
Children of every race and creed still love this old poem
about Christmas. Every year, we are deluged by requests
for books about Christmas.

501 On City Streets: Anthology of Poetry, edited by Nancy
Larrick.   Photographs by David Sagarin.   M. Evans,
1968. $4.95   (Bantam Pathfinder, 1969, pb $.75)
RL: Varied-mainly elementary   IL: 4-adult BSMP
A splendid collection of poems about the city chosen by young
people with the help of the editor and illustrated with excellent and appropriate photographs of city streets and situations.
Very popular. The paperback edition has an especially eye-
catching cover.

502 On These I Stand, by Countee Cullen.   Harper, c1947.
$4.95
RL: Varied: mainly adult IL: JH-adult   BMP
An anthology of the poems of the famous black poet (for whom
the Countee Cullen Library in Harlem was named) selected
by the poet himself just before his death in 1946. Some of
these will seem dated and artificial to the young of the 70s
but most will endure and be enjoyed for a long time to come.

503 One Hundred Plus American Poems, edited by Paul
Molloy.   Scholastic, 1970.   pb $.75
RL: Varied   IL: 5-adult   BSMP
A heart-warming collection of poems mostly modern but some
Longfellow, Amy Lowell and Whittier. The variety is such

that anyone must find at least one poem he would like and
most will find many. It concludes with a section of rhyming
riddles with the answers at the end for those who couldn't
guess the right word. It also includes several pages of notes
about some of the poems and poets which make the works
discussed much more meaningful. There are many photographs throughout the book, some directly illustrative of a
poem (e. g. , "Brooklyn Bridge") others evocative of the meaning. These photographs are the award winners in a photography contest run by Scholastic Magazine from 1964 to 1969.
All in all a rich book and one of the best buys in this bibliography.

504   The Panther and the Lash (Poems of Our Times), by
      Langston Hughes. Knopf, 1967. $4. 50 (pb $2. 50)
      RL: 6   IL: 6-adult   BSMP
This superb and highly readable book of poetry speaks directly
to black people of all ages about today's problems. Very
popular on the bookmobile especially with the young and in
all high schools.

505   The Pocket Book of Verse, edited by Morris E. Speare.
      Washington Square Press, 1940. pb $. 60
      RL: Varied, mainly 6 and above IL: JH-adult B
An inexpensive edition of many classic favorites.

506   Poems, illustrated by Victor Lazzaro. Grosset and
      Dunlap Early Start Wonder Book, c1965. $. 50
      RL: 1-2   IL: Read aloud-3   BS
Using only 107 words, this little book gives seven poems by
Rossetti, Stevenson and Tennyson and two traditional poems:
Star Light, Star Bright and I Had a Little Nut Tree. Gaily
illustrated with both city and country scenes, this is a real
find and very popular both with pre-school children, who
memorize the poems, and with beginning readers.

507   Poems, edited by Louis Untermeyer. Illus. by Joan
      Walsh Anglund. Western, Golden Press, 1959. pb
      $. 75
      RL: Varied, mainly 5-6 IL: 4-HS   BS
A very varied collection of fairly easy poetry especially useful because of the way the poems are arranged in categories;
for example, People; Unforgettable stories, etc.

508   Poetry from Black Africa, edited by Langston Hughes.
      Indiana University Press, c1963. $5. 95 (pb $1. 75)
      RL: Varied, mainly high IL: JH-adult   BMP

An extraordinary collection of poetry from all over Africa
ranging from anonymous oral traditional to sophisticated modern poets. Surprisingly popular in spite of the reading level.

509 **Poetry of Rock**, edited by Richard Goldstein. Bantam
    Books, c1969. pb $1
    RL: 5   IL: 5-adult   BS
A fascinating collection of rock lyrics with commentary whose
words are highly relevant to the youth of today. I was interested to find that I found most of these lyrics readable and
interesting and many are indeed poetry. This is a much
fuller collection and richer book on the whole than Favorite
Pop Rock Lyrics [481] and Pop Rock Lyrics 2 [511] and
... 3 [512] but it lacks their many photographs, which are
a real lure with junior high and high school non-readers.
All these books are excellent for introducing poetry to students who have been convinced they won't like it.

510 The Poetry of Soul, edited by A. X. Nicholas. Bantam,
    c1971. pb $1
    RL: 4   IL: 6-adult   *BSMP
A description of the black world as depicted in the lyrics of
soul music selected by the black poet, A. X. Nicholas. The
lyrics are arranged in four sections: Black World as Passion, Black World as Pain, Black World as Protest and
Black World as Celebration. I'm not sure how popular this
book will be but, if I were trying to help black children as
a teacher or librarian I'd certainly read it with interest.
I've seen teenagers go hungry to buy the record they wanted.
The music speaks to them and many a child who is illiterate will
know the words to all the top songs.

511 Poetry U.S.A.: 105 American Poems, edited by Paul
    Molloy. Scholastic, c1968. pb $.75
    RL: Varied   IL: JH-adult   BS
Another collection of American poems similar to number 503.
In this one, the print is smaller, there are far fewer photographs and the poems chosen don't seem to have as broad an
appeal. However, it is worth having for variety's sake.

512 Pop-Rock Lyrics 2; and
    Pop-Rock Lyrics 3, edited by Jerry L. Walker. Scho-
    lastic, c1970, 1971. pb $.60 each

                               BS
More pop-rock lyrics and more photographs of popular singers
and rock groups. See also 481.

514   Ramblers, Gamblers & Lovers: A Book of Poetry,
        edited by Lawrence Swinburne.   Illus. by Ferd Son-
        dern.   McGraw-Hill Reading Shelf Series, c1968.
        pb $1. 60
        RL: 4-5   IL: 4-adult   BS
An unusual collection of poems and ballads, this is bound to
have at least one selection any reader will like and most
will enjoy them all.   Among the ballads are "Casey at the
Bat, " "Frankie and Johnny" and "The Shooting of Dan
McGrew. " Among the poems are several by Stephen Vincent
Benét and Langston Hughes.   My favorite is a modern version of the Pied Piper called "Pete Piper and the Rats"
which I had never seen before and which would be very successful in any slum area.   Illustrated with good pen and ink
drawings.

515   Read-Aloud Mother Goose, illustrated by Judy Stang.
        Grosset & Dunlap Read-Aloud Wonder Book, c1957.
        pb $. 39
        RL: 3-4   IL: Read aloud-2   BS
All children need Mother Goose as a basic part of an English-
speaking heritage and many of the children the School Volunteers encounter have never heard of the rhymes.   This version has a picture on every page and is very popular.

516   Reflections on a Gift of Watermelon Pickle & Other
        Modern Verse, edited by Stephen Dunning, Edward
        Luedes and Hugh Smith.   Scott, Foresman, 1966.
        $2. 50
        RL: 5-6   IL: 5-adult   S
An unusual collection of modern poetry arranged tastefully
and with more humor than is usual.   Among the poets are
Eve Merriam, Phyllis McGinley and Dorothy Parker.   Magnificent photographs help to stimulate interest and enjoyment.

517   The Secret Place and Other Poems, by Dorothy Aldis.
        Illus. by Olivia H. H. Cole.   Putnam, c1925.   Scho-
        lastic, 1962.   pb $. 50
        RL: 3   IL: Read aloud-4   BS
A lovely poetry-picture book with an intriguing title.   The
poems are on subjects that will interest any child and it is
very much liked both as a read-aloud and as a book to read
to oneself.

518   Selections from Brian Wildsmith's Mother Goose.
        Scholastic, c1964.   pb $. 95
        RL: 3-4   IL: Read aloud-2   BS

Children love Wildsmith's illustrations. The colors are the
kind they use themselves. Too many underprivileged children are never exposed to Mother Goose rhymes although
they should be a part of every child's heritage. This book
is a good selection.

519 Some of the Days of Everett Anderson, by Lucille
      Clifton. Illus. by Evaline Ness. Holt, Rinehart,
      c1970. $3.95 (Owlet, pb $1.25)
      RL: 3   IL: Read aloud-4   BSM
Poems and pictures illustrate some of the days and thoughts
of a happy black six year old. Everett's feelings about his
father and mother and the dark are shared by all children
but this book will mean most to black children who will relish seeing themselves in a book.

520 Soulscript: Afro-American Poetry, edited by June Jor-
      dan. Doubleday Zenith, c1970. $3.95 (pb $1.95)
      RL: Varied, mainly HS   IL: JH-adult   *BSM
A very interesting selection of poetry by a noted black poet.
Most of the poets in this volume are still alive although there
are a few classic examples of Jean Toomer, Langston Hughes,
Claude McKay and Countee Cullen. With its intriguing title,
good print and poetry on contemporary events, this book will
be very popular. In fact many of the poems in it by LeRoi
Jones, Ishmael Reed and Julius Lester are already known and
well-liked in the Women's House of Detention on Riker's Island.

521 Spin a Soft Black Song: Poems for Children, by Nikki
      Giovanni. Illus. by Charles Bible. Hill & Wang,
      c1971. $5.50
      RL: 3-4   IL: Read aloud-4   *SM
Many of the situations in these poems are the universal ones
of childhood but on the whole both the poems and the illustrations are clearly meant for black children who will feel very
much at home with the book and enjoy it.

522 Story Poems, compiled by Louis Untermeyer. Washing-
      ton Square Press, 1966. $.95
      RL: Varied, but mainly HS   IL: JH-adult   BS
These story poems are difficult going for many but students
will struggle to read a poem like "The Highwayman" and
others of these stories. It is also an excellent book from
which to read aloud to younger children who will love hearing
a story poem such as "The Pied Piper."

523   That Was Summer, by Marci Ridlon.   Illus. by Mia
        Carpenter.   Follett, 1969. $3.48
        RL: 3   IL: Read aloud-6   *SMP
It is a delight to find these poems on such an easy reading
level.   They are especially aimed at city children although
many will appeal to any child.   I'm glad to note that quite
a few of the poems have humor.   Many also have a catchy
rhythm that children will enjoy.

524   This Street's for Me, by Lee Bennett Hopkins.   Illus.
        by Ann Grifalconi.   Crown, 1970. $3.50
        RL: 3   IL: Read aloud-4   *SMP
A book of poems for city children which are simple enough
to inspire children to write about their own experiences.

525   Twenty-Six [26] Ways of Looking at a Black Man and
        Other Poems, by Raymond Patterson.   Illus. by
        Lawrence F. Sykes.   Universal Pub.   Award, c1969.
        pb $.95
        RL: Varied: mainly 6   IL: 5-adult   *BSMP
This simple direct poetry on contemporary themes is often
bitter but also has dignity, passion and even some humor.
It has been an instant success on the bookmobile.

526   What Have I Got?, by Mike McClintock.   Illus. by
        Leonard Kessler.   Harper, Early I Can Read, 1961.
        $1.95
        RL: 1-2   IL: Read aloud-3   BS
A boy tells in rhyme what he has in his pocket and then
imagines what he can do: catch fish, catch a bandit; rocks
are gold, etc.   By the author of A Fly Went By [994].

527   Where Have You Been?, by Margaret Wise Brown.
        Illus. by Barbara Cooney.   Hastings, 1952. $2.50
        (Scholastic, 1968, pb $.50)
        RL: 2   IL: Read aloud-3   BS
Simple verses about familiar birds and animals, well liked
by young children.

528   Woody and Me, by Mary Neville.   Illus. by Ronni
        Solbert.   Pantheon, 1966. $2.95
        RL: 2-3   IL: 2-5   S
Excellent blank verse written the way children talk.

529   Yours Till Niagara Falls, edited by Lillian Morrison.
        Illus. by Marjorie Bauernschmidt.   Scholastic,
        (abridged).   pb $.50

RL: 4   IL: 4-HS   BS

Autograph verses and rhyming games. Easy poetry with a wide appeal to many ages. Very useful for the end of a period in reading help programs.

ADVENTURE STORIES

530 Adventure Stories, by Charles L. Coombs. Pocket
     Books, Lantern Press, c1969. pb $.50
     RL: 5-7   IL: 5-HS   BS
Adventure is where you find it according to this author.
Consequently, his stories have very varied backgrounds--
sometimes humdrum, sometimes exotic. The quality is uneven but all have some suspense and most have great appeal
to teenagers.

531 The Big Green Thing, by Miriam Schlein. Illus. by
     Elizabeth Dauber. Grosset Easy-To-Read Wonder
     Book, c1963. $.60
     RL: 2   IL: Read aloud-3   BS
A good easy-to-read story for younger children about a mysterious green object which proves to be a kite.

532 A Boy Ten Feet Tall, by W. H. Canaway. Ballantine,
     pb c1961. OP
     RL: 5   IL: JH-adult   BS
This story of an orphan boy's trek the length of Africa is
very popular. In fact, it is so much liked that the title has
become a catch word for pride and courage with the staff.
It was made into a popular movie.

533 The Bushbaby, by William Stevenson. Illus. by Victor
     Ambrus. Houghton-Mifflin, c1965. $3.95 (Bantam,
     pb $.75)
     RL: 6   IL: 6-adult   BSMP
An unusual story of a young English girl who travels through
the African wilds with a native tracker to keep her bushbaby
(monkey) safe. An exciting adventure story with many dimen-
sions--colonial, racial and generational.

534 Calico, by Virginia Lee Burton. Houghton Mifflin,
     1941. $3.40 (Scholastic, 1968, pb $.60)
     RL: 3   IL: Read aloud-4   BS
A wonderful western with colorful language and illustrations

like a comic book.   The wonder horse foils the plans of a
gang of desperadoes.   Children love the humor and suspense.
A classic.

535 Call It Courage, by Armstrong Sperry.   Illus. by Dom
     Lupo.   Macmillan, c1940. $4.50 (Collier, 1971,
     pb $.75)
     RL: 6   IL: 6-adult   BSMP
About a Polynesian boy who is determined to conquer his
fear of the sea or die, this exciting story is very much liked
by boys and men.

536 The Count of Monte Cristo, edited by W. Kottmeyer
     et al.   McGraw, c1952. $1.48
     RL: 4   IL: 4-HS   BS
The exciting story of revenge in France in the nineteenth
century in an easy version that is very popular even with
good readers.

537 Dark Sea Running, by George Morrill.   Adapted by
     Lawrence Swinburne.   Illus. by Nat White.   McGraw
     Reading Shelf Series, 1968.   pb $1.60
     RL: 5   IL: JH-adult   *BS
A spell-binding story of World War II, this concerns the
crew of a tanker whose captain goes mad from grief.   Highly
relevant right now as the atrocities in it can relate to what
has been going on in Viet Nam.

538 Fail-Safe, by Eugene Burdick and Harvey Wheeler.
     Abridged by Stephen M. Joseph.   Noble & Noble,
     Falcon, 1967.   pb $.56
     RL: 5-6   IL: 6-adult   *BS
A thriller about a future possibility.   Our bombers are mis-
takenly sent to bomb Russia.   Can they be stopped in time?
Once well into this story, no one can lay it down.   It will
be very popular.

539 The Flight of the Doves, by Walter Macken.   Macmillan,
     1968. $4.50 (Collier, pb $.95)
     RL: 5-6   IL: 5-adult   *BS
Everyone loves a chase story and this one of two children on
the run in Ireland from a cruel stepfather is a real thriller.
It was to be made into a movie.

540 Look Out for Pirates, by Iris Vinton.   Random, 1961.
     Beginner. $2.50
     RL: 3   IL: 3-6   BS

This adventure story about pirates is a slightly harder Easy-
To-Read book than most.   It is enormously popular especially
with boys.   I have used it with great success with junior high
non-readers.

541   The Most Dangerous Game.   Edited by Richard
        Connell, et al.   Berkeley, Highland Books, 1957.
        pb $.50
        RL: Adult   IL: HS-adult   B
An excellent collection of adventure stories.

542   Rat Patrol #1: Target for Tonight, by David King.
        Paperback Lib., c1967. pb $.60
        RL: 5   IL: 5-adult   BS
An exciting combat novel based on the well-known TV series.
It is interesting to see TV stimulate an interest in reading.
This title and several others relating to TV series are car-
ried by request and are popular.

543   Robin Hood of Sherwood Forest, edited by Ann McGovern.
        Illus. by Arnold Spilka.   Paperback version illustrated
        by Tracy Sugarman.   Crowell, 1968. $4.50 (Scho-
        lastic, pb $.60)
        RL: 4-5   IL: 4-HS   *BS
Favorite adventures of the legendary outlaw who robbed the
rich and fed the poor.   This easy version of the old tales
will be very popular; possibly, also with adults.

544   Shane, by Jack Schaefer.   Houghton Mifflin, c1949.
        $3.50 (Bantam Pathfinder, 1963, pb $.50)
        RL: 6   IL: 6-adult   B
A Western thriller set in the 1890s about the rivalry between
the cattlemen and the homesteaders, this was made into an
outstanding movie.   It is popular with boys and men.

545   Toby Tyler; or, Ten Weeks with a Circus, by James
        Otis. (abridged), c1930. Scholastic, 1969. pb $.75
        RL: 4-5   IL: 4-JH   *BS
Toby, an orphan whose foster home is not very happy, is
thrilled to have a chance to run off to work in a circus.   He
soon learns that most of the circus glamor is surface glamor
but he makes some good friends and finally gets back to a
home that now looks quite different from what it did before.
Most of today's children only know of circuses through television, but a circus still has great glamor.   This abridgement of an old classic has excitement and pathos and
will be popular.

546 Tom Sawyer, Detective, by Mark Twain. (pseud. of
        Samuel Clemens) (abridged, c1959) Scholastic, 1968.
        pb $.60
        RL: 6   IL: 6-JH   BS
Too bad this timeless classic is so difficult for many who
would enjoy it.   It is popular with good readers and can be
used successfully with adults in tutorial programs.   This is
only a portion of the original book.

547 Treasure Island, by Robert Louis Stevenson. Illus. by Dom
        Lupo. Doubleday, 1961. $1.75 (Scholastic, pb $.75)
        RL: 7   IL: 6-adult   B
Difficult reading for many but a good classic to carry as it
is one that children want to reach for.   This edition of the pirate
story has very good print and dramatic illustrations to lure
the reader on.

548 Up Periscope, by Robb White.   Doubleday, 1956.
        $3.75 (Scholastic, 1960, pb $.60)
        RL: 6   IL: 6-adult   B
A tense fictional story of an American submarine in the battle for the Pacific in World War II.

ANIMAL STORIES

549 Bambi, by Felix Salten.   Simon and Schuster, c1929.
        $2.95 (Grosset, Tempo, 1964, pb $.50)
        RL: 5   IL: General   BS
The life story of an orphan deer, this book is only moderately
popular but we carry it because of several requests and because adults read it as well as children.   We also like to
carry a small selection of the best in each category of literature.   Bambi is certainly one of the classics among animal
stories.   There is a great and unmet need for animal stories
of good calibre on a low reading level.   Books of the calibre
of Benjie [870] or Runaway Slave [1527] are needed for children and adults who want to read about animals but are not
looking for Disney.   When I see the number of dogs and cats
on city streets and in city homes, I realize how much people
care about animals and how good a market there would be
for the right kind of book.

550 Black Beauty to Read Aloud, by Anna Sewell.   Adapted

and abridged by Felix Sutton. Illus. by Robert
Frankenburg. Grosset Read-Aloud Wonder Book,
1960. pb $.49
    RL: 4   IL: 3-JH   BS
This classic horse story is very old-fashioned but has never
lost its appeal. Children who have never seen a horse except on TV borrow this regularly. It is both easy and sentimental and very popular.

551 Bristle Face, by Zachary Ball. Holiday, 1962. $3.95
     (Scholastic pb $.60)
    RL: 6   IL: 4-7   BS
The story of a boy in Tennessee and his ugly looking mutt
who saves him from a panther. The interest level of most
dog stories seems to be below the reading level, leading to
frustration. We carry a few by request but long to have
some easy ones.

552 Broken Fang, by R. G. Montgomery. Illus. by Carl
     Ballantine. Scholastic, 1935. pb OP
    RL: 6   IL: 4-7   B
Story of a boy's trust in his dog. See comment on 551 above.

553 The Call of the Wild and White Fang, by Jack London.
     Bantam Pathfinder, 1967. pb $.50
    RL: 7   IL: 4-adult   B
The classic story of a pet dog which is kidnapped and who
learns to survive in the wilds of Alaska. This and the additional story have been loved for years but their reading
level is far too high for most of the bookmobile's clientele
and for the students whom the School Volunteers are helping.
See 554 and 555 below.

554 The Call of the Wild, by Jack London. Adapted by
     Warren Halliburton. McGraw-Hill Reading Shelf,
     1968. pb $1.60
    RL: 6   IL: 4-adult   BS
555 The Call of the Wild, by Jack London. Adapted by
     Versa Plummer. Noble & Noble Falcon, 1968.
     pb $.75
    RL: 5   IL: 4-adult   BS
I am grateful for these two adaptations of Jack London's
famous stories [see 553]. 555 has been quite popular on
the bookmobile and in the School Volunteer Programs. An
easy version such as this can lead a poor reader to attempt
other stories by the same author once his interest has been
aroused.

556 The Curious Cow, by Esther K. Meeks. Illus. by Mel
    Pekarsky. Follett, 1960. $1.25
    RL: 2-3   IL: Read aloud-3   BS
A humorous story of a cow whose curiosity leads her into
adventures and misadventures. Also available in French and
German. See Book List classification 4.

557 The Digging-est Dog, by Al Perkins. Illus. by Eric
    Gurney. Random House Beginner Book, 1967. $1.95
    RL: 3   IL: Read aloud-4   BS
A silly but popular easy-to-read book about a dog who doesn't
know how to dig. Not exactly the easy animal story I had in
mind but it is borrowed by young dog lovers.

558 Dog Stories, edited by David Thomas. Pocket Books,
    Lantern Press, 1964. pb $.50
    RL: 5-7   IL: 4-adult   BS
Fourteen very varied dog stories. Dog lovers who are good
readers will devour all these stories. If they are used in a
tutoring program, it would be wise for the tutor to read the
book first and help the student to choose a story which fits
his interest and reading level. Some of the stories have
real quality and some don't.

559 Flip, by Wesley Dennis. Illustrated by the author.
    Viking Seafarer, c1962. pb $.65
    RL: 3   IL: Read aloud-4   BS
Flip, the colt, finds his courage and jumps the brook which
has always been too much for him before. Very much liked
and even young children seem to get the analogy and gain
confidence. Lovely black and white illustrations.

560 Gentle Ben, by Walt Morey. Illus. by John Schoenherr.
    Dutton, 1965. $3.95 (Grosset, Tempo, pb $.60)
    RL: 5-6   IL: 4-HS   B
A well-written story of a boy and his pet Kodiak bear, this
is popular because of the TV series based on the book. However, it can stand on its own merits and is also borrowed by
young people and adults who have never heard of the series.
Excellent black and white illustrations.

561 Gertie the Duck, by Nicholas P. Georgiady and Louis G.
    Romano. Illus. by Dayra Wilson. Follett Beginning
    To Read Book, 1966. $1.25
    RL: 2   IL: Read aloud-3   BS
Gertie the duck lays her eggs in such an awkward spot that
it changes people's lives. Not only do the babies hatch but

people learn to slow down and be friendly for their sake.
Small children find this a very satisfying story. Also available in Spanish. See Book List Classification 4.

562 Gray Wolf, by Rutherford Montgomery. Houghton
     Mifflin, c1949. OP (Scholastic, 1963, pb $.60)
     RL: 5   IL: 5-HS   BS
An exciting adventure story of the king of the wolf pack by a
Western writer who is popular with teenagers.

563 Great Stories About Animals, edited by Eleanor M.
     Edwards. Lion, 1968. $3.99 (pb $1)
     RL: 5   IL: 5-adult   BS
An interesting collection of stories about animals on not too
high a reading level.

564 Grizzwold, by Syd Hoff. Harper I Can Read Book, 1963.
     $2.50
     RL: 2   IL: Read aloud-3   BS
Grizzwold is a bear who loses his forest home because all
the trees are cut down but finally finds a refuge in a National
Park. Very popular and can be used to introduce ecological
studies.

565 The Hole in the Hill, by Marion Seyton. Illus. by
     Leonard Shortall. Follett, 1959. $1.25
     RL: 2-3   IL: Read aloud-4   BS
The prehistoric Stone family search for a pet. Children love
Shortall's cartoon-like illustrations.

566 The Incredible Journey, by Sheila Burnford. Illus. by
     Carl Burger. Bantam, c1961. pb $.60
     RL: 6   IL: 6-adult   B
A sentimental animal story which is popular with a wide age
range.

567 Indian Two Feet and His Horse, by Margaret Friskey.
     Illus. by Ezra Jack Keats. Scholastic, c1959. pb
     $.50
     RL: 2   IL: Read aloud-4   BSM
With superb illustrations by Ezra Jack Keats, Two Feet's
determination to have a horse will interest many children
who care nothing for horses.

568 Joey's Cat, by Robert Burch. Illus. by Don Freeman.
     Viking, 1969. $3.50
     RL: 2-3   IL: Read aloud-4   SMP

Joey's mother finally permits his cat and kittens in the house.
A family story with credible characters on a popular subject.

569 Lassie Come Home, by Eric Knight. Grosset, Tempo,
     1960. pb $.60
     RL: 7   IL: 4-adult   B
This moving story of a boy and a dog in Scotland leads to
much frustration. Everyone who sees it assumes that it is
based on the TV series which was named for it and rushes
to borrow it. In almost every case, the vocabulary and the
Scotch dialect defeat them. I am therefore grateful for 570
below.

570 Lassie Come Home, by Eric Knight. Edited by Doris
     Duenewald. Grosset, 1970. $1.50
     RL: 3-4   IL: 4-adult   BS
A valuable adaptation of 569, above, which makes the story
available to the many children who cannot read the original.

571 Little Vic, by Doris Gates. Illus. by Kate Seredy.
     Viking, 1951. $3.95 (Washington Square Press,
     Archway, 1968, pb $.50)
     RL: 5-6   IL: 5-adult   BSMP
The courage of Pony, the black boy hero of this story, in
the face of vicissitude and discrimination, makes this story
of a race horse into a story of wide appeal even to those
who have never seen a horse except on TV.

572 The Lonesome Bear, by Harrison Kinney. Illus. by
     Howard Price. Scholastic, c1949. (pb 1968 $.60)
     RL: 4-5   IL: 4-6   BS
A family "adopts" a friendly bear who becomes a hero. A
silly story but children like it, especially boys.

573 Momo's Kittens, by Mitsu and Taro Yashima. Viking,
     c1961. $3.50 (Seafarer, 1971, pb $.75)
     RL: 3   IL: Read aloud-2   *BSMP
A picture book about a little girl and her kittens which is
listed for its superior illustrations and because the family
involved is a Japanese one in Los Angeles. There are increasing numbers of Japanese children in the city schools on
both coasts. Any child who likes cats will love this book.

574 No Bark Dog, by Stanford Williamson. Illus. by Tom
     O'Sullivan. Follett Beginning To Read Series, 1962.
     $1.25
     RL: 2   IL: Read aloud-3   BS

Children like this silly story about a dog who doesn't know
how to bark and the low vocabulary and high repetition level
fill a need in reading skills.

575 Old Whirlwind: A Davy Crockett Story, by Elizabeth
     Coatsworth. Scholastic, 1964. pb $.50
     RL: 4   IL: 4-HS   BS
A good dog story as well as easy-to-read historical fiction.

576 Old Yeller, by Fred Gipson. Illus. by Carl Burger.
     Harper, c1956. $4.37 (pb $.60)
     RL: 6   IL: 5-adult   BS
An excellent dog and family story, made famous by a Disney
movie that has wide appeal.

577 Pet Show, by Ezra Jack Keats. Macmillan, c1971.
     $4.95
     RL: 2-3   IL: Read aloud-3   *BSMP
Archie's cat (the hero of Hi Cat [392]) finally wins a blue
ribbon in the pet show. The story of this one is slight and
rather silly but the illustrations of inner city life are, as
usual with Mr. Keats, superb, and children love them.

578 Project Cat, by Nellie Burchardt. Illus. by Fermin
     Rocker. Watts, 1966. $3.50 (Scholastic, pb $.50)
     RL: 4   IL: 3-JH   BSMP
Girls who live in a housing project take care of a homeless
cat and scheme to adopt her in spite of project rules. This
is popular with boys as well as girls and especially popular
with children from housing projects who long for dogs and
cats and are not allowed to have them.

579 The Red Pony, by John Steinbeck. Illus. by Wesley
     Dennis. Viking, c1938. $3.50 (Bantam Pathfinder,
     1960, pb $.60)
     RL: 6-7   IL: 6-adult   BS
This story of a boy and his pony has many dimensions and
a lot of insight into human nature and the gap between generations. It is a book which will be read for years to come
and appeals to adults as well as to boys and girls. It is
especially valuable in School Volunteer high school programs
because it is on all the high school reading lists and is both
more interesting and easier than most for a poor reader.

580 Reggie's No-Good Bird, by Nellie Burchardt. Illus. by
     Harold Berson. Watts, 1967. $3.50 (Washington
     Square Press, Archway, pb $.60)

RL: 4   IL: 3-JH   BSMP
Reggie, the project troublemaker, adopts a bird he has hurt
thoughtlessly and finds himself doing all sorts of things for
his pet.   The picture on the dust jacket of the hard cover
edition could be any one of a dozen places in Bedford-
Stuyvesant.

581   The Several Tricks of Edgar Dolphin, by Nathaniel
      Benchley.   Illus. by Mamoru Funai.   Harper I Can
      Read, c1970. $2.50
      RL: 2   IL: Read aloud-JH   BS
The story of a clever dolphin who figured out how to escape
from his tank into the sea.   A recent series for children
about dolphins on TV has now interested many children who
have never seen the sea or the ocean and its inhabitants.

582   Skip, by Aileen N. Fisher.   Scholastic, c1958.   pb $.60
      RL: 5   IL: 4-HS   BS
The moving dilemma of a girl whose dog becomes blind and
who protects him and cares for him at the sacrifice of her
own plans and desires.   This has great appeal to dog lovers
and also to high school girls who are interested in the heroine.

583   Star of Wild Horse Canyon, by Clyde Robert Bulla.
      Illus. by Grace Paull.   Crowell, c1953. $3.95
      (Scholastic, 1966, pb $.50)
      RL: 3   IL: 4-7   BS
Large easy-to-read type tells of a boy who earns and trains
his own horse.   Not as popular as when westerns were all
over the TV screen but still worth carrying.

584   The Story About Ping, by Marjorie Flack.   Illus. by
      Kurt Wiese.   Viking, c1933. $2.50 (Seafarer, 1970,
      pb $.95)
      RL: 3-4   IL: Read aloud-3   BS
A satisfying story about a little duck who lives on a Chinese
riverboat, this book is much loved by children from three
through third grade.   An excellent read-aloud for a group of
children.

585   Surprise in the Tree, by Sara Asheron.   Illus. by
      Susan Perl.   Grosset Easy-to-Read Wonder Book,
      1965. $.69
      RL: 2   IL: Read aloud-4   BS
A popular story about a boy who tries to rescue a kitten and
winds up having to be rescued himself.

586   Too Many Bozos, by Lilian Moore.   Illus. by Susan
       Perl.   Golden Read-It-Yourself Book, c1960. $1.95
       RL: 2-3   IL: Read aloud-3   BS
A lovely humorous story of a boy who is determined to have
a pet.   Excellent read-aloud since adults can enjoy it also.

587   Too Many Dogs, by Ramona Dupré.   Illus. by Howard
       Baer.   Follett, 1960. $1.59
       RL: 2-3   IL: Read aloud-4   BS
Two family dachshunds bring home another dog and her nine
puppies.   An exceptionally easy to read dog story.

588   Too Many Pockets, by Dorothy Levenson.   Illus. by
       Ruth Wood.   Grosset Easy-To-Read Wonder, 1963.
       $.59
       RL: 2-3   IL: Read aloud-3   BS
This story about a kangaroo and her baby is very popular.

589   Waggles and the Dog Catcher, by Marion Belden Cook.
       Illus. by John Peterson.   Scholastic, c1951. pb 1963 $.60
       RL: 2-3   IL: Read aloud-4   BS
Waggles is loveable whether he is white and black or black
and white and children enjoy his triumph when he eludes the
dog catcher and finds a home.

590   What Mary Jo Wanted, by Janice May Udry.   Illus.
       by Eleanor Mill.   Whitman, 1968. $3.75
       RL: 3   IL: Read aloud-5   BSMP
Children enjoy learning how Mary Jo got what she wanted (a
dog).   The book does not minimize the responsibilities of
having a dog, an important matter in many families.   The
illustrations are heartwarming.

591   What Whiskers Did, by Ruth Carroll..   Scholastic,
       c1965. pb $.60
       RL: No Text   IL: Pre-school-4   BS
Enchanting pictures tell the story of a runaway puppy who becomes involved with a fox and a rabbit family and then finally
returns to his forlorn master.   This is loved by children and
is also a wonderful conversation piece for a one-to-one tutorial situation.

ANTHOLOGIES

592 <u>American Negro Short Stories</u>, edited by John Henrik
     Clarke.   Hill & Wang, American Century Series,
     c1969.   pb $1.95
     RL: Varied   IL: HS-adult   BMP
An anthology of short stories by Negro authors written during
the last seventy-five years.   They vary in quality but almost
all reflect the bitterness the plight of the American Negro
has inspired.   Many are therefore strong meat.   This book
moves slowly on the bookmobile but is much appreciated by
the adults who borrow it.

593 <u>Arrow Book of Famous Stories</u>, by James Baldwin.
     Scholastic, 1963.   pb OP
     RL: 4   IL: 4-adult   BS
A useful collection of famous tales.   Short stories like these
are especially helpful in reading help programs since a story
can be finished and discussed in one session, giving the pupil a sense of accomplishment.

594 <u>Best Short Shorts</u>, edited by Eric Berger.   Scholastic,
     1958.   pb $.60
     RL: 6   IL: JH-adult   BS
Thirty-five fast moving stories contained in two to four pages,
this is excellent material for giving variety to pupils in reading help sessions.   It is also popular on the bookmobile with
teenagers and adults.

595 <u>The Black American Experience</u>, edited by Frances S.
     Freedman.   Bantam, c1970.   pb $.95
     RL: Varied   IL: JH-adult   BSMP
Arranged in five sections starting with "The Uprooting" from
Africa and continuing to "We March" in the present day, this
valuable anthology of black literature presents a moving picture of black courage and talent.   Of the many books of black
literature on this list, this is the richest and most compre-
hensive.   A must for public and high school libraries.

596 <u>The Black Hero</u>, edited by Alma Murray and Robert
     Thomas.   Photographs by John Shearer.   The Scho-
     lastic Black Literature Series, c1970.   pb $1.80
     RL: Varied   IL: JH-adult   *BSMP
This book was published in cooperation with the Los Angeles
City Schools and is intended as a textbook.   However, it has
an attractive appearance and many photographs.   It contains

poems, essays and selections from fiction by black authors
which will interest many people.   It is unfortunate that the
very first selection, "The Wonderful World of Law and
Order" by Ossie Davis, is an essay on a very high reading
level so that an independent but not very skilled reader would
undoubtedly become discouraged without realizing that there
are many selections he would enjoy in the balance of the
book.

597   Black on Black, edited by Arnold Adoff.   Macmillan,
        c1970. $5.95   (Collier, pb $.95)
        RL: Varied   IL: 6-adult   *BSMP
An anthology of writings by black Americans dealing mainly
with modern times although there are some excerpts from
the writings of Frederick Douglass.   This book is one that
poor readers will stretch for if introduced to it by excerpts
read aloud.   Although much of it is understandably bitter,
nevertheless the total effect is a positive one.   As an American, I am proud that these writers are fellow Americans.
With so many anthologies appearing just now, there is necessarily some duplication.   However, although the authors
in this volume are the same as in many others, the selections are very different from most.   I found Baldwin's
"Unnameable Objects, Unspeakable Crimes" new to me and
very powerful indeed.

598   Black Voices: An Anthology of Afro-American Litera-
        ture, edited by Abraham Chapman.   St. Martin's
        Press, 1968. $8.50   (New American Library, Men-
        tor, pb $1.50)
        RL: Adult   IL: HS-adult   BSMP
Another splendid collection of fiction, autobiography, poetry
and essays by Afro-American authors.   This book should be
on all reading lists for high school students.   Unfortunately,
the print of the paperback edition is exceptionally small which
will inhibit many people from enjoying it.

599   The Black Woman, edited by Toni Cade [Bambara].
        New American Library, Signet, c1970.   pb $.95
        RL: Adult   IL: HS-adult   BSM
Another very varied collection, this time about and by black
women--mainly young women.   Most of the essays are very
sophisticated and will mean little to the average black woman
borrower on the bookmobile or the average high school girl
in a Volunteer program.   However, some of the stories and
poems are very moving and the whole book breathes a spirit
of rebellion against conditions that exist today for black

women, a spirit that is increasingly evident in Harlem and
Bedford-Stuyvesant.

600 Christmas Gif', compiled by Charlemae Rollins.   Illus.
     by Tom O'Sullivan.   Follett, c1963. $4.95
     RL: Varied   IL: Universal   BM
An anthology of Christmas poems, songs and stories written
by and about blacks.   This is much more than a seasonal
book, however.   Stories like the Black Madonna are relevant
and moving at any time of the year.   The line drawings add
depth to the text.

601 Courage, edited by Stephen Dunning and Dwight L. Bur-
     ton.   Scholastic Literature Anthology, c1960.   pb $1
     RL: Varied   IL: 6-adult   *BS
Thirty-one stories and poems highlighting various kinds of
courage both physical and mental.   Good reading for an individual and also good reading aloud for a group.   See 617
for comment on the Scholastic Literature Anthologies.

602 Crossroad Series (Breaking Loose, In Other's Eyes,
     Playing It Cool, Tomorrow Won't Wait).   Noble &
     Noble, various dates.   pb $1.48 each
     RL: 5-6   IL: 5-HS   S
Relevant themes for older students in short selections ranging
from poetry to excerpts from plays.   Well liked and not a
textbook format.

603 Famous Stories, edited by Edward W. Dolch, Marguerite
     P. Dolch and Beulah F. Jackson.   Illus. by Yolande
     Cuypens-Fransen.   Garrard, 1955. $2.69
     RL: 4   IL: 2-6   S
The simple vocabulary makes these short stories very acceptable for short reading periods.   Children feel secure
with these stories and find them interesting.

604 The Funny Bone, edited by Susan Gamer.   Illus. by
     Renzo Bartolomucci.   McGraw-Hill, Reading Shelf
     Series, c1970.   pb $1.84
     RL: 4-5   IL: 5-adult   *BSMP
This is an aptly named book.   As the reader will recall, if
you hit your funny bone, the pain is exquisite.   This collection of short stories is full of that ironic pain.   Some selections are better than others but there is great variety and
a student can be led from one of these excerpts to reading
the book from which it came.

605 <u>Gateway Series</u>. Macmillan, all c1966. pb $1.36 each.
     <u>A Family Is a Way of Feeling</u>, edited by Marjorie B.
     Smiley, Florence B. Freedman, and John J. Marca-
     tante; <u>Who Am I?</u>, edited by Smiley, Domenica
     Paterno, and Betsy Kaufman; <u>Coping</u>, edited by
     Smiley, Freedman, Jacqueline Titles, and Marcatante;
     <u>Stories in Song and Verse</u>, edited by Smiley, Richard
     Corbin, and Marcatante.
These four books contain a very diversified collection of prose
and poetry which really excites junior and senior high school
students. Some of the material is very unusual such as
poems written by other junior and senior high students in
New York public schools. Other material, such as excerpts
from Jackie Robinson's biography are so interesting that the
student becomes eager to read the whole book from which
the excerpt came. The books have many interesting photographs. These books have so much to offer the general public as well as students that it would be great to have them
available and marketed but omitting on the cover and title
page any mention of an English literature and language arts
program. I know many people on the bookmobile who would
borrow or buy them with eagerness. Two more books in the
series on RL:8 and RL:9 have been published but the School
Volunteers have not yet tried them out.

606 <u>The Gift of Christmas</u>, edited by Norma Ruedi Ains-
     worth and Miriam Lee. Illus. by Ethel Gold. Scho-
     lastic, c1965. pb $.50
     RL: 4-5   IL: 4-adult   BSMP
A rich collection of Christmas stories and poems including
the "Legend of the Black Madonna." Illustrated in color.

607 <u>Impact Series</u>, edited by Charlotte K. Brooks. Holt,
     c1968. pb $1.60 to $1.84
     RL: 5-6   IL: 5-HS   SMP
     <u>At Your Own Risk</u>, edited by Lawana Trout and Allan
     D. Pierson; <u>Cities</u>, edited by Edith G. Stull; <u>I've
     Got a Name</u>, edited by Charlotte K. Brooks and
     Lawana Trout; <u>Larger Than Life</u>, edited by Edith G.
     Stull.
Another varied series of anthologies of stories and poems
and photographs with great variety. <u>At Your Own Risk</u> and
<u>Cities</u> could well interest adults; <u>Larger Than Life</u> is a
mixture of folk and fairy stories and <u>I've Got a Name</u> is
somewhat more for adolescents. The School Volunteers have
found this series useful and popular.

608 <u>Junk Day on Juniper Street</u>, by Lilian Moore. Illus.
     by Arnold Lobel. Parents, 1969. $3.95
     RL: 2-3   IL: Read aloud-4   *SMP
Seven easy-to-read stories, many of them with humor, this
is a valuable addition to the easy-to-read library.

609 <u>Moments of Decision</u>, edited by Helen F. Olson. Illus.
     by Orin Kincade. Scholastic Literature Anthology,
     1961. pb $.60
     RL: Varied: mainly 6   IL: 6-HS   *SP
Another Scholastic literature anthology, this has a rich collection of poems and stories including that old favorite <u>The
Lady or the Tiger</u>. The book is excellent for an individual
reader and many of the stories and poems are also excellent
for reading aloud and for group discussions.

610 <u>The Outnumbered</u>, edited by Charlotte Brooks. Dela-
     corte, c1967. $4.95 (Dell Laurel Leaf, pb $.50)
     RL: Varied: 6 and up   IL: JH-adult   *BSMP
Edited by the supervising director of English in the Washington public schools, this uniquely valuable book has thirteen
stories and essays about minority groups in America. It
includes Willa Cather on the Bohemian immigrants, Benét on
the Irish, Longfellow and Malamud on the Jews and stories
about Assyrians, Indians, Italians and Puerto Ricans as well
as blacks. It serves to remind the reader that, except for
the Indians, we have all been immigrants once and that it is
essential that we all have respect for the other man and his
heritage. It concludes with the Langston Hughes poem, "Let
America Be America Again." A great job of selecting pieces
and a book that could really affect people's lives if all junior
high students were exposed to it.

611 <u>The People Downstairs and Other City Stories</u>, by
     Rhoda Bacmeister. Illus. by Paul Galdone. Coward-
     McCann, 1964. $3.97   BSMP
This invaluable book has sixteen stories and several poems
about city children of all kinds, black and white and healthy
and handicapped and Catholic and Protestant. It is very well
liked in the School Volunteer program and would be popular
on the bookmobile in paperback.

612 <u>Personal Code</u>, edited by Robert E. Shafer and Verlene
     C. Bernd. Illus. by Gabe Keith. Scholastic Litera-
     ture Anthology, c1961. pb $1
     RL: 6-7   IL: 6-adult   *SMP

A varied and thought provoking collection of stories and one
or two poems all of which deal with the subject of integrity.
This is a wonderful collection for a tutoring program in a
junior high or high school.

613   Read-Aloud Cowboy and Indian Stories, compiled by
      Oscar Weigle. Illus. by William Wiesner. Grosset
      Read-Aloud Wonder Book, c1959. pb $.49
      RL: 3-4   IL: 3-6   BS
Cowboys and Indians are not as popular as they were but they
still have enough fans to make it worth carrying this title at
this price.

614   Read-Aloud Train Stories, illustrated by Art Seiden.
      Grosset Read-Aloud Wonder Book, c1957. pb $.49
      RL: 3-4   IL: 3-6   B
Trains still seem to have their loyal fans even in a generation which rarely sees a track except for the subway.

615   Rescue Stories, edited by A. L. Furman. Pocket Books,
      Lantern Press, 1964. pb $.50
      RL: 6   IL: 6-HS   BS
A collection of short stories to do with the theme of rescuing
people. There is great variety and suspense. Many poor
readers will enjoy a short story who are too scared to tackle
a whole book.

616   Right On: An Anthology of Black Literature, edited by
      Bradford Chambers and Roberta Moon. New American
      Library, Mentor, c1970. pb $.95
      RL: Varied   IL: 6-adult   *BSMP
This collection of plays, poetry and fiction is a powerful
statement about the oppression and suffering of the black people in America. Except for the two poems "For My People"
and "If We Must Die," virtually all the material is different
from that of the other anthologies in this section. Although
some of the selections are difficult reading, most are not
and in any event, the interest in the subject matter will overcome any reading problems for most black students. Divided
into three sections, Oppression, Resistance and Black Is
Beautiful, the last of which is the weakest of the three. The
book would have a better balance and more effect if some of
the more humorous and positive black literature which exists
had been included.

617   Scholastic Literature Anthologies. Various editors,
      various dates. pb $1 each

RL: Varied   IL: 6-adult   SMP

There are twelve titles in this series. I have investigated and used the following with success: Family, Moments of Decision, Personal Code, Small World, Success and Survival. For individual comments, see under titles in this section. The series as a whole is so valuable and has so much to offer that I am sure there would be a good market for them among the general public if they had really eye-catching covers and the words "Scholastic Literature Unit" were left off.

618 Small World, edited by Robert Smith, Jane Sprague and Stephen Dunning. Scholastic Literature Anthology, c1964. pb $.60
      RL: 6-7   IL: 6-adult   *SMP
Short stories and essays focusing on understanding peoples of many cultures in a diminishing world. Well done and not preachy. Pen and ink illustrations. See comment on Personal Code [612].

619 Stories by Jesse Stuart, adapted by Lawrence Swinburne. Illus. by F. Sondern. McGraw-Hill Reading Shelf Series, 1969. pb $1.60
      RL: 4-5   IL: 6-adult   *BS
An easy adaptation of entertaining stories of the Kentucky mountaineers.

620 Success, edited by Dr. Robert Shafer and Verlene Bernd. Scholastic Literature Anthology, c1964. pb $1
      RL: Varied   IL: JH-adult   BSMP
This is a fascinating collection of stories, some true and some fiction, which lead the reader to try to make his own definition of what constitutes success. It has very high reader interest. The last story in it, "Flowers for Algernon," which was published previously and separately, has been a surefire success with high school students of every reading level.

621 Survival, edited by James R. Squire. Scholastic Literature Anthology, c1960. pb $1
      RL: Varied   IL: JH-adult   *SM
This is a highly varied collection of stories to do with one kind or another of survival. A book like this can be very valuable in a tutorial program if the tutor reads it first and suggests titles that individual students will enjoy. Many inner city students will feel encouraged by "Truth Is Beauty,"

one of the stories and almost anyone will thrill to the stories
of Eddie Rickenbacker and Admiral Byrd.

622   Take the Short Way Home and Other Stories, edited by
        John Durham. Illus. by Robert Swanson.   McGraw-
        Hill, City Limits Series, 1968.   pb $1.60
        RL: 5   IL: 6-adult   *BSMP
Six spellbinding stories of great variety and appeal.   Anyone
who reads the first story will want to read the rest and all
are thought-provoking.

623   The Unfinished Journey, by Theresa Oakes and M.
        Jerry Weiss.   McGraw-Hill, c1967. $5.95
        RL: Varied, 5-up   IL: JH-adult   SMP
An excellent collection of plays, poetry, essays and fiction
dealing with the experience of minority groups in America.
The format is textbook-like with questions after each selection and it is therefore not suitable for the bookmobile but
the material is so thought-provoking that it is well worth
having for use in a one-to-one situation or for group discussion among good readers at the high school age.   The School
Volunteers have found the first selection, Me Candido, a play
about a homeless Puerto Rican boy, excellent for motivating
poor readers who are caught by Candido's plight and dignity.
The Outnumbered [610] and We Too Belong [625] are on the
same theme but, with one exception, are of entirely different
material.

624   Voices of Man.   Addison-Wesley, c1969.   pb
                                                      *SMP
        Homecoming, edited by G. M. Goff (intended for
        grade 10);   This Is Just to Say, edited by Goff
        (grade 10);   I Have a Dream, edited by B. J. Kinnick
        and J. Perry (grade 11);   Let Us Be Men, edited by
        Kinnick and Perry (grade 11);   Eyes of Love, edited
        by V. L. Medeiros, Jr. (grade 12);   The Drinking
        Gourd, edited by V. L. Medeiros, Jr. and D. B.
        Boettcher (intended for grade 12).
This is an interesting series designed to create an English
literature course for the high school years out of modern
materials which will seem relevant to todays students, especially those in ghetto areas.   It contains poetry, plays,
essays and fiction and has photographs and reproductions of
modern art.   The publisher has designated the grade for
which the various volumes are intended.   The School Volunteers have used selections from all the different volumes
with junior high and high school students.   The reading level

is varied, mainly five and up but the interest level is high
enough to motivate a poor reader.   This is a valuable series
somewhat similar to Macmillan's Gateway Series [605] and
Holt's Impact Series [607].

625   We, Too Belong, edited by Mary Turner.   Dell, Laurel
        Leaf, c1969.   pb $.60
        RL: Varied: mostly 6-7   IL: 6-adult   *BSMP
Another anthology about minorities on the same lines as The
Outnumbered [610] and Unfinished Journey [623] and again
with virtually no repetition of the material in those books.
This collection doesn't seem to me to be quite so effective
but it has many good things in it and will be well liked.

626   Young and Black in America, compiled by Rae Pace
        Alexander.   Random, c1970. $3.95
        RL: Varied   IL: 6-adult   SMP
Eight men and women (Frederick Douglass, Richard Wright,
Daisy Bates, Malcolm X, Jimmy Brown, Anne Moody, Harry
Edwards and David Parks) tell in vivid language what it meant
to them to be young and black in America.   Some of these
excerpts from autobiographies are available in other collections but the way they have been grouped here with new and
current material (Jimmy Brown and David Parks) has a telling effect.   This book is already very popular in inner city
schools.

CAREER STORIES

627   A Cap for Mary Ellis, by Hope Newell.   Harper, c1953.
        $3.50 (Berkley Highland, 1967, pb $.50)
        RL: 5-6   IL: 5-HS   BSMP
The story of two black girls who are the first of their race
to attend a previously segregated nursing school, this book
has a lot of action on many fronts.   Although it is nearly
twenty years old, it does not seem very dated since hospital
stories of life and death and courage and learning are timeless.   It is very popular with the many girls who dream of
becoming nurses.

628   Fire on Sun Mountain, by Molly C. Gorelick and Jean
        B. Graeber.   Ritchie, 1967. $2.95
        RL: 3   IL: 4-HS   *S

This is a fictionalized account of the work of a helicopter
pilot helping to fight a dangerous brush fire in California.
The controlled vocabulary is stilted but the action is so exciting that it will carry most students along. Illustrated with
photographs of fire-fighting situations.

629 Hit Parade of Nurse Stories, edited by Eleanor Van
     Zandt. Scholastic, 1964. pb $.50
     RL: 6   IL: 5-HS   BSMP
An interesting collection on a very popular subject.

630 Hold Fast to Your Dreams, by Catherine Blanton.
     Messner, 1955. $3.79 (Washington Square Press,
     Archway, pb $.60)
     RL: 5   IL: 5-HS   BSMP
This book was the cause of a hot debate among the bookmobile
staff. It tells the story of a black girl who wants to make
dancing her career and who is very talented. It also tells
of the injustice and discrimination she encounters, of the
loyal friends who fight for her and of her eventual triumph.
The book was included in our list by majority vote but feelings
ran high. One person felt that it would probably depress a
girl in a similar situation. Others felt that the fact that justice won out in the end was the most important factor and
that reading about the difficulties incurred would armor a
child who later encountered them. It is very popular with
teenage girls.

631 Mary Ellis, Student Nurse, by Hope Newell. Harper,
     c1958. $3.79 (Berkley, Highland, 1968, pb $.50)
     RL: 5-6   IL: 5-HS   BSMP
This is a sequel to A Cap for Mary Ellis [627] and has great
appeal especially to black girls interested in becoming nurses
as many of them are in elementary and junior high school.
There is a real need for more multi-ethnic books (both fact
and fiction) in this subject area.

632 Nancy Kimball, Nurse's Aide, by Carli Laklan. Illus.
     by John N. Barron. Doubleday, Signal, 1962. $3.50
     RL: 4   IL: 6-HS   BS
Nancy Kimball learns about hospitals and nursing and does a
lot of growing up in the process. A good book for motivating
junior high school girls who are interested in the field of
nursing.

633 Nat Dunlap, Jr., Medic, by Evelyn L. Fiore. Illus.
     by Dick Kohfield. Doubleday, Signal, 1964. $3.50

RL: 4   IL: 6-HS   BS
A good story which describes what life is like for a beginning
doctor.

634 On Your Toes, Susie!, by Lee Wyndham.   Illus. by
     Jane Miller.   Scholastic, 1958.   pb $.60
     RL: 5   IL: 4-JH   BS
Girls seem interested in ballet stories and ballet even in deprived areas.

635 Serving in the Peace Corps, by Carli Laklan.   Double-
     day, Signal, 1970. $3.50   (Semaphore pb $1.75)
     RL: 4   IL: 6-adult   *BSMP
This fictional account of three girls on three different assign-
ments in the Peace Corps will be very popular and should
help to motivate many teenagers.   The photographs of Peace
Corps volunteers in the field make the stories real.

636 Student Nurse, by Bernard and Marjorie Palmer.   Moody
     Press, 1960.   pb $.60
     RL: 4-5   IL: 4-JH   BS
A good fictional story on nurses' training.

637 Susie and the Ballet Family, by Lee Wyndham.   Illus.
     by Jane Miller.   Scholastic, c1955.   pb $.60
     RL: 5   IL: 5-JH   BS
A sequel to On Your Toes, Susie! [634] and an equally good
story for would-be ballet stars.

FAIRY TALES, FOLK TALES, MYTHOLOGY

638 The Adventures of Silly Billy, by Tamara Kitt.   Illus.
     by J. Elgin.   Grosset Easy-to-Read Wonder Book,
     c1961. $.59
     RL: 2-3   IL: Pre-school-non-reading 7 BS
Based on a familiar folk tale;   very popular because of the
upside down picture on the cover, this has humor and encourages the reader to feel that he is more intelligent than
the people in the story.

639 The Adventures of Spider, by Joyce Cooper Arkhurst.
     Little, c1964. $3.95   (Scholastic, 1970, pb $.75)
     RL: 4   IL: Read aloud-JH   *BSMP

An exceptionally useful book of African folk tales because
they are well told and relatively easy to read.   Children can
read and enjoy these themselves and a reading help volunteer
can use a story and finish it in one session.   Many of the
stories have humor and the illustrations are entertaining as
well as colorful.

640   Adventures of the Greek Heroes, by Mollie McLean and
          Anne Wiseman.   Illus. by Wirold T. Mars.   Houghton
          Mifflin, c1961. $4.25
          RL: 3-4   IL: 3-adult   S
Eighteen of the Greek myths told on a very easy reading
level.   These stories of Hercules and Perseus and Theseus
and Jason have illustrations that resemble a Greek frieze
and the format is suitable for any age.   They are very popular with children from the fifth grade through high school.

641   African Myths and Legends, edited by Kathleen Arnott.
          Illus. by Joan Kiddell-Monroe.   Walck, c1963. $6
          RL: 3-4   IL: 3-JH   *SMP
A collection of thirty-four very short stories.   It is rare to
find stories at this reading level with such an appeal to older
reluctant readers.   The brevity of the stories makes them
especially valuable as a treat at the end of a hard work session of reading help.

642   Ali Baba and the Forty Thieves, retold by Ned Hoopes.
          Illus. by Unada Bliewe.   Dell, Yearling, c1968.   pb
          $.75
          RL: 5-6   IL: 4-adult   BS
Good format;   well-written and with good illustrations, this
is only moderately popular because most of our clientele have
never encountered the Arabian Nights whereas they have all
heard of Cinderella and other fairy tales.

643   Anansi the Spider Man, by Philip M. Sherlock.   Illus.
          by Marcia Brown.   Crowell Co., c1954. $3.75
          RL: 4   IL: Universal   BSM
These wonderful folk tales came via Jamaica from Africa.
They have a universal quality and are requested by many who
remember hearing them told as children.   Everyone enjoys
their wit and humor.

644   Andersen's Fairy Tales, edited by Freya Littledale.
          Illus. by John Fernie.   Scholastic, c1966.   pb $.60
          RL: 5   IL: 4-adult   B
Too difficult for many fifth and sixth graders who love fairy

tales but liked by good readers and adult women who still
(many of them) love fairy tales and say so frankly.

645 Apollo, by Katherine Miller.   Illus. by Vivian Berger.
     Houghton, 1970. $3.95
     RL: 3-4   IL: 3-HS   S
The Apollo myths are retold with drama and grace.   While
retaining the flavor of the ancient tales, the author still
reaches today's children, probably because she knows them
well being herself a School Volunteer.   The handsome woodcuts enhance the text.

646 The Big Jump and Other Stories, by Benjamin Elkins.
     Illus. by Katherine Evans.   Random, Beginner, c1958.
     $1.95
     RL: 2-3   IL: Read aloud-5   BS
An excellent trio of stories that are like folk tale riddles.
They are very popular and can be used with older non-readers.
This is also a good set of stories for story-telling groups.

647 The Bigger Giant, retold by Nancy Green.   Illus. by
     Betty Fraser.   Scholastic, c1963.   pb $.50
     RL: 2-3   IL: K-4   BS
An Irish fairy tale about a giant whose clever wife outwits a
bigger giant.   A wonderful cover picture makes this a very
popular item.

648 Black Fairy Tales, by Terry Berger.   Illus. by David
     Omar White.   Atheneum, c1969. $4.75
     RL: 5-6   IL: 4-adult   *SMP
Ten very unusual fairy stories from Africa.   Some like "The
Serpent's Bride" are very much like the European story
"Beauty and the Beast."   Others are distinctly African.   All
will be enjoyed by anyone who likes fairy tales.   The black
and white illustrations are exotic and striking.

649 Black Folktales, by Julius Lester.   Illus. by Tom
     Feelings.   Baron, c1969. $4.50 (Grove pb $.95)
     RL: 4   IL: 5-adult   BSMP
Folk tales from Africa, from slavery days and from modern
times told with zest and humor--sometimes bitter humor in
fresh and biting language.   Several of these stories would be
rated X in the movies.   Others are appropriate to any age.
All have superb illustrations.

650 The Boy, the Cat and the Magic Fiddle, by Tamara
     Kitt.   Illus. by William Russell.   Grosset, c1964

Easy-To-Read-Wonder Book, $.59
RL: 2   IL: Read aloud-5   BS
A popular easy-to-read fairy tale. The repetition which helps
the child to read the book is so natural, it seems an intrinsic
part of the story.

651 The Boy Who Fooled the Giant, by Tamara Kitt. Illus.
     by William Russell. Grosset Easy-To-Read Wonder
     Book, c1962. $.69
     RL: 2   IL: Read aloud-5   BS
Everyone likes to see the little guy lick the big guy. This
folk tale of a boy who saves the town from a giant is very
popular and can be used with older non-readers.

652 The Case of the Marble Monster and Other Stories,
     by I. G. Edmunds. Illus. by Sanae Yamazaki.
     Bobbs-Merrill, 1961. OP (Scholastic, 1967, pb
     $.50)
     RL: 4   IL: 4-adult   BSM
A collection of folk tales all involving a legendary judge in
Japan named Ooka. This could be an excellent book in a
story-telling program or to read aloud to a group of varied
ages. The title misleads many children and adults on the
bookmobile since they assume it is a collection of mystery
stories. More valuable to the School Volunteers than on the
bookmobile since it needs introducing, but is well liked once
started.

653 Cinderella, by Evelyn Andreas. Grosset & Dunlap,
     1964. Nursery Treasure Books. $1
     RL: 4   IL: Pre-school-6   BS
The one hardcover book that we can't keep in stock and the
one heroine everyone seems to have heard of.

654 Congo Boy, by Mollie Clarke. Illus. by Beatrice
     Darwin. Scholastic, 1965. pb $.50
     RL: 3   IL: Read aloud-5   BSM
An African folk-tale, this is only moderately popular on the
bookmobile. It is actually mainly the adults we serve who
are interested in Africa. It seems pretty remote to most
New York City children. However, children enjoy it when
it is read aloud to them and it can have great appeal if it
is told by a storyteller who acts out some of the incidents
in the story.

655 The Crane Maiden, by Miyoko Matsutani. Illus. by
     Chihiro Iwasaki. Translated by Alvin Tresselt.

Parents, 1968. $3.95
RL: 4   IL: Read aloud-6   *SMP
An extraordinarily beautiful book which tells a Japanese fairy
tale of a crane who turns into a girl to help an elderly couple
in need. The illustrations have the colors children love.
This would also appeal to adults.

656   The Dancing Palm Tree and Other Nigerian Folktales,
      by Barbara Walker. Illus. by Helen Siegl. Parents,
      c1968. $3.95
      RL: 5   IL: Read aloud-adult   *BSMP
These are very meaty folk-tales, both unusual and unusually
interesting. A good story teller could hold a group spellbound
with one of them and they will make thoughtful conversation
pieces with junior high, high school and adult groups. It
would be a rare child who would borrow them to read on his
own.

657   The Emperor's New Clothes, by Hans Christian Ander-
      sen. Illus. by Virginia Lee Burton. Houghton Mifflin,
      c1949. $4.07 (Scholastic pb $.75)
      RL: 3-4   IL: Read aloud-6   BS
Only a child will tell the truth about the emperor's new and
non-existent clothes. A brightly illustrated edition of a very
popular story that every child should know.

658   Fairy Tales to Read Aloud, by Hans Christian Andersen.
      Compiled by Oscar Weigle. Illus. by Jill Elgin.
      Grosset, Read-Aloud Wonder Books, c1960. pb $.49
      RL: 4   IL: Read aloud-6   BS
Andersen's most famous fairy tales; "The Ugly Duckling,"
"The Emperor's New Clothes" and ten more in a version that
fills a real need. This book is much enjoyed by the many
children who want to but cannot read the original.

659   Famous Folk Tales to Read Aloud, by Mabel Watts.
      Illus. by Serio Leone. Grosset, Read-Aloud Wonder
      Book, c1961. pb $.49
      RL: 4   IL: Read aloud-JH   BS
In spite of the title, more of these stories are unfamiliar
than not but the book is valuable for its variety and its appeal to many different interest levels.

660   Favorite Fairy Tales to Read Aloud, illustrated by
      William Wiesner. Grosset, Read-Aloud Wonder Book,
      1958. pb $.49
      RL: 4   IL: Read aloud-6   BS

Another popular easy version of fairy tales. All the Read-
Aloud Fairy Tale books are borrowed until they fall apart.

661   Fire on the Mountain and Other Ethiopian Stories, by
      Harold Courlander and Leslau Wolf. Illus. by Robert
      W. Kane. Hold, c1950. $3.27
      RL: 5   IL: Universal   BSM
An excellent collection of folk tales from Ethiopia, this is
not much borrowed on the bookmobile because of its hardcover format. However, our teenage story tellers love telling stories from it in the summer programs and the stories
are then very popular with all ages.

662   Five Chinese Brothers, by Claire Huchel Bishop. Illus.
      by Kurt Wiese. Scholastic, 1938. pb $.60
      RL: 3   IL: Read aloud-4   BSM
Each of the five brothers in this famous folk tale had a magic
trait which enabled him to survive. This story is loved by
all small children who savor its humor.

663   A Ghost, a Witch and a Goblin, illustrated by Rosalind
      Fry. Scholastic, 1970. pb $.50
      RL: 3   IL: Read aloud-5   *BS
Three folk tales, (one of them part of the Russian Baba
Yaga folktale series) tell of how a human triumphed over
supernatural beings.

664   The Golden Phoenix and Other French-Canadian Fairy
      Tales, by Marius Barbeau. Retold by Michael Horn-
      yansky. Walck, c1958. (Scholastic pb: see 680)
      RL: 5   IL: 4-adult   BS
A good group of fresh fairy tales which are quite unusual.
It has a lot of humor and the hero often goes through many
unexpected vicissitudes before the standard happy ending.
Many of the stories are excellent to read aloud to a group
of children of different ages and some of the stories are useful with older non-readers.

665   Grimm's Fairy Tales, edited by Nora Kramer. Illus.
      by Carol Wilde. Scholastic, c1962. pb $.60
      RL: 5   IL: 5-adult   BS
Many adult women borrow these fairy tales which are too difficult reading for the fifth and sixth graders who also love them.

666   Grimm's Fairy Tales to Read Aloud, compiled by Oscar
      Weigle. Illus. by Roberta Carter. Grosset & Dunlap,
      c1963. pb $.49

RL: 4   IL: Read aloud-6
A large print and easier version of the above with many illustrations, this edition is very popular.

667 The Hat-Shaking Dance and Other Stories, by Harold
     Courlander. Illus. by Enrico Arno. Hale, Cadmus,
     c1957. $3.50
     RL: 6   IL: Read aloud-adult   BSM
Twenty-six wonderful folk tales from the Gold Coast about
Anansi the spider. The format is excellent for any age
group and so are the stories. Very popular with story
tellers and their audiences.

668 Hercules and Other Tales from Greek Myths, by Olivia
     E. Coolidge. Illus. by David Lockhart. Scholastic,
     c1949. (abridged) 1960. pb $.60
     RL: 6   IL: 5-adult   BS
This book has been used with great success in reading help
programs in junior high and high schools. On the bookmobile
it often leads to frustration since so many of the older elementary children who want to read it, cannot. See 640 and
645 for easier books of Greek myths.

669 The Iguana's Tail--Crick Crack Stories from the
     Caribbean, by Philip Sherlock. Illus. by Giola
     Flammenghi. Crowell, c1969. $3.95
     RL: 5   IL: Read aloud-adult   *BSMP
This collection of unusual folk tales--I have encountered them
nowhere else--is told with real suspense. It could be used
very effectively in a storytelling session and also to inspire
children of different ages to make up and tell their own
stories.

670 Indian Tales, by Jaime DeAngulo. Hill & Wang, 1969.
     American Century Series, $4.50 (pb $1.95)
     RL: 5   IL: Read aloud-adult   *BSMP
An unusual collection of Indian folklore. The content is of
universal interest. It is illustrated with black and white line
drawings which add a great deal and are the kind of pictures
which will inspire children to draw their own.

671 Jack and the Beanstalk, illustrated by William Wiesner.
     Scholastic, 1969. pb $.50
     RL: 2-3   IL: Read aloud-4   BS
Everyone has heard of Jack and wants to read his story. He
and Cinderella and Red Riding Hood seem to be the three
stories every child knows and enjoys.

672   John Henry: An American Legend, by Ezra Jack Keats.
      Pantheon Books, 1965. $3.95
      RL: 5   IL: Read aloud-JH   BS
This superb version of the American legend should be in
every school and library in the country.   I have seen a good
story teller hold junior high children spellbound with the tale
of John Henry's prowess.

673   Juan Bobo and the Queen's Necklace, by Pura Belpré.
      Illus. by Christine Price.   Warne, 1962. $2.95
      RL: 5   IL: Read aloud and universal   BSMP
A beguiling Puerto Rican folk tale, this is very popular in
the School Volunteer program and, when introduced, moves
well on the bookmobile in spite of the hard cover format.

674   Kantchil's Lime Pit and Other Stories from Indonesia,
      by Harold Courlander.   Illus. by Robert Kane.   Har-
      court, c1950. $3.50
      RL: 5-6   IL: 4-adult   SMP
This group of folk tales is too exotic to be popular on the
bookmobile and has to be introduced by an adult in the School
Volunteer Program.   Then it is popular for it has traditional
folk tale humor.   It is fascinating to run across stories like
"Pamudjo's Feast" which also occur in a different form in
the stories about Anansi and stories like "The Hunter of
Perak" which in a European version is why one can't count
one's chickens before they are hatched.   I have used "The
Tiger's Tail" with both junior high and high school students
in group discussions of pacificism and non-violence and later
heard them recommend the book to their friends.

675   King Midas and the Golden Touch, by Al Perkins.
      Illus. by Harold Berson.   Random House, Beginner
      Series, c1969. $1.95
      RL: 2-3   IL: 2-JH   BS
Everyone loves gold.   This easy-to-read version of the Greek
myth about the king who loved gold too much for his own good
is very popular.   It is also very valuable since it is often
one of the first books that children who are reading easy books
encounter which has some idea content and philosophical value.
After a diet of Go, Dog, Go and The Cat in the Hat (valuable
as those books are as education tools) this one opens doors
to a larger world.

676   The King's Wish and Other Stories, by Benjamin Elkin.
      Illus. by Leonard Shortall.   Random House, 1960,
      Beginner Series. $1.95

RL: 2-3   IL: Read aloud and K-4   BS
This book has three folk tale-like stories about a king and
his three sons.   It is an excellent book for reading help programs and much liked on the bookmobile.

677 Lucky and The Giant, by Benjamin Elkin.   Illus. by
     Brinton Turkle.   Childrens Press, 1962. $2.75
     (Scholastic, 1969, pb $.50)
     RL: 2-3   IL: Read aloud-5   BS
Lucky outwits the giant in this popular folk tale.   This one
is also enjoyed by junior high and high school non-readers.

678 The Magic Fish, by Freya Littledale.   Illus. by Ed
     Arno.   Scholastic, 1967.   pb $.50
     RL: 3   IL: Read aloud, pre-school to 6   BS
A version of the well-known folk tale about the fisherman
whose wife was too greedy, this is very popular as is any
book to do with wishing.

679 The Magic Listening Cap, by Yoshiko Uchida.   Har-
     court, Brace, Voyager, c1955. $3.50   (pb $.75)
     RL: 5   IL: 5-HS   BSM
A collection of Japanese folk tales illustrated with delicate
pen and ink drawings.   Many are excellent for reading aloud
or for storytelling.   In reading help sessions older children
can be intrigued with some of the Japanese words introduced
and then be led to think about language.

680 The Magic Tree and Other Tales, by Marius Barbeau.
     Retold by Michael Hornyansky.   Illus. by Arthur Price.
     Scholastic, 1958.   pb $.60
     RL: 5   IL: Read aloud-6   *BS
This book contains nine unfamiliar fairy tales full of action
and humor, a most unusual thing in fairy tales.   It could be
a wonderful read-aloud or storytelling book for a wide age
range.   It is a paperback version of The Golden Phoenix
[664].

681 Myths and Legends of Many Lands, edited by Nicola
     Ann Sissons.   Illus. by Robert Todd.   Lion, 1962.
     $3.99 (pb $1)
     RL: 5-6   IL: 5-adult   BS
A good collection of non-Greek myths and legends with black
and white illustrations.   Useful with many different age groups.

682 Nine Witch Tales, edited by Abby Kedabra (!).   Illus.
     by John Fernie.   Scholastic, 1968.   pb $.50

RL: 4-5   IL: 4-adult   BS
This is an excellent and varied collection of scary stories
about witches.   Children really enjoy it and so do the adults
who like fairy stories.

683 Oté: A Puerto Rican Folk Tale, by Pura Belpré.
     Illus. by Paul Galdone.   Pantheon, c1969. $3.95
     RL: 3-4   IL: Read aloud-3   BSM
The story of a near-sighted devil who steals a family's food
and how he was outwitted by the smallest child, this has
dramatic illustrations.   It is a fine story for story telling
but not so appropriate for a child to read to him or herself.
In general, the age that can and wants to read fairy tales
prefers fairy princess and princesses to devils and small
children.

684 Perez y Martina, by Pura Belpré.   Warne, 1961.
     $3.50
     RL: 4-5   IL: Read aloud-adult   BSM
A Puerto Rican folk tale, the love story of a mouse and a
cockroach.   Puerto Ricans who already know the story, love
it.   The children who are not familiar with it, however, dislike it since it is about objects they loathe.

685 The Piece of Fire and Other Haitian Tales, by Harold
     Courlander.   Illus. by Beth and Joe Krush.   Har-
     court, 1942. $3.50
     RL: 4-5   IL: Read aloud-adult   BSM
As the author of these folk tales rightly says, "folk tales are
meant to be told and dramatized rather than read."   This
collection strikes me as quite unusual with much more belly-
laugh humor and surprise endings than any other collection
I have read.   It can seem both relevent and funny to today's
teenagers;   see for example the story, "The Lizard's Big
Dance."

686 Prince and Princess Stories to Read Aloud, by Oscar
     Weigle.   Illus. by Sergio Leone.   Grosset and Dunlap
     Read-Aloud Wonder Books, c1964.   pb $.49
     RL: 3-4   IL: 3-6   BS
A collection of good but less familiar fairy stories.

687 Puss in Boots, by M. Jean Craig.   Illus. by Robert
     Jones.   Scholastic, 1966.   pb $.50
     RL: 2-3   IL: Read aloud-6   BS
This is a welcome retelling of this fairy tale since the reading level is low enough to make it comfortable for many non-
readers.

688 Read-Aloud Fairy Tales, illustrated by Laszlo Matulay.
     Grosset, c1957. pb $.39
     RL: 3-4   IL: Read aloud-6   BS
This collection has all the old favorites--Cinderella, Jack
and the Beanstalk, Puss in Boots, etc., and is very popular.

689 Read-Aloud Nursery Tales, illustrated by Ann Wolf.
     Grosset, c1957. pb $.49
     RL: 3   IL: Read aloud-3   BS
A nice collection of old favorites like Henny Penny and The
Three Little Pigs with many pictures and large print. This
is easier to read than any of the other titles in this series.

690 Rod Serling's Triple W: Witches, Warlocks and Were-
     wolves, edited by Rod Serling. Grosset & Dunlap,
     1963. OP
     RL: 6-7   IL: 6-adult
A grisly and extremely popular group of horror stories by
various authors.

691 Shan's Lucky Knife, by Jean Merrill. Illus. by Ronni
     Solbert. Hale, 1960. $2.97 (Scholastic pb $.60)
     RL: 5   IL: 5-adult   BSM
The classic story of the country bumpkin who outwits the city
slicker in an Oriental (Burmese) setting.

692 Six Foolish Fishermen, by Benjamin Elkin. Illus. by
     Bernice Myers. Hale, 1957. $2.43 (Scholastic,
     1968. pb $.50
     RL: 2   IL: Read aloud-4   BS
A counting story of six fishermen who thought one of their
number was missing. Children find it both humorous and inspiring to realize that they are smarter than the fishermen.

693 Stone Soup, by Ann McGovern. Illus. by Nola Langner.
     Scholastic, 1968. pb $.60
     RL: 2   IL: 2-JH   BS
The old folk tale describing how a hungry wayfarer tricks an
old lady into feeding him by telling her he can produce soup
from a stone. This story in different versions has been enjoyed for hundreds of years.

694 Stories About Giants, Witches and Dragons to Read
     Aloud, compiled by Oscar Weigle. Illus. by Sergio
     Leone. Grosset Read-Aloud Wonder Books, 1964.
     pb $.49
     RL: 3-4   IL: Read aloud-6   BS

Another popular collection of fairy stories in this useful
series.

695 A Story, A Story, by Gail E. Haley. Atheneum, c1970.
      $5.95
      RL: 3   IL: Read aloud-4   *SMP
This African folk tale explains how Anansi the "spider man"
first managed to obtain stories for the people of earth from
the Sky God. Some of the African names and terms may
throw children off but a good storyteller will find that this
colorful book is much enjoyed. It is time for all American
children to have the opportunity to relish the African tales,
as well as the European fairy tales and Greek myths. The
woodcut illustrations are both unusual and appropriate. Their
color is dazzling.

696 The Superlative Horse, by Jean Merrill. Illus. by
      Ronni Solbert. W. R. Scott, c1961. $3.75 (Scho-
      lastic, pb OP)
      RL: 5   IL: 5-adult   BSM
A Chinese folk tale with superb illustrations that intrigue
anyone interested in drawing.

697 Tales from the Green Fairy Book, edited by Andrew
      Lang. Scholastic, 1965 (abridged). pb $.60
      RL: 5   IL: 4-adult   BS
This book and its companion, Tales from the Red Fairy
Book [698] lead to a great deal of frustration since so many
children reach for them and find them too difficult. However, we carry them for our better readers and they have
a steady circulation among adult women who seize on them,
saying "I still love fairy stories."

698 Tales from the Red Fairy Book, edited by Andrew
      Lang. Scholastic, 1965 (abridged). pb $.60
      RL: 5   IL: 4-adult   BS
See 697 above.

699 Three Bears, edited by Margaret Hillert. Illus. by
      Irma Wilde. Follett, Just Beginning to Read Series,
      1963. $1.25
      RL: Pre-primer IL: Read aloud-2   BS
Another useful Follett pre-primer, this is a colorfully illustrated forty-five word version of the classic story of Goldi-
locks.

700 The Three Billy-Goats Gruff, illustrated by Susan Blair.

Scholastic, c1963. pb $.50
RL: 2-3   IL: Read aloud-2   BS
All children seem to love this old Norwegian story of the
goats and the troll. It is especially good for story hours
with its repetition and noise effects.

701 Three Giant Stories, edited by Lesley Conger. Illus.
     by Rosalind Fry. Scholastic, 1968. pb $.50
RL: 3   IL: Read aloud-5   BS
Two traditional folk tales, "The Brave Little Tailor" and
"The Giant and the Cobbler," and one original story, "How
Big-Mouth Wrestled the Giant," appeal to a wide audience.
Children, to whom size matters a great deal, love giant
stories and these are on a pleasantly easy reading level.

702 Three Goats, edited by Margaret Hillert. Illus. by
     Mel Pekarsky. Follett, Just Beginning To Read
     Series, 1963. $1.25
RL: Pre-primer IL: K-2   BS
Another Follett pre-primer with a vocabulary of thirty-six
words to re-tell the story of the Billy Goats Gruff.

703 The Three Visitors, by Marjorie Hopkins. Illus. by
     Anne Rockwell. Parents, 1967. $3.95
RL: 3   IL: Read aloud-6   *BSMP
A little Eskimo girl unselfishly aids three visitors and in the
end, her deeds create the light to bring her great-grandmother
safely home. For such a simple vocabulary, the language is
extraordinarily vivid and poetic and the theme will carry the
unfamiliar setting even for children who normally shrink from
unfamiliar situations. A beautiful book which adults will also
enjoy. An excellent family read-aloud.

704 The Three Wishes, by M. Jean Craig. Illus. by
     Rosalind Fry. Scholastic, 1968. pb $.60
RL: 2-3   IL: Read aloud-4   BS
Wishing is a popular sport--anytime, anywhere. Children
love to laugh at the story of how the woodcutter and his wife
wasted their three wishes and love to feel how much better
they could handle such an opportunity. A very good conversation piece for school volunteers who would like, without
prying, to get to know their pupils better.

705 The Three Wishes, edited by Ricardo E. Alegría.
     Translated by Elizabeth Culbert. Illus. by Lorenzo
     Homar. Harcourt, Brace, c1969. $3.50
RL: 4-5   IL: Universal   BSMP

Another rich collection of Puerto Rican folk tales with woodcuts by a well-known Puerto Rican artist. This is an excellent book. There can not be too many Puerto Rican books
right now, the demand is so great and the supply as yet so
small.

706   The Tiger and the Rabbit and Other Tales, edited by
       Pura Belpré. Illus. by Tomie de Paola. Lippincott,
       c1965. $3.95
       RL: 4   IL: Universal   BSMP
A great read-aloud and story telling book by a very well-
known Puerto Rican author and librarian who has run pioneering Spanish and English storytelling programs in New York
City. Striking black and white illustrations.

707   A Treasury of Stories to Read Aloud, compiled by
       Oscar Weigle. Illus. by Andrae Goblin. Grosset,
       1962. pb $.49
       RL: 3-4   IL: Read aloud-6   BS
A collection of unusual folk tales that can interest a wide
age range. This book is useful for tutoring programs and
popular on the bookmobile.

708   The Ugly Duckling, by Hans Christian Andersen. A
       new English version by Lilian Moore. Illus. by
       M. Barnett. Scholastic, 1969. pb $.60
       RL: 3   IL: Read aloud-5   BS
There never was a child who didn't love the story of the
ugly duckling. What child doesn't wonder if he is one and
one, furthermore, that may never turn into a swan? This
is a lovely poetic version of the old tale on an easy reading
level.

709   The Ugly Duckling and Two Other Stories, by Hans
       Christian Andersen. Adapted by Lilian Moore. Illus.
       by Trina Schart Hyman. Scholastic, 1969. pb $.50
       RL: 3   IL: Read aloud-5   BS
It is good to have these well-written versions of three classic
fairy tales on so low a reading level. The book has a lovely
cover and imaginative illustrations.

710   When the Drum Sang--An African Folk Tale, by Anne
       Rockwell. Parents, c1970. $3.95
       RL: 2-3   IL: Read aloud-4   *BSMP
Little girls will relate to the heroine of this African tale
which has both suspense and a satisfying happy ending.
Children will like the very colorful illustrations.

711 Why the Sun Was Late, by Benjamin Elkin.   Illus. by
     Jerome Snyder.   Parents, c1966. $3.95
     RL: 2   IL: Read aloud-6   SMP
A good folk tale with dramatic illustrations explains why the
fly can go buzz, buzz, buzz and why the sun was once late
in rising.

712 The Wisest Man in the World, by Benjamin Elkin.
     Illus. by Anita Lobel.   Parents, 1968. $3.95
     RL: 4-5   IL: Read aloud-6   S
This lovely fable of King Solomon and the bee will appeal to
a wide age range especially because of the various tests to
which the Queen of Sheba put King Solomon.   Children love
riddles especially those such as the ones in this book which
are as applicable today as in Solomon's time.   For example,
how would you tell which were boys and which were girls if
fifty children dressed alike and with hair alike were brought
before you?

FAMILY STORIES

713 All-of-a-Kind Family, by Sydney Taylor.   Illus. by
     Helen John.   Follett, c1951. $4.95   (Dell Yearling,
     1969, pb $.65)
     RL: 4-6   IL: 4-HS   BSMP
This book is popular with a great many children even though
they know nothing of Jewish family life.   All children love
stories about happy families and often very deprived children
seem to derive a vicarious sense of security from stories of
this type.   This one, now a classic, is about a Jewish family
on the lower East Side in the days before World War I.   A
child who likes this book can often be lured into the library
to get the hardcover sequels to it.   Both it and its sequel
More All-of-a-Kind Family (also a Dell Yearling pb) can be
enjoyed by a wide age range since there is both teenage and
adult romance as well as the adventures of elementary school
children.   The format, however, is childish.

714 And Now Miguel, by Joseph Krumgold.   Illus. by Jean
     Charlot.   Crowell, c1953.   (Appollo, 1970, pb $1.65)
     RL: 5-6   IL: 4-adult   BMP
Miguel prays to St. Isidro for something he wants very badly
and then learns that one is not always happy to get one's wish.

A beautiful story of a Mexican-American sheep herding family
with wise insight into the human heart.

715   Ann Aurelia and Dorothy, by Natalie Savage Carlson.
      Illus. by Dale Payson.   Harper & Row, c1968.
      $4.95   (Dell Yearling $.75)
      RL: 4   IL: 3-7   BSMP
A thoroughly satisfying story of two friends at school and the
choice one of them has to make between her real mother and
a kind foster mother.   It celebrates the things that middle
graders feel are really important--safety patrols, Halloween
costumes, school expeditions, friendship, and family.

716   The Bear Scouts, by Stan and Jan Berenstain.   Random
      Beginner, 1967. $1.95
      RL: 2-3   IL: Read aloud-4   BS
Many city children, as well as country children, look to the
day when they can become cub scouts or Brownies.   This
book is useful in telling something about the subject.   The
rhymes in which the story is told help a faltering reader
and the illustrations are wonderful.   Unfortunately, the story
itself which makes father out to be a fool is pretty silly and
just what most children don't need.

717   Becky, by Julia Wilson.   Illus. by John Wilson.
      Crowell, c1966. $3.75
      RL: 3   IL: Read aloud-5   BSMP
Becky longs for a very special doll but the one she wants is
too expensive.   How she gets her doll seems a little far-
fetched but girls really love this book.   What child doesn't
like to hear about a wish come true?

718   Behind the Magic Line, by Betty Erwin.   Illus. by
      Julia Iltis.   Little, c1969. $4.95
      RL: 4-5   IL: 4-JH-adult   *BSMP
This is a most unusual story of a black family in the city
and their adventures when they move to California.   It combines humor, fantasy and excitement.   It would be very popular on the bookmobile in paperback.   I would recommend
this strongly to any adult who did not come from the inner
city and who was planning to work with inner city families
such as the one portrayed in this book.   The father is rarely
home, the oldest boy is in trouble with the police and the
family, living below the poverty line, is on and off welfare.
Nevertheless it is a wonderful family with warmth, loyalty
and courage and will have the same appeal to older girls
and women as Roosevelt Grady [764].

719 Big Cowboy Western, by Ann Herbert Scott. Illus. by
Richard W. Lewis. Lothrop, c1965. $3.95
RL: 3   IL: Read aloud-2   BSMP
Westerns are out of style right now with older children but
the five, six, and seven year olds still want guns with which
to go "Pow, Pow, Pow." This is a satisfying story of a boy
in a housing project and how he finds a horse to go with his
cowboy suit.

720 Binky Brothers and the Fearless Four, by James
Lawrence. Illus. by Leonard Kessler. Harper I
Can Read, 1970. $2.50
RL: 2-3   IL: Read aloud-4   *BS
A new family moves into the neighborhood of the four boys
who call themselves prime mystery solvers. The Fearless
Four are unfriendly but the younger brother of one of them
is friendly and manages to mystify the older ones. A story
of sibling rivalry and humor. See also 1134, about the same
group of children.

721 Blue Willow, by Doris Gates. Illus. by Paul Lantz.
Viking, Seafarer, 1940. pb $.75
RL: 5   IL: HS-adult   B
This moving story of a migrant worker's family was intended
for children but is very popular with girls and older women.

722 Carol, by Frieda Friedman. Illus. by Mary Barton.
Morrow, c1950. Scholastic, 1966. pb $.60
RL: 4-5   IL: 4-JH   BS
This book is by an author who is very popular even though
her books came out a while ago. All of her books are about
children of a low income level, but with solid family background, living in New York. Girls love these books. This
one is about a girl who resents having to move to the city
because of her father's job but who finally finds new friends
on the city streets.

723 Cotton in My Sack, by Lois Lenski. Lippincott, c1949.
$4.82 (Dell Yearling, 1966, pb $.65)
RL: 5   IL: Older girls and women BSP
This is a heart-warming and realistic but dated story of
family life on a share-cropping farm. Older girls like it
because they can empathize with the heroine. Older women
like it because for many it is the story of their youth. I
wish the format was adult, as many more women would then
borrow it and enjoy it.

724   Did You Carry the Flag Today, Charley?, by Rebecca
      Caudill.   Illus. by Nancy Grossman.   Holt, c1966.
      $3.50   (Owlet pb $1.45)
      RL: 3-4   IL: Read aloud-4   BS
Charley Cornett is the youngest of ten children in an Appala-
chian family.   His older brothers and sisters explain to him
as he starts school that each day the most helpful child is
picked to carry the flag.   In spite of many humorous misadventures, Charley finally gets to carry the flag.   This book
is a wonderful read-aloud for a mixed group of children--
the younger ones can hardly wait to hear what happens and
the older ones relish the humor.

725   Dot for Short, by Frieda Friedman.   Illus. by Carolyn
      Haywood.   Morrow, c1947. $4.50 (Scholastic, 1959,
      pb $.50)
      RL: 4   IL: 3-JH   BS
A heart-warming story about a taxi driver's family who live
under the El in New York City.   The people are real and
the situations are universal.   Girls love this.

726   Ellen and the Gang, by Frieda Friedman.   Illus. by
      Jacqueline Tomes.   Morrow, 1963. $3.95
      RL: 4   IL: 4-HS   BSMP
Ellen lives in a housing project and when her best friend
goes to camp, falls in with a poor group of older boys and
girls who use her for a fall guy.   This is a family story
rich in values and with much to say on the subject of honesty
and loyalty.   A very popular book.

727   Evan's Corner, by Elizabeth Starr Hill.   Illus. by
      Nancy Grossman.   Holt, 1967. $3.95   (Owlet pb
      $1.45)
      RL: 3-4   IL: Read aloud-4   BSMP
This quiet story of a boy in an over-crowded New York
apartment who finally acquires a corner of his own is justly
popular with all children and especially with those who also
live in close quarters with their brothers and sisters.

728   Family, edited by M. Rockowitz.   A Scholastic Litera-
      ture Anthology, Scholastic, 1969.   pb $1
      RL: 5-7   IL: 5-adult   BSMP
An excellent anthology, consisting of short stories and excerpts from autobiographies and novels, centered around the
theme of family relationships.   There is enough variety so
that there is something for almost every taste and most selections are thought-provoking.   This kind of book can be

used to lead a student or borrower to reading the books from
which these excerpts were chosen.

729 A Family Is a Way of Feeling, edited by Marjorie B.
     Smiley, Florence B. Freedman and John S. Marca-
     tante. Macmillan, c1966. $1.36
     RL: 4-5   IL: 5-adult   BSMP
Another anthology with family as the theme. This one includes poems as well as stories and excerpts from novels
and biography. The selections are not quite as varied as
in 728 since virtually every one is about a family or child
who is poor but the book is popular and has been used with
great success in the New York School Volunteer Program in
both junior high and high schools for several years. Illustrated with many photographs.

730 Five Friends at School, by Peter Buckley and Hortense
     Jones. Holt, Holt Urban Social Studies, 1967. $3.50
     RL: 2-3   IL: Read aloud-3   BSM
One of the first books to use photographs of children in a
city setting. The pictures accurately reflect the kind of
neighborhood we serve. Children are thrilled to see themselves and all the children who have borrowed it relate to
it. This is a very useful book since it can be used as a
read-aloud (showing the pictures) or a conversation piece or
as a book for the child to read to himself. See also 783,
below, in the same series.

731 Friday Night Is Papa Night, by Ruth A. Sonneborn.
     Illus. by Emily Cully. Viking, c1970. $3
     RL: 3   IL: Read aloud-4   BSMP
An excellent Puerto Rican family story. Papa has to work
away from home and can only come home on Friday nights.
This Friday he doesn't come--where is he? All ends well
and the picture of family love will be warming even, or
perhaps especially, to children from families who are not
fortunate enough to have this.

732 Gracie, by Suzanne Roberts. Illus. by Marilyn Miller.
     Doubleday & Co., 1965. $3.50
     RL: 4   IL: 6-adult   BSP
Popular with older girls and adults, this story of a migrant
worker family generates real excitement when the hero tries
to unionize the workers.

733 The Green Thumb Story, by Jean Fiedler. Illus. by
     Wayne Blickenstaff. Scholastic, c1952. pb $.50

RL: 3   IL: Read aloud-3   BS
Peter's mother tells him he needs a "green thumb" to make
a garden but with a neighbor's help he does create one and
learns what having a green thumb really means. Inner city
children are eager to grow things and love a teacher who
gives them the opportunity to plant something even in a
flower pot on a dark window sill.

734 Gypsy Girl's Best Shoes, by Anne Rockwell. Parents,
      c1966. $3.95
      RL: 2-3   IL: Read aloud-4   SMP
No one has time to watch a little gypsy girl dance in her
new red shoes. Finally she dances for a squirrel and makes
some new friends. New shoes mean a great deal to all
girls. The city setting is realistic but not dreary. This
would be popular in paperback.

735 Have You Seen My Brother?, by Elizabeth Guilfoile.
      Illus. by Mary S. Andrew. Follett, c1962. $1.25
      RL: 2   IL: Read aloud-3   BS
Although written for young, beginning readers, the movement
of this story is enough to retain the interest of a ten- or
eleven-year-old slow reader with a sense of humor.

736 Hooray for Jasper, by Betty Horvath. Illus. by Fermin
      Rocker. Grolier-Watts, 1966. $3.95
      RL: 3   IL: 2-5   BSMP
How a small, black boy proves his worth. Story has implications for all children. See also Jasper Makes Music [739].

737 Hurry Up, Slowpoke, by Crosby Newell. Illus. by the
      author. Grosset Easy-To-Read Wonder Book, c1961.
      $.59
      RL: 3   IL: Read aloud and K-4   BS
This humorous story has so much appeal that it can overcome the fact that it is about a family of mice. Normally,
we never carry books about mice. A mouse immediately
reminds a ghetto child of rats and unpleasant experiences.
Fortunately, the entertaining pictures are not very mouselike
and the book is consistently popular.

738 The Janitor's Girl, by Frieda Friedman. Illus. by
      Mary Stevens. Morrow, c1956. $3.75 (Scholastic,
      1966, pb $.60)
      RL: 5   IL: 4-JH   BS
A very popular story with an unstressed lesson in the acceptance of individuals. The city setting adds flavor.

739 Jasper Makes Music, by Betty Horvath. Illus. by
    Fermin Rocker. Watts, 1967. $3.95
    RL: 3   IL: 2-5   BSMP
Jasper finds a way to earn a guitar. A good family story.
See Hooray for Jasper [736].

740 Jasper the Drummin' Boy, by Margaret Taylor
    Burroughs. Illus. by Ted Lewin. Follett, 1970.
    $2.95
    RL: 3-4   IL: 2-6   *SM
This story of a boy who drummed wherever he went, church
or school or whatever, was first published in 1947. It has
been revised but the basic story is as likeable as ever and
full of rhythm. Boys who find it hard to sit still in school
will like this one.

741 Jerry the Newsboy, by Leonard Shortall. Morrow,
    c1970. $3.95
    RL: 2-3   IL: 1-4   *SMP
Jerry helps out on his uncle's newsstand and Pedro, a Puerto
Rican shoeshine boy, saves the day in an emergency.

742 Joel Is the Youngest, by Judith Ish-Kishor. Illus. by
    Jules Gottlieb. Washington Square Press, Archway,
    1954. pb $.60
    RL: 4   IL: 3-6   *BSMP
A good story of Jewish family life, this book will be appreciated by many children who hate, as Joel does, being left
behind or looked down on as the youngest. Joel's family has
things in common with families everywhere and the setting
could be Brooklyn or a small town anywhere in the United
States.

743 José's Christmas Secret, by Joan M. Lexau. Illus.
    by Don Bolognese. Dial Press, 1963. $3.50
    RL: 4-5   IL: 5-JH   BSMP
This heartwarming book about a fatherless Puerto Rican family tells how ten-year-old José tries to be the man of the
family and succeeds in providing a Christmas surprise.
Very popular with children and volunteers alike in the School
Volunteer program, it is passed by on the bookmobile due to
its hardcover format and size which lead children who would
enjoy it to think it is a picture book for younger children.

744 A Kiss for Little Bear, by Else Holmelund Minarik.
    Illus. by Maurice Sendak. Harper I Can Read Book,
    1968. $2.50

RL: 2   IL: Read aloud-3   BS
One of a series of books about a little bear and his family.
These books seem to give many deprived children a cozy
feeling of secure family life. The illustrations go with and
enhance the text which has a slender story line.

745 Let Papa Sleep, by Crosby Bonsall and Emily Reed.
     Grosset Easy-To-Read Wonder Book, c1963. $.69
     RL: 2-3   IL: Read aloud-3   BS
A humorous easy-to-read book about life with father that is
very popular with the young.

746 A Letter to Amy, by Ezra Jack Keats. Harper, c1968.
     $4.95
     RL: 2-3   IL: Read aloud-3   BSMP
Peter invites Amy to his birthday party and gets a surprise.
Without in any way prettying up the inner city, Mr. Keats
finds and shows that there is beauty there. What his books
about Peter and his family and friends mean to all city children, and especially to Afro-American children, cannot be
overestimated. See 397, 760 and 782.

747 Lillie of Watts, by Mildred Pitts Walter. Illus. by
     Leonora E. Prince. Ritchie, c1969. $3.95
     (pb $1.95)
     RL: 3   IL: Read aloud-4   *BSMP
A first-rate story about a girl who learns that cats can be
kind and that her mother really loves her. Children will
like the large warm family in this book and empathize with
Lillie's ups and downs.

748 The Little Brown Hen, by Patricia Miles Martin. Illus.
     by Harper Johnson. Crowell, 1960. $3.25
     RL: 3   IL: Read aloud-4   *BSMP
Willie finds his pet hen has hatched an unusual birthday
present for his mother. A happy story with good illustrations on a useful reading level. Boys and girls like this
one. Although it is a country story, I have tried it on city
children with great success.

749 Little Runner of the Long House, by Betty Baker.
     Illus. by Arnold Lobel. Harper I Can Read, c1962.
     $2.50
     RL: 2-3   IL: Read aloud-3   BSMP
Little Runner is an Iroquois Indian but any child will recognize the happiness he shares with his mother and baby
brother in this story of the way the Iroquois celebrate the
New Year.

750 **Little Women** (abridged), by Louisa M. Alcott. Illus.
by Gabe Keith. Scholastic, 1968. pb $.75
RL: 6   IL: 6-HS   BS
The famous story of a family in Concord in Civil War days.
A good abridgement with large print, this is one classic that
is really read.

751 **Mama's Bank Account**, by Kathryn Forbes. Harcourt,
c1943. $2.95 (pb $.75)
RL: 5   IL: 6-adult   BS
A warm story of a Norwegian-American family with very
little money but lots of spunk, this is very popular with
adults. It has exceptionally good print for a paperback.

752 **Maria**, by Joan M. Lexau. Illus. by Ernest Crichlow.
Dial Press, 1964. $3.50
RL: 3-4   IL: Read aloud-5   BSMP
Young Maria Rivera receives a very special gift doll. This
is a moving story of a Puerto Rican family in New York. The
illustrations are especially beautiful. It should be in paperback.

753 **Meet Miko Takino**, by Helen Copeland. Illus. by Karl
Werth. Lothrop, 1963. $3.28
RL: 2-3   IL: 2-5   SMP
A charming story about a boy of Japanese background in New
York who "adopts" American grandparents for a school party.
Thoroughly pleasant reading.

754 **Melindy's Medal**, by Georgene Faulkner and John Becker.
Illus. by Elton C. Fax. Messner, c1945. $3.50
(Washington Square Press, Archway, 1967, pb $.59)
RL: 4   IL: 4-7   BSMP
This story of a black girl and her family in a Boston housing
project was read by the entire staff since one member wanted
it removed on the ground that it condescended to black people.
However, after much debate the majority felt it had many
positive values to give to city children and it was allowed to
stay. I am glad because Melindy's courage can mean a lot
to girls of any color.

755 **Moy Moy**, by Leo Politi. Scribner, c1960. $4.37
RL: 3   IL: Read aloud-2   SMP
Moy Moy (little sister in Chinese) and her family celebrate
the Chinese New Year in Los Angeles. Beautiful soft illustrations and one of a handful of books about Chinese Americans.

756 A New Home for Billy, by May Justus. Illus. by Joan
     Balfour Payne. Hastings, 1966. $3.25
       RL: 3-4   IL: Read aloud-6   BSMP
Many, many city children wish they could move to the country like Billy and his family. A book with a satisfying happy
ending.

757 The Noonday Friends, by Mary Stolz. Illus. by Louis
     S. Glanzman. Harper, 1965. $4.95 (pb $.95)
       RL: 5-6   IL: 5-HS   BSMP
A family story with depth which includes a multi-ethnic friend-
ship. There are many colorful characters in this Greenwich
Village story.

758 One Kitten Is Not Too Many, by Dorothy Levenson.
     Illus. by Carl and Mary Hauge. Grosset Easy-To-
     Read Wonder Book, 1964. $.69
       RL: 2-3   IL: Read aloud-5   BS
This humorous story of a family with too many cats is popular with younger children and yet still useful for older non-
readers since the situation is ageless.

759 Pablo's Mountain, by Albert Johnston. Universal Press
     Award, c1953. pb OP
       RL: 6-7   IL: 6-adult   BSMP
The sensitive story of a Mexican boy's adolescence in El
Barrio. A fictional parallel to Down These Mean Streets
but with a warm relationship between father and son. A
good and popular book. I hope it will soon be back in print.

760 Peter's Chair, by Ezra Jack Keats. Harper, c1967.
     $4.95
       RL: 2-3   IL: Read aloud-3   BSMP
Another in this lovely group of books about Peter and his
family. This one is especially valuable as it takes up a
problem troubling many children--i.e., will the new baby
steal my place?

761 A Present from Rosita, by Celeste Edell. Illus. by
     Elton Fax. Messner, 1952. OP (Washington Square
     Press, Archway, 1967, pb $.60)
       RL: 5   IL: 4-JH   BSMP
This is one of my favorite books and girls like it as much
as I do. It is about a Puerto Rican widow and her three
children: Pablo, Rosita and Victor. Victor is often in
trouble but the relationship between him and the rest of the
family is a warm one. In spite of the fact that the family

has very little money and suffers many misfortunes through
hurricanes and illness, the book is not a sad one.   The first
half takes place in Puerto Rico and gives a good picture of
life in a Puerto Rican village.   The second half is set in
New York City and is a realistic picture of what an emigrating
Puerto Rican family may encounter.   Although this book was
published in 1952, it is not out of date.

762   A Quiet Place, by Rose Blue.   Illus. by Tom Feelings.
        Grolier, Watts, 1969. $3.95
        RL: 3-4   IL: 3-JH   BSMP
The local library is a quiet refuge for Mathew whose foster
home is warm but crowded and noisy.   Many children will
understand Mathew's sad feelings when the library is closed
for repair and he feels lost.   In a way, it's an older version
of Evan's Corner [727] and will be relished by quiet girls and
boys and will bore the active ones to tears.   It is written by
an author who really knows her black family and the Feelings
illustrations are, as usual, superb.

763   Ready-Made Family, by Frances Solomon Murphy.
        Illus. by Moneta Barnett.   Scholastic, c1953.   pb $.50
        RL: 4   IL: 5-JH   BS
The suspenseful story of a family of three orphans and how
they come to trust their foster parents.   Girls eat this one
up.

764   Roosevelt Grady, by Louisa R. Shotwell.   Illus. by
        Peter Burchard.   World, 1963. $3.95   (Grosset &
        Dunlap, Tempo, pb $.60)
        RL: 5-6   IL: HS-adult   BMP
This heart-warming story of a migrant family was intended
for junior high boys and girls who never borrow it but it has
great appeal to older girls and women who can identify with
Roosevelt's mother and her dreams of a stable life with a
future.   The black and white illustrations add a great deal
to the book's attraction.

765   Rosa-Too-Little, by Sue Felt.   Doubleday, c1950.
        $3.50
        RL: 3   IL: Read aloud-3   SMP
A little Puerto Rican girl longs to be old enough to join the
library.   This is a good family read-aloud book with excellent illustrations of city scenes.   It would be very popular on
the bookmobile in a Dell Yearling or Holt Owlet format.

766   Runaway Alice, by Frances Salomon Murphy.   Illus. by

Mabel Jones Woodbury.   Scholastic, c1951.   pb $.60
RL: 4   IL: 4-JH   BS
A very popular book with girls, an orphan finally finds the
right foster home.

767 Sam, by Ann Herbert Scott.   Illus. by Symeon Shimin.
      McGraw, 1967. $3.95
      RL: 3-4   IL: Read aloud-4   SMP
A beguiling story about a little boy whose whole family is
too busy to play with him.   The illustrations are especially
popular with mothers.

768 Sea Beach Express, by George Panetta.   Illus. by
      Emily McCully.   Harper, c1966. $3.95
      RL: 3   IL: 2-5   SMP
A heartwarming story of an Italian family's trip to Coney
Island.   En route they acquire on loan a small Puerto Rican
boy who enhances their day.   The book portrays lots of
drama and happiness in little things.   A good read aloud
book.

769 Sidewalk Story, by Sharon Bell Mathis.   Illus. by Leo
      Carty.   Viking, c1971. $3.95
      RL: 3-4   IL: Read aloud-6   *BSMP
Lilly-Etta's best friend is Tanya.   Tanya's family is being
evicted for non-payment of rent.   Lilly-Etta tries every way
she can think of to help and finally succeeds beyond her
wildest dreams.   A wonderful story of friendship with very
real people and good illustrations.   A must for private and
suburban schools and will be very popular in city schools.

770 Something Special, by David Tucker.   Illus. by Eliza-
      beth Dauber.   Grosset Easy-To-Read Wonder Book,
      c1970. $.59
      RL: 2   IL: Read aloud-3   BSM
Billy's friend, Pablo Serrano, often has something special at
his house because his father owns a pet shop.   When, after
many small adventures, Billy finds his friend's house, he
and the reader are surprised to find what the something special is this time.

771 Soo Ling Finds a Way, by June Behrens.   Illus. by
      Taro Yashima.   Golden Gate, 1971. $4.50
      RL: 3   IL: Read aloud-4   *SMP
The happy ending in this story of a Chinese family's dilemma
will please children very much but I doubt if they will like
the illustrations.   However, stories that relate to our Chinese-

American children are few and far between and this is a nice
one. I hope we shall soon have one about a Chinese-American scientist. There are many distinguished ones and many
people are not aware of the fact.

772 The Spider Plant, by Yetta Speevack. Illus. by Wendy
     Watson. Atheneum, 1965. $3.25 (Washington
     Square Press, Archway, pb $.50)
     RL: 5   IL: 5-JH   BSMP
An excellent story about a Puerto Rican family's move to
and in New York. This book centers around the twelve-year-
old daughter Carmen. The people are credible and the situations interest any schoolgirls and have special meaning for
other children who have been uprooted. This title was well-
liked on the bookmobile and in the School Volunteer program
when it was well introduced in hardcover--now that it is out
in paperback, it will be very much in demand.

773 Striped Ice Cream, by Joan M. Lexau. Illus. by John
     Wilson. Lippincott, 1968. $3.11 (Scholastic pb
     $.60)
     RL: 4   IL: 3-6   BSMP
A realistic story about a large family living on the poverty
line, this book has warmth and action and suspense. How I
wish all Joan Lexau's many good books about different families could be put into appropriate paperback format so that
the many children who would enjoy them would seek them out.
This one is now in paperback and will be very popular.

774 A Sundae with Judy, by Frieda Friedman. Illus. by
     Carol Wilde. c1949, Scholastic, 1963. pb $.60
     RL: 5   IL: 5-7   BSM
Eleven-year-old Judy finds fun and excitement helping out in
her Dad's New York City candy store and makes friends with
a Chinese-American family.

775 Sunflowers for Tina, by Anne Norris Baldwin. Illus.
     by Ann Grifalconi. Four Winds Press, 1970. $4.50
     RL: 4   IL: Read aloud-4   *SMP
This story about a little girl and her grandmother is quite
far-fetched but the illustrations by Ann Grifalconi are superb
and the book also deals with the longing for a garden which
is wide spread among city children everywhere.

776 Sweet Flypaper of Life, by Roy de Carava and Langston
     Hughes. Hill and Wang, c1955. pb $1.50
     RL: 5-6   IL: 5-adult   BSMP

When the messenger of the Lord arrived with a telegram for
Sister Mary Bradley saying "Come home," she sent back
word she was too tangled up in living and too needed by her
grandchildren to leave. In beautifully chosen words and winning photographs, the book shows the family she couldn't
leave and through them, the Harlem of 1955. The people are
much the same as in 1972, human nature being what it is,
but expectations were lower in those days and there were
few militants.

777   Tino, by Marlene Fanta Shyer.   Illus. by Janet Palmer.
        Random, 1969. $3.95
        RL: 3-4   IL: 3-JH   BSMP
A delightful story about a Puerto Rican boy who tries to hatch
an egg in a New York City apartment. Its humor and abundant conversation hold the interest of students who dislike
books.

778   Tony's Treasure Hunt, by Holly and John Peterson.
        Scholastic, c1964.   pb $.60
        RL: 2-3   IL: 3-5   BS
Easy-to-read story about a treasure hunt and birthday party.

779   Trouble After School, by Jerrold Beim.   Illus. by Don
        Sibley.   Scholastic, c1957.   pb $.60
        RL: 5   IL: 5-HS   BS
An eighth grader learns how to handle his after-school problems in a story boys like. The title has great appeal.

780   Two Is a Team, by Lorraine and Jerrold Beim.   Illus.
        by Ernest Grichlow.   Harcourt, c1945. $3.50
        RL: 2-3   IL: Read aloud-3   SMP
One of the earliest of the multi-ethnic books, this story of
two boys who fight and then are reconciled is well liked by
each new generation of children.

781   Umbrella, by Taro Yashima.   Viking, c1958. $3.37
        (Seafarer, 1970, pb $.75)
        RL: 3   IL: Read aloud-2   SMP
Momo, age three, finally gets a chance to use her birthday
umbrella. Superb and imaginative pictures of city life depict the story of a child with a great deal in common with
any little girl any time anywhere.

782   Whistle for Willie, by Ezra Jack Keats.   Viking, 1969.
        $3.50 (Seafarer pb $.75)
        RL: 3   IL: Read aloud-3   BSMP

This lovely story of a little boy who learns to whistle is
beloved by all children.   The illustrations in the paperback
edition have all the wonderful color of the original hardcover
edition.

783   William, Andy and Ramon, by Peter Buckley and Hor-
      tense Jones.   Holt, 1966, Textbook. $3.48
      RL: 2-3   IL: 1-3   BSMP
William's grandmother and cousin come to live with William
and his family in a housing project.   Andy and Ramon and
their families make surprises for the newcomers to make
them feel welcome.   The book is heavily illustrated and full
of good will and happy families;   children like this picture
of themselves.   This is a textbook but luckily most children
do not realize that.   See also 730.

FOREIGN PEOPLE

784   Bemba: An African Adventure, by Andrée Clair.   Illus.
      by Harper Johnson.   Harcourt Voyager, 1957.   pb
      $.60
      RL: 5   IL: 5-adult   BMP
An unusual story of a boy in French Africa in the 1930's and
his encounters with another culture.   Popular only with good
readers because of the alien culture which makes it difficult
going.   An interesting book for a high school or adult reading
program in spite of the young format.   Adults who have borrowed it have liked it.

785   Bernardine and the Water Bucket, by Aileen Olsen.
      Illus. by Nola Langner.   Abelard-Schuman, c1966.
      $3.50
      RL: 3   IL: Read aloud-4   BSMP
This book about a girl's first independent trip to the village
for water gives a vivid and warm picture of life on a small
Caribbean island.   Children love the story and it is an excellent family read-aloud.

786   Big Horse, Little Horse, by Martha Goldberg.   Illus.
      by Joe Lasker.   Scholastic, c1960.   pb $.50
      RL: 3   IL: 3-6   BSMP
An appealing story of a Mexican boy who helps his family in
a crisis.   This has special interest for Spanish-speaking

families but all children like the story and the illustrations.
It is another good family read-aloud.

787   The Blanket, by A. A. Murray.   Vanguard Press,
      1966. $4.95
      RL: 6   IL: JH-adult   BS
This is a thriller about murder in Africa and how differently
two cultures view it.   It is much liked by the staff and by
those who borrow it on their recommendation.

788   François and the Langouste: A Story of Martinique,
      by Ethel Sadowsky.   Illus. by Herbert Danska.
      Little, 1969. $3.75
      RL: 3-5   IL: Read aloud-4   *BSMP
This story of why a little boy is late for school gives a
vivid picture of life on Martinique through a plot which will
hold children's attention and sympathy.   The French cultural
background will also be much appreciated by the many Haitian
children who have come to this country.

789   The Good Earth, by Pearl S. Buck.   Simon & Schuster
      Pocket Books, 1931.   pb $.95
      RL: Adult   IL: HS-adult   BM
The story of a Chinese peasant of the 1920s and his family,
this is a classic.   It appeals to high school students and
adults who can empathize with Wang Lung's ambition and his
wife's joys and sorrows.   Although the setting is exotic, the
emotions and experiences are universal.

790   Josefina February, by Evaline Ness.   Scribner, c1963.
      $4.37
      RL: 2-3   IL: Read aloud-5   BSMP
This is the handsomely illustrated story of a little girl in
Haiti.   She loves her burro but is finally willing to give him
up in order to get her grandfather a badly needed pair of
new shoes.   The book is factual and realistic rather than
sentimental and is much appreciated by all children but especially by the many Haitian children who have recently come
to New York.

791   Little Pear, by Eleanor Lattimore.   Harcourt, c1931,
      c1959. $3.95 (Voyager, 1969, pb $.75)
      RL: 3-4   IL: Read aloud-4   BSM
This story of a little boy in rural China was written years
ago by the daughter of an American missionary.   There is
a desperate need for books about Chinese children with whom
the children pouring into the United States via Hong Kong can

identify. Once it is explained that this is a story of long ago, all children love it, for Little Pear is irresistible. This would be an ideal book to read aloud to a group of pre-school or younger elementary children. Older elementary children might well find the story a little young unless they had a special interest in it because of the setting.

792 Ootah's Lucky Day, by Peggy Parish. Illus. by
   Mamoru Funai. Harper I Can Read, 1970. $2.50
   RL: 2   IL: Read aloud-5   *BSMP
Ootah goes hunting by himself and kills a walrus and avoids a polar bear. He has proved himself. Wide interest range.

793 Rosa, by Leo Politi. Scribner, 1963. $4.95
   RL: 3   IL: Read aloud-3   SMP
Rosa, a little Mexican girl, has many lonely moments and longs to have a doll for company but is even happier to receive a baby sister instead. Lovely illustrations interest children with Spanish background even if they come from a different part of the Spanish-speaking world.

794 Seven Grandmothers, by Reba Paeff Mirsky. Illus. by
   W. R. Mars. Follett, 1955. $4.95 (Dell Yearling,
   1970, pb $.75)
   RL: 5   IL: 4-JH   *BSM
Nomusa, a young Zulu girl, is torn between the old ways of witch doctors and the new ways of white men. This book paints a warm picture of Zulu family life and the story is such that the reader wants to turn the page even though the events related are not big ones. It will interest adults also. See also Thirty-One Brothers and Sisters [797].

795 The Sheep of the Lai Bagh, By David Mark. Illus. by
   Lionel Kalish. Parents, 1967. OP
   RL: 2-3   IL: Read aloud-3   SM
City children will like the pictures of a park in India and country children will know how important it is to mow the lawn. All will like the story of a sheep's victory over a machine and the very colorful illustrations which remind one of a circus.

796 Sumi's Prize, by Yoshiko Uchida. Illus. by Kazue
   Mizamara. Scribner, c1964. $4.50
   RL: 3   IL: 3-5   SM
A beautifully illustrated story about a boy in Japan who tries to win a prize. There are two more books about Sumi with the same author and illustrator: Sumi and the Goat and the

Tokyo Express and Sumi's Special Happening.

797 Thirty-One Brothers and Sisters, by Reba Paeff Mirsky.
     Illus. by W. T. Mars.   Follett, 1952. $4.95 (Dell
     Yearling, 1969, pb $.75)
     RL: 5   IL: 5-JH   *BSM
The story of Nomusa, the daughter of a Zulu chief, will delight all tomboy girls.   It also gives a deeply interesting
picture of a totally different way of life.   This may well
mean that the book will interest boys and girls in junior and
senior high.   Excellent black and white illustrations.   See
also 794.

798 Tiger on the Mountain, by Shirley L. Arora. Illus.
     by Hans Guggenheim.   Follett, c1960.   Scholastic,
     1963. pb OP
     RL: 5-6   IL: 4-adult   BSM
An exciting and moving story of an Indian boy in the mountains of India who is the first of his family to learn to read.
He has to take on adult responsibilities and braves danger
to help feed his family.   A wonderful family read-aloud.

799 Tuesday Elephant, by Nancy Garfield. Illus. by Tom
     Feelings.   Crowell, c1968. $3.95
     RL: 2-3   IL: Read aloud-4   SM
A touching story of a boy in Kenya with simple, sensitive
illustrations.

800 Two Pesos for Catalina, by Ann Kirn. Rand, 1962.
     $3.50 (Scholastic, pb $.60)
     RL: 3   IL: Read aloud-4   BS
Catalina has two pesos to spend.   She finally decides on a
pair of shiny new shoes.   The setting is Mexico, the dilemma
a common one and the love of new shoes universal among
children.   Another good family read-aloud.

HISTORICAL FICTION

801 The African, by Harold Courlander. Crown, c1967.
     $5.95
     RL: 7   IL: JH-adult   *BSMP
An extraordinary novel, this is the story of a slave from before his capture in Africa through slavery in the West Indies

and America and his later escape. Simply told, the book
has the ring of authenticity. It is by a noted storyteller who
is an expert on African history and African folklore.

802   And Then We Heard the Thunder, by John Oliver Kil-
       lens. Knopf, 1962. $7.95 (Coronet Communications,
       Inc., Paperback Library, 1971, pb $1.25)
       RL: 7   IL: HS-Adult   *BSMP
This is a very powerful novel about anti-Negro discrimination
in World War II. The characters are so believable and the
reader becomes so emotionally embroiled in the action that
reading it is an experience.

803   And What of You, Josephine Charlotte, by Elizabeth Wither-
       idge. Illus. by Barbara McGee. Atheneum, c1969. $4.25
       RL: 6   IL: 5-adult   *SMP
This story of a slave girl in the 1800's who wants her freedom, even though she loves her kind mistress, has both romance and adventure. It would be popular both with girls
who love dates and clothes (there is a lot about clothes and
wedding dresses) and also with girls and older women who
are interested in history.

804   The Apple and the Arrow: The Legend of William Tell,
       by Mary and Conrad Buff. Houghton Mifflin, c1951.
       $3.73 (Scholastic, 1951, pb $.60)
       RL: 5   IL: 5-HS   BS
The format of this book is too young. However, it has good
illustrations and the story of William Tell's gamble to win
freedom for his country is still a very exciting one and one
(that in different forms) still goes on.

805   April Morning, by Howard Fast. Adapted by Dora F.
       Pantell. Noble & Noble (Falcon Books), 1970. $.56
       RL: 4-5   IL: JH-adult   *BS
A wonderful historical novel about a day in Lexington when a
boy meets the Redcoats and becomes a man. Exciting and
honest, this adapted version should be very popular.

806   The Autobiography of Miss Jane Pittman, by Ernest J.
       Gaines. Dial, 1971. (Bantam, 1972, pb $1.25)
       RL: 5   IL: 5-adult   *BSMP
A superb novel in the form of an autobiography which tells
the story of a black woman whose life spans the years from
slavery to the tense days of the Civil Rights movement.
Very simply told, the effect of this book is cumulative and
at the end, intensely moving. Must reading for everyone

and already very popular.

807 Ben-Hur, by Lew Wallace.   Adapted by Willis Lindquist.
    Illus. by Charles Beck.   Scholastic, 1960, pb $.60
    RL: 5   IL: 5-adult   BS
An adapted edition of the famous story of the Jewish leader
who became a galley slave and whose sister and mother
were cured by Jesus.   It is very popular.   I persuaded most
of the staff to read it.   They were very much interested in
the religious implications and started recommending it.   Then
the movie came to our neighborhood and it was very much in
demand.   The movie has gone now but it is still an exciting
and popular story.

808 Benjamin in the Woods, by Eleanor Clymer.   Illus. by
    William Russell.   Grosset Easy-To-Read Wonder
    Book, c1962.   OP
    RL: 2-3   IL: Read aloud-4   BS
A pioneer boy is lonely until a new family joins the settlement.   This useful easy-to-read book has humor as well as
history and can be used with older non-readers.

809 Black Courage, by A. E. Schraff.   Illus. by Len Ebert.
    Macrae, 1969. $3.95
    RL: 5   IL: 5-HS   *SM
The stories of twenty-one black heroes of the West are told
with a great deal of fictitious dialogue to lend interest.   I
am bothered by the writing in this book but the facts of the
men's lives are authentic and collections of short materials
like these are always very valuable in Reading Help programs.
Since the interest value of the stories varies greatly, it
would be wise for a tutor to read the book first and pick out
the stories which he finds most appealing.

810 Black Soldier, by John Clarke.   Illus. by Harold James.
    Doubleday, Signal, c1968. $3.50 (Doubleday,
    Semaphore, pb $1.75)
    RL: 4   IL: 4-adult   *BSMP
The fictionalized account of many black soldiers in World
War II, a story, to quote the dust jacket, "of shame and
glory."   This book will be of great interest to many boys
facing the draft or thinking of volunteering.   Older boys
might go on from this book to And Then We Heard the
Thunder [802].

811 Black Thunder, by Arna Bontemps.   Beacon, c1936
    and c1963.   pb $2.45

RL: 6-7   IL: JH-adult   *BSMP
A moving vivid novel about Gabriel Prosser's slave revolt in
Virginia in 1800.

812 Bond of the Fire, by Anthony Fon Eisen.   World,
     c1965. $4. 95   (Dell Yearling pb $. 75)
     RL: 7   IL: 5-adult   B
This is a very unusual book which brings to life the world
of early man in the Glacial Age.   Ash, the young hero,
tames a dog whom he eventually breeds to a she wolf.   With
the dog's help in hunting, he enables his tribe to survive
several natural catastrophes and with the dog's love and de-
votion, he learns to understand the power of love and trust.
The format attracts children too young to really understand
the story but many read it for the exciting adventures.   If
teenagers who are curious are introduced to this book by an
enthusiast, they like it very much.   See also 826 and 827.

813 Boy on the Mayflower, by Iris Vinton. Illus. by Jon
     Nielsen.   Four Winds. $2. 50   (Scholastic, 1957,
     pb $. 35)
     RL: 5   IL: 5-JH   BS
Good historical fiction helps to bring the Pilgrim days alive.

814 Brady, by Jean Fritz. Illus. by Lynd Ward. Coward-
     McCann, 1960. $4. 25   (Scholastic, 1966, pb $. 60)
     RL: 5   IL: 5-adult   BS
A very exciting story of a boy in Pennsylvania whose father
is connected with the Underground Railway.   His confrontation
with the fact of slavery is thought-provoking.

815 Bronco Charlie: Rider of the Pony Express, by Henry
     V. Larom.   Illus. by Wesley Dennis.   McGraw-Hill,
     1951. $2. 75   (Scholastic, 1966, pb $. 50)
     RL: 3   IL: 4-JH   BS
A realistic account of a young pioneer who winds up riding
the pony express.   So written that it is easy for even an
inner city boy to picture himself as the hero.

816 By Secret Railway, by Enid La Monte Meadowcroft.
     Illus. by Dom Lupo.   Crowell, 1948.   (Scholastic,
     1966, pb $. 75)
     RL: 5   IL: 5-adult   BS
An excellent fictional story of the underground railroad.
Both fictional and factual books to do with Afro-American
history are being requested more and more.   This is a good
one since it can appeal to a wide age range.

817   Canalboat to Freedom, by Thomas Fall.   Illus. by
      Joseph Cellini.   Dial, 1966. $3.95
      RL: 5-6   IL: 5-JH   *BSMP
I enjoyed this story of an indentured Scotch boy who gets involved with the Underground Railroad and I think many other
adults would.   The characters are both interesting and moving.

818   Captain Blackman, by John A. Williams.   Doubleday,
      c1972. $6.95
      RL: 6   IL: 6-adult   *BMP
An extraordinary tour de force, this novel starts with Captain
Abraham Blackman as he is seriously wounded in Vietnam because of an action he took to protect his men.   Thereafter
he drifts in and out of a coma as he relives in a hallucinating dream the role of a black soldier in every one of America's wars starting with Lexington and the Revolution.   The
book brings home the part that black soldiers have played in
the battle for freedom and the freedom and equality of opportunity they have been promised each time they were needed.
This book will be very popular indeed with black people and
should be read by all adult Americans.

819   Caroline and Her Kettle Named Maud, by Miriam E.
      Mason.   Illus. by Joseph Escourido.   Macmillan,
      1951. $3.95   (Scholastic, 1965, pb $.60)
      RL: 3-4   IL: 2-5   BS
Children almost always seem to like books by this author.
In this story a pioneer girl outwits a wolf with her kettle.
Girls empathize with the tomboy heroine.

820   The Children Who Stayed Alone, by Bonnie Bess Wor-
      line.   Illus. by Walter Barrows.   McKay, c1956.
      (Scholastic, c1965, pb $.60)
      RL: 4   IL: 4-JH   BS
Many, many girls in underprivileged families are forced by
their family's poverty to assume adult responsibilities before
they are out of elementary school.   I have seen fifth graders
in charge of marketing and cooking for their younger siblings.
They and their friends love this kind of story, the story of
a pioneer girl who is forced by circumstance to share with
her younger brother the care of five younger children of the
family through a blizzard and other perils.   The book has the
added dimension of a very warm family relationship (always
popular with children) and a very happy ending.

821   Confessions of Nat Turner, by W. Styron.   Modern
      Library, c1967. $2.95   (New American Library,

Signet, pb $1.25)
RL: Adult   IL: Adult   BM
Although this story of a famous slave revolt and the confession and death of its leader is a very controversial book, it was much requested and the comments on it were almost uniformly favorable--"very exciting," "I liked it," etc. Only a few militant areas produced objections. We showed them Black Thunder and other books to prove that we carried several points of view.

822 Day of Glory, by Philip Spencer. Illus. by Peter
     Burchard. Scholastic, c1955. pb $.75
     RL: 5   IL: 5-adult   BS
The exciting story of the day that started the American Revolution told hour by hour in such dramatic fashion that it is a real spell binder. Excellent for reading to a group and popular with boys from sixth grade on up.

823 Down the Mississippi, by Clyde Robert Bulla. Illus.
     by Irwin Hoffman. Crowell, c1954. $3.50 (Scholastic, c1961, pb $.60)
     RL: 4   IL: 4-HS   BS
The story of a boy in 1850 on a homestead on the Mississippi. The boy wants to be a riverman against his farmer father's wishes. He finally gets his wish. The story has lots of action and can be enjoyable and interesting to many different ages and maturity levels. In the School Volunteer program it often leads to interesting discussions about careers or family relationships. It has been one of the all time favorites both on the bookmobile and in the School Volunteer program.

824 Drinking Gourd, by F. N. Monjo. Illus. by Fred
     Brenner. Harper, I Can Read Series, c1970. $2.50
     RL: 3   IL: Read aloud-5   *BSMP
An exciting story of the Underground Railroad told from the point of view of a boy whose father was involved in helping escaping slaves on their way.

825 Edge of Two Worlds, by Weyman Jones. Illus. by
     J. C. Kocsis. Dial, c1968. (Dell, pb $.75)
     RL: 5   IL: 5-adult   BMP
Calvin, on his way from Texas East with a wagon train, is the only survivor of an Indian attack. He is lost and starving on the prairie when he falls in with an old sick Indian who helps him. Eventually he learns to trust and admire the Indian, Sequoyah, and both are finally rescued by

Sequoyah's son. The story of the famous Cherokee who invented a written language for his people is a fascinating one
that appeals to older boys and adults.

826   Fire-Hunter, by Jim Kjelgaard. Illus. by Ralph Ray.
      Holiday House, c1951. (Scholastic, 1966, pb $.60)
      RL: 6-7   IL: 5-adult   B
In this fascinating story of prehistoric man, Hawk the young
spear maker learns how to create a bow and arrow, how to
tame and make use of wild dogs, how to smoke meat and
how to use a snake's venom. Authentic history (except for
the telescoping into one life of what must have taken generations) the author makes the story full of action and excitement. Popular with teenagers.

827   First to Ride, by Pers Crowell. McGraw, c1948.
      (Scholastic, 1959, pb $.60)
      RL: 6   IL: 6-adult   BS
An exciting fictional account of the first man to domesticate
a horse. The dramatic black and white drawings bring to
life the age of the woolly mammoth. This book is popular
with teenagers and can sometimes be used to widen the interests of horse crazy girls of whom there are many in the
inner city even though they never see a live horse.

828   Flaming Arrows, by William O. Steele. Illus. by
      Paul Goldone. Harcourt, c1957. $3.95 (Voyager,
      1971, pb $1.15)
      RL: 4-5   IL: 4-JH   BS
One of the most exciting books I have read in years, this
story of pioneer life in Tennessee in Indian days has authenticity and depth. The Indians are not downgraded (their at-
tacks are rightly looked on as warfare) and the ethical dilemma of how to treat a traitor's family and moral leadership
against a mob are not contrived but an integral part of the
story.

829   Follow the Free Wind, by Leigh Brackett and Lawrence
      Swinburne. Illus. by Nat White. McGraw-Hill, Read-
      ing Shelf II, 1970. $1.60
      RL: 4-5   IL: 4-adult   *BSMP
A fictional account of the life of Jim Beckworth who was a
real person, a mountain man in the first half of the 19th
Century. He was a fur trapper who was adopted by the Crow
Indians. He was happy for a while but, as a black man, he
never felt truly at home in either the Indian or the white
man's world. At the end of his life, he died trying to make

peace between the Crows and the whites.   This is an exciting
book which will interest people even if they do not think they
care about history or the West.

830   Freedom Road, by Howard Fast.   Crown, 1969. $3.95
      (c1944, Bantam, 1969, pb $.75)
      RL: 8   IL: HS-adult   BSMP
A stirring novel about the Reconstruction era, this is well
written and so moving I could hardly bear to finish it.   Very
popular on the bookmobile.

831   The House of Sixty Fathers, by Meindert De Jong.
      Illus. by Maurice Sendak.   Harper & Row, 1956.
      (Dell Yearling, 1970, pb $.75)
      RL: 5-6   IL: 5-adult   BSMP
The tense and thrilling story of a young Chinese boy during
World War II who becomes separated from his family and
whose courage and endurance finally bring him to a reunion
with his parents.   A deeply moving story which has great
appeal to young people.   In a Signet or Archway format it
would be very popular with adults.   Those whom we have
persuaded to read it have loved it.

832   Johnny Tremain, by Esther Forbes.   Houghton Mifflin,
      c1943. $3.95   (Dell, Laurel, 1968, pb $.75)
      RL: 7   IL: 7-adult   B
An exciting story of a young boy during pre-Revolutionary
times in America.   Good format;   story is appealing to
adults.

833   Jubilee, by Margaret Walker.   Houghton Mifflin,
      Bantam, 1966.   pb $.95
      RL: Adult   IL: HS-adult   BMP
A powerful Civil War story of a black woman from her birth
in slavery to her life after emancipation, by the well known
black poet. .

834   Just Like Abraham Lincoln, by Bernard Waber.   Hough-
      ton Mifflin, 1964. $3.73
      RL: 2-3   IL: 1-4   S
A small boy sees the man next door who looks just like Lincoln.   An unusual way to arouse interest in Lincoln's life by
the author of the very popular Lyle books.

835   A Lantern in Her Hand, by Bess Streeter Aldrich.
      Hawthorn, c1928. $3.50   (Scholastic, 1956, pb $.75)
      RL: 6   IL: 6-adult   BS

This novel of pioneering on the prairie is a popular and useful book since it appeals to such a wide age-range.

836 The Magic Tunnel, by Caroline D. Emerson. Illus. by
     Jerry Robinson. Four Winds, c1940. $3.25 (Scholastic, 1964, pb $.60)
     RL: 5   IL: 4-JH   BS
Two children take a magic subway train which lands them
back in New Amsterdam. After many suspenseful adventures
they manage to return to the 20th century. A book which
brings New York City history alive. The modern beginning
of the story hooks children who normally shrink from historical fiction.

837 North Winds Blow Free, by Elizabeth Howard. Morrow,
     c1949.
     RL: 5   IL: 5-HS   BSMP
Elspeth McLaren was very sad when her father sold their
farm in Michigan and moved to Canada to help escaped slaves
to get a new start in an alien land. Before too long, though,
she was as deeply involved as he in the fight for freedom
and justice for black people. Believable characters, warm
family relationships and romance make this a very popular
book with girls from fifth grade on up.

838 Ol' Prophet Nat, by Daniel Panger. Blair, c1967.
     $4.95 (Fawcett pb OP)
     RL: 6   IL: 6-adult   BSMP
This little-known account of Nat Turner's rebellion is a
spellbinder. Told in direct language as if by Nat himself it
has real suspense even though the reader, of course, knows
that the rebellion was a failure. In 1967, the book had to
be introduced even in black areas, so few people knew who
Nat Turner was. It caught on fast and was and is still very
popular.

839 Old Whirlwind: A Davy Crockett Story, by Elizabeth
     Coatsworth. Macmillan, c1953. (Scholastic, 1964,
     pb $.50)
     RL: 4   IL: 4-HS   BS
A good dog story as well as good easy historical fiction about
a frontier hero.

840 On to Freedom, by Mary Kennedy Carter. Illus. by
     Joyce Owens. Hill and Wang, Challenger, c1970.
     $1 (dist. by Random)
     RL: 5   IL: 5-HS   *BSMP

A fictional account of Robert Small's seizure of the boat, the <u>Planter</u>, and his escape to freedom in Civil War Days, told from the point of view of a thirteen-year-old slave boy who escapes with him. This not very well written account makes the whole event (which, of course, really happened) seem improbable but the book has excitement and is on a popular subject so it will probably be well liked. See 1375, 1415 and 1548 for more authentic versions of the story.

841 <u>One Week of Danger</u>, by Cateau De Leeuw. Illus. by
     Kurt Werth. Scholastic, 1959. pb $.60
     RL: 5   IL: 4-HS   BS
A very exciting adventure story about the Kentucky frontier with enough fast action to interest older boys.

842 <u>Page Boy of Camelot</u>, by Eugenia Stone. Illus. by
     Mort Künstler. Follett, 1949. (Scholastic, 1967,
     pb $.50)
     RL: 5   IL: 4-HS   BS
An interesting story of a boy's adventures at King Arthur's Court which has real appeal for boys. It can be used almost as a sequel to <u>The Sword in the Tree</u> [856] with older boys who are making rapid progress in reading.

843 <u>The Perilous Road</u>, by William O. Steele. Illus. by
     Paul Galdone. Harcourt, Brace, 1958. $3.95
     (Voyager pb $.75)
     RL: 6   IL: 5-HS   BSP
A very exciting and unusual story about the Civil War illustrating many different points of view but especially the "war is hell" aspect. It can be used to start a discussion of pacifism, dissent and violence. The protagonist is a young boy whose family is divided in its sympathies between the North, the South, and pacifism.

844 <u>Powder Keg</u>, by Donald E. Cooke. Illus. by Harve
     Stein. Holt, Rinehart, 1953. OP (Scholastic, 1967,
     pb $.60)
     RL: 5   IL: 5-HS   BS
An action packed story of a boy's adventures and heroism in the Revolution.

845 <u>The Price of Liberty</u>, edited by Phyllis R. Fenner.
     Illus. by William R. Lohse. Morrow, 1960. $3.95
     RL: Varied, mostly 6 up   IL: 6-HS   SP
There is already a lot of talk about the Bicentennial and an increasing interest in the Revolution. This is a good and

varied collection of stories about the subject which will be
enjoyed if well introduced.

846   The Railroad to Freedom, by Hildegarde H. Swift.
        Illus. by James Daugherty.   Harcourt, Brace, c1932,
        1960. $4.25
        RL: 6   IL: 6-adult   SMP
An exciting fictional account of the life of Harriet Tubman.
It is very well done but some children may find the dialect
in it difficult.   Others find the story so suspenseful that the
dialect doesn't bother them.   It is interesting to note that
this book was published in 1932 when books on this subject
were rare indeed.

847   The Red Badge of Courage, by Stephen Crane.   Illus.
        by Herschel Levit.   Macmillan, c1895, 1962.   (Lan-
        cer pb $.60)
        RL: 7   IL: 6-adult   B
This classic story of a young man's experiences in the Civil
War has universal implications.   It doesn't move often on
the bookmobile but the young people and adults who do read
it are enthusiastic.

848   Riding the Pony Express, by Clyde Robert Bulla.   Illus.
        by Grace Paull.   Crowell, c1948. $3.50 (Scholas-
        tic, 1963, pb $.60)
        RL: 3-4   IL: 3-JH   BS
A ten-year-old goes out West in 1860 to find his father and
winds up in many adventures.   Another easy-to-read Bulla
book that can be of real interest to a seventh- or eighth-
grade slow reader.

849   Sam the Minuteman, by Nathaniel Benchley.   Illus. by
        Arnold Loble.   Harper, I Can Read Series, 1969.
        $2.50
        RL: 3   IL: 3-6   BS
The story of Sam and how and why he fought at the battle of
Lexington told in simple language, this book makes history
real.

850   Samax the Gladiator, by Robert Faraday.   Dell, 1964.
        OP
        RL: 5   IL: 4-JH   B
A fast moving story of two boys who are whisked by magic
back to early Rome, we carry this to add variety.   The occasional good reader who picks it up is very enthusiastic and
is often sparked by it to go to the library for more on Rome.

851 <u>Silence Over Dunkerque</u>, by John R. Tunis.   Morrow,
     1962. $4.59   (Scholastic, 1968, pb $.60)
     RL: 5-6   IL: 5-adult   BS
An exciting story of two British soldiers in World War II
marooned in Nazi Europe after Dunkerque.   This book has
two great virtues: first, it is by a sports author that boys
have confidence in, therefore, if it's by Tunis they'll read it
and, in this instance, move into a different brand of literature.   Secondly, without stating anything or preaching any
morals, the plot teaches tolerance and an appreciation of a
two culture situation;   in this instance, British soldiers learn
to like and respect the French.

852 <u>Silver for General Washington: A Story of Valley Forge</u>,
     by Enid LaMonte Meadowcroft.   Illus. by Lee Ames.
     Crowell, c1957.   (Scholastic, 1964, pb $.75)
     RL: 4-5   IL: 3-JH   BS
A twelve-year-old boy meets the rigors of winter at Valley
Forge and helps smuggle supplies for Washington out of
Philadelphia.   An exciting story of the Revolution which is
well liked by boys through junior high school.

853 <u>Snow Treasure</u>, by Marie McSwigan.   Illus. by André
     LaBlanc.   Dutton, 1942. $3.95   (Scholastic, 1958,
     pb $.75)
     RL: 5   IL: 4-JH   BS
An exciting story (based on fact) of how Norwegian children
conspired successfully to help defeat the Nazi invaders.

854 <u>Spies of the Revolution</u>, by Katherine and John Bakeless.
     Lippincott, c1962. $4.25   (Scholastic pb $.60)
     RL: 6   IL: JH-adult   B
TV and James Bond have aroused interest in espionage in
every circle.   These stories are borrowed mainly by older
boys and adults.   Black and white illustrations add interest.

855 <u>A Star Pointed North</u>, by Edmund Fuller.   Harper &
     Row, Perennial, 1946. $.75
     RL: 7   IL: HS-adult   *BMP
A rich imaginative novel of the life of Frederick Douglass.
Not easy reading but hard to lay down once into it.   See
also 858, 1417, 1418 and 1495.

856 <u>The Sword in the Tree</u>, by C. R. Bulla.   Illus. by
     Paul Galdone.   Crowell, c1956. $3.50   (Scholastic
     pb $.75)
     RL: 4   IL: 4-JH   BS

An exciting story with great suspense laid in the days of
King Arthur. It can be used with older non-readers with
great success.

857 Tejanos, by Ed Foster. Illus. by Bill Negron. Hill &
     Wang Challenger (Distributed by Random), 1970. pb
     $1
     RL: 5   IL: 4-JH
This slender volume (forty-eight pages) tells the story of the
battle for the Alamo from the point of view of a young Mexican boy whose father died in the Alamo with the brave de-
fenders battling for independence. It is a dramatic story
and I found it very interesting to learn that Mexicans fought
on both sides in the battle.

858 There Once Was a Slave, by Shirley Graham. Messner,
     c1947. OP
     RL: 6   IL: 6-adult   SMP
An excellent but somewhat sentimental fictionalized version
of the life of Frederick Douglass. Far easier to read than
his own Narrative, it covers also much more of his life. It
has been very popular. Many of today's readers would probably prefer A Star Pointed North [855]. Again, however,
that is more difficult reading than this.

859 We Were There at the Battle for Bataan, by Benjamin
     Appel. Illus. by Irv Doktor. Grosset, c1957. $2.95
     (Tempo pb OP)
     RL: 5   IL: 5-HS   BS
A vivid account of World War II in the Philippines told by
two American youngsters caught there after Pearl Harbor.

860 We Were There at the Normandy Invasion, by Clayton
     Knight. Grosset & Dunlap, c1956. (Tempo pb OP)
     RL: 5   IL: 5-HS   BS
An exciting story of a French boy's experiences in the Normandy invasion. Popular with a wide age range. Illustrated.

861 White Sails to China, by Clyde Robert Bulla. Illus. by
     Robert G. Henneberger. Crowell, c1955. $3.50
     (Scholastic, 1965, pb $.60)
     RL: 3-4   IL: 4-JH   BS
A most unusual book about a boy of clipper ship days who
wants to drop out of school to escape strict guardians. It
poses many ethical questions. I have used this book successfully with high school and young adult slow readers and it
holds their interest.

862 Young Vikings, by Jack Coggins. Scholastic, 1966.
     pb $.50
     RL: 4-5   IL: 5-JH   BS
This story of a brave Viking boy and his crew has many
thrills. The illustrations by the author are vivid and lure
the reader on. Vikings may seem remote from city streets
but, in fact, they do seem to capture the imagination of many
city boys. Many third and fourth graders reach for this but
find it too difficult. We need an easy book on Vikings similar to Clyde Bulla's The Sword in the Tree on the Arthurian
era.

HUMAN EXPERIENCES

863 Aesop's Fables, retold by Ann McGovern. Illus. by
     A. J. McCloskey. Scholastic, c1963. pb $.60
     RL: 5   IL: 5-adult   S
People have been learning about human nature, especially
their own, from these fables for generations. "Sour grapes"
and other quotations from them are part of our language.
This book is very useful and much enjoyed in a one-to-one
situation in Reading Help Programs. This edition is not
colorful enough to move well on the bookmobile.

864 All Except Sammy, by Gladys Vessayan Cretan. Illus.
     by Symeon Shimin. Little, c1966. $3.50
     RL: 3   IL: 3-6   S
Everyone in his family except Sammy is musical. He plays
baseball and feels left out. The setting in this book is middle class but feeling left out knows no class and I include
this book because what ended Sammy's lonely feelings was a
picture at the Museum. The feeling for art among school
children today is very strong and genuine and I hope this
book will lead other boys to museums.

865 Apt. 3, by Ezra Jack Keats. Macmillan, c1971. $5.95
     RL: 3   IL: Read aloud-4   *BSMP
The illustrations in this book, soft and grey and every color
of a rainy day, would interest any art-loving person of any
age. They have a haunting quality. The story is about two
boys who find a new friend, a blind man and has both suspense and warmth.

866   A Bargain for Frances, by Russell Hoban.   Illus. by
        Lillian Hoban.   Harper, c1970. $2.50
        RL: 3   IL: Read aloud-4   BS
Frances learns about greed and bargains that are no bargains
and her friend learns to put friendship ahead of doll's dishes
in this entertaining and popular story.

867   Bear for the FBI, by Melvin Van Peebles.   Trident
        Press, New York, 1968. $4.50
        RL: 7   IL: HS-adult   BS
A novel, which reads like an autobiography about growing up
in Chicago in the black middle class at the time of World
War II.   Although some of the vocabulary is difficult, many
poor readers enjoy this book when persuaded to try it because the hero's experiences are such universal ones and
yet very interesting.   He confronts the school bully, he and
his friends long to "make out" with girls etc. and the author
brings an extra dimension to the telling that makes one want
to read on.

868   Beautiful Junk: A Story of the Watts Tower, by Jon
        Madigan.   Photographs by Barbara and Lou Jacobs.
        Little, Brown, c1968. $3.95
        RL: 3   IL: 3-adult   SMP
A young boy hates the look of the junk around where he lives
and smashes bottles in anger at his surroundings.   He sees
an old man gather up the broken glass and other debris as if
it were precious and carry it away.   He follows him and
finds the famous Watts towers--junk turned into something
beautiful by a creative man.

869   Benito, by Clyde Robert Bulla.   Illus. by Yalenti
        Angelo.   Crowell Co. , c1961. $3.50
        RL: 3   IL: 3-JH   BSMP
A realistic story of a Mexican-American boy's life in Southern
California and his successful struggle to become an artist.
A good book which is much borrowed by Puerto Rican chil-
dren who like the Spanish name and then like the story even
when they find the hero is not Puerto Rican.

870   Benjie, by Joan M. Lexau.   Illus. by Don Bolognese.
        Dial, c1964. $3.95
        RL: 3   IL: 2-4   BSMP
A wonderful book that ought to be in paperback.   This is the
heartwarming story of a boy whose love for his grandmother
overcomes his overwhelming shyness.   Popular in School
Volunteer programs but does not do well on the bookmobile

because it is in hardcover.

871 <u>Benjie on His Own</u>, by Joan M. Lexau. Illus. by Don
Bolognese. Dial, c1970. $3.95
RL: 3-4 IL: K-5 BSMP
This sequel to <u>Benjie</u> tells about Benjie grown old enough for
school and confronting some very real problems. His grandmother becomes very ill and has to go to the hospital. Happily, he learns that people pitch in to help even in a big city
and that neighbors do care even if they don't know your name.
I'd like to see this book in a Dell Yearling kind of format. It would be very popular then. This way, many children who would really enjoy it and be helped by it, will pass
it up thinking it's a baby book.

872 <u>The Big Wave</u>, by Pearl Buck. Illus. by Kazue Miza-
mura. John Day, c1947. (Scholastic pb $.60)
RL: 5 IL: 5-adult BSMP
This is an extraordinary book. In less than a hundred pages,
the author tells the story of a Japanese boy whose family is
drowned in a tidal wave. He learns to face death with courage and the future with hope. The illustrations are delicate
and exotic but the story has universal implications. It has
been very popular with adults on the bookmobile.

873 <u>Boy Wanted</u>, by Ruth Fenisong. Illus. by Lili Cassel-
Wronker. Harper, 1964. $2.95
RL: 4-5 IL: 4-JH and older poor readers
especially girls and women *SMP
The story of an orphan boy in the Bahamas will seem exciting
to middle graders and moving to older readers. The poverty
depicted is very real and reminds me of Sidney Poiter's description of his boyhood in Nassau. Fortunately, he didn't
have a villainous aunt and uncle like the ones in this book.

874 <u>Bread and Jam for Frances</u>, by Russell Hoban. Illus.
by Lilliam Hoban. Harper & Row, 1964. $3.50
(Scholastic pb $.50)
RL: 3 IL: Read aloud-3 BS
A popular and funny story about a bear who learns that there
is such a thing as too much bread and jam. Good for younger
children.

875 <u>Brooklyn Story</u>, by Sharon Bell Mathis. Illus. by
Charles Bible. Hill & Wang Challenger (distributed
by Random), c1970.
RL: 5 IL: 5-HS *BSM

A story of a boy and girl who live with their grandmother in Bedford-Stuyvesant. Their mother, whose absence has never been explained to them, comes home for a visit during the course of which the lives of the entire family are changed. The setting is authentic (the author grew up in Bedford-Stuyvesant) and the time covers the period of Martin Luther King's assasination which almost all inner city children remember as traumatic. The story deals with mental illness and family loyalties.

876   Brown Girl, Brownstones, by Paule Marshall. Avon,
      1959.   pb $.95
      RL: 6   IL: JH-adult   *BSMP
The story of a West Indian girl growing up in Brooklyn. Her mother is willing to sacrifice anything, including her father's self-respect, to the goal of home ownership and material success. The relationship between the two generations gives this superb novel universal value.

877   The Carrot Seed, by Ruth Krauss. Illus. by Crockett
      Johnson. Harper & Row, 1945. $3.50 (Scholastic
      pb $.35)
      RL: 2   IL: Read aloud-3   BS
A small boy is sure his carrot will grow in spite of everyone's jeers and, in fact, it does. Many city children have a love for growing things and like this story. Any book illustrated by Crockett Johnson is popular. Children reach for his pictures.

878   The Cool World, by Warren Miller. Fawcett, c1959.
      pb $.75
      RL: 5-6   IL: 6-adult   BSMP
This frank story of an eighth grader in Harlem who is a "cool" gang leader is one of the three most popular books in the School Volunteer programs in junior and senior high schools. It is also very popular on the bookmobile with teenagers and adults. Although fiction, it is an accurate picture of life in the inner city. Although the "hero," who is very likeable, sleeps with his girl and winds up peddling marijuana cigarettes, the book is highly moral in its attitude. He winds up finding a new life in a reform school that resembles the Wiltwyck School which gave Floyd Patterson, the boxing champion, when he was a delinquent youth, the ambition to become a useful citizen.

879   Crow Boy, by Taro Yashima. Illus. by the author.
      Viking, c1955. $3.50 (Seafarer, 1970, pb $.75)

RL: 3-4   IL: Read aloud-5   BSMP
A Japanese story of a lonely boy who seems to have nothing
to contribute but who ends up admired by his schoolmates
and teacher. Unusual illustrations.

880 Cry, the Beloved Country, by Alan Paton.   Scribner,
     1948. $3.95   (pb $1.65)
RL: Adult   IL: Adult   BMP
A black South African parson leaves his country home and
goes to the city in search of his son who seems to have disappeared. He finds him in jail about to be tried for murder-
ing a white man who has worked all his life for justice for
the black race. This beautiful and tragic story of South
Africa is far too difficult for most of our clientele but is
something for them to reach for. Often if the first chapter
is read aloud, even a poor reader will be caught up in the
story and struggle to finish it.

881 Cry the Beloved Country, by Alan Paton.   Edited by
     Felicia Komai.   Friendship Press, c1955.   pb $.75
                                                  BM
An abridged and slightly easier version of the above.

882 Doc Stops a War, by Ben Lucius Burman.   Reader's
     Digest Services, Inc.   Pegasus.   pb
RL: 2-3   IL: Read aloud-4   *BSP
This book is an excerpt from High Water At Catfish Bend,
adapted for beginning readers by L. A. Thomas. A flood
strands a number of natural enemies (such as the fox and the
hen) on a small island. How they learn to live and let live
makes a wonderful story. The format of the book is excellent with large print and bright pictures. Many people are
interested in exposing children to books on the theme of
peace. This is excellent for that purpose. For more books
on the subject ranging from picture books to books on the
high school interest level, see the magazine, School Library
Journal, October 1970.

883 The Egypt Game, by Zilpha Keatley Snyder.   Illus. by
     Alton Raible.   Atheneum, c1967. $3.95   (pb $.95)
     RL: 5   IL: 4-7   BSMP
This very unusual book is not widely popular but means a
great deal to those who do like it--that is, rather lonely
imaginative girls in the upper elementary grades or in junior
high school. A group of imaginative children create a pretend world based on what they have learned at school about
life and religion in early Egypt. They experience good times

and some very real and justified terror. The book has quiet
humor. The children involved are black and white and
Chinese-American and all are very real.

884   Fables of Lafontaine, by Jean de La Fontaine. Transl.
      and illus. by Richard Scarry. Doubleday, 1964.
      $3.25
      RL: 2-3   IL: Read aloud-HS Non-readers   S
Every child should have the chance to hear these stories
whose characters have become part of the language. This
version is not very well told but it is easy to read and has
the same kind of pictures that are so well liked in numbers
5 and 142. A very useful book for a short change of pace
or a start to meaningful conversation in a Reading Help program.

885   Fifty Thousand Names for Jeff, by Anne Snyder. Illus.
      by L. Carty. Holt, 1969. $3.50
      RL: 4   IL: 3-6-non-reading JH-HS   *SMP
When I read a review of this book, it sounded so contrived
I didn't want to read it. However, this story of a boy who
through luck and diligence wins a fight over a housing project actually carries conviction. It has suspense, the people
are real and hopefully it will inspire other young activists.

886   Follow My Leader, by James B. Garfield. Illus. by
      Don Sibley. Viking, c1957. $3.95 (Scholastic,
      1967, pb OP)
      RL: 5   IL: 4-JH   BS
Jimmy, blinded in a firecracker accident, learns many new
things--how to get around with a cane and a guide dog, how
to read Braille and, most important, that you cannot be happy until you quit hating.

887   Free As a Frog, by Elizabeth J. Hodges. Illus. by
      Paul Giovanopoulos. Addison-Wesley (Addisonian),
      1969. $3.25
      RL: 3   IL: Read aloud-4   *SMP
A lovely story of a shy six-year-old who gains confidence
from a frog. Like the book What Mary Jo Shared, the story
has a universal quality many children will appreciate. Unusual black and white illustrations.

888   Go Tell It on the Mountain, by James Baldwin. Dial,
      c1953. $4.95 (Dell Laurel pb $.95)
      RL: Adult   IL: Hs-adult   BM
James Baldwin's exciting novel of life in a Harlem preacher's

family and the relationships of the different generations.
This is also available in a Falcon Book edition at an easier
reading level. See 175.

889 Headed for Trouble, by Barbara Rinkoff. Illus. by
     Don Bolognese. Knopf, c1970. $4.50
     RL: 5   IL: 4-JH   *BSMP
Books with trouble in the title always seem to be very popular with boys and this one will be no exception. Matt, an
orphan deserted by his father, is sent to a home for boys.
A younger boy who is his companion on the trip to the home
attaches himself to Matt, who thinks he's a nuisance but
finally learns, through his friendship, not to run away from
life. Lots of action carries the story along fast.

890 Heidi, by Johanna Spyri. Illus. by John Fernie.
     Scholastic, c1959. pb $.75
     RL: 5   IL: 5-6   B
The classic story of the little Swiss girl who pines for her
mountain home is still very popular with girls of today.

891 Heidi to Read Aloud, by Johanna Spyri. Adapted for
     the Grosset Read-Aloud Wonder Book series. pb
     $.49
     RL: 3-4   IL: 4-6   BS
Large print and simpler language make this version useful
and popular with poor readers.

892 His Enemy, His Friend, by John R. Tunis. Wm.
     Morrow, 1967. $4.95 (Avon pb $.75)
     RL: 5-6   IL: 5-adult   BSP
This book is a little hard for a poor reader to get into with
its unfamiliar setting (occupied France in World War II) but
once in, he is hooked. It is a gripping story of justice,
revenge and brotherhood. It is also an excellent sports
story. The account of the soccer game is a real thriller.
The book raises important issues for today and would be an
excellent basis for a discussion group on the high school
level.

893 How to Find a Friend, by Sara Asheron. Illus. by
     Susan Perl. Grosset Easy-To-Read Wonder Book,
     c1964. OP
     RL: 2   IL: Read aloud-3   BS
Many beginning readers reach for this looking for the answer
which the title implies. However, this is a fictional account
of a boy in a new neighborhood whose wandering dog provides

an introduction and it is much liked.

894 I Should Have Stayed in Bed, by Joan M. Lexau. Illus.
     by Syd Hoff.   Harper & Row, I Can Read Series,
     1965. $3.50
     RL: 2   IL: Read aloud-4   BSMP
Everyone has bad days and good days and this book about a
bad day that turned good is very popular.

895 J. T. , by Jane Wagner.   Photographs by Gordon Parks,
     Jr. Van Nostrand Reinhold, c1969. $4.95   (Dell
     Yearling pb $. 75)
     RL: 3   IL: 3-adult   BSMP
A moving story of a boy's relationship with his mother and
with a stray sick cat whom he tries to save.   It can be read
on many levels and involves the generation gap and the meaning of life and death.   The black family, grandmother, mother
and child, are real and appealing as are also a Jewish store-
keeper and his wife who play a major part in the story.
This story first appeared as a ballad and then as a TV program.   Now it has become a book which is read and reread.

896 Jeffrey at Camp, by Syd Hoff.   Putnam, 1968. $3.29
     RL: 3   IL: 2-5   SMP
A funny story of a boy at camp whose only interest is in eat-
ing and what happens to him.   Many children being sent to
camp are frightened and don't know what to expect.   This
book fills a real need since it is on not too high a reading
level and the camp pictures and situations are universal ones.

897 The Landlord, by Kristin Hunter.   Avon, 1969.   pb
     $.95
     RL: Adult   IL: HS-adult   BM
The son of a Jewish mother becomes the landlord of a tene-
ment in a black ghetto and finds his identity.   This was especially popular when the movie based on it came out.   However, it is a wise and witty book with universal insights into
human relationships and it is still in demand now that the
movie has been forgotten.   See also 1056 and 1107 by the
same author.

898 Let's Be Enemies, by Janice M. Udry.   Illus. by
     Maurice Sendak.   Harper & Row, c1961. $2.90
     (Scholastic pb $. 75)
     RL: 2-3   IL: 2-3   BS
A popular picture book that opens doors in reading help sessions in the early grades.   It is on the Publishers for Peace

list.   See the annotation for 882.

899   The Lilies of the Field, by William E. Barrett.   Illus.
      by Burt Silverman.   Doubleday, 1962. $3.50   (Pop-
      ular pb $.50)
      RL: 6   IL: JH-adult   BM
This warm and appealing story of the power of faith was the
basis for the popular movie with Sidney Poitier as the hero.
Illustrated with pen and ink drawings.

900   Little Boy Who Lives Up High, by John and Lucy Haw-
      kinson.   Hale, c1967. $2.55
      RL: 2-3   IL: Read aloud-3   BSMP
Living up high in the sky is a new human experience and one
that is not yet well understood.   Is it good or bad for people
to live up high?   Ricky doesn't question his life but reports
on what it's like to live in one of the top floors of a high
rise apartment in a way to interest all children.

901   A Little Princess, by Frances Hodgson Burnett.
      Scribners, c1904, c1938. $6   (Grosset Tempo pb
      $.60)
      RL: 6   IL: 6-HS   B
Girls still love to cry over this story of the orphan girl and
her proud struggle to survive.   For an abridged version,
get Sara Crewe pub. by Scholastic Book Services.

902   The Lollipop Party, by Ruth A. Sonneborn.   Illus. by
      Brinton Turkle.   Viking, c1967. $2.95
      RL: 3   IL: Read aloud-3   BSMP
Tomas is unexpectedly left alone to cope with what could be
a frightening experience.   Instead, the stranger proves to be
a friend and all turns out happily.   Children, especially
Puerto Ricans, love this.   Should be in paperback.

903   Look to the River, by William Owens.   Illus. by Ferd
      Sondern.   Adapted by Ray L. Trautman.   McGraw-
      Hill Reading Shelf, c1963, c1970. $1.60
      RL: 5   IL: 5-adult   *BSMP
A boy, bound by his own word to a farmer, runs away after
a wandering peddler who is the only man who can prove that
the boy has not stolen a watch found in his belongings.   The
boy gets involved with a chain gang and learns the meaning
of courage and loyalty.

904   The Looking-Down Game, by Leigh Dean.   Illus. by
      Paul Giovanopoulos.   Funk & Wagnalls, 1968. $3.95

RL: 3-4   IL: 3-6   BSMP
A shy boy is lonely because his family has moved to a different part of the city.   He looks down to discover another
world--ants, beetles, etc.   The book expresses feelings
common to all children and is well liked.

905 Marty and Printer's Measure, by Paddy Chayefsky.
     Adapted by Warren Halliburton.   Illus. by Wolfgang
     Otto.   McGraw Reading Shelf I Series Original, 1956,
     c1968. $1.60
     RL: 4-5   IL: 7-adult   BS
Two television plays adapted into two easy-to-read long short
stories.   Both selections are suspenseful and the characters
are appealing and real.   One concerns a man so ugly that no
girl wants to date him and the other deals with automation
and loyalties.   Both are well liked.

906 Mary Jo's Grandmother, by Janice M. Udry.   Illus. by
     Eleanor Mill.   Whitman, c1970. $3.75
     RL: 3   IL: Read aloud-5   *BSMP
Mary Jo goes to visit her grandmother and faces a crisis
bravely when her grandmother falls and is hurt just as a
blizzard arrives.   Girls will love this, especially those who
already know Mary Jo.

907 Member of the Gang, by Barbara Rinkoff.   Illus. by
     Harold James.   Crown, 1968. $3.50 (Scholastic
     pb $.60)
     RL: 5   IL: 5-HS   *BSMP
An exciting story of the pressures on a boy in an impoverished neighborhood to join a gang and look cool with his peers
at an age when his family, who is pressuring him to do well
in school, do not seem to understand his problems.   Will be
very popular.

908 Miguel's Mountain, by Bill Binzen.   Coward McCann,
     1968. $3.69
     RL: 3   IL: Read aloud-4   SMP
Miguel's Mountain is a mound of earth in New York.   The
story tells how the "mountain" was allowed to remain for
children to play on after Miguel wrote the mayor.   The book
is illustrated with attractive photographs and though Miguel
is young, it can be used with older boys who also like to
play on snow mountains.

909 Mr. Pine's Purple House, by Leonard Kessler.   Grosset
     and Dunlap Easy-To-Read Wonder Book Series, 1965.
     $.69

RL: 2   IL: Read aloud-4   BS
A good, funny read-aloud and easy-to-read story about the
struggle to be different.

910 My Side of the Mountain, by Jean George.   Dutton,
        c1959. $3.95 (Scholastic, 1969, pb $.75)
        RL: 6   IL: 6-HS   *B
A modern city boy learns to survive alone in a mountain
wilderness. This book has suspense and excitement. It is
also like a survival manual with black and white sketches by
the author of useful wild plants and traps and other utensils
that the boy fashioned out of wilderness materials. The
Outward Bound Survival Camp Program has scholarship money
for inner city youth and this book may well inspire some to
apply. Certainly the boy in the story (who has considerable
confidence to start with) ends up with unshakeable self-con-
fidence and a great deal of education by the end of his experience.

911 The Nitty Gritty, by Frank Bonham.   Illus. by Alvin
        Smith.   Dutton, c1968. $3.95
        RL: 5   IL: 4-adult   BSMP
Charlie Mathews dreams of escaping from Dogtown, the slum
in which he lives, by going off with his uncle, a wanderer
whose glamor has the Mathews family bemused. He learns
in this story how hard it is to make a quick hit and how un-
wise it is to pin your hopes on a dreamer. The book has
unusual depth, humor and excitement and is popular even in
hard cover.

912 No Place to Play, by Paul Newman.   Illus. by David
        Lockhart.   Grosset & Dunlap Easy-To-Read Wonder
        Book, c1969. $.69
        RL: 2-3   IL: Read aloud-3   BSM
Three boys who are in the way wherever they go, finally
manage to build a clubhouse out of an old crate. The story
has humor and appeals to early graders.

913 No Promises in the Wind, by Irene Hunt.   Illus. by
        Richard Taylor.   Follett, c1970. $4.95 (Grosset
        Tempo, pb--no illustrations, $.95
        RL: 5-6   IL: 5-adult   *BSP
An inspiring story of love and courage in the great depres-
sion of the 1930s. Two brothers, one fifteen and one ten,
are forced out of their home by their father's harsh despair
at his inability to find work. They meet all kinds of people
and gradually learn tenderness and tolerance even toward

their father. The many adult characters in the book and the
simple direct writing make the story one which will appeal
to people of any age who will read the story on different
levels of interest and maturity.

914 The Off-Islanders, by Nathaniel Benchley. Adapted by
      J. Olsen. Illus. by A. Crane. McGraw-Hill Reading
      Shelf II Series, 1968. $1.72
      RL: 4-5   IL: 6-adult   BS
A simplified version of an entertaining comedy about a Russian submarine stranded on Nantucket Island, this story, which
was made into the movie The Russians Are Coming ... !,
tells the reader in a humorous way, a lot about human nature, whether Russian or American. Good fun. There are
all too few books with humor for older readers on this reading level.

915 Old Ramon, by Jack Schaefer. Illus. by Harold West.
      Houghton, c1960. $2.50 (pb $.50 OP)
      RL: 5-6   IL: 6-adult   B
This story of the gentle relationship between a young boy and
a wise old sheepherder is well written in direct language.
It is popular with young people and adults.

916 A Patch of Blue, by Elizabeth Kata. Popular Library,
      1968. $.60
      RL: 6   IL: 6-adult   BSMP
I had thought this novel about the blind white girl who falls
in love with the black man who befriends and understands her
might go out of vogue after the movie, which was based on
it, had gone by. However, it is still very much in demand
with every age from sixth grade on up. Even though the
print of our edition is awful, one reader recommends it to
another. It is a book that would be popular in a large print
edition.

917 The Pearl, by John Steinbeck. Viking, c1945. $4.95
      (Bantam pb $.60)
      RL: 6   IL: 6-adult   BS
This suspenseful story of a Mexican pearl diver has great
appeal and is borrowed by a wide age range.

918 Queenie Peavy, by Robert Bruch. Illus. by Jerry
      Lazare. Viking, 1966. $3.50 (Scholastic,
      pb $.60)
      RL: 5-6   IL: 5-JH   BS
This very unusual book tells the story of a girl who lives in

a fantasy and defies the world in order to avoid the unpleasant truth that her father is in jail because he deserves to be. Queenie Peavy is a girl of real quality. Other girls will be fascinated by her and, in the end, inspired by her courage.

919   Shadow of a Bull, by Maia Wojciechowska. Illus. by Alvin Smith. Atheneum, c1964. Alladin, 1970. pb $.95
      RL: 6   IL: 5-HS   BSP
The situation of Manolo, whose father was a great Spanish bullfighter and who is expected to follow in his father's steps, may seem remote to most Americans. But the situation of living up to an adult's uncongenial expectations is very common for many children. In spite of the exotic setting, the suspense in this book is such that once a reader is well launched, he cannot bear to lay it down. Very popular especially at the junior high age.

920   The Sniper, by Martin J. Hamer. Illus. by S. Hollingsworth. McGraw-Hill, City Limits Series, c1970. pb $1.96
      RL: 4-5   IL: 5-adult   BSMP
The story of a boy and girl who learn to know and trust each other in the course of an inner city riot, the book ends in tragedy. A real spellbinder.

921   Song of the Empty Bottles, by Osmond Molarsky. Illus. by Tom Feelings. Walck, 1968. $4.75
      RL: 4   IL: 3-7   *BSMP
Thaddeus loves to hear Mr. Andrews play his guitar and sing songs at the Neighborhood House. He longs for a guitar of his own but his mother says there is no money for anything extra. How Thaddeus earns his guitar is a credible and heart-warming story which may well inspire other children and which they will certainly enjoy reading.

922   Stevie, by John Steptoe. Harper & Row, 1969. $3.27
      RL: 3   IL: Read aloud-5   BSMP
This is a lovely book about a very common youthful experience. A boy is saddled with having to have a younger child as a companion and considers him a nuisance. When the younger child moves away, the boy realizes how much affection there was between them and how much he misses him. The author, an eighteen-year-old boy from Bedford-Stuyvesant, has also illustrated the story in color and his pictures are strong and warm and memorable. I am a little puzzled as to what age group will appreciate this book but it will be a real inspiration

to the teenagers on the bookmobile and to the junior high
and senior high boys and girls whom the school volunteers
are helping. If John Steptoe can write and illustrate books
and be published, why can't others? There is a world of
talent waiting. [1972: Stevie has proved to be unexpectedly
popular with nine- and ten-year-old boys.]

923   Take It or Leave It, by Osmond Molarsky.   Illus. by
      Trina Scharr Hyman.   Walck, c1971. $4.75
      RL: 3   IL: Read aloud-6   *BSMP
Chester is a champion swapper and he swaps all day long
finally ending his day with a poor bargain in order to find a
good home for a puppy.   This funny cheerful story portrays
an authentic urban scene with rich children with their fancy
toys (submarines, boomerangs, unicycles) and poor children
with home made scooters meeting and mixing unaffectedly in
the park.

924   Tambourines to Glory, by Langston Hughes.   Hill &
      Wang, American Century Series, c1958.   pb $1.75
      RL: 6   IL: HS-adult   BM
A wonderful book, almost as funny as the Simple Stories
[938 and 961], this is about two women in Harlem who decide
to get off home relief by starting a church.   They are successful beyond their wildest dreams with riotous consequences.
A highly realistic picture of life in Harlem and of human nature anywhere.   It was written, the author said, as "a fictional exposé of certain ways in which religion is misused
... by unscrupulous leaders who might be called 'gospel
racketeers'."

925   Teacup Full of Roses, by Sharon Bell Mathis.   Viking,
      c1972. $4.50
      RL: 5-6   IL: 6-adult   *BSMP
A searing story of a family, the father of which is a cripple
and the mother can only think of and care for her eldest son
who is a drug addict.   The book centers on the second son,
a high school dropout about to graduate from night school,
who is trying to be the responsible man of the family.   The
protaganists are black but the problems and emotions are
universal ones.   Like Howard Street [1062], this is an authentic picture of inner city conditions.   Unlike Howard Street,
the reader cares for and respects the characters involved
which makes the story a tragedy.   This book will be very
popular with the young and also with any adult who is introduced to it.

926 That Was Then, This Is Now, by S. E. Hinton. Viking,
     c1971. $3.95 (Dell pb $.75)
     RL: 5-6   IL: 5-adult   BSP
This shattering book is the story of the friendship between
two boys in a low-income area. Mark, an orphan, is like
an adopted brother to Bryon and both are much on their own
with no father and with Bryon's mother either working or ill.
The area they live in is full of violence and as the two grow
older, their attitudes start to differ and in an explosive finish
they part company. The book is realistic, the dialogue is
street language and appropriate to the situation; the result
is haunting literature.

927 Their Eyes Were Watching God, by Zora Neale. Negro
     University Press, c1937, 1965. $11 (Fawcett, Pre-
     mier, pb $.75)
     RL: 5-6   IL: Adult   BM
A spellbinding novel about the life of a black woman in Florida in the 1920s and 30s, this book has extraordinarily vivid
language and haunting imagery. It takes maturity to appreciate. If I were a teacher of an adult elementary class, I
should read the first twenty-one pages aloud. I would be
willing to bet that every woman in the class would finish the
book.

928 To Kill a Mockingbird, by Harper Lee. Lippincott,
     1960. $5.50 (Popular Library, 1960, pb $.60)
     RL: 6   IL: 6-adult   BMP
This suspenseful novel of law and justice in the South is popular with a wide range of people.

929 Tomás Takes Charge, by Charlene Joy Talbot. Illus.
     by Reisie Lonette. Lothrop, c1966. $3.95 (Avail-
     able in paperback under title Children in Hiding,
     Scholastic, $.75)
     RL: 4   IL: 4-JH   BSMP
Two Puerto Rican children, a boy and a girl whose father
has disappeared, manage to set up housekeeping in an empty
building in a deserted area. In spite of their problems, the
story is a warm one with suspense and then a happy ending
as they find a home. Especially popular with girls.

930 A Tree Grows in Brooklyn, by Betty Smith. Harper,
     c1943. $7.95 (Popular Library, pb $.95)
     RL: 7   IL: JH-adult   B
This story of adolescence in a Brooklyn slum is popular and
relevant still. It would be very much in demand in a large

print version as many of our senior citizens who would enjoy
it cannot read the fine print. This book is also available in
an adapted and abridged edition--Noble & Noble, Falcon, pb
$.56 BS. See 175.

931 West Side Story, by Irving Shulman. Simon & Schuster,
      Pocket Books, c1961. pb $.75
      RL: 6   IL: 6-adult   BSMP
Romeo and Juliet transported to the West Side of Manhattan
and changed into Puerto Ricans and Americans. This is a
novelized version of the very successful play and movie of
the same name and is very popular with teenagers and adults.
An abridged and adapted version is also available on a slightly
easier reading level: West Side Story by Irving Shulman,
adapted by F. Price. Noble & Noble, Falcon, pb $.56 BSMP.

932 What Mary Jo Shared, by Janice May Udry. Illus. by
      Eleanor Mill. Whitman, 1966. $3.25 (Scholastic,
      pb $.60)
      RL: 2-3   IL: Read aloud-4   BSMP
A delightful story of a shy girl who finds something different
to share with her class. This book is loved when children
are introduced to it. On the bookmobile, however, the children who are able to read it pass it by, thinking from the
format that it is a baby book. It would be very popular in
the Dell Yearling format.

933 When Carlos Closed the Street, by Peggy Mann. Illus.
      by Peter Burchard. Coward, 1969. $3.86
      RL: 3-4   IL: 3-7   BSMP
Black and Puerto Rican boys make their own play street in
New York City and create a monumental traffic jam. The
book has humor and suspense and is very popular.

934 A Wonderful, Terrible Time, by Mary Stolz. Harper,
      c1967. $4.50 (Scholastic pb $.75)
      RL: 4-5   IL: 3-6   *BSMP
A wonderful story of two girls, best friends, who unexpectedly
have a chance to go to camp. The book tells of their camp
adventures and how each reacts to the new experience. The
story is full of action, the characters are likeable and believable and girls will love it.

935 Zeely, by Virginia Hamilton. Illus. by Symeon Shimin.
      Macmillan, c1967. $4.95 (Collier pb $.95)
      RL: 4-5   IL: 4-HS   *BSMP
A curious haunting story of a young girl's visit to some

relatives in the country.   She sees a beautiful tall black woman whom she imagines to be an African princess.   In the end
Zeely, the tall beauty helps her to see the difference between
fantasy and reality and that the latter is worth finding.   A
book that girls of many ages can enjoy.

HUMOR (Fiction)

936   Albert the Albatross, by Syd Hoff.   Harper, I Can
         Read, c1961. $2.50
         RL: 2-3   IL: Read aloud-3   BS
One of the funniest of the easy-to-read books, this story of
an albatross who is mistaken for a lady's hat is very popular.

937   Arty the Smarty, by Faith McNulty.   Illus. by Albert
         Aquino.   Grosset, Easy-To-Read Wonder Book, c1962.
         $.69
         RL: 2-3   IL: Read aloud-3   BS
Arty is a smart fish who has fun being the leader and fooling
other fish.

938   The Best of Simple, by Langston Hughes.   Hill & Wang,
         American Century Series, c1961. $4.50. pb $1.95
         RL: 6-adult   IL: HS-adult   BM
Much in demand, these humorous stories of life in Harlem
still have a great deal of insight for today's world even though
they first came out twenty years or more ago.   They revolve
around a character called Simple who, however, belies his
name.

939   Billy Brown, The Baby Sitter, by Tamara Kitt.   Illus.
         by Rosalind Welcher.   Grosset, Easy-To-Read Wonder
         Book, 1962. $.69
         RL: 2-3   IL: Read aloud-4   BS
A funny easy-to-read poem about a small boy who is stuck
with having to take care of the baby.   Very popular and as
much fun for the grown-up reader as it is for the children.

940   Bird in the Hat, by Norman Bridwell.   Scholastic, 1964.
         pb $.60
         RL: 2-3   IL: Read aloud-3   BS
How a bird and a cat learn to live together;   the cartoonlike
illustrations make this very popular.

941   The Boy Who Would Not Go to School, by Munro Leaf.
      Scholastic, c1935, c1963.   pb $.60
      RL: 3-4   IL: Universal   BS
A funny story with pen and ink drawings of a boy who won't
go to school and what happened to him.   An excellent family
read-aloud.

942   Caps for Sale, by Esphyr Slobodkina.   Scholastic, c1947.
      pb $.60
      RL: 3   IL: Read aloud-3   BS
This cheery tale of the peddler who outwitted some thieving
monkeys is very well liked.

943   The City Boy, by Herman Wouk.   Doubleday, c1948.
      (Dell, Laurel, 1964, pb $.75)
      RL: 6-7   IL: HS-adult   BM
A very funny story of a young Jewish boy's adventures at
home in the Bronx and at summer camp that ends in being
a moving account of a father and son relationship.   It is a
measure of how universal the humor is in this one that the
all black staff in Bedford-Stuyvesant liked it so much that
their recommendation has made it surprisingly popular with
other adults.

944   The Clumsy Cowboy, by Jean Bethell.   Illus. by Shel
      and Jan Haber.   Grosset Easy-To-Read Wonder Book,
      c1963.   OP
      RL: 2-3   IL: Read aloud-4   BS
The clumsy cowboy turns into a hero.   A funny story that can
be used with junior high nonreaders.

945   The Day Joe Went to the Supermarket, by Dorothy
      Levenson.   Illus. by Jessica Zemsky.   Grosset,
      Easy-To-Read Wonder Book, c1963. $.69
      RL: 2-3   IL: 2-4   BS
This slapstick story of a boy who knocks over half the items
in a supermarket as he pursues some soap for his mother is
popular with third and fourth graders who grasp the humor.
Younger children are frightened by the fear that Joe will be
punished for his carelessness.

946   Gordon the Goat, by Murro Leaf.   Scholastic, 1971.
      pb $.60
      RL: 2-3   IL: Read aloud-3   BS
A captivating tale based on the follow-the-leader theme helps
children to think for themselves.   By a very popular author
whose funny illustrations children love.

947 Hello Henry, by Ilse-Margret Vogel. Parents, 1965.
      $3.95
      RL: 3   IL: Read aloud-3   *BSMP
Two children get lost in a supermarket. Many slum areas
have no supermarkets but all children will like this imaginative story about friendship. It is a very popular subject.
The illustrations are good and the price is pleasantly low.

948 Homer Price, by Robert McCloskey. Viking, 1943. $3
      (Scholastic, 1962, pb $.75)
      RL: 5   IL: 4-JH   BS
A modern classic of tall tales and humor, this can be used
in tutoring programs with any age level above grade 3. It
is a truly funny book.

949 Hooray for Henry, by Jean Bethell. Illus. by Sergio
      Leone. Grosset & Dunlap, Easy-To-Read Wonder
      Book, 1966. $.69
      RL: 2   IL: Read aloud-4   BS
A funny story about an awkward boy who finally wins a prize
at the school picnic. Very popular.

950 I Was a Lonely Teen-ager, by Carole Katchen. Scholas-
      tic, c1965. pb $.50
      RL: 6   IL: 6-HS   BS
It's good to see a humorous approach to a rather unhappy age.
This book is a little sophisticated for many of the girls who
come on the bookmobile but the title, the subject matter and
the comical line drawing illustrations make it popular even
so.

951 Kenny's Monkey, by Susan Singer. Scholastic, 1969.
      pb $.50
      RL: 1-2   IL: Read aloud-3   BS
Humor is always popular and this story carries a subtle lesson.

952 Lentil, by Robert McCloskey. Viking, c1940. $3.50
      (Scholastic, c1969. pb $.60
      RL: 4-5   IL: Read aloud-5   BS
The humorous story of a boy who learns to play the harmon-
ica. This is a good read-aloud book.

953 The Little Fish That Got Away, by Bernadine Cook.
      Illus. by Crockett Johnson. W. R. Scott, 1956. $3
      (Scholastic pb $.60)
      RL: 2   IL: Read aloud-3   BS

With comical illustrations, this is a deservedly popular fish
story.

954   The Man Who Didn't Wash His Dishes, by Phyllis
         Krasilovsky.   Illus. by Barbara Cooney.   Doubleday,
         1950. $3.50   (Scholastic pb $.50)
         RL: 3-4   IL: Read aloud-3   BS
What happens when an old man refuses to wash his dishes.
A popular book on a subject familiar to every child.

955   Mr. Pine's Mixed Up Signs, by Leonard Kessler.
         Grosset, Easy-To-Read Wonder Book, 1961. $.69
         RL: 2-3   IL: Read aloud-5   BS
This funny story is full of street signs every child is familiar
with.   It is also useful for older non-readers.

956   More Homer Price, by Robert McCloskey.   Scholastic,
         1968.   pb $.75
         RL: 5   IL: 4-JH   BS
This book drawn from "Centerburg Tales" is a sequel to
Homer Price [948] and just as funny.   Homer is a wonderful
character and both books are marvelous to read aloud since
their humor can be enjoyed on many levels.

957   My Mother is Lost, by Bernice Myers.   Scholastic,
         1970.   pb $.50
         RL: 2   IL: Read aloud-3   BS
An entertaining story of two boys who romp through a department store on the way to the Lost and Found to look for their
mothers.   With humorous pictures, it is very popular with
aggressive children and frightens timid children.

958   Nobody Listens to Andrew, by Elizabeth Guilfoile.   Illus.
         by Mary Stevens.   Follett, Beginning-To-Read Series,
         c1957. $1.25   (Scholastic, 1967, pb $.60)
         RL: 2   IL: Read aloud-3   BS
Nobody listens to Andrew although he has something pretty
interesting to say.   Children relish this funny story.   We
need many more like it on this reading level.

959   The Off-Islanders, by Nathaniel Benchley.   Adapted by
         J. Olsen.   Illus. by A. Crane.   McGraw Reading
         Shelf II Series, 1968.   pb $1.72
         RL: 4-5   IL: 6-adult   BS
A simplified version of an entertaining comedy (made into a
movie) about a Russian submarine stranded on Nantucket
Island.   Both the Russians and the Islanders demonstrate

their humanity in a satisfying way that makes for many laughs.

960   Olaf Reads, by Joan Lexau.   Dial, c1961. $3.25
      (Scholastic pb $.60)
      RL: 2   IL: Read aloud-3   BS
Children enjoy this funny story which demonstrates why learning to read is important and useful.

961   Simple's Uncle Sam, by Langston Hughes.   Hill & Wang,
      c1965. $3.95 (American Century Series, pb $1.75)
      RL: 6-adult   IL: HS-adult   BMP
Another collection of these superb stories which combine humor with wisdom and which are very popular with people over
thirty.   They must be introduced to younger people who then
recommend them to their peers.

962   Stop That Ball, by Mike McClintock.   Random, Beginner.
      1959. $2.50
      RL: 2-3   IL: Read aloud-4   BS
An excellent rhyming story with humor and suspense which
can be used with non-readers through high school with great
success.   It has been one of the most successful books in
the reading help program.

963   Surprise in the Tree, by Sara Asheron.   Illus. by Susan
      Perl.   Grosset, Easy-To-Read Wonder Book, c1962.
      $.69
      RL: 2   IL: Read aloud-4   BS
A popular story about a boy who tries to rescue a kitten and
winds up being rescued himself.

964   Surprising Pets of Billy Brown, by Tamara Kitt.   Illus.
      by Rosalind Welcher.   Grosset, Easy-To-Read Wonder
      Book, c1962. $.69
      RL: 2   IL: Read aloud-4   BS
A very amusing story in rhyme about a boy who decides to
put on his own pet show.   Parents who read it to their children enjoy the humor too.

965   Too Much Noise, by Ann McGovern.   Illus. by Simms
      Taback.   Houghton Mifflin, 1967. $3.75 (Scholastic
      pb $.60)
      RL: 2-3   IL: Read aloud-3   BS
A cumulative and humorous story about a man who learns
that a noise is loud or soft according to the point-of-view.
Excellent for storytelling and for sharpening childrens' ears.

966 What Good Luck! What Bad Luck!, by Remy Charlip.
       Scholastic, 1969.   pb $.60
       RL: 2-3   IL: Read aloud-4   BS
A very comical book in which the hero has good luck on one
page and bad luck on the next. This one is a real favorite
both on the bookmobile and in the School Volunteer program.

967 Who Took the Farmer's Hat?, by Joan L. Nodset.
       Illus. by Fritz Siebel.   Harper, 1963. $3.95
       (Scholastic, 1968, pb $.75)
       RL: 2   IL: Read aloud-2   BS
A wonderful picture story of a farmer's missing hat that becomes a bird's nest. This was popular in hardcover and
will be even more so in paperback.

MAKE-BELIEVE AND FANTASY

968 Alice in Wonderland, by Lewis Carroll. Illus. by John
       Tenniel.   Penguin, Puffin, 1960.   pb $1.25
       RL: 5-6   IL: 3-adult   B
The famous story of the little girl who fell down the rabbit
hole into a magic world run by the red queen and other chess
pieces is and will always be popular.   This edition, a paperback version of the original, is well done but too difficult for
most of the children who want to borrow it.

969 Alice in Wonderland to Read Aloud, by Lewis Carroll.
       Adapted by Oscar Weigle.   Illus. by Sergio Leone.
       Grosset Read-Aloud Series, c1963.   pb $.49
       RL: 3   IL: 3-6   BS
This easy and inexpensive version fills a real need.   So many
children want to read the classics and cannot.   This series is
the answer.   Hopefully they may later progress to the real
thing.

970 Andy and the Lion, by James Daugherty.   Viking,
       Seafarer, c1938, c1966.   pb $.75
       RL: 3-4   IL: 3-7   BS
A fantasy about a boy who reads about lions and then sees
his dreams come true.   This modern version of the story of
Androcles and the lion is very popular.

971 Arrow Book of Ghost Stories, edited by Nora Kramer.

Scholastic, c1960. pb $.60
RL: 4   IL: 4-JH   BS
A very popular collection of stories.   Ghosts are very popu-
lar with all elementary and junior high children.

972   The Arrow Book of Spooky Stories, edited by Edna
      Mitchell Preston. Illus. by Erwin Hoffmann. Scho-
      lastic, c1962. pb $.50
      RL: 4   IL: 4-JH   BS
A useful and popular collection of not very scary ghost stories.
This kind of book is popular on the bookmobile and can also
be used in reading help programs with high school and adult
pupils.

973   Babar Loses His Crown, by Laurent de Brunhoff.
      Random, Beginner, c1967. $1.75
      RL: 2-3   IL: Read aloud-3   BS
Babar, the elephant king, loses and finally regains his crown
in a chase story that takes him and his elephant family all
over Paris.   Small children find this one full of suspense
and older ones are impressed by how hard the elephant children try to help to recover the lost crown.   It is good to see
popular characters like Babar and Celeste and their children
show up in easy to read stories.

974   The Cat in the Hat, by Dr. Seuss.   Random House,
      Beginner, c1957. $2.50
      RL: 2-3   IL: K-3   BS
A story in rhyme, this is one of the very first easy-to-read
books with humor and imagination ever to be published.   It
tells of a girl and a boy, confined to the house by bad
weather, who have a magic visitor, a cat who can perform
humorous wonders.   This is very popular with most children
although some shy ones seem almost to be frightened by the
illustrations.

975   Charlotte's Web, by E. B. White.   Illus. by Garth
      Williams.   Harper & Row, c1952. $3.95 (Dell,
      Yearling, 1968, pb $.75)
      RL: 5   IL: 5-adult   B
An unusual book and an excellent one for family read-aloud
sessions; every child should have an opportunity to read or
hear Charlotte's Web.   Much of the humor is adult but children will be enthralled by the story.   This is the story of a
spider whose ingenuity rescues a pig from becoming bacon.
The book confronts the fact of death in a natural and reassuring fashion but many children weep for the spider because

they have become so involved with her struggles.

976 Chitty Chitty Bang Bang, by Ian Fleming. Random,
      1964. $3.95 (New American Library, Signet, 1968,
      pb $.75)
      RL: 5   IL: 5-JH   B
A family read-aloud story, this story of a magical car has
great appeal but is somewhat frustrating to a librarian or
teacher since so many young children reach for it (due to the
movie) and then find they cannot read it. Illustrated by the
author.

977 Clifford the Big Red Dog, by Norman Bridwell. Scho-
      lastic, c1963. pb $.50
      RL: 2-3   IL: Read aloud-4   BS
Everyone loves Clifford, the big red dog whose house dwarfs
most people and who needs a swimming pool to bathe in. The
illustrations are wonderful and the book is fun to read aloud.

978 Clifford Gets a Job, by Norman Bridwell. Scholastic,
      1965. pb $.50
      RL: 3   IL: Read aloud 4   BS
See above. In this one, Clifford tries to be self-supporting
with disastrous consequences at first, then he winds up a
hero.

979 Clifford's Halloween, by Norman Bridwell. Scholastic,
      c1966. pb $.50
      RL: 2-3   IL: Read aloud-4   BS
Clifford decides to be a ghost on Halloween. Children enjoy
this story all year round.

980 Clifford's Tricks, by Norman Bridwell. Scholastic,
      c1969. pb $.50
      RL: 2-3   IL: Read aloud-4   BS
It's wonderful to get a new Clifford book. This one has lots
of humor and a dramatic rescue.

981 Corduroy, by Don Freeman. Illus. by the author.
      Viking, c1968. $3.50 (Seafarer pb $.95)
      RL: 3   IL: Read aloud-4   BSMP
Corduroy, a small teddy bear, longs to be chosen by a child
and taken home. After some comical adventures in the department store where he is on sale, he is bought by a girl
who understands his longing. Little girls love this story and
all children recognize how important it is to be wanted. One
of the top sellers in children's books.

982 <u>The Cowboy</u>, by John Peterson. Scholastic, 1967. pb
     $.50
     RL: 2-3   IL: Read aloud-3   BSMP
An imaginative boy pretends that he and his cat are cowboys.
A new generation of would-be cowboys is appearing and this
book is very popular. It has good illustrations.

983 <u>Curious George</u>, by Hans A. Rey. Houghton Mifflin,
     c1941. $3.75 (Scholastic, 1965, pb $.60)
     RL: 3-4   IL: Read aloud-4   BS
George, a beguiling monkey, gets into all kinds of trouble because of his curiosity about everything he sees or hears but
the stories all end happily because the man in the yellow hat,
his friend, comes to the rescue. This is the first of the
series. All children love <u>Curious George</u>. No matter how
many copies we have, there are never enough. Even very
shy children request him by name. As one little boy said
to me, "Curious George is my friend."

984 <u>Curious George Gets a Medal</u>, by Hans A. Rey. Hough-
     ton Mifflin, c1957. $3.95 (Scholastic pb $.60)
     RL: 3   IL: Read aloud-4   BS
George gets into a lot of trouble at home, on a farm and in
a museum but winds up helping out the space program and
ends up a hero.

985 <u>Curious George Goes to the Hospital</u>, by Margaret and
     Hans A. Rey. Houghton Mifflin, c1966. $3.75
     (Scholastic pb $.50)
     RL: 3   IL: Read aloud-4   BS
George swallows a piece of his jig-saw puzzle and has to go
to the hospital to have it removed. A must, this book can
make the difference between terror and confidence to a child
going to the hospital for the first time.

986 <u>Curious George Learns the Alphabet</u>, by Hans A. Rey.
     Houghton Mifflin, c1963. $3.50
     RL: 2-3   IL: 1-4   BS
Delightful pictures illustrate a rather young text in which
humor extends the appeal beyond the beginning grades. Helpful in teaching phonics.

987 <u>Curious George Rides a Bike</u>, by Hans A. Rey. Hough-
     ton Mifflin, c1952. $3.75 (Scholastic pb $.60)
     RL: 2-3   IL: Read aloud-4   BS
George rides his new bike and gets into trouble but winds up
the hero of the animal show.

988   Curious George Takes a Job, by Hans A. Rey.   Houghton
        Mifflin, c1947. $3.50   (Scholastic pb $.60)
        RL: 3-4   IL: Read aloud-4   BS
George gets a job as a window washer but is too curious for
his own good.   However, he finally winds up on top of his
world as the star in a movie about himself.

989   Danny and the Dinosaur, by Syd Hoff.   Harper & Row,
        I Can Read, c1958. $2.50
        RL: 2-3   IL: Read aloud-4   BS
All children seem to like dinosaurs and this easy-to-read fiction about one who comes alive and befriends some children
is very popular with many age groups.

990   Doctor Dolittle Tales, by Hugh Lofting.   Lippincott,
        c1920.   (Scholastic, 1968, pb $.60)
        RL: 4   IL: Read aloud-6   BS
These stories about the famous animal doctor from Puddleby-
on-the-Marsh are a wonderful family read-aloud.   They are
banned by many black people and there is no doubt that the
author, who loved children and animals, also reflected the
attitudes of a British Colonial officer in the early 1900's.
However, there is nothing in the stories themselves that
shows animosity to black people (although there is some patronizing in one book) and children so enjoy the adventures
of Gub-gub, the pig, Dab-dab the duck and Polynesia the par-
rot that it seems too bad to deprive them.   This book is very
popular on the bookmobile.

991   Elbert the Mind Reader, by Barbara Rinkoff.   Illus. by
        Paul Galdone.   Lothrop, c1967. $3.50   (Scholastic
        pb $.50)
        RL: 4   IL: 4-JH   BS
Elbert's mind reading gets him his heart's desire--to get into
a football game.   It also gets him into a pickle.   A good, fantastic and humorous sport story.

992   The Enormous Egg, by Oliver Butterworth.   Illus. by
        Louis Darling.   Little, Brown, c1956. $4.25   (Scho-
        lastic pb $.50)
        RL: 5   IL: 4-7   BS
This science fantasy about a dinosaur's egg which hatches in
modern day Connecticut has an extraordinary fascination and,
once they have started it, even poor readers stick with it to
the end.

993   A Fish Out of Water, by Helen Palmer.   Illus. by

P. D. Eastman. Random House Beginner, 1967.
$2.50
RL: 2   IL: Read aloud-4   BS
A boy's pet fish grows until he is too big for any tank but a
swimming pool. A funny fantasy in easy-to-read form, deservedly popular.

994 A Fly Went By, by Mike McClintock. Illus. by Fritz
     Siebel. Random House Beginner Books, 1958. $1.95
     RL: 3   IL: Read aloud-4   BS
A fly is frightened by a frog who was frightened by a cat who
was frightened by a dog--and so on. A popular easy-to-read
story whose moral is implicit and whose rhymes help the slow
reader.

995 Freddy the Detective, by Walter R. Brooks. Knopf,
     c1932. (Scholastic, 1965, pb $.60)
     RL: 5   IL: Read aloud-6   B
There are sixteen books in print about Freddy the pig and
the other wonderful animals on Mr. Bean's farm. The animals can talk and engage in all kinds of enterprises. The
Freddy books have humor, action and a lot of wisdom about
human nature. They are wonderful books to read aloud as
children of different ages can enjoy them on different levels
and the reader enjoys them too. They are not easy reading
but once a child is hooked by Freddy, he will be a reader
for life. More Freddy books should be in paperback. This
book has Freddy solving a mystery and is full of suspense.

996 Georgie, by Robert Bright. Illus. by the author.
     Doubleday, c1944. $3.50 (Scholastic pb $.60)
     RL: 3   IL: Read aloud-4   BS
Georgie, the friendly ghost has been popular since 1944 and
still is in 1973.

997 Ghost Named Fred, by Nathaniel Benchley. Illus. by
     Ben Schecler. Harper & Row, c1968. $2.50
     RL: 2-3   IL: Read aloud-3   BS
Ghosts are very popular and this easy, humorous story is
much in demand.

998 The Ghosts Who Went to School, by Judith Spearing.
     Illus. by Marvin Glass. Atheneum, 1966. $3.95
     (Scholastic pb $.60)
     RL: 4   IL: 4-6   BS
Humorous; very popular "ghost" story about two ghosts who
go to school.

999   The Green Song, by Doris Troutman Plenn.   Illus. by
        Paul Galdone.   David McKay, 1954. $3.95
        RL: 4   IL: 4-adult   BSMP
A wonderful fable of a Puerto Rican coqui (tree toad) and his
adventures on a trip to New York.   Enjoyable to many ages
on different levels.   Would be very popular in good paperback
format.   Excellent family read-aloud.

1000   Harold and The Purple Crayon, by Crockett Johnson.
         Harper & Row, 1955. $2.50 (Scholastic, 1966, pb
         OP
         RL: 2-3   IL: Read aloud-4   BS
Harold uses his purple crayon to take him on exciting adventures.   This imaginative book can be used with any age non-
reader by a tutor with insight.   It is also very popular with
young children.   See also Harold's ABC [1001] and A Picture
for Harold's Room [1011].

1001   Harold's ABC, by Crockett Johnson.   Illus. by Crockett
         Johnson.   Harper, 1963. $2.50
         RL: 2-3   IL: K-3   BS
Harold uses his purple crayon again, this time to illustrate
the alphabet in a most unusual way.   All children love this
book and it is especially good for teaching the alphabet to an
older child.   Harold's humor is appealing to any age.

1002   The House on East 88th Street, by Bernard Waber.
         Houghton Mifflin, 1962. $3.50
         RL: 3   IL: Read aloud-4   BS
A very popular book about a friendly crocodile called Lyle,
this is sought out by children even when hard to find on the
bookmobile.   The Lyle books almost rival the Curious George
books in popularity.   See also 1008 and 1009.

1003   I Can Lick 30 Tigers Today, by Dr. Seuss.   Random
         House, c1969. $3.50
         RL: 3   IL: Read aloud-4   S
Three imaginative stories on a fairly easy reading level, these
are very popular with boys almost all of whom love the Dr.
Seuss books.

1004   The Little Witch, by Margaret Mahy.   Illus. by Charles
         Mozley.   Watts, c1970. $4.95
         RL: 3   IL: Read aloud-3   *S
This unusual picture book will delight children, especially city
children.   The little witch's gifts bring enchantment to the city
and the witch winds up safe and happy in her mother's arms.

The colors in the book are a delight.

1005 Lonesome Boy, by Arna Bontemps. Illus. by Feliks
      Topolski. Houghton Mifflin, c1955. $3.25
      RL: 4-5   IL: 4-adult   BS
This brief story is almost like a jazz fantasy. The story of
a lonesome boy who learns that it is dangerous to get lost in
music, it has a haunting satisfying quality. Boys who like it
read it over and over. It is popular with a wide age range
when attention is called to it.

1006 The Lorax, by Dr. Seuss. Random, c1971. $3.50
      RL: 4   IL: Read aloud-4   BSP
The old master tells a funny story and at the same time gives
a superb lesson in ecology. The Once-ler destroys a landscape in order to manufacture a perfectly useless object which,
however, everyone wants to buy simply because it is available.
Children love this one and get the message. A must for every
library.

1007 Lorenzo, by Bernard Waber. Houghton Mifflin, 1961.
      $1.95 (Scholastic pb $.60)
      RL: 3   IL: Read aloud-4   *BS
An entertaining story about a fish who loses and then finds
his family. By the author of the Lyle books, this book will
appeal to children who will learn a little about life underseas
in the bargain.

1008 Lovable Lyle, by Bernard Waber. Houghton Mifflin,
      1969. $3.95
      RL: 3-4   IL: Read aloud-4   BS
An especially good "Lyle" story about being liked and not liked
because of one's appearance and reputation. See 1002 and
1009.

1009 Lyle, Lyle, Crocodile, by Bernard Waber. Houghton
      Mifflin, 1965. $3.50
      RL: 3-4   IL: Read aloud-4   BS
Children love this funny story of a crocodile who lives with
a family in a brownstone house in New York City. See also
1002 and 1008.

1010 Petunia's Christmas, by Roger Duvoisin. Knopf, 1952.
      $4.59 (Scholastic, 1967, pb OP)
      RL: 3   IL: Read aloud-4   BS
This story of the brave goose who earns the money to save
her gander from becoming a Christmas dinner has lots of

suspense. It is very popular all year round.

1011 A Picture for Harold's Room, by Crockett Johnson.
         Harper & Row, 1960. $2.50 (Scholastic pb $.60)
         RL: 3-4   IL: 3-JH   BS
An entertaining sequel to Harold and the Purple Crayon
[1000]. The illustrations appeal to any age and the book can
therefore be used with older non-readers who need a touch of
humor.

1012 Pippi Longstocking, by Astrid Lindgren. Illus. by
         Louis S. Glanzman. Viking, 1950. $3.50 (Scholas-
         tic, 1959, pb $.75)
         RL: 4   IL: 4-7   BS
Pippi Longstocking is a Swedish Supergirl who lives alone and
manages her own life handily. She is very popular with elementary school children. Pippi in the South Seas and Pippi
Goes on Board are also available through Viking.

1013 Rabbit and Skunk and the Scary Rock, by Carla Stevens.
         Illus. by Robert Kraus. Scholastic, 1962. pb $.50
         RL: 2   IL: Read aloud-3   BS
Children love the silly rabbit and skunk in this story and en-
joy the feeling of being wiser than they are. We also carry
Rabbit, Skunk and the Spooks in our seasonal collection.

1014 Sam and the Firefly, by Philip D. Eastman. Random
         House, Beginner, 1958. $2.50
         RL: 2   IL: K-4 and older non-readers   BS
This is one of the most imaginative and popular of the easy-
to-read books. It is the story of a mischievous firefly who
creates chaos with his misleading sky writing but in the end
saves the day. It has proved invaluable in reading help programs with children of many different age groups. It is also
much liked on the bookmobile.

1015 Thirteen Ghostly Tales, edited by Freya Littledale.
         Illus. by Wayne Blickenstaff. Scholastic, c1960.
         pb $.50
         RL: 5   IL: 4-JH   BS
Any kind of ghost tale is always in demand. This collection
does not live up to its name since the ghosts mainly turn out
to be frauds or mistakes but the title ensures its being borrowed.

1016 A Tiny Family, by Norman Bridwell. Scholastic,
         c1968. pb $.50

RL: 2-3   IL: Read aloud-4   BS
Another story, by the author of the Clifford books, which
deals with size. In this one, a family of tiny creatures have
to cope with the human world which to them is a world of giants.
The story has suspense as well as humor and is very popular.

1017 Violet Tree, by Doris Troutman Plenn. Illus. by
      Johannes Troyer. Farrar, Straus, 1962. $3.25
      RL: 4   IL: Read aloud-5   *S
This very unusual book tells of the adventures of a fighting
cock, a hen and a horse in Puerto Rico. The language is
poetic and the story is like a folk tale. This book is unlikely to be popular but there will be some children who will
want to read and reread it. Like The Green Song [999] by
the same author, this book is a wonderful family read-aloud
story.

1018 Where the Wild Things Are, by Maurice Sendak.
      Harper, c1963. $4.95 (Scholastic pb $.95)
      RL: 3   IL: Read aloud-4   BS
A little boy is sent to his room as a punishment for being
naughty. He has a fantasy of sailing off to where the wild
things (fantastic animals) are. He finally sails back to his
room, rid of his anger, just in time for supper. Some children find the illustrations in this book very frightening so I
never suggest it to a child. However, it is worth making it
available for a child to choose for himself as it seems to
mean a great deal to the boys and girls who do like it.

1019 Will You Come to My Party?, by Sara Asheron. Illus.
      by Susanna Suba. Grosett, Easy-to-Read Wonder
      Book, c1961. $.69
      RL: 2-3   IL: Read aloud-4   BS
How the grey squirrel gave a party. All children like parties
and books about parties.

1020 The Witch Next Door, by Norman Bridwell. Four
      Winds, 1965. $2.50 (Scholastic pb $.50)
      RL: 2   IL: Read aloud and K-3   BS
Funny text and pictures about a helpful witch and some stupid
people who didn't want her living near them because she was
"different." Very popular with the young and should be in
every elementary school.

1021 The Wizard of Oz, by L. Frank Baum. Illus. by Paul
      Granger. Scholastic, 1958. pb $.60
      RL: 5   IL: 3-6   BS

The classic story of the little Kansas girl whom a tornado
blew to the magic kingdom of Oz is still very popular. Many
children have seen the movie version of this on TV and welcome it as an old friend.

1022   The Wizard of Oz to Read Aloud, by L. Frank Baum.
       Adapted by Oscar Weigle. Illus. by Robert Patter-
       son. Grosset, Read Aloud Wonder Book. $.49
       RL: 3-4   IL: 4-6   BS
An abridged and easier version with large print and many
illustrations that is very popular.

1023   Yellow Submarine, by Max Wilk. World, 1969.   OP
       (New American Library, Signet, pb $.95)
       RL: 6-7   IL: 5-HS   BS
The story of the Beatles' movie. This book is still in
demand and many children stretch to read every word.

MINORITIES

1024   American Negro Short Stories, edited by John Henrik
       Clarke. Hill & Wang, American Century Series,
       c1969. pb $1.95
       RL: Varied   IL: HS-adult   BSMP
An anthology of short stories by Afro-American authors written during the last seventy-five years. They vary in quality
but almost all reflect the bitterness inspired by the treatment
of black people in America. Many are therefore strong meat.
This book moves slowly on the bookmobile but is much appreciated by the adults who borrow it.

1025   And Then We Heard the Thunder, by John Oliver Killens.
       Alfred A. Knopf, c1962. $7.95 (Coronet Communica-
       tions, Inc., Paperback Library, 1971, pb $1.25)
       RL: 7   IL: HS-adult   *BSMP
This is a very powerful novel about anti-Negro discrimination
in World War II. The characters are so believable and the
reader becomes so emotionally embroiled in the action that
reading it is an experience.

1026   Another Country, by James Baldwin. Dial, c1962.
       $5.95 (Dell pb $1.25)
       RL: Adult   IL: HS-adult   BSM

There is a small but steady demand among adults and teenagers for all of Baldwin's books. This story of two tragic
interracial love affairs shocks many of the older generation
but is very popular with the young.

1027 Anything Can Happen, by George and Helen Papashivily.
      Harper, c1945. $4.95 (Avon Camelot pb $.50)
      RL: 5-6   IL: JH-adult   BS
An Armenian immigrant boy finds his way in America.
Cheerful and popular.

1028 The Autobiography of an Ex-Coloured Man, by James
      Weldon Johnson. Knopf, c1912. $4.95 (Hill &
      Wang, American Century Series, 1960, pb $1.95)
      RL: Adult   IL: Adult   BSMP
A novel about a fair-skinned black boy who discovers life on
both sides of the color line before he makes a decision as to
how to live. Beautifully written and easier to read than the
format indicates, it is increasingly popular on the bookmobile.

1029 The Autobiography of Miss Jane Pittman, by Ernest J.
      Gaines. Dial, c1971. (Bantam, 1972, pb $1.25)
      RL: 5   IL: 6-adult   *BSMP
A superb novel in the form of an autobiography which tells
the story of a black woman whose life spans the years from
slavery to the tense days of the Civil Rights movement.
Very simply told, the effect of this book is cumulative and
at the end, intensely moving. Must reading for everyone
and already very popular.

1030 The Black American Experience, edited by Frances S.
      Freedman. Bantam, c1970. pb $.95
      RL: Varied   IL: JH-adult   BSMP
Arranged in five sections starting with The Uprooting from
Africa and continuing to We March in the present day, this
valuable anthology of black literature presents a moving pic-
tuer of black courage and talent. Of the many books of black
literature on this list, this is the richest and most compre-
hensive. A must for public and high school libraries.

1031 The Black B C's, by Lucille Clifton. Illus. by Don
      Miller. Dutton, 1970. $3.95
      RL: 6   IL: Read aloud-JH   *BSMP
This outstanding book has a poem and a picture relating to
black history for each letter of the alphabet and also a paragraph expanding on and explaining the initial word. For example, under B for books, after the poem there is a short

paragraph about the first black poets and novelists in this
country followed by a list of outstanding contemporary black
writers. Such a list might well lead readers of this book on
to books of the writers listed. The illustrations are superb
and the whole book is inspiring.

1032   The Black Hero, edited by Alma Murray and Robert
       Thomas. Photographs by John Shearer. Scholastic,
       The Scholastic Black Literature Series, c1970. pb
       $1.80
       RL: Varied   IL: JH-adult   *BSMP
This book was published in cooperation with the Los Angeles
City Schools and is intended as a textbook. However, it has
an attractive appearance and many photographs. It contains
poems, essays and selections from fiction by black authors
which will interest many people. It is unfortunate that the
very first selection, "The Wonderful World of Law and Order"
by Ossie Davis, is an essay on a very high reading level so
that an independent but not very skilled reader would undoubtedly become discouraged without realizing that there are
many selections he would enjoy in the balance of the book.

1033   Black on Black, edited by Arnold Adoff. Macmillan,
       c1968. $5.95 (Collier pb $.95)
       RL: Varied   IL: 6-adult   *BSMP
An anthology of writings by black Americans, the book deals
mainly with modern times although there are some excerpts
from the writings of Frederick Douglass. This book is one
that poor readers will stretch for if introduced to it by excerpts read aloud. Although much of it is understandably
bitter, nevertheless the total effect is a positive one. As an
American, I am proud that these writers are fellow Americans. With so many anthologies appearing just now, there
is necessarily some duplication. However, although the authors in this volume are the same as in many others, the
selections are very different from most. I found Baldwin's
"Unnameable Objects, Unspeakable Crimes" new to me and
very powerful indeed.

1034   Black Voices: An Anthology of Afro-American Litera-
       ture, edited by Abraham Chapman. St. Martin's
       Press, 1968. $8.50 (New American Library,
       Mentor, pb $1.50)
       RL: Adult   IL: HS-adult   BSMP
Another splendid collection of fiction, autobiography, poetry
and essays by Afro-American authors. This book should be
on all reading lists for high school students. Unfortunately,

the print of the paperback edition is exceptionally small which
will inhibit many people from enjoying it.

1035   Black Voices from Prison, by Etheridge Knight and
       other inmates of Indiana State Prison.   Merit Path-
       finder, c1970.   pb $2.45
       RL: Varied, 5-8   IL: 6-adult   BM
An extraordinary collection of essays, short stories, poems
and taped interviews by some of the inmates of Indiana State
Prison.   Etheridge Knight, the principal author can write
well and movingly at times but most of the work is not up
to Cleaver's Soul On Ice which is much quoted in the book.
However, it is a book well worth reading since the problem
of America's prisons and prisoners is one that is daily af-
fecting more and more lives in cities all over the country.
As Knight says "Small wonder that 75% of all ex-convicts return to crime.   Men are put in prison for the protection of
society, it is said, but is it being protected when 90% of all
the men in prison will at one time or another be released
and when 75% of them return to crime?"

1036   The Black Woman, edited by Toni Cade [Bambara].
       New American Library, Signet, c1970.   pb $.95
       RL: Adult   IL: HS-adult   BSM
Another very varied collection, this time about and by black
women, mainly young women.   Most of the essays are very
sophisticated and will mean little to the average black woman
borrower on the bookmobile or the average high school girl
in a Volunteer Program.   However, some of the stories and
poems are very moving and the whole book breathes a spirit
of rebellion against conditions that exist today for black wom-
en, a spirit that is increasingly evident in Harlem and Bedford-Stuyvesant.

1037   Bloodline, by Ernest T. Gaines.   Dial, 1968. $4.95
       RL: Mainly 5   IL: JH-adult   BM
Five long short stories which depict black life in the South in
the recent past.   The reading level is easy because the author
writes so directly and with a great deal of conversation but
the stories have depth, humor and maturity and a moving
quality in their compassion that lingers in the reader's mind.

1038   Blueschild Baby, by George Cain.   McGraw-Hill,
       c1970. $4.95   (Dell pb $.95)
       RL: 7   IL: JH-adult   *BM
A raw brutal novel which seems to be autobiographical, this
is the story of a black boy who is a basketball star, a "token

nigger" at school and college and finally a convict, a junkie
and a rapist.   Like Howard Street [1062], this is a vivid picture of some aspects of life in the inner city.   Although the
reader is held by the writing, the protagonist is so sorry for
himself that the reader finds it hard to sympathize with him
even when at the end, he kicks the drugs cold turkey.   It
will be interesting to see how popular this is.

1039   Blue Willow, by Doris Gates.   Illus. by Paul Lantz.
          Viking, Seafarer, 1940.   pb $.75
          RL: 5   IL: HS-adult   B
This moving story of a migrant worker's family was intended
for children but is very popular with girls and older women.

1040   The Book of Numbers, by Robert Deane Pharr.
          Doubleday, 1969. $5.95   (Avon pb $1.25)
          RL: 6-7   IL: HS-adult   *BM
An astonishing comic novel, by an ex-waiter, about two
waiters who create a successful numbers racket in a Southern
town.   The book is fun to read and makes the reader want to
know what happens next although it is a bit too long and the
women are a bit too beautiful to be credible.

1041   Call Me Bronko, by Rosa K. Eichelberger.   Illus. by
          Hedley Rainnie.   Morrow, c1955.   (Scholastic, 1965,
          pb $.45)
          RL: 4   IL: 5-HS   B
A very different view of America, the adventures of a young
Polish refugee in New York.   This book must be pushed but
once it is started in a group of boys its popularity is evident.

1042   Candita's Choice, by Mina Lewiton.   Illus. by Howard
          Simon.   Harper, c1959. $3.95
          RL: 5   IL: 5-JH   BSMP
This is a well-written and interesting story about a young
Puerto Rican girl and her adaptation to New York.   The
School Volunteers find it popular since they can introduce it
on a one-to-one basis.   On the bookmobile, the fact that it
is hardcover limits its usefulness.   It should be in paperback.

1043   Cane, by Jean Toomer.   Harper, c1923, 1969. $.95
          RL: Adult   IL: Adult   BM
This black classic of poems and stories about the South is
difficult reading and is mainly borrowed by teachers and
Vista personnel but we feel that the bookmobile should offer
a few titles which are difficult but are books to stretch up
to.

1044 Captain Blackman, by John A. Williams. Doubleday,
      c1972. $6.95
      RL: 6   IL: 6-adult   *BMP
An extraordinary tour de force, this novel starts with Captain
Abraham Blackman as he is seriously wounded in Vietnam because of an action he took to protect his men. Thereafter he
drifts in and out of a coma as he relieves in a hallucinating
dream the role of a black soldier in every one of America's
wars starting with Lexington and the Revolution. The book
brings home the part that black soldiers have played in the
battle for freedom and the freedom and equality of opportunity
they have been promised each time they were needed. This
book will be very popular indeed with black people and should
be read by all adult Americans.

1045 The Cay, by Theodore Taylor. Doubleday, c1969.
      $3.95 (Avon, Camelot, pb $.75)
      RL: 5-6   IL: 5-adult   BSMP
Eleven-year-old Phillip's ship is torpedoed in World War II
and he is rescued by a black sailor who saves his life and
teaches him to survive on a tiny Caribbean cay. Phillip,
whose Virginian mother had taught him never to trust black
people, learns to love and respect black Timothy and so does
the reader.

1046 The Cotillion, by John Oliver Killens. Trident Press,
      c1971. (Simon & Schuster Pocket Book, pb $1.25)
      RL: Adult   IL: Adult   *BM
A ribald and hilarious novel about what happens when a socially ambitious black mama's daughter falls in love with a
"black is proud and beautiful" young man. The theme may
sound special but social climbers have existed since society
began and the book can be enjoyed by anyone with a sense of
humor. This will be very popular with teenagers as well as
adults. The cover picture is an eye-catcher for young people.

1047 Daddy Was a Numbers Runner, by Louise Meriwether.
      Prentice-Hall, 1970. Paper Edition. $5.95
      RL: 5   IL: JH-adult   BSM
A novel that brings to life the Harlem of the 30s as seen by
a young girl. The people are real, the situations are real
and the reader cannot help but empathize with the characters.
Most readers don't think of it as fiction but as a true story.
As a result, since it is not a happy story, some don't like
it. If every white American would read it, the world would
be a better place.

1048 The Day Luis Was Lost, by Edna Barth. Illus. by
        Lilian Obligado. Little, Brown, c1971. $3.50
        RL: 3   IL: Read aloud-4   *BSMP
Luis, a little Puerto Rican boy who has just come to New
York and is a little frightened both by school and the city,
gets lost on his way to school. He is very late but instead
of a scolding receives a warm welcome. His appearance
gives his class perfect attendance! A cheerful story for a
newcomer to read.

1049 A Different Drummer, by William Melvin Kelley.
        Doubleday, c1959. (Anchor, 1969, pb $1.25)
        RL: 7   IL: 6-adult   BM
This is a curious book. Laid in a south central state, it
tells of a black family and a white family and a town where
all the blacks suddenly move out so that not one is left. An
adaptation of the book was on national television in 1969 and
we carried it after that because of several requests. It is a
book that takes awhile to get into but it is hard to lay it down
once started. However, it has never moved very well.

1050 Don't Look At Me That Way, by Caroline Crane. Ran-
        dom House, 1970. $3.95
        RL: 5-6   IL: 6-HS   *BSMP
Rose is a young Puerto Rican girl who goes to work for an
"Anglo" taking care of her two young children. She hopes to
earn enough money to send her ailing mother on a visit to
Puerto Rico. Her mother dies and Rosa quits her job to take
care of her young brothers and sisters. This sounds like
straight gloom and the picture of life in El Barrio is a real
one but as in real life there are moments of excitement and
happiness, even moments of fun, and the book ends on a note
of hope.

1051 Eagle Feather, by Clyde Robert Bulla. Illus. by Tom
        Two Arrows. T. Y. Crowell, c1953. $3.95
        (Scholastic, 1965, pb $.60)
        RL: 3   IL: 3-JH   BSMP
All Bulla's books have unusual depth and maturity and are
well liked. This is a realistic story about a modern Indian
boy. It is illustrated in good pen and ink drawings by a
Navaho artist on the reservation in Arizona.

1052 The Empty Schoolhouse, by Natalie Savage Carlson.
        Illus. by John Kaufmann. Harper, c1965. $4.50
        (Dell Yearling, pb $.75)
        RL: 5   IL: 5-adult   BSMP

This superb book goes unread because both the hardcover and paperback format convince the clientele it is intended for young children. In an adult format, we wouldn't be able to keep it in stock. Older girls and adults who are persuaded to read it are uniformly enthusiastic. It is a dramatic story about the integration of the parochial schools in Louisiana and centers around a brave and likeable black family. The black and white illustrations are superb.

1053 Enrique, by Pablo Figueroa. Illus. by Bill Negron.
      Hill & Wang, Challenger, c1970. pb $1
      RL: 4   IL: 4-JH   *BSMP
The exciting and moving adventures of a Puerto Rican boy who comes to New York, this book is believable and has a lot of suspense.

1054 Garbage Can Cat, by Victor Sharoff. Illus. by Howard
      N. Watson. Westminster, c1969. $3.95
      RL: 2-3   IL: Read aloud-4   *BSMP
The story of a small boy and a cat, this is one of several books dominated by the effects of urban renewal. Even when, as in this story, the family finds a better place to live (statistically only twenty-five per cent of those displaced do), removal is traumatic. This book, however, ends happily and city children and pet lovers will find it very satisfactory.

1055 The Girl From Puerto Rico, by Hila Colman. Morrow,
      c1961. $4.95 (Dell Laurel, pb $.50)
      RL: 5   IL: 5-HS   BSMP
This story of a Puerto Rican family who move to New York is not as understanding of either the Puerto Rican or child's point of view as one would like but there are not many books yet about Puerto Ricans for this age group and the girls, both Puerto Ricans and others, do like it and do borrow it.

1056 God Bless the Child, by Kristin Hunter. Scribner,
      c1964. OP (Bantam, 1967, pb $.75)
      RL: 5-6   IL: HS-adult   *BM
A tragic novel of a girl growing up "cool," fighting with everything she has to get rich and finding at the end what is worthwhile and what is not.

1057 Going to Meet the Man, by James Baldwin. Dial,
      c1965. $5.95 (Dell pb $.75)
      RL: 6   IL: JH-adult   BM
A group of powerful short stories mainly about life in Harlem, this book is an excellent starting point for many poor readers

who have heard of Baldwin but find his essays and novels difficult reading because of vocabulary.   The language in these
stories is very direct and the reader is plunged into the scene
and the story right from the beginning.

1058   Gracie, by Suzanne Roberts. Illus. by Marilyn Miller.
       Doubleday & Co. , 1965. $3.50
       RL: 4   IL: 6-adult   BSP
Popular with older girls and adults, this story of a migrant
worker family generates real excitement when the hero tries
to unionize the workers.

1059   Harlem--Voices from the Soul of Black America, edited
       by John Henrik Clarke.   New American Library,
       Signet, c1970.   pb $.95
       RL: Varied   IL: HS-adult   *BSMP
These twenty short stories by black New York writers are
very interesting in themselves and also give a brief chrono-
logical picture of black literature since World War I starting
with the Harlem Renaissance in the twenties and ending with
an excerpt from Daddy Was a Numbers Runner which was
published in December 1970.   Unlike Right On (see 1101 below), which is pretty much unrelieved gloom and bitterness,
this collection has great variety and will, therefore, have
more impact.

1060   The Hit, by Julian Mayfield.   Vanguard, 1969. $3.50
       (Belmont pb $.95)
       RL: 6   IL: HS-adult   *BM
A well written well-plotted novel of the numbers game by a
man who knows his Harlem.   With humor and suspense, this
will be very popular.

1061   Home to Harlem, by Claude McKay.   Harper, c1928.
       OP   (Simon & Schuster Pocket Books, c1956, pb $.50)
       RL: 7   IL: HS-adult   BSMP
A classic story of post-war Harlem by the black poet, this
came out years ago but is still very popular.   People who
have never heard of McKay borrow it because of the title,
like it and recommend it.

1062   Howard Street, by Nathan C. Heard.   Dial, c1968.
       $4.95 (New American Library, pb $.95)
       RL: 6   IL: Adult   BM
This is a novel of life in a section of the slums of Newark,
N. J.   The characters are mostly pimps, prostitutes, drug
addicts and corrupt police.   I did not enjoy reading it but it

does have power and credibility. The sex and violence are
not dragged in for effect but are an intrinsic and necessary
part of the story, probably of any story written about this
segment of society. The book is extremely popular with
young adults apparently on a word of mouth kind of publicity
since I have not seen the book advertised at all.

1063   Hurricane: The Story of a Friendship, by Dorothy
        Whitney Ball. Hale, 1966. $2.11 (Grosset & Dun-
        lap, Tempo, pb $.60)
        RL: 6   IL: 5-adult   BSMP
A suspenseful story of interracial friendship in a small Florida town.

1064   I Am Here: Yo Estoy Aqui, by Rose Blue. Illus.
        by Moneta Barnett. Watts, c1971. $4.95
        RL: 2-3   IL: Read aloud-4   *BSMP
In English with some Spanish words, this is the story of the
first school day of a little Puerto Rican girl who has just
moved to New York City. She is naturally frightened and ill
at ease but her troubles end when she finds a Spanish-speaking
teacher assigned to translate for her and to help her to feel
at home. This is a lovely and reassuring book. In how many
schools would this be a true experience for a Spanish-speaking
newcomer?

1065   I Am Maria, by Toby Talbot. Illus. by Eleanor Mills.
        Cowles, c1969. $3.50
        RL: 3   IL: Read aloud-4   *BSMP
This story of a girl from the Dominican Republic who is terrified and resentful of New York and then finds a friend will
have great appeal to the many immigrants we serve. It
should be in paperback.

1066   Invisible Man, by Ralph Ellison. Modern Library,
        1952. $2.95 (New American Library, Signet, pb
        $1.25)
        RL: Adult   IL: HS-adult   BSMP
This extraordinary novel of a black man's experiences in the
South and the North is one of the great books of American
literature.

1067   It Happened to Anita, by Ruth Faux. Illus. by Adriana
        Saviozzi. Dodd, Mead, 1967. $3.50
        RL: 2-3   IL: Read aloud-4   BSMP
Based on a true experience, this story of a little Panamanian
girl who got lost on her first shopping trip in New York City

has great appeal for girls.

1068   Jazz Country, by Nat Hentoff.   Harper & Row, 1965.
       $3.95 (Dell pb $.50)
       RL: 6   IL: 6-adult   BSMP
An authentic and thought-provoking novel of the world of jazz
with an excellent format.   Very popular both with teenagers
and adults.

1069   Jokers Wild, by Mary Sullivan.   Photographs by
       Michael H. Roberts.   Field Educational Pub. Hap-
       penings Series, c1970. $2.56
       RL: 4-5   IL: 6-HS   BSMP
This book starts with thirty-five pages of excellent photographs
of black people--mainly teenagers.   Then follows a story of
a boy whose gay and spendthrift mother is driving her children
out of the home.   Randy winds up sleeping in an abandoned
house, sustained by the friendship of his rock band group.   A
quiet and authentic picture of poverty and of boys trying to
make something of themselves under very tough circumstances.
See comment on Happenings Series [1288].

1070   José's Christmas Secret, by Joan M. Lexau.   Illus.
       by Don Bolognese.   Dial Press, 1963. $3.50
       RL: 4-5   IL: 5-JH   *BSMP
This heartwarming book about a fatherless Puerto Rican family tells how ten-year-old José tries to be the man of the
family and succeeds in providing a Christmas surprise.   This
very real picture of the economic stresses of a fatherless
family is very popular.   However, it is passed by on the
bookmobile due to its hardcover format and size which leads
children who would enjoy it to think it is a picture book.

1071   The Journey, edited by Alma Murray and Robert
       Thomas.   Illus. by Diane and Leo Dillon, Tom
       Feelings, George Ford, and Alvin Hollingsworth.
       Scholastic, The Scholastic Black Literature Series,
       c1970.   pb $1.80
       RL: Varied   IL: 6-adult   *BSMP
Still another anthology of black literature (see 1030, 1032-34,
1059 and 1101).   Yet again, there is very little overlapping.
Virtually all of these selections are interesting and some are
memorable.

1072   Journey All Alone, by Deloris Harrison.   Dial, c1971.
       $4.95
       RL: 5   IL: 5-adult   *BSMP

A story of family life in Harlem written from the point of
view of a teenage girl. It is a story full of sadness and
courage and will interest readers of every age. I hope it will
soon be out in paperback.

1073 Julie's Heritage, by Catherine Marshall. McKay,
     c1957. $4.75 (Scholastic, 1969, pb $.75)
     RL: 6   IL: 6-HS   BSMP
This story of a black girl in an integrated high school in a
Northern city has depth and insights for both races. It is
very popular with girls.

1074 The Learning Tree, by Gordon Parks. Harper, c1963.
     $6.95 (Fawcett, Crest, 1969, pb $.95)
     RL: Adult   IL: HS-adult   BSMP
An enthralling novel about a black boy growing up in a prairie
town. It was made into an excellent movie by its author, the
well-known photographer and poet. See also 1371 and 1381.

1075 Letters to a Black Boy, by Bob Teague. Walker &
     Co., c1968. $4.50 (Lancer pb $.75)
     RL: 6   IL: HS-adult   *BSMP
This moving series of letters by the well-known TV news-
caster to his son tells what it was like for the author to grow
up black in America and what he hopes for his son. It also
has universal overtones in the father-son relationship and
much tenderness. Highly recommended for all adults and
also for all high school students.

1076 Little Vic, by Doris Gates. Illus. by Kate Seredy.
     Viking, c1951. $3.95 (Washington Square Press,
     Archway, 1968, pb $.60)
     RL: 5-6   IL: 5-adult   BSMP
The courage of Pony, the black boy hero of this story, in the
face of vicissitudes and discrimination, make this story of a
race horse into a story of wide appeal even to those who have
never seen a horse except on TV.

1077 The Man Who Cried I Am, by John A. Williams.
     Little, Crown, 1967. $6.95 (New American Library,
     Signet, 1968, pb $.95)
     RL: Adult   IL: Adult   BM
A powerful novel of a writer's black experience in America
by an author who is becoming very much respected by the
critics. This is also a roman à clef and many who read it
come to the conclusion that the CIA and the FBI played a
part in the deaths of Malcom X and Martin Luther King.

See also Captain Blackman [1044] by the same author.

1078 Marchers for the Dream, by Natalie Savage Carlson.
      Illus. by Alvin Smith.   Harper, c1969. $3.50
      RL: 4   IL: 4-adult   *BSMP
The story of two participants in the Poor People's March on
Washington, Bethany and her great-grandmother, this book
will appeal to all ages in underprivileged areas.   The characters are real and courageous and the housing problem, which
is the center of the plot, is one that strikes home to many
people these days.   If, as I hope, this book comes out in
paperback, it should be done in an adult format.   Many older
women will enjoy it.   This book is by the author of The
Empty Schoolhouse [1052].   Both books should be required
reading in every school in the country as should Mary Jane
[1079].

1079 Mary Jane, by Dorothy Sterling.   Doubleday, c1959.
      $3.95   (Scholastic pb $.75)
      RL: 6   IL: 5-HS   BSMP
This is a story of courage and friendship based on true incidents which took place when some junior high schools in
Nashville were integrated.   It is a deeply moving book and
one of the most popular I have ever seen in inner city schools
and on the bookmobile.   Girls who are behind in reading
struggle to read it and it is so universally popular that it is
creating a common background for black girls everywhere.
It is equally a must for white children.

1080 Mexicali Soup, by Katherine Hitte and William D.
      Hayes.   Illus. by Anne Rockwell.   Parents, c1970.
      $3.95
      RL: 3   IL: Read aloud-3   *BSMP
There are all too few books available about Spanish-American
families.   This one is about a Mexican-American family, but
whether Mexican, South American or Puerto Rican, children
will recognize the dilemma of newcomers as to what new customs to adopt and what old ideas to discard.   The children
in this book discarded so many old ideas that their soup became nothing but water.   Both the story and the illustrations
have humor and the book could be a good basis for a group
discussion.

1081 Mira! Mira!, by Dawn C. Thomas.   Illus. by Harold
      L. James.   Lippincott, c1970. $3.50
      RL: 3   IL: Read aloud-3   *BSMP
Little Ramon from Puerto Rico finds New York full of

surprises; some good, like snow and some frightening, like elevators.   Children from the island who remember their first impressions will emphathize with Ramon and other children will be interested to think of a world where snow and high rise buildings don't exist.

1082   My Dog Is Lost, by Ezra Jack Keats and Pat Cherr.
       Crowell, 1960. $3.50   (Scholastic pb $.50)
       RL: 2-3   IL: Read aloud-5   BSM
A Puerto Rican boy who speaks no English makes many friends while looking for his lost dog.   This has been a very useful book for reading help programs but it moved slowly on the bookmobile because of its hardcover format.   It is a delight to have this book in paperback.

1083   My House Is Your House, by Toby Talbot.   Illus. by
       Rod Weaver.   Cowles, c1970. $3.95
       RL: 4-5   IL: Read aloud-JH   *BSMP
Juana, a Puerto Rican girl just beginning to put down roots in Manhattan after the move from Puerto Rico, learns the meaning of home.   The story involves urban renewal, marijuana and a fire and has suspense and credibility.

1084   My Sweet Charlie, by David Westheimer.   New Ameri-
       can Library Signet, c1965.   pb $.75
       RL: 6-7   IL: 6-adult   BM
This is another instance of a book made popular by a movie but whose popularity has endured.   This story of a highly educated black man from the North who by curious circumstance becomes stranded in a winter-bound resort on the Gulf Coast with an uneducated pregnant young white girl seems contrived and not too credible.   However, the author makes one want to continue reading and the book has been very popular on the bookmobile.

1085   New in the City, by Muriel Stanek.   Illus. by Paul
       Brewer.   Whitman, 1965. $2.75
       RL: 3   IL: 3-6   S
Story about a new boy lately arrived in the city.   This is popular with the many children who have recently come to New York and who can empathize with the problems the little boy encounters.

1086   North Town, by Lorenz Graham.   Crowell, c1965.
       $4.50
       RL: 6   IL: 6-adult   BSMP
The Williams family, driven from their Southern home by

the tensions created by the school desegregation decision and
by their desire to give their son the kind of education the
South won't allow him to have, move to Detroit. There they
run into the kind of problems any uprooted family would encounter aggravated by a severe illness of Mr. Williams as a
result of the physical beating he was subjected to in the South.
The family is a likeable one, their problems are real and not
exaggerated and the reader is filled with admiration and sympathy for the brave way in which they tackle their difficulties.

1087 Not Without Laughter, by Langston Hughes. Knopf,
       c1930. $6.95 (Macmillan, Collier, 1969, pb $1.50)
       RL: Mainly 6   IL: JH-adult   BMP
This moving autobiographical novel by the noted poet tells of
his childhood in a small Kansas town. He was raised by his
grandmother who gave him the determination to be a credit
to his race but never to return hate for hate because hatred
"sours your soul." The book first appeared in 1930 and was
recently reissued. Anything by Langston Hughes is in demand.

1088 Nothing but a Man, by Jim Thompson. Popular Library,
       1970. pb $.60
       RL: 6   IL: HS-adult   BM
This novel was written from the scenario of a prize-winning
movie and seems rather simplistic. It concerns a black section gang leader who settles down in a southern town in order
to marry the local minister's daughter with whom he has
fallen in love. He wants to be respected as a man. His
father-in-law lives by compromise. Popular with teenagers
and adults.

1089 On Being Black: Writings by Afro-Americans, edited
       by Charles T. Davis and Daniel Walden. Fawcett
       Premier, c1970. pb $.95
       RL: Varied   IL: 6-adult   BSMP
A rich anthology of prose and verse by black Americans from
Frederick Douglass to the present. Although this is one of
several anthologies of black writers on this list, by and large,
except for a few famous poems such as If We Must Die and
For My People, the selections do not overlap. This in itself, of course, is a testimonial to how much good material
there is. This book has a full measure.

1090 One Summer in Between, by Melissa Mather. Harper
       & Row, 1967. $5.95 (Avon, Camelot, pb $.60)
       RL: 6   IL: JH-adult   BMP
A black girl from South Carolina who has never been out of

the South takes a job with a family in Vermont as part of her research for a course in sociology. The result is humorous, fascinating, revealing and thought-provoking.

1091 The Ordeal of Running Standing, by Thomas Fall. McCall Pub. Co., c1970. $6.95 (Bantam, 1971, pb $.95)
RL: 6-7   IL: JH-adult   *BMP
Ordinarily I wouldn't dream of offering our clientele in either program a book about an American Indian of the 1880's. However, this remarkable book has on the cover a picture of an Indian split down the middle; the left half is almost white and dressed in white man's clothes, the right half is reddish bronze with feathers, breech cloth and war paint. The book probes the dual culture problem of minority groups in a way that is relevant and exciting and tragic. The fictional story of a very intelligent Indian who tries to adapt to the white man's values, the book tied in with so many others on the list, I felt obliged to offer it. It made me think especially of Brown Girl, Brown Stones [876], God Bless the Child [1056], and Black Think--My Life as a Black Man and a White Man [428], by Jesse Owens among others. See what you think.

1092 The Outnumbered, edited by Charlotte Brooks. Delacorte, c1967. $4.95 (Dell Laurel Leaf, pb $.50)
RL: Varied-6 and up   IL: JH-adult   *BSMP
Edited by the supervising director of English in the Washington public schools, this uniquely valuable book has thirteen stories and essays about minority groups in America. It includes Willa Cather on the Bohemian immigrants, Benet on the Irish, Longfellow and Malamud on the Jews and stories about Assyrians, Indians, Italians and Puerto Ricans as well as blacks. It serves to remind the reader that, except for the Indians, we have all been immigrants once and that it is essential that we all have respect for the other man and his heritage. It concludes with Langston Hughes' poem Let America Be America Again. A great job of selecting pieces and a book that could really affect people's lives if all junior high students were exposed to it.

1093 The Outsiders, by S. E. Hinton. Viking, c1967. (Dell Laurel, Leaf, pb $.60)
RL: 5-6   IL: 6-adult   BSP
The outsiders are a defiant group of long-haired leather jacket "greasers," so called by the affluent world across the tracks, who feel doomed to a world of juvenile delinquency, reform

school and prison by the poverty and lack of family backing
in their environment.   This suspenseful novel, by a seventeen-year-old author, has an authentic ring and is a real
spellbinder.   It is very popular.

1094   Pablo's Mountain, by Albert Johnston.   Universal Pub.,
       Award, 1967. pb OP
       RL: 6-7   IL: 6-adult   BMP
A sensitive story of a Mexican boy's adolescence in El Barrio
(East Harlem).   A fictional parallel to Down These Mean
Streets but with a warm relationship between father and son.
A very good and popular book.   I hope it will soon be back
in print.

1095   The Pancho Villa Rebels, by Mary W. Sullivan.   Photo-
       graphs by Donald Armfield.   Field Educational Pub.
       Inc., Happenings Series, c1970. $2.56
       RL: 4   IL: 6-HS   *BSM
This book starts with approximately thirty pages of photographs of Mexican-Americans and their environment in a city.
Then there is a story about Mexican-American teenagers
which revolves around a rock band and a girl who is ashamed
of her Spanish heritage.   The story is simplistic but the book
will certainly be useful since it will surely interest teenage
reluctant readers and since it does have a positive attitude
toward dual culture situations.   See comment on Happenings
Series [1288].

1096   A Patch of Blue, by Elizabeth Kata.   Popular Library,
       1968. $.60
       RL: 6   IL: 6-adult   BSMP
I had thought this novel about the blind white girl who falls
in love with the black man who befriends and understands her
might go out of vogue after the movie which was based on it
had gone by.   However, it is still very much in demand with
every age from sixth grade on up, even though the print of
our edition is awful.   One reader recommends it to another.
It is a book that would be very popular in a large print edition.

1097   Plain Girl, by Virginia Sorensen.   Illus. by Charles
       Geer.   Harcourt, Voyager, 1955.   pb $.50
       RL: 5   IL: 5-HS   BSP
A moving story of an Amish girl's search for the right way
to cope with the clash of two cultures and with the generation
gap.   It has many parallels for other minority children and
is well liked once it is introduced.   The picture on the cover

leads most readers to think it is historical fiction from which
many poor readers shy away.   When I explain that the girl
dresses that way in today's world because her parents want
her to, interest is immediately sparked.

1098   A Present from Rosita, by Celeste Edell. Illus. by
        Elton Fax.   Washington Square Press, Archway,
        c1952.   pb $.50
        RL: 5   IL: 4-JH   BSMP
This is one of my favorite books and girls like it as much
as I do.   It is about a Puerto Rican widow and her three
children: Pablo, Rosita and Victor.   Victor is often in
trouble, but the relationship between him and the rest of the
family is a warm one.   In spite of the fact that the family
has very little money and suffers many misfortunes through
hurricanes and illness, the book is a happy one.   The first
half takes place in Puerto Rico and gives a good picture of
life in a Puerto Rican village; the second half is laid in
New York and is a realistic picture of what an emigrating
Puerto Rican family may encounter.

1099   Rattrap, by Mary Sullivan.   Photographs by Donald
        Armfield.   Field Educational Pub. Happenings Series,
        c1970. $2.56
        RL: 4   IL: 6-HS   BSMP
Another teenage band story about impoverished youngsters
whose families are having a struggle to find and hang onto
decent housing.   One boy's home has been destroyed by an
urban renewal project and his grandfather forced into an old
folks home.   One girl, whose family is fighting to hang onto
their home, lives on a street slated to be condemned by the
city.   In the rather simplistic story, the kids learn how to
take community action and whom to trust and whom not to.
See comment on Happenings Series [1288].

1100   Return to Ramos, by Leo Cardenas.   Illus. by Nilo
        Santiago.   Hill and Wang, Challenger Books, c1970.
        pb $1
        RL: 5-6   IL: 6-adult   *BMP
Juan José Ramos has lived for thirty years in Ramos for half
the year and (since he couldn't find work to support his family in his home town) gone on the road with his family to pick
crops the rest of the year.   His oldest daughter who is doing
very well at school, persuades him to leave her in Ramos.
He returns to find that his dead mother cannot be buried in
the local Catholic cemetery solely because she is Mexican-
American and that his daughter is a leader of a group of

Chicano students who are determined to get decent treatment.
His instinct is not to demonstrate or to protest but in the
end, the determination and courage of the young move him to
speak out against injustice.   This brief story rings with sincerity.

1101   Right On: An Anthology of Black Literature, edited by
       Bradford Chambers and Roberta Moon.   New Ameri-
       can Library, Mentor, c1970.   pb $.95
       RL: Varied   IL: 6-adult   *BSMP
This collection of plays, poetry and fiction is a powerful
statement about the oppression and suffering of the black people in America.   Except for the two poems "For My People"
and "If We Must Die," virtually all the material is different
from that of the other anthologies in this section.   Although
some of the selections are difficult reading, most are not
and in any event, the interest in the subject matter will overcome any reading problems for most black students.   Divided
into three sections, Oppression, Resistance and Black Is
Beautiful;   the last section is the weakest of the three.   The
book would have a better balance and more effect if some of
the more humorous and positive black literature which exists
had been included.

1102   Roosevelt Grady, by Louisa R. Shotwell.   Illus. by
       Peter Burchard.   World, 1963. $3.95 (Grosset &
       Dunlap, Tempo, pb $.60)
       RL: 5-6   IL: HS-adult   BMP
This heart-warming story of a migrant family was intended
for junior high boys and girls who never borrow it but it has
great appeal to older girls and women who can identify with
Roosevelt's mother and her dreams of a stable life with a
future.   The black and white illustrations add a great deal
to the book's attraction.

1103   Santiago, by Pura Belpré.   Illus. by Symeon Shimin.
       Warne, c1969. $3.95
       RL: 3   IL: Read aloud-4   BSMP
Santiago, a young newcomer to New York, is lonely for the
lovely pet hen he had to leave behind in Puerto Rico and constantly boasts about her at school.   One classmate always
disbelieves and downgrades him.   How Santiago finally con-
vinces him of the beauty of his pet is a story with many dimensions that can be used with older non-readers.   The author, Pura Belpré, is a noted Puerto Rican storyteller who
has worked for years with the New York Public Library and
really knows her audience.

1104 <u>Seven in a Bed</u>, by Ruth A. Sonneborn. Illus. by Don
      Freeman. Viking, c1968. $2.95
      RL: 3   IL: Read aloud-3   BSMP
A newly arrived Puerto Rican family finds that seven in a bed
is too many. A humorous story that children enjoy and that
gives a picture of warm family life. Should be in paperback.

1105 <u>The Siege of Harlem</u>, by Warren Miller.   Fawcett
      Premier, c1964.   pb $.75
      RL: Adult   IL: JH-adult   BM
This is a sardonic and clever fantasy which tells of a time
when Harlem becomes an independent state and takes on the
rest of New York City. Its good humored wit, which bears
little relationship to the kind of speeches made by today's
militants, nevertheless makes vivid the many injustices suffered so long by the people of Harlem. This book came out
several years ago and is now a black classic which has a
small but steady demand from older people. Everyone likes
humor and many more would borrow it and enjoy it if it were
called to people's attention.

1106 <u>Snakes</u>, by Al Young. Holt, Rinehart, c1970. $4.95
      RL: 5   IL: JH-adult   *BSM
MC lives with his grandmother in Detroit and lives for his
music and his friends. He manages to graduate from high
school and to have enough success with his music to feel able
to leave for New York with high hopes for the future. A
beautiful story of growing up that will be very popular with
black teenagers and young adults. In its warmth and the
loving relationship between MC and his grandmother, it has
much in common with <u>Bear for the FBI</u> [867], but MC's experiences are much more deeply affected by his color and
poverty. Much of the conversation in the book is street
language which will bother some readers and make the book
more popular with others.

1107 <u>Soul Brothers and Sister Lou</u>, by Kristin Hunter.
      Scribner, c1968. $4.50 (Avon Books, 1970, pb
      $.75)
      RL: 5-6   IL: 5-adult   BSMP
The story of a courageous teenager coping with life in a
Northern ghetto, this is a wonderful book which accurately
mirrors life in the inner city as seen through her eyes.
Although some of the story is tragic (poverty and death) there
are many constructive elements. It is somewhat similar to
<u>Soul City Downstairs</u> [1320], but much deeper and more re-
warding. Highly recommended.

1108 The Souls of Black Folk, by W. E. B. DuBois.
      Fawcett Premier, c1953, c1961.   pb $.75
      RL: Adult   IL: HS-adult   BSMP
Subtitled essays and sketches, this beautiful classic has had
"a greater effect upon and within the Negro race in America
than any single book published ... since Uncle Tom's Cabin,"
according to James Weldon Johnson. It is still highly relevant. I have heard it quoted from twice in the last month by
black leaders and ministers. It is a searching into the dilemma of being black in America and a proud statement of
what it means to be black. This paperback is the twenty-
sixth edition.

1109 Sound of Sunshine, Sound of Rain, by Florence Parry
      Heide. Illus. by Kenneth Longtemps. Parents,
      c1970. $3.95
      RL: 3   IL: 6-HS   *SMP
A most unusual book. A blind boy goes to the park and makes
friends with an ice cream vendor who tells him how beautiful
the world is. The little boy doesn't know what color his
friend's skin is. This enrages his bitter sister who wishes
the world was blind so that she would not be discriminated
against because of her black skin. A haunting book which
should stimulate some interesting discussions.

1110 South Town, by Lorenz Graham. Follett, 1958. $4.98
      (New American Library, Signet, 1965, pb $.60)
      RL: 6   IL: 5-adult   BSMP
The story of a black family in the South which is driven out
of town by the tensions created by the changing atmosphere
which follows the Supreme Court school decision of 1954.
This book has suspense, drama and realistic and attractive
characters. It appeals to a wide age range. The hardcover
sequel North Town [1086], tells what happens to the Williams
family in Detroit and is also excellent. See also Whose
Town [1126].

1111 The Spider Plant, by Yetta Speevack. Illus. by Wendy
      Watson. Atheneum, 1965. $3.25   (Washington
      Square Press, Archway, pb $.50)
      RL: 5   IL: 5-JH   BSMP
An excellent story about a Puerto Rican family's moves to
and in New York. This book centers around the twelve-year-
old daughter Carmen. The people are credible and the situations interest any schoolgirl and have special meaning for
other children who have been uprooted. This title was well-
liked on the bookmobile and in the School Volunteer program

when it was well introduced in hardcover--now that it is out
in paperback, it will be even more in demand.

1112 The Spook Who Sat by the Door, by Sam Greenlee.
      Allison & Busby Ltd. , c1969. (Bantam pb $. 95)
      RL: Adult   IL: JH-adult   BM
Styled the first black nationalist novel, this is a story of the
first black man in the CIA. Freeman, the hero, deliberately
learns as many CIA techniques as possible and then uses them
to organize a black underground throughout America. The
book ends on a note of defiance. It is extremely popular on
the bookmobile.

1113 The Tall One, by Gene Olson. Dodd, 1956. $3. 95
      RL: 5-6   IL: 5-HS   *SMP
A good basketball story with depth to it. Miles Talbert,
seven feet tall, feels like a freak and is often treated like
one. Bill Washington, a member of the only black family in
town is accepted by some and not by others. The emotions
involved are not overstressed and there is plenty of action.

1114 Tell Me How Long the Train's Been Gone, by James
      Baldwin. Dial, c1968. $6. 95 (Dell pb $1. 25)
      RL: Adult   IL: HS-adult   BM
The story of a man who came out of Harlem to become a
famous actor, this is one of Baldwin's most popular novels.

1115 That Bad Carlos, by Mina Lewiton. Illus. by Howard
      Simon. Harper, 1964. $3. 79
      RL: 5-6   IL: 4-JH and older slow readers   BS
A heart-warming story of a newly arrived Puerto Rican boy's
adventures in New York and in growing up. I know from my
school volunteer experiences how very much appreciated this
book is especially by Puerto Rican boys and girls but it moves
slowly on the bookmobile due to the fact that it is only available in hardcover.

1116 Third Generation, by Chester Himes. New American
      Library, Signet, c1954. pb $. 75
      RL: Adult   IL: Adult   BM
A hard-hitting story of an intense middle-class black family's
inter-relationships. This is serious fiction by the author of
many detective stories. See Cotton Comes to Harlem [1145],
Hot Day, Hot Night [1153], and others.

1117 Tres Casas--Tres Familias, by Edna Beiler. Illus.
      by Ezra Jack Keats. Friendship Press, 1964.

pb $1.75
RL: 5-6   IL: 5-adult   BSMP
This book is very expensive for a paperback. However, its
format is exceptional in that it is appropriate for any age
level and has excellent paper and good print. It tells the
story of a Cuban refugee family, a Puerto Rican family who
emigrate to Chicago, and a Mexican-American family in south
Texas. The characters in the stories are real; the situations
they face with courage are also real and the outcome of each
family's dilemma is hopeful as well as believable. There is
no patronizing here on the part of the author. However, this
book must be introduced as people assume from the title that
it is in Spanish.

1118 Trina, by Patricia Miles Martin. Illus. by Robert L.
      Jefferson. Scholastic, c1967.   pb $.50
      RL: 4   IL: 4-JH   BSMP
A lonely Mexican girl finds a friend and learns English. Although the setting of this story is remote to city children (a
town in Colorado) the language problem is one that many of
our children encounter and the book's attitude is both positive
and realistic.

1119 Troubled Summer, by Ben Haas. Hale, 1966. $3.81
      (Grosset & Dunlap, Tempo, pb $.60)
      RL: 6   IL: 6-adult   BSMP
The exciting story of Freedom Riders in a Southern town seen
through the eyes of a Negro boy who has come (with cause) to
hate whites and is torn between his hatred and his admiration
for the young white leader who risks his life for justice for
the blacks. A very relevant story for today as the problems
it poses are still with us.

1120 The Unfinished Journey, by Theresa Oakes and M.
      Jerry Weiss. McGraw-Hill, c1967. $5.95
      RL: Varied, 5-up IL: JH-adult   SMP
An excellent collection of plays, poetry, essays and fiction
dealing with the experiences of minority groups in America.
The format is textbooklike with questions after each selection
and it is therefore not suitable for the bookmobile but the
material is so thought-provoking that it is well worth having
for use in a one-to-one situation or for group discussion
among good readers at the high school age. The School
Volunteers have found the first selection, Me Candido, a play
about a homeless Puerto Rican boy, excellent for motivating
poor readers who are caught by Candido's plight and dignity.
Note that The Outnumbered [1092] and We Too Belong [1121]

are on the same theme and, with one exception, are entirely
different material.

1121 We Too Belong, edited by Mary Turner. Dell Laurel
      Leaf, c1969.   pb $. 60
      RL: Varied, mostly 6-7 IL: 6-adult   *BSMP
Another anthology about minorities on the same lines as The
Outnumbered [1092] and Unfinished Journey [1120], and again
with virtually no repetition of the material in those books.
This collection doesn't seem to me to be quite so effective
but is has many good things in it and will be well liked.

1122 What's Wrong with Julio?, by Virginia H. Ormsby.
      J. B. Lippincott, 1965. $2. 95
      RL: 2-3   IL: Read aloud-4   BSMP
Julio doesn't want to learn English or participate in anything
because he misses his parents.   When the other children
understand and help him, he opens up.   One of the very few
really low reading level books to include Puerto Rican children.
Especially useful in bilingual sections of the city, the book
has a picture page of Spanish and English words at the end.

1123 Where Did You Come From?, by J. Koch.   Hale.
      $2. 79
      RL: 5   IL: 4-HS   *BSMP
A black boy, new in the neighborhood, is asked where he
comes from and tells of both his African and American heritage.   This unusual book gives pride to black children.

1124 White Elephant for Sale, by Edna Beiler.   Illus. by J.
      Gretger.   Friendship Press, 1967.   pb $1. 75
      RL: 4-5   IL: 4-HS   BSMP
Three short stories set in different locales having a central
theme of children (white, Indian, Mexican) facing poverty
realistically.   No happy endings but a good, involving, and
challenging collection which will even hold adult interest.

1125 Who Will Be My Friends?, by Sydney Hoff.   Harper
      Early I Can Read Series, 1960. $1. 95
      RL: 1-2   IL: Read aloud-2   BS
Freddy moves to a new neighborhood but manages to make
friends.   A popular book on a very important subject.

1126 Whose Town?, by Lorenz Graham.   Crowell, 1969.
      $4. 50
      RL: 5-6   IL: 5-adult   *BSMP
This superb book is a sequel to South Town and North Town.

The Williams family, around whom all three books revolve,
was forced to flee the South at the end of the first book. In
the second they lived through some tough times in Detroit but
finally seem to be getting on pretty well. In Whose Town,
they live through the Detroit riots. David Williams, who has
just graduated from school and gotten a scholarship to college,
is under great pressure to join a militant black group. He
and his friends have to figure out where they stand. This is
a very exciting and yet a very thoughtful book and, in my
judgment, a must for every high school library in the country.
Both this book and its predecessor, North Town should be in
paperback.

1127   Wild Boy, by Thomas Fall. Illus. by Leo Summers.
       Dial, 1965. $3.50 (Scholastic pb $.60)
       RL: 5-6   IL: 5-adult   BSMP
Roberto, half Spanish, half Indian comes of a family that lives
in the wilderness and traps and trains wild horses. Roberto
is torn between his white and Indian heritage and finally re-
jects them both because both involve cruel and bloodthirsty
fighting. He escapes from the white fort, starts a prairie
fire to prevent an Indian massacre and goes off to the wilderness again with a magnificent stallion he has tamed. A very
exciting story with many levels of interest.

1128   Will I Have a Friend?, by Miriam Cohen. Illus. by
       Lillian Hoban. Macmillan, 1967. $3.95 (Collier
       pb $.95)
       RL: 2-3   IL: Read aloud-2   BSMP
Jim is worried that he won't be able to make friends on his
first day at school but happily he finds a friend and all is
well.

1129   Willy Wong: American, by Vanya Oakes. Illus. by
       Mrs. T. Weda Yap. Messner, 1967. $3.50
       (Washington Square Press, Archway, pb $.50)
       RL: 5-6   IL: 4-7   BSMP
A very nice family story about a Chinese-American boy in
San Francisco. There is a good deal of action and suspense.
Willy, who at first feels that his two cultures are in conflict
learns at the end to enjoy and be proud of both.

1130   Young and Black in America, compiled by Rae Pace
       Alexander. Random, c1970. $3.95
       RL: Varied   IL: 6-adult   SMP
Eight men and women (Frederick Douglass, Richard Wright,
Daisy Bates, Malcom X, Jimmy Brown, Anne Moody, Harry

Edwards and David Parks) tell in vivid language what it meant
to them to be young and black in America. Some of these excerpts from autobiographies are available in other collections
but the way they have been grouped here with new and current
material (Jimmy Brown and David Parks) has a telling effect.
This book is already very popular in inner city schools.

MYSTERY STORIES

1131   The Acid Nightmare, by M. E. Chaber.   Holt, Pace-
       setter, c1967. $3.50
       RL: 4-5   IL: 4-HS   BS
An up-to-date mystery about LSD by a well-known mystery
writer, this has an adult format.   It is very popular with
sixth grade on up.   Although it has a controlled vocabulary,
it appeals to good readers as well as poor ones.

1132   Against Time!, by Roderic Jeffries.   Harper, c1964.
       $3.79   (Scholastic, 1968, pb $.60)
       RL: 5   IL: 5-adult   BS
A truly exciting detective story about a kidnapping solved by
police team work.   A thriller that appeals to a wide age
range.

1133   Ax, by Ed McBain.   Adapted by James Madigan.
       Illus. by W. Otto.   McGraw-Hill, Reading Shelf
       Series. $1.60
       RL: 4-5   IL: 5-adult   BS
An exciting up-to-date detective story by a popular author in
a good adaptation for easy reading.

1134   The Bamboo Key, by L. A. Wadsworth.   Grosset,
       Tempo, c1948.   pb $.50
       RL: 5   IL: 5-HS   BS
An adequate teenage mystery;   more good ones are needed.

1135   Big Max, by Kin Platt.   Illus. by Robert Lopshire.
       Harper, I-Can-Read Series, c1965. $2.50
       RL: 2-3   IL: K-4   BS
How Big Max, the world's greatest detective, found the missing elephant.   Very popular.   A lovely detective story for the
younger set.

1136 Binky Brothers, Detectives, by James Lawrence.
      Illus. by Leonard Kessler. Harper, I-Can-Read
      Series, c1968. $2.50
      RL: 2-3   IL: Read aloud-3   BSMP
This funny mystery story could also be titled Younger
Brother's Triumph and will have special appeal for younger
siblings everywhere.

1137 Blues for a Black Sister: Superspade #6, by B. F.
      Johnson. Paperback Library, 1971. pb $.75
      RL: 6   IL: JH-adult   B
The latest in a series of mystery novels about a super black
detective called Superspade who drives a fancy car, leads a
very fancy sex life and always gets his man after hair-raising
adventures. The series is very popular with boys and men
from seventh grade on up. This one suggests that the Mafia
have been feeding jazz stars dope in order to keep them under
the Mafia's control and that the many accidents and suicides
in the music field are due to miscalculations on the part of
the Mafia. It's an interesting theory but the book is imitation
James Bond.

1138 The Boy's Book of Great Detective Stories, by Howard
      Haycraft, ed. (Abridged) Berkley, Highland Book,
      1964. pb $.50
      RL: Adult   IL: JH-adult   B
Too bad this collection is labelled the "Boy's Book" as many
adults would enjoy it. Now it is mainly borrowed by exceptionally good readers of whom we don't have many.

1139 The Case of the Aluminum Crutch, by Lester Heath.
      Dell, 1963. pb OP
      RL: 5   IL: 5-HS   B
A mystery adventure about a boy detective, this book is much
in demand although it is not very credible. There is an unmet need for good, modern mystery stories for children and
young people.

1140 The Case of the Cat's Meow, by Crosby Bonsall.
      Harper I Can Read Series, c1965. $2.50
      RL: 2   IL: Read aloud-3   BSMP
Who stole the cat? A bunch of backyard detectives, real
boys, solve a mystery. This easy-to-read mystery has instant appeal even to non-readers and is a very motivating
book. It has humor and action.

1141 The Case of the Dumb Bells, by Crosby Bonsall.

Harper I Can Read, c1966. $2.50
RL: 2   IL: Read aloud-3   BSMP
Another in the same series as 1140 and equally popular.

1142   The Case of the Hungry Stranger, by Crosby Bonsall.
Harper I Can Read, c1963. $2.50 (Scholastic,
1969, pb $.60)
RL: 2   IL: Read aloud-3   BSMP
This time the boys are trying to find out who stole Mrs.
Meech's pies. Again the same series but even better this
time since it is in paperback. We are grateful because we
can afford forty copies of this one instead of ten. Also
available in Spanish--See Category IV.

1143   Cases of Sherlock Holmes, adapted by W. Kottmeyer
et al. McGraw-Hill, Webster Division. $1.48
RL: 4   IL: 4-HS   BS
This is an invaluable book for the many junior high and high
school students who cannot read the original.

1144   Cop's Kid, by Scott Corbett. Illus. by Jo Polseno.
Little, Brown, c1963. $3.95
RL: 4   IL: 4-7   S
A fast moving mystery with real children in a real setting
and lots of action. This is very popular when one child has
been persuaded to read it but would move very fast in paperback.

1145   Cotton Comes to Harlem, by Chester Himes. Putnam,
1965. OP (Dell, 1970, pb $.75)
RL: 6   IL: HS-adult   BM
A ribald funny murder mystery laid in Harlem with many
racial incidents and much excitement. It is now (1970) also
a very good movie. It has always been very popular on the
bookmobile as are all of Chester Himes detective stories
about his two black detectives, The Grave Digger and Coffin
Ed. This one has a plot based on a fraudulent imitation of
Garvey's Back to Africa movement. The bookmobile has
carried the following mysteries by Himes with great success.
I list them here. The paperback editions go in and out of
print but are always very popular when they are available.
Blind Man with a Pistol (Putnam, c1966), Cotton Comes to
Harlem (Putnam, 1965), The Heat's On (Putnam, c1966),
Hot Day, Hot Night (Dell, c1969, pb), Pinktoes (Putnam,
c1965), A Rage in Harlem (Avon, c1965, pb), The Real Cool
Killers (Avon, c1959, pb), Run, Man, Run (Putnam, c1966).

328 Read for Your Life

1146 Deathman, Do Not Follow Me, by Jay Bennett. Hawthorne, c1968. $3.95 (Scholastic, 1969, pb $.60)
RL: 6   IL: 6-adult   BSM
A mystery story laid in Brooklyn about a stolen Van Gogh. It starts off well with interesting characters and good suspense but grows less credible toward the end. It is popular in Brooklyn, however, because the setting is familiar. We still need many more good mysteries for grades three through high school.

1147 Emil and the Detectives, by Erich Kastner. Illus. by Walter Triel. Doubleday, c1930. $3.95 (Scholastic, 1955, pb $.60)
RL: 5   IL: 5-7   B
This old German story is well written and still popular for its suspense but we certainly need modern detective stories on this reading level. The Hardy boys, though not up to date, are still popular and would be a godsend in paperback.

1148 Encyclopedia Brown, Boy Detective, by Donald J. Sobol. Illus. by Leonard Shortall. Nelson, c1963. $2.95 (Scholastic, 1965, pb $.35)
RL: 4   IL: 4-6 and can be used with JH and HS poor readers   BS
A wonderful book of short stories about a boy detective which challenge the student's ability to solve a problem. This book and its sequels are very popular. The sequels are as follows:
Encyclopedia Brown and the Case of the Secret Pitch
    Nelson c1965, $2.95
Encyclopedia Brown Finds the Clues
    Nelson 1966, $2.95 (Scholastic, 1966, pb $.50)
Encyclopedia Brown Gets His Man
    Nelson 1967, $2.95 (Scholastic, 1968, pb $.50)
Encyclopedia Brown Keeps the Peace
    Nelson 1969, $2.95
Encyclopedia Brown Saves the Day
    Nelson 1970, $2.95 (Archway, 1971, pb $.60)
Encyclopedia Brown Solves Them All
    Nelson 1971, $2.95 (Rand, 1971, pb $1)
Encyclopedia Brown Strikes Again
    Nelson 1965, $2.95 (Scholastic, 1966, pb $.50)
Encyclopedia Brown Tracks Them Down
    Nelson 1971, $2.95
We can't have too many Encyclopedia Browns, they are so popular and for the School Volunteers so useful.

1149 Fist Against the Night, by Burton Goodman. Illus. by
Robert Swanson. McGraw-Hill, 1970, City Limits II
Series. pb $1.60
RL: 4-5 IL: 5-adult *BMP
An absorbing story of two boys, one black, one white, linked
by their toughness and fortuitous circumstances to the murder
of a candy-store owner on the edge of Harlem. The people
are believable and there is suspense right up to the last page.

1150 The Heat's On, by Chester Himes. Dell, 1967. pb
OP
RL: 5-6 IL: HS-adult BM
Another of Chester Himes' tough, humerous and ribald detec-
tive stories about two black police detectives in New York
City. His books have a depth and breadth that show how
superficial and trashy books like the Superspade books (see
1137) are. However, both kinds of books are very popular.

1151 Hiroshi's Wonderful Kite, by George Heller. Illus. by
Kyuzo Tsugami. Silver Burdett, c1968. $2.98
RL: 2-3 IL: 2-JH SMP
A boy of Japan becomes a hero when he uses his kite as a
signal to help catch a thief. Simple clear illustrations and
a suspenseful story help children to empathize with a boy of
a different culture.

1152 The Homework Caper, by Joan Lexau. Illus. by Syd
Hoff. Harper, I Can Read, c1966. $2.50
RL: 2 IL: Read aloud-2 BSM
Bill's homework disappears but his friend, Ken, finally solves
the mystery. Bill also decides to be nicer to his little sis-
ter. This is very popular.

1153 Hot Day, Hot Night, by Chester Himes. Dell, c1969.
pb $.95
RL: 5-6 IL: HS-adult BM
All Himes' detective stories have interesting things to say on
race relations. This one focuses on riots and what causes
them and is excellent.

1154 In Black and Whitey, by Ed Lacy. Lancer, 1967.
pb $.75
RL: 6 IL: JH-adult BS
An exciting mystery by a well known author deals in addition
with racial issues. This is an honest and constructive book
as well as a spellbinder.

1155 In the Heat of the Night, by John Ball. Harper &
      Row, 1965. $5.95 (Bantam, 1967, pb $.75)
      RL: 6   IL: 6-adult   BSMP
Detective thriller about a black detective in a Southern town,
the book is as good as the movie was, which is saying a lot.
A very popular title.

1156 The Listening Walls, by Margaret Millar. Adapted by
      George McMillin. Noble & Noble, Falcon Books.
      pb $.75
      RL: 4-5   IL: 5-adult   *BS
A very suspenseful mystery story about a death which may
be a suicide or may be murder. This is an abridged and
adapted version of the original and will be very popular.

1157 Me and Arch and the Pest, by John Durham. Illus. by
      Ingrid Fetz. Four Winds, c1970. $4.50
      RL: 4   IL: 4-JH   *BSMP
One of the best books on this list, this engaging mystery has
humor, taut suspense and believable and appealing characters.
Two young boys from Watts, one white and one black get involved with a dognapping ring. This book will be justly popular especially when it comes out in paperback. It is well
written, the story is easy to get into and the excitement goes
on building right to the last page.

1158 Moment of Untruth, by Ed Lacy. Lancer, c1964. pb
      OP
      RL: 6   IL: Adult   BM
Another popular mystery story by a popular author. A black
detective goes to Mexico on a job and gets involved in more
than he expected.

1159 The Mysterious Schoolmaster, by Karin Anckarsvard.
      Translated by Annabelle MacMillan. Illus. by Paul
      Galdone. Harcourt, Voyager, c1955. $4.25
      (pb $.75)
      RL: 6   IL: 5-JH   BS
A good thriller for older children even though it is set in
Scandinavia. We badly need good modern mysteries in paper-
back on every reading level.

1160 The Mystery Man, by Scott Corbett. Illus. by Nathan
      Goldstein. Little, Brown, c1970. $4.95
      RL: 5-6   IL: 4-JH   *S
A puzzle left by an old man is solved by a twelve year old who
foils the old man's greedy nephews. Not great but up to date
at least.

1161 The Mystery of Dolphin Inlet, by James Holding.
      Macmillan, 1968. $4.50
      RL: 5   IL: 5-HS   BS
An exciting mystery for young people laid in Florida. Although the setting is remote to many, the story gets underway with so much action that the reader is held from the
start.

1162 Mystery of the Fat Cat, by Frank Bonham. Illus. by
      Alvin Smith. Dutton, c1968. $3.95 (Dell pb $.75)
      RL: 5   IL: 4-HS   BSMP
This is a wonderful book, a fast exciting mystery in authentic
ghetto surroundings. It is very popular even in hardcover
and really motivates a lot of boys to read. I am delighted
to see it in paperback.

1163 The Mystery of the Flooded Mine, by Willard Manus.
      Illus. by James Dwyer. Doubleday, Signal, 1964.
      $3.50
      RL: 4   IL: 5-HS   BS
An adequate mystery for teenagers on a satisfyingly easy
reading level. The locale is very remote for our clientele
but it is popular.

1164 Puzzle of the Talking Monkey, by L. A. Wadsworth.
      Rinehart, 1947. (Grosset & Dunlap, Tempo, 1963,
      pb $.50)
      RL: 6   IL: 5-adult   BS
A reasonably exciting mystery on a fairly low reading level.
We badly need more really good mysteries on an easy reading
level.

1165 The Rocking Chair Ghost, by Mary Jane. Illus. by
      Tomic dePaola. Lippincott, 1969. $2.95
      RL: 3-4   IL: 2-4   *BSMP
This easy-to-read mystery about a missing stamp box and a
mysteriously rocking chair is the next step up for children
who enjoyed stories like Big Max and The Case of the Hungry
Stranger.

1166 The Rooftop Mystery, by Joan M. Lexau. Illus. by
      Syd Hoff. Harper I Can Read, 1968. $2.50
      RL: 2-3   IL: Read aloud-3   BSMP
On moving day, Sam's sister Iris has her doll stolen. A
wonderful humorous read-aloud mystery. Every child loves
this one.

1167 Run, Man, Run, by Chester Himes.   Putnam, 1966.
      OP (Dell, 1969, pb $.75)
      RL: 6-7   IL: HS-adult   BM
A well written violent and hair-raising detective story by the
well-known black writer.   A drunken New York City detective
shoots two black men and then tries to cover up.   There is
suspense right up to the last line on the last page.   Very
popular with adults.

1168 Runaway Black, by Ed McBain.   Fawcett, 1969. pb
      $.75
      RL: 6   IL: Adult   BM
An excellent detective story by a well-known author.   Very
popular.

1169 Schoolhouse Mystery, by Gertrude C. Warner. Illus.
      by David Cunningham.   Whitman, 1965. $2.95
      RL: 4   IL: 4-HS   S
This book is one of a series of mysteries about a large family in Massachusetts.   Although it is not very exciting, the
author does make the reader want to turn the page and I
have used it successfully with a variety of children.   The
adventures of many different aged children with whom the
reader can identify are balanced with enough romance to interest a high school student and enough action to keep a
younger child from being bored.

1170 The Secret Three, by Mildred Myrick.   Illus. by
      Arnold Lobel.   Harper & Row, I Can Read Series,
      1963. $2.50
      RL: 2   IL: K-4   BS
Another popular mystery in this excellent series.

1171 The Shark Bites Back, by Stephen Joseph.   Illus. by
      Robert Weaver.   McGraw-Hill, Reading Shelf Series,
      1970. $1.72
      RL: 5   IL: 5-adult   *BSMP
A very exciting story about the murder of two hippies who
were involved with the drug trade.   The reader is kept
guessing for a long time as to who did it.   The detectives
are interesting as people and the book has a lot of suspense.
It will be very popular.

1172 Sleep in Thunder, by Ed Lacy.   Grosset & Dunlap,
      Tempo, 1964. pb $.60
      RL: 5   IL: 5-HS   BSMP
An excellent and exciting detective story about a Puerto Rican

boy in Spanish Harlem who is an inadvertent witness to a
murder and does not trust the police.   One of our most useful and popular mysteries.

1173   Spice Island Mystery, by Betty Cavanna.   Morrow,
        c1969. $4. 81
        RL: 6-7   IL: JH-HS   *BSMP
An unusual mystery by a very popular teenage author, this
story is laid on the island of Grenada.   Marcy, the West
Indian heroine, comes back from school in the United States
to find that many of her former school mates are involved
in a mysterious business deal.   Excellent characterization
and good suspense will make this popular.   Paperback publishers please note--good mysteries like this are rare.

1174   The Stolen Ruler, by Eric Johnson.   Illus. by June
        Goldsborough.   Lippincott, c1970. $3. 50
        RL: 3   IL: Read aloud-3   *BSMP
A mystery story in first grade.   Claude learns how to find
the evidence to prove that the stolen ruler is his and all the
boys involved decide friendship is more important than rulers.
Older children would find the story too moral but younger
children will enjoy it.

1175   Stories of Edgar Allan Poe, adapted by Glenn Munson.
        Illus. by Art Wolfson.   McGraw-Hill, Reading Shelf
        Series, pb 1968. $1. 60
        RL: 4-5   IL: 4-adult   *BS
Seven of Poe's most exciting stories in a simplified fast-
moving version.   Will be very much in demand.

1176   Two Minute Mysteries, by Donald Sobol.   Scholastic,
        1969.   pb $. 50
        RL: 5-6   IL: JH-HS   S
Quickie mysteries in which clues are provided and the reader
is challenged to solve the puzzle.   Answers are given in case
he fails.   An excellent book for high school students at the
end of a tutorial session.

SCIENCE FICTION

1177   Andy Buckram's Tin Men, by Carol Ryrie Brink.
        Illus. by W. T. Mars.   Viking, c1966. $3. 50

(Grosset & Dunlap, 1967, Tempo, pb $.50)
RL: 5   IL: 4-JH   BS
An unusual science fiction fantasy about robots by a good
author. The characters are real, the format is excellent
and the subject seems endlessly popular. A good family
read-aloud, this story can be enjoyed on different levels.

1178   Caves of Steel, by Isaac Asimov.   Fawcett, c1954.
       (Crest, 1970, pb $.75)
       RL: 6-7   IL: 6-adult   BS
A fascinating murder mystery laid in the very distant future
when people live in vast underground cities with communal
meals and a controlled climate and never venture into the
open air. This is not only an exciting story but also has
great relevance for today as the hero faces the fact that man
has almost exhausted earth's resources and must emigrate to
other worlds to survive. Very popular with teenagers and
adults including many who read it for the story and skip all
the words they can't understand.

1179   City of Gold and Lead, by John Christopher.
       Macmillan, c1967. $4.25 (Collier pb $.95)
       RL: 5-6   IL: 5-adult   BS
This is the second volume of an enthralling trilogy of stories
laid over a hundred years from now. Civilization as we know
it has been destroyed and the earth is ruled by monsters
called Tripods who come from outer space. This has nothing
like the depth and ethical and philosophical implications of the
best science fiction but is justly popular for its suspense and
action. Good escape literature.

1180   The Day the Space Ship Landed, by Beman Lord.
       Illus. by Harold Benson.   Walck, c1967. $4.25
       RL: 2-3   IL: 2-5   S
A good book on a very low reading level on a subject of growing interest to today's students who are looking for adventures
in space.

1181   Fahrenheit 451, by Ray Bradbury.   Simon & Schuster.
       $4.95 (Ballantine Books, c1950, pb $.95)
       RL: 6-7   IL: 6-adult   BS
A story about Montag the fireman, in the far future when all
houses are fireproof and it is the job of firemen to burn books
(because books upset people, give them ideas and make them
unhappy) rather than to save lives. A thought-provoking science fiction adventure story which explores the nature of happiness and which has a chilling chase at the end. Very

popular with teenagers and young adults.

1182   **First on the Moon**, by Hugh Walters.   Criterion, 1960.
         OP (Grosset, Tempo, 1962, pb $. 60)
         RL: 5   IL: 5-adult   BS
Suspenseful science fiction story with thought-provoking implications for world peace.   Although this story of a Russian
and an American space ship competing to be first on the
moon may seem dated in view of the Apollo flights, the questions it raises are relevant today, not only in space but in
environmental problems and in the problems of war and peace.
The action and excitement of the story have made this very
popular with the young and it has been an excellent basis for
discussion groups.

1183   **The Forgotten Door**, by Alexander Key. Illus. by
         Dom Lupo. Westminster, c1965. $3. 50   (Scholas-
         tic, 1965, pb $. 60)
         RL: 5   IL: 4-JH   BS
A boy falls onto our planet from one with a more advanced
civilization.   He has a dangerous and unhappy time before
he escapes from earth back to his home planet.   Here
science fiction is used to give an imaginative look at some
of man's traits.

1184   **Great Stories of Space Travel**, edited by Groff Conklin.
         Grosset, Tempo, c1963.   pb $. 60
         RL: HS   IL: HS-adult   B
This group of stories is difficult reading for most of our
clientele but science fiction fans seem to be a determined
bunch.   They borrow it and work hard to read it and seem
to feel that it is worth the effort.

1185   **The Illustrated Man**, by Ray Bradbury.   Doubleday,
         1951.   OP (Bantam, 1952, pb $. 75)
         RL: 7   IL: 6-adult   B
A series of science fiction stories that are enormously exciting in themselves and are also thought-provoking and full
of wisdom.   This is a valuable book since it is very popular
with teenagers and stretches both their minds and their vo-
cabularies.   It is also an excellent book for high school age
discussion groups because of the issues it raises.   Stories
like The Other Foot are as timely as today's newspaper headlines.

1186   **Miss Pickerell and the Geiger Counter**, by Ellen
         MacGregor. Illus. by Paul Galdone.   McGraw-Hill,

336 Read for Your Life

RL: 5   IL: 3-7   BS
The Miss Pickerell books are a wonderful mixture of science,
fantasy and humor. Miss Pickerell is a sturdy matter-of-
fact spinster who becomes involved in fantastic scientific adventures. Although the reading level of the stories is high,
I include them on the list because they are such wonderful
books to read aloud to a group of children of varied ages
and because they reach children who think they don't like
books because they don't like fairy or animal stories. This
one is the first of the series and in it, Miss Pickerell discovers uranium.

1187 Miss Pickerell Goes to the Arctic, by Ellen McGregor.
Illus. by Paul Galdone. McGraw-Hill, 1954. $3.95
(Scholastic pb $.60)
RL: 4   IL: 3-7   BS
Miss Pickerell gets involved in a rescue mission to the Arctic. This book is especially valuable since it is the easiest
to read of the Miss Pickerell books. If a poor reader can
manage this one, it can give him the confidence and interest
to conquer the others.

1188 Miss Pickerell Goes to Mars, by Ellen MacGregor.
Illus. by Paul Galdone. McGraw-Hill, c1951. $3.83
(Scholastic pb $.60)
RL: 5   IL: 3-7   BS
Miss Pickerell collects rocks on a successful and hilarious
visit to Mars.

1189 Miss Pickerell Goes Underseas, by Ellen MacGregor.
Illus. by Paul Galdone. McGraw-Hill, 1957. $3.83
(Scholastic pb $.60)
RL: 5   IL: 3-7   BS
Miss Pickerell goes underseas to rescue her collection of
rocks from Mars which went down on a ship that foundered.

1190 More Stories from the Twilight Zone, by Rod Serling.
Bantam, Pathfinder, 1963. pb $.60
RL: 5-6   IL: 5-adult   BS
Fascinating and very popular science fiction stories. See
also 1191, 1196 and 1201.

1191 New Stories from the Twilight Zone, by Rod Serling.
Bantam, Pathfinder, 1962. pb $.60
RL: 5-6   IL: 5-adult   BS
Very popular stories of the fantastic that appeal to a wide age
range.

1192   The Other Side of Nowhere, by Murray Leinster.
        Berkley, 1964.   pb OP
        RL: 7   IL: JH-adult   B
An exciting science fiction adventure story which is popular
even though the vocabulary is difficult for many.   Science
fiction readers seem highly motivated in their reading.

1193   Out of the Sun, by Ben Bova.   Holt, Rinehart &
        Winston, Pacesetter Series, 1968. $3.27
        RL: 4   IL: 5-adult   BS
New fighter planes fall apart when sent after mysterious objects spotted on Air Force Defense radar screens.   Another
of this useful series.   This one is an exciting science fiction
adventure story with wide age range appeal and is just the
right length for poor readers.

1194   Planet of the Apes, by Pierre Boulle.   Signet, 1962.
        pb $.60
        RL: 6-7   IL: 6-adult   B
This book had a burst of popularity when the movie from it
first appeared.   However, although not quite so much in demand now it still moves well with science fiction fans of
whom there are many.   This story of a planet in the far future where men are beasts and apes are intelligent and effective, stimulates a lot of discussion among our teenage
helpers on the bookmobile.

1195   The Pool of Fire, by John Christopher.   Macmillan,
        c1968. $4.25   (Collier pb $.95)
        RL: 5-6   IL: 5-adult   BS
The last of the trilogy begun in The White Mountains [1205]
Will and his friends have many hair-raising adventures before
they finally win the battle against the alien Tripods who mean
to destroy the earth.   Then, the battle won, they find they
must start a new and even harder task: to keep men from
destroying each other and themselves.   A science fiction
thriller laid in the distant future which has great relevance
for our time.

1196   Rod Serling's Twilight Zone Revisited, by Rod Serling.
        Adapted by Walter B. Gibson.   Grosset, Tempo,
        1964.   pb OP
        RL: 5-6   IL: 5-adult   BS
A very popular group of stories about the supernatural.   Sus-
penseful, but not too gory.   Very popular as are all the Rod
Serling books.

1197   The Runaway Robot, by Lester del Rey.   Illus. by
       Wayne Blickenstaff.   Scholastic, 1965.   pb $.75
       RL: 5   IL: 4-JH   BS
A boy and his robot friend refuse to be parted and have many
exciting adventures trying to reach earth.   A popular science
fiction story.

1198   Science Fiction Stories, by Richard M. Elam, Jr.
       Pocket Books, Lantern.   pb $.60
       RL: 5-6   IL: 5-HS   BS
This collection of stories is both useful and popular because
it is easier to read than the books by Ray Bradbury and
Arthur Clarke, yet the format is adult compared to 1197
above.   However, the content is geared to young adults and
has neither the depth nor the universality of really good
science fiction.

1199   The Secret of the Martian Moons, by Donald A.
       Wollheim.   Grosset, Tempo, 1963.   pb OP
       RL: 6   IL: 5-adult   BS
This story of life on Mars and its moons is full of action
and suspense.   The plot stimulates the imagination and a
sense of wonder.   Too bad that the author seems to feel that
a desire for combat and domination are manly virtues.   Very
popular with teenagers and some adults.

1200   Star Trek, adapted by James Blish.   Bantam, 1967.
       pb $.60
       RL: 5-6   IL: 5-adult   BS
Another collection of science fiction stories, more popular
than 1198 because they are not geared to any one age group
and because they are based on a very long-lived and popular
TV show.   These stories are quite easy to read compared to
much science fiction and a person who has enjoyed this book
can often be led on to other more meaty stories of the same
kind.   Star Trek Nos. 2 and 3 are also available at the same
price.

1201   Stories from the Twilight Zone, by Rod Serling.
       Bantam, 1960.   pb $.60
       RL: 5-6   IL: 5-adult   BS
These unusual stories of the fantastic are not the usual science
fiction fare but appeal to science fiction buffs as well as to
many other audiences.   The Serling books are among the
most consistently popular on the bookmobile with a wide age
range.

1202   Trapped in Space, by Jack Williamson. Illus. by
        Robert Amundsen. Doubleday, Signal. $3.50
        (Doubleday, Semaphore, 1968.   pb $1.75)
        RL: 4   IL: 4-HS   BSMP
An interesting science fiction story.   The choice of the crew
of the spaceship, which seems to be based on ethnic backgrounds, strains credibility but once launched, the story carries the reader along.   There is a real demand for easy
science fiction of this type.

1203   Tunnel Through Time, by Lester Del Rey. Illus. by
        Hal H. Frenck. Westminster. $4.75 (Scholastic,
        1966, pb $.60)
        RL: 6   IL: 5-JH   BS
Another exciting science fiction story for young people by the
author of The Runaway Robot.   This one is about two boys
whose time machine lands them in the age of the dinosaurs.

1204   2001: A Space Odyssey, by Arthur C. Clarke.   New
        American Library, Signet, c1968.   pb $.95
        RL: 6-7   IL: 6-adult   BS
Arthur Clarke is a scientist as well as one of the most admired writers in the field of science fiction.   Many of his
imaginative stories (like Jules Verne's) have proved later to
be pictures of the future and indeed, he predicted moon land-
ings at a time when no one else thought such a thing would
be feasible for generations.   This book is a novelized version
of the movie he made with Kubrick and has dazzling photographs reproduced from the movie.   Many readers simply
skip the scientific language and descriptions and follow the
plot.   The movie and Apollo missions have made this very
popular.

1205   The White Mountains, by John Christopher.   Macmillan,
        c1967. $4.95 (Collier pb $.95)
        RL: 6-7   IL: 6-adult   BS
This story is laid in the Alps, one hundred years from now,
in a world which is run by the "Masters" who operate in
huge mechanical tripods.   The "Masters" have enslaved man-
kind and on the whole most men are prosperous and happy
and don't miss their lack of freedom.   Three very human
and likeable boys about to reach the age of enslavement, set
out to escape their fate or to fight back in a spellbinding
novel which is the first of a notable trilogy.   See also 1179
and 1195.

1206   Wonderful Flight to the Mushroom Planet, by Eleanor

Cameron. Illus. by Robert Henneberger. Little,
Brown, c1954. $3.75 (Scholastic, 1966, pb $.75)
RL: 5   IL: 4-JH   BS
Two boys build a homemade space ship for a mysterious
little man who sends them to find a new planet. This one
has all the charm of dreams come true and is very popular
with older elementary children and junior high students.

SPORTS STORIES

1207 All-Scholastic Sports Stories, edited by Stanley Pashko.
      New American Library, Signet, 1962. pb $.50
      RL: 5   IL: 4-adult   BS
A good collection of short stories for sports fans. There is
good variety both in the sports covered and in the style of
writing.

1208 Anchor Man, by Jesse Jackson. Harper & Row,
      c1947. $4.50 (Dell, 1970, pb $.65)
      RL: 5   IL: 5-HS   BSMP
A good book which will interest track fans and other junior
high and high school students both because of interracial con-
flicts and the exciting story.

1209 Arrow Book of Sports Stories, edited by Tony Simon.
      Scholastic, c1969. pb $.60
      RL: 4-5   IL: 6-HS   BS
This collection of sports stories has great variety and includes a story about a soapbox derby. It is especially popular in the reading help programs where short stories are
more in demand than on the bookmobile.

1210 Barney Beagle Plays Baseball, by Jean Bethell. Illus.
      by Ruth Wood. Grosset, Easy-To-Read Wonder Book,
      1963. $.59
      RL: 2   IL: 2-4   BS
One of the few baseball books at this reading level, this humorous story is very popular.

1211 Baseball Flyhawk, by Matt P. Christopher. Illus. by
      Foster Caddell. Little, 1963. $3.25
      RL: 3-4   IL: 3-6   BSMP
This suspenseful baseball story about a Puerto Rican boy is

very popular with boys. It should be in paperback.

1212 Baseball Spark Plug, by Jack Zanger. Illus. by
      Francis Chauncy. Doubleday, Signal, c1963. $3.50
      RL: 4   IL: 6-HS   BS
A really exciting story about an odd man out who finally gets
to be part of the gang. It focuses on baseball but is also
enjoyed by non-sport fans.

1213 Bearcat, by Henry A. Bamman and Robert J. White-
      head. Illus. by James Andrews. Field Educational
      Publications, c1967. Checkered Flag Series. $1.92
      RL: 2-3   IL: 4-HS   *S
The poorest of a good series, this highly improbable story
of villainy in a classic car race will still interest most boys
since it has action and suspense. The controlled vocabulary
is rather stilted but it is good to have material of high school
interest on this reading level. See 1217 for annotation on
this series.

1214 Break for the Basket, by Matt Christopher. Illus. by
      Foster Caddell. Scholastic, c1960. pb $.60
      RL: 4   IL: 4-JH   BS
A shy boy is helped to success on the basketball court by an
artist who feels that he is a failure and whose career is rescued by the boy he befriended. A story with depth that would
be much more popular in an older format.

1215 Bucket of Thunderbolts, by Gene Olson. Dodd, Mead,
      1959. OP (Willow Pyramid, 1966, pb $.50)
      RL: 5   IL: 6-HS   BSMP
A story of sports car racing and racial prejudice and growing
up. The story is laid in California and one of the boys is a
Mexican-American. This is an action-packed thriller and very
well liked.

1216 The Challenger, by Frank Waldman. World, 1955.
      OP (Grosset, Tempo, 1963, pb OP)
      RL: 6   IL: 5-adult   BS
A behind the scenes story of a Golden Gloves champion. Not
very credible but very popular on the bookmobile.

1217 The Checkered Flag Series, by Henry A. Bamman and
      Robert J. Whitehead. Illus. by James Andrews.
      Field Educational Publications, Inc. , various dates.
      $1.92 per volume
      RL: 2-3 through 4-5   IL: 5-HS   BS

The Checkered Flag series consists of eight books, all on
the theme of automobile or motorcycle racing. The stories
have a controlled vocabulary ranging in difficulty from grades
2-3 to grades 4-5. The plots are somewhat simplistic and
the dialogue often stilted but there is plenty of action and
suspense and I am sure that the books will be very popular.
They are aimed at an age group that is deeply interested in
cars and in racing. Even in the inner city, boys yearn for
fast cars. The publisher says that the series was carefully
designed especially to attract poor readers and boys who dislike books and in general the format, print and illustrations
serve his purpose. However the first thing the reader sees
on opening the book is a disagreeable form glued to the inside
cover proclaiming that the book belongs to X School District
and asking the teacher to evaluate the condition of the book
and how the pupil has treated it (Good, fair, poor, bad are
the terms used). I can think of nothing calculated quicker to
repel a reluctant reader. Look under the following titles for
comment on the individual books: Bearcat, 500, Flea, Grand
Prix, Riddler, Scramble, Smashup, and Wheels.

1218   Chicano Cruz, by William Cox. Bantam, c1972. pb
       $.75
       RL: 5-6   IL: 6-adult   BSMP
Mando Cruz and Jack Kelly and Sandy Roosevelt and Gilbert
Jones are all rookies trying to make good in baseball. Cruz
is a Chicano, Roosevelt is black and the other two are
Wasps. All have family and financial problems pressing
them to be first in competition. Although the cast of characters makes the book sound contrived, the writing is good,
the young men are likeable and credible and the author makes
the reader care a great deal how the story comes out. Since
there are several love stories involved, this book will be
very popular with girls as well as boys and men.

1219   City High Champions, by William Heuman. Dodd,
       Mead and Co., 1969. $3.75
       RL: 4-5   IL: 6-HS   BSMP
An exciting basketball story about a Puerto Rican boy in an
inner city school. Same characters as 1220 below.

1220   City High Five, by William Heuman. Dodd, Mead and
       Co., c1964. $3.25
       RL: 5   IL: 6-HS   BSMP
An excellent basketball story in a city high school centering
around a Puerto Rican hero. It should be in paperback.

1221   The Contender, by Robert Lipsyte.   Harper & Row,
        1967. $3.50 (Bantam, 1969, pb $.75)
        RL: 3-4   IL: 4-HS   BSMP
An unusually fine novel about boxing and the choices a Harlem
dropout has to make.   The picture of life in Harlem is very
real and so is the suspense.   Especially recommend for private and suburban schools.   Boys will find it enthralling and
gain a lot of understanding of the problems faced by their
black peers.   It is very popular on the bookmobile and in
School Volunteer programs.

1222   Crooked Arm and Other Baseball Stories, compiled by
        Tony Simon.   Scholastic, c1968.   pb $.50
        RL: 5   IL: 5-HS   BS
Nine stories about boys and baseball that will appeal to fans.
We carry this to add variety.   Adequate but not noteworthy.

1223   Don and Donna Go to Bat, by Al Perkins.   Illus. by
        B. Tobey.   Random House Beginner, c1966. $1.95
        RL: 2-3   IL: Read aloud-4   BS
Very popular easy-to-read baseball story about a girl twin
who pinch hits successfully for her ailing brother.   There is
now a Cinderella League which is the equivalent of the Little
League for boys and some mothers may feel that this book
downgrades the female sex.

1224   Drag Strip, by William C. Gault.   Dutton, 1959.
        $3.95 (Berkley, Highland, 1963, pb $.50)
        RL: 6   IL: 6-HS   BSMP
Boys in the inner city are as interested in car racing as boys
in the suburbs.   This is an exciting racing story in which
interracial relationships and tensions add another dimension
to the book.

1225   Fast Break Forward, by Les Etter.   Illus. by Francis
Chauncy.   Hastings, 1969. $4.95
        RL: 5   IL: 5-HS   SMP
A good basketball story which also deals with the issue of
militancy.   The black hero has an athletic scholarship and
thinks that he has a future.   His younger brother is convinced
that no one gives you anything--you've got to take it.   Well
liked in the School Volunteer programs, this would be very
popular on the bookmobile in paperback.

1226   The Fighting Southpaw, by "Whitey" Ford, Yogi Berra,
        and Jack Lang.   Pratt, 1962. $.50
        RL: 5   IL: 5-adult   BS

A baseball story about a rookie pitcher's rise and fall, this
book has a special appeal for left-handed people. At the end,
Whitey Ford gives pitching tips and there is a short account
of each of the left-handed pitchers in the Baseball Hall of
Fame.

1227 500, by Henry A. Bamman and Robert J. Whitehead.
        Illus. by James Andrews. Field Educational Pub.,
        Checkered Flag Series, c1968. $1.92
        RL: 4   IL: 4-HS   *BS
A story of racing at the Indianapolis 500, this has a lot of
authentic detail on how drivers have to qualify for the race
and what control it takes to drive in it. There is also some
suspense and an unusual ending in which the hero does not
win but counts himself lucky to be alive to race again. See
1217 for comment on this series.

1228 Flea, by Henry A. Bamman and Robert J. Whitehead.
        Illus. by James Andrews. Field Educational Pub.,
        Checkered Flag Series, c1969. $1.92
        RL: 3-4   IL: 4-HS   *BS
An unusual racing story, this book tells how two dune buggies
are raced over the desert from Tijuana to La Paz in Mexico.
The prize is $5,000 and, even more important, a contract to
manufacture the winning buggy. The story has suspense and
plenty of action as the men encounter all kinds of hazards in
the desert. See 1217 for comment on this series.

1229 Floorburns, by John F. Carson. Dell, Mayflower,
        1957. pb OP
        RL: 5   IL: 6-HS   BS
A prima donna ball player learns team play in a basketball
story with depth and suspense by a popular author. Good
format.

1230 Free Throw, by Mike Neigoff. Illus. by Fred Irvin.
        Whitman, 1968. $3.25
        RL: 3-4   IL: 4-JH   BSMP
Problems of a black boy who has come from an all black
school in adapting to being part of an integrated basketball
team. By a popular sports fiction author.

1231 Go Team Go, by John R. Tunis. Morrow, c1954.
        $4.95 (Scholastic, 1969, pb $.60)
        RL: 6   IL: 6-HS   BSM
Multi-ethnic basketball story with excitement and ethical implications. Some of the players get involved with a gambling

---

ring. The first team refuses to obey the coach's rules because they think themselves indispensable. The coach wins the season with his second string players--including a black boy and changes the climate of public opinion.

1232 Grand Prix, by Henry A. Bamman and Robert J. Whitehead. Illus. by James Andrews. Field Educational Publications, Inc., Checkered Flag Series, c1969. $1.92
RL: 4   IL: 4-HS   *BS
This story of racing cars in the Grand Prix race in California is unusual in that the hero doesn't win. It is full of authentic detail about car racing and has some suspense but is chiefly notable for making clear that car racing is like many other contests, "you can't win 'em all," and mature men take that fact in their strides. See 1217 for comment on this series.

1233 Guards for Matt, by Beman Lord. Walck, 1961. $4.25
RL: 3   IL: 3-JH   S
Good, easy basketball story about a boy who has to wear glasses. Will appeal to sports fans as well as all boys who wear glasses.

1234 Here Comes the Strikeout, by Leonard P. Kessler. Harper, 1965. $2.50
RL: 2-3   IL: 2-6   BSMP
Bobby always strikes out. Finally he learns to practice and winds up with a triumph. A very popular easy-to-read baseball story.

1235 Highpockets, by John R. Tunis. Illus. by Charles Beck. Morrow, 1948. $4.95 (Scholastic, 1964, pb $.60)
RL: 6   IL: 6-adult   BS
An exciting sports story about a loner who finally learns team play by an extremely popular author.

1236 Hit and Run, by Duane Decker. Morrow, c1949. $4.50
RL: 5-6   IL: 5-adult   BSMP
The last of a series of baseball books about the "Blue Sox," this tells of a good ball player who has a chip on his shoulder because he is short. He finally learns self-control by watching his teammate, the first black man in the big leagues, handle unwarranted jeering, booing and rough play. This

would be a very popular book in paperback and doesn't seem
dated in spite of its age and the many black baseball stars in
the leagues.

1237   Hit Parade of Sports Stories, edited by Dick Friendlich.
       Scholastic, 1966.   pb $.50
       RL: 5   IL: 6-HS   BS
A good collection which even includes stories about girls, a
rare occurrence in most sports anthologies.

1238   Hot Rod Rodeo, by Robert Sidney Bowen.   Criterion,
       1964. $3.95   (Scholastic pb $.45)
       RL: 6   IL: 6-JH   BS
A story about hot rods and robbery and much excitement.

1239   Jake, by Alfred Slute.   Lippincott, c1971. $3.93
       (pb $1.95)
       RL: 4   IL: 3-JH   *BSMP
An exciting baseball story about an eleven year old who has
had to learn to be tough, he has been thrown so much on his
own.   In the end, he learns that there are other important
qualities beside courage, honesty and toughness.   Very satisfying and will be very popular.

1240   "Keeper" Play, by Mark Porter.   Grosset & Dunlap,
       Tempo, 1960.   pb OP
       RL: 6   IL: 6-HS
Sports story with many ethical implications.

1241   Kick, Pass and Run, by Leonard Kessler.   Harper,
       I Can Read Series.   OP
       RL: 2   IL: Read aloud-4   BS
Very popular easy-to-read football story.   One of the few on
this reading level so we hope it will soon be back in print.

1242   The Kid Comes Back, by John R. Tunis.   Illus. by
       George Meyerricks.   Morrow, 1946. $4.75   (Scho-
       lastic, 1968, pb $.60)
       RL: 6   IL: 6-adult   BS
A war hero returns to big-league baseball and faces some
tough decisions.   Has suspense and action.

1243   The Kid from Tomkinsville, by John R. Tunis.   Illus.
       by Jay Barnum.   Harcourt, c1940. $3.95   (Berkley,
       1964, pb OP)
       RL: 6   IL: 6-adult   BS
Another excellent baseball story from this outstanding author.

Even non-sport fans find him interesting.

1244 The Kid Who Batted 1,000, by Bob Allison and Frank Ernest Hill, c1959. Scholastic, 1968. pb $.60
RL: 6   IL: 6-HS   BS
Humor and fantasy in a baseball story.

1245 Last One In Is a Rotten Egg, by Leonard Kessler. Harper & Row I Can Read Series, c1969. $2.50
RL: 2   IL: Read aloud-5   BSMP
The portable public swimming pools in New York City have made swimming available to many children who never before had the opportunity. This is an excellent book about a boy who conquers his fears of the deep water and other things in life by learning to swim. Very well done.

1246 Pro Football Rookie, by Haskel Frankel. Illus. by Charles Leise. Doubleday, Signal, c1964. $3.50
RL: 4   IL: 4-HS   S
TV has made football a very popular subject even to city children who never have a chance to play it. This is a popular story of a rookie who makes good.

1247 Quarterback's Aim, by Beman Lord. Illus. by Arnold Spilka. Walck, 1960. $4.25 (pb $.75)
(Scholastic, 1965, pb $.50)
RL: 3-4   IL: 3-6   BS
How a skinny quarterback makes the team--a popular subject.

1248 Relief Pitcher, by Dick Freundlich. Westminster, 1964. $3.75 (Scholastic pb $.60)
RL: 6   IL: 6-HS   BS
This story of baseball rivalry in the minors is a useful book for slow readers in high school but very little baseball or football fiction is as popular as non-fiction.

1249 Requiem for a Heavyweight, by Rod Serling. Adapted by James Olsen. Illus. by Ferd Sondern. McGraw-Hill, Reading Shelf Series I, c1968. pb $1.60
RL: 4-5   IL: 5-adult   *BSP
An adaptation of a well known story of the living death of a prizefighter. The characters are pretty stereotyped but the language and emotions are vivid and the story will interest a great many boys and men.

1250 Riddler, by Henry A. Bamman and Robert J. Whitehead. Illus. by James Andrews. Field Educational

Pub. Inc. , Checkered Flag Series, c1967. $1.92
RL: 2-3   IL: 4-HS   *BS
This is an automobile story with a lot of twists and would
interest boys who are not crazy about cars.   Two young men
buy an old Cadillac to enter it in a car rally and become
embroiled with a plot to steal some missing jewels.   There
is action and suspense and three or four riddles to solve.
See 1217 for comments on this series.

1251   Schoolboy Johnson, by John R. Tunis.   Morrow, 1958.
       $5.25   (Berkley, 1963, pb $.45)
       RL: 5   IL: 5-HS   BS
The story of a big league player who finally learns that handling his temper is as important as handling the ball.   Another
good sports story by this popular author.   Poor readers who
love sports and are being hounded by their teachers to read
something are delighted to discover the Tunis books.

1252   Scramble, by Henry A. Bamman and Robert J. White-
       head.   Illus. by James Andrews.   Field Educational
       Pub. Inc.   Checkered Flag Series, c1969. $1.92
       RL: 3   IL: 4-HS   *BSMP
This is an exciting story about motorcycle racing.   One of
the heroes is a Mexican-American boy.   This is one of the
best written and tightly plotted books in this series.   See
1217 for comments on this series.

1253   Screwball, by Alberta Armer.   World, 1963. $4.95
       (Grosset, Tempo, 1965, pb $.50)
       RL: 5-6   IL: 5-JH   BS
A sensitive story of an awkward twin who finally finds his
own field of interest in the soapbox derby.   Well liked and
appeals to girls as well as boys if introduced.

1254   Smashup, by Henry A. Bamman and Robert J. White-
       head.   Illus. by James Andrews.   Field Educational
       Pub. Inc.   Checkered Flag Series, c1967. $1.92
       RL: 2-3   IL: 5-HS   BS
Two boys buy a smashed up sports car and repair it hoping
to race it in sports car races.   They become reckless and
get into trouble in their first venture on the highway but are
taken in hand by a famous racing car driver who teaches
them that skill and control are more important than speed.
See 1217 for comment on this series.

1255   The Tall One, by Gene Olson.   Dodd, c1956. $3.95
       RL: 5-6   IL: 5-HS   SMP

A good basketball story with depth to it. Miles Talbert,
seven feet tall, feels like a freak and is often treated like
one. Bill Washington, a member of the only black family
in town is accepted by some and not by others. The emotions
involved are not overstressed and there is plenty of action.

1256   Time for Gym, by Jerrold Beim. Illus. by Tom Quinn.
        Houghton Mifflin, 1968. $2.20
        RL: 3   IL: 2-4   *SMP
A simple story about athletic rivalry and team work that appeals to boys. The format is textbook-like. In attractive
paperback format this book would be very popular.

1257   Touchdown for Tommy, by Matt Christopher. Illus.
        by Foster Caddell. Scholastic, 1959. pb $.50
        RL: 4   IL: 3-6   BSMP
An orphan boy, who wants his foster parents to adopt him,
learns about fair play on and off the football field. The author is always in demand.

1258   The Twenty-Third Street Crusaders, by John F. Car-
        son. Farrar, Straus, 1958. $3.95 (Scholastic
        pb $.60)
        RL: 6   IL: 6-HS   BSMP
Basketball turns a teen gang in trouble with the law into a
team. Exciting and sensitive story--unusual in that it also
reveals the fallability of adults.

1259   Two-Wheeled Thunder, by William C. Gault. Scholas-
        tic, c1962. pb $.60
        RL: 5-6   IL: 5-young adult   BS
A well written story of racing rivalry as well as engineering
rivalry in the motorcycle world. This one has many dimensions of what it means to be a loser in either life or racing
and is very popular with teenagers and young adults.

1260   A Uniform for Harry, by Caary Jackson. Illus. by
        June Goldsborough. Follett, c1962. $1.25
        RL: 3   IL: 2-5   BS
Harry helps his big league hero solve his batting problems
by his sharp observation on TV and thereby wins a uniform.
Good story with humor, suspense and imagination.

1261   Wheels, by Henry A. Bamman and Robert J. White-
        head. Illus. by James Andrews. Field Educational
        Pub. Inc. Checkered Flag Series, c1967. $1.92
        RL: 2-3   IL: 4-HS   *BS

Wheels White, a hot rod racer and top mechanic is asked to
help with a big racing car which seems jinxed. He and the
owner are attacked by men who want to keep the big car from
racing but after a thrilling mountain race, they get away due
to Wheels' skillful driving. This, like many of this series
is so simplistic and naive, it insults the intelligence of most
of the people with whom we work. However, books like this
do fill a need. They are easy to read and full of action and
a functional illiterate who reads three or four of these in a
row has so improved his reading that he can then move on
to something with more content.

1262 Winning Pitcher, by Mark Porter. Grosset, Tempo,
      c1962. pb OP
      RL: 5   IL: 5-HS   BS
A story about high school baseball rivalries with lots of action by a popular author.

1263 Wonder Boy, by William Heuman. Scholastic, 1964.
      pb $.60
      RL: 5   IL: 5-adult   BS
A fearful catcher learns that concern for his friend and pro-
tege can cure his terror. An exciting baseball story by a
popular sports writer.

1264 The Year the Yankees Lost the Pennant, by Douglass
      Wallop. Adapted by Warren Halliburton. Illus. by
      Renzo Bartolomucci. McGraw-Hill Reading Shelf I
      Series, 1961. pb $1.72
      RL: 4-5   IL: 5-adult   *BS
An adaptation of the popular novel and play of the man who
sold his soul to the devil so that he could become a big league
ball player and his team could win the pennant. Humorous,
popular and very well done.

TEENAGERS

1265 Angelita Nobody, by Lawrence Swinburne. Illus. by
      Norman Nodel. McGraw-Hill, City Limits Series,
      c1968. pb $1.84
      RL: 5   IL: 6-adult   *BSMP
Angelita is the daughter of a black woman and a white man.
On the whole, the family is close knit and happy but one

evening when Angelita has already been hurt by her boyfriend,
there is a family row and Angelita runs away. By the time
she is found by her family, she has found herself and learned
to stand on her own two feet. Although the story has many
improbabilities, it will be popular; it has suspense, likeable
people and moves fast.

1266   Big Band, by Haskel Frankel. Illus. by J. W.
         McDaniel. Doubleday, Signal, c1965. $3.50
         RL: 4   IL: JH-HS   BS
A boy wants to drop out of school to play the trumpet. He
makes a different decision after an exciting summer touring
with a band. A good story on a subject of great interest to
many teenagers.

1267   A Birthday Present for Katheryn Kenyatta, by Charlie
         L. Russell. Illus. by Lee Morton. McGraw-Hill,
         City Limits Series, c1970. pb $1.60
         RL: 4-5   IL: JH-adult   *BSMP
Katheryn Kenyatta's Daddy finally grows up on her third
birthday. This is a good story for a discussion group. It
will interest almost all young people and especially athletic
stars.

1268   Call It Courage, by Armstrong Sperry. Illus. by
         Dom Lupo. Macmillan, c1940. $4.50 (Collier,
         1971, pb $.75)
         RL: 6   IL: 6-adult   BSMP
The story of a Polynesian boy who is determined to conquer
his fear of the sea or die, this exciting story is very much
liked by boys and men.

1269   Charley Starts from Scratch, by Jesse Jackson.
         Harper, c1958. $3.79 (Dell Yearling, 1968, pb
         $.75)
         RL: 5   IL: 5-HS   BSMP
An excellent sequel to Anchor Man [1208] this book portrays
realistically the adventures of a young boy who has just graduated from high school and is starting out on his own. The
format is too young for the boys who are the natural audience
for this story. The book would be very popular in an Archway or Signet format.

1270   Chico, by Lawrence Swinburne. Illus. by Robert
         Carter. McGraw-Hill, City Limits Series, 1968.
         pb $1.72
         RL: 5   IL: 5-HS   *BSMP

A strange, not very credible book about a Puerto Rican boy whose ex-convict Anglo father sends for him to come to New York and how they finally get to know and respect each other. I think many teenagers would find this book interesting and suspenseful and overlook the lack of credibility.

1271 Chile Peppers, by Mary W. Sullivan. Photographs by
      Donald Armfield. Field Educational Pub. Inc.,
      Happenings Series, c1970. $2.56
      RL: 3-4   IL: 6-HS   BSMP
This book starts out with thirty-seven pages of photographs of Chicanos and their surroundings. They are authentic but there is not one that shows the beauty that can be seen in both the people and the places. I think of Sweet Flypaper of Life [776] and The World's Friends [121] for comparison. The story which follows is excellent. The Chile Peppers are a high school band and the teenagers involved have the kind of problems and aspirations which will interest other teenagers whether Chicano or not.

1272 The Comeback Guy, by C. H. Frick. Harcourt,
      Voyager, c1961. pb $.75
      RL: 6   IL: 6-HS   BS
A show-off athlete has his come-uppance and finally wins his way back to self-respect. The sport is track but the subject is universal. High school boys like this one.

1273 Cool Cat, by Frank Bonham. Dutton, c1971. $3.95
      (Dell pb $.75)
      RL: 5-6   IL: 6-HS   *BSMP
Buddy Williams and his friends hope to make money in the summer doing odd-job hauling with their second hand truck. But they run into both trouble and mysteries with the Machete gang and a cool cat, Cal Brown whom they cannot figure out. In the end and after much action and suspense, they solve the mystery of who is peddling drugs in Dogtown. An exciting book which takes place in the same milieu (Dogtown) as The Mystery of the Fat Cat [1162] and The Nitty Gritty [911].

1274 Daddy-Long-Legs, by Jean Webster. Century, c1912.
      $2.95 (Grosset, Tempo, pb $.60)
      RL: 6   IL: 6-HS   BS
Daddy Long-Legs is the story of an orphan girl who is sent to college by an unknown benefactor. The Cinderella theme is always a popular one and this book has humor and charm but it seems astonishing that a story written about a teenager

in 1912 should be as popular as this is in the 1970s with
both boys and girls on the bookmobile.

1275 Danger at Mormon Crossing, by Roger Barlow.
        Grosset & Dunlap, Tempo, 1963.   pb $.50
        RL: 6   IL: 6-HS   BS
A not very realistic teenage adventure story about going down
rivers on rafts in the Rockies.   However, it is well-liked in
spite of its shortcomings.

1276 Detour For Meg, by Helen D. Olds.   Washington Square
        Press, Archway, 1967.   pb $.50
        RL: 6   IL: 6-HS   BS
An excellent teenage novel with ethical implications, this is
popular with girls from the sixth grade through high school.

1277 Don't Look At Me That Way, by Caroline Crane.
        Random House, 1970. $3.95
        RL: 5-6   IL: 6-HS   *BSMP
Rosa is a young Puerto Rican girl who goes to work for an
"Anglo" taking care of her two young children.   She hopes
to earn enough money to send her ailing mother on a visit
to Puerto Rico.   Her mother dies and Rosa quits her job to
take care of her young teenage brothers and sisters.   This
sounds like straight gloom and the picture of life in El Barrio is a real one but as in real life there are moments of
excitement and happiness, even moments of fun, and the book
ends on a note of hope.

1278 A Dream to Touch, by Anne Emery.   Macrae Smith,
        c1958. $3.95   (Berkley, Highland, pb OP)
        RL: 6   IL: 6-HS   BS
A story about a girl who wants to go to college and to become a soloist with the Chicago Symphony Orchestra.   One
boy friend shares her dream but her "steady" insists that
only money brings happiness.   Teenage romantic novels are
extremely popular with girls from sixth grade on up even
(or perhaps especially?) when they portray a life very remote
from an inner city girl's situation.   This author writes well
and makes the reader want to turn the page.   She also offers
unobtrusive ethical advice which is very much welcomed by
our adolescent readers.

1279 Dropout, by Jeanette Eyerly.   Lippincott, c1963.
        $3.25   (Berkley, Highland, pb $.60)
        RL: 6   IL: 6-HS   BS
Two teenagers decide to drop out of school to get married.

A suspenseful story which girls like very much.   The author
is a popular and dependable one and girls learn to ask for
her books.

1280   Enrique, by Pablo Figuroa.   Illus. by Bill Negron.
        Hill & Wang, Challenger, c1970.   pb $1
        RL: 4   IL: 4-JH   *BSMP
The exciting and moving adventures of a Puerto Rican boy
who comes to New York, this book is believable and has a
lot of suspense.

1281   Escape from Nowhere, by Jeanette Eyerly.   Lippincott,
        c1969. $3. 95   (Berkley, Highland, pb $. 60)
        RL: 6   IL: 6-HS   BSP
Another popular novel about a teenage girl and drugs by the
author of Dropout [1279].   The setting is very middle class
but teenagers are interested in any well-written book on this
subject.

1282   Fifteen, by Beverly Cleary.   Illus. by Joe and Beth
        Krush.   Morrow, c1956. $5. 50   (Scholastic, 1967,
        pb $. 60)
        RL: 5   IL: 6-HS   BS
A babysitting job wins fifteen-year-old Jane her first date.
This entertaining story of young love really hooks non-readers
in the early teens.   It has magic.

1283   First Love, edited by Gay Head.   Scholastic, 1963.
        pb $. 60
        RL: 6   IL: 6-HS   B
Fourteen short stories depicting the experiences of first love.
See 1284.

1284   First Love, by Mina Lewiton.   David McKay, 1952.
        $4. 50   (Grosset, Tempo, 1966, pb $. 50)
        RL: 5   IL: 6-HS   B
A seventeen year old must choose between two young men
who declare their love.   Both these books are very popular.

1285   For Boys Only, edited by Eric Berger.   Scholastic,
        1960.   pb $. 60
        RL: 7   IL: 7-HS   BS
A dozen adventure, sports and mystery stories.   Boys and
girls both like this title.

1286   For Girls Only, edited by Sylvie Schuman.   Scholastic,
        1957.   pb $. 50

RL: 7   IL: 6-HS   BS
Eleven short stories about teenage romance. This is a very
popular title.

1287 Gang Girl, by H. Samuel Fleischman. Illus. by
        Shirley Walker. Doubleday, Signal, c1967. $3.50
        RL: 4   IL: 5-HS   BSMP
Maria Gomez is unhappy at home where life is drudgery and
harsh words from a disagreeable stepfather. She joins a
gang which looks like freedom and good times but finds in
the end that it is worse than home and that home has many
redeeming features. The story is a little simplistic, not in
the same class as books like Journey All Alone and Daddy
Was a Numbers Runner, but both boys and girls find it very
exciting.

1288 Happenings Series. Field Educational Pub. , Inc. ,
        various dates.
        RL: 3-4 IL: 4-HS SM & BSM (depending on title)
This is a series with four titles (thus far), two about Chicano
teenagers and two about black teenagers. All the stories are
focussed around teenage bands--a very popular subject with
teenagers everywhere and especially in the inner city. Although the stories have a controlled vocabulary, they have
suspense and credibility and a great deal more flavor than
the Checkered Flag series [1217] from the same publisher.
They will certainly be very popular. The publishers say
that the books have been especially designed to attract reluctant readers. The outside format is good; the print is
excellent. Each book starts out with thirty-five to forty
photographs of life in a black or Chicano area. This varies
from title to title but in general the photos are poor and give
little idea of the beauty of the people or the squalor which
often surrounds them. The first thing the reader sees on
opening the book is an unpleasant form which asks the teacher
to evaluate the condition of the book and how the pupil has
treated it. The end section contains questions which seem
to be based on the premise that a poor reader has very little
intelligence. However, the books are very popular if used
properly. We paste heavy paper over the form at the front
and cut out (physically) the questions at the back. In some
junior high schools which have photography programs, students have been inspired by the photographic essays in front
to go out and do a photographic survey of the people and surroundings in their own area. For comment on the individual
titles see Chile Peppers [1271], Jokers Wild [1292], The
Pancho Villa Rebels [1303], and Rattrap [1310].

1289 Harlem Summer, by Mary Elizabeth Vroman. Putnam,
      c1967. $3.49 (Berkley, Highland, pb $.50)
      RL: 6   IL: 6-HS   BSMP
A very popular up-to-date story of a southern boy's summer
in Harlem. The characters are believable and the situations
are real and exciting.

1290 High School Drop Out, by John Clarke. Illus. by
      Albert Micale. Doubleday, Signal, c1964. $3.50
      (Semaphore pb $1.75)
      RL: 4   IL: 6-HS   BS
Good and popular story of the problems of being a high school
dropout.

1291 Jazz Country, by Nat Hentoff. Harper & Row, c1965.
      $3.95 (Dell pb $.50)
      RL: 6   IL: 6-adult   BSMP
An authentic and thought-provoking novel of the world of jazz
with an excellent format. Very popular both with teenagers
and adults.

1292 Jokers Wild, by Mary Sullivan. Photographs by
      Michael H. Roberts. Field Educational Pub. Hap-
      penings Series, c1970. $2.51
      RL: 4-5   IL: 6-HS   BSMP
This book starts with thirty-five pages of excellent photographs
of black people, mainly teenagers. Then follows a story of
a boy whose gay and spendthrift mother is driving her children out of the home. Randy winds up sleeping in an abandoned house, sustained by the friendship of his rock band
group. A quiet and authentic picture of poverty and of boys
trying to make something of themselves under very tough circumstances. See comment on Happenings Series [1288].

1293 Journey All Alone, by Deloris Harrison. Dial, c1971.
      $4.95
      RL: 5   IL: 5-adult   *BSMP
A story of family life in Harlem written from the point of
view of a teenage girl. It is a story full of sadness and
courage and will interest women of every age. I hope it
will soon be out in paperback.

1294 Julie's Heritage, by Catherine Marshall. McKay,
      c1957. $4.75 (Scholastic, 1969, pb $.75)
      RL: 6   IL: 6-HS   BSMP
This story of a black girl in an integrated high school has
depth and value for children of both races. Very popular
with girls.

1295   The Loner, by Ester Weir.   Illus. by Christine Price.
          McKay, 1963. $3.75   (Scholastic pb $.50)
          RL: 5   IL: 6-HS   B
The story of a boy who is on his own but finally finds friendly
adults who help him to find himself.

1296   The Long Haul and Other Stories, by John Durham.
          Illus. by Norman Nodel.   McGraw-Hill, City Limits
          Series, 1968.   pb $1.60
          RL: 4-5   IL: 6-HS   *BSMP
Five top notch short stories about young people, some exciting, some moving and some funny.

1297   Mary Jane, by Dorothy Sterling.   Doubleday, c1959.
          $3.95   (Scholastic pb $.75)
          RL: 6   IL: 5-HS   BSMP
This is a story of courage and friendship based on true incidents which took place when some junior high schools in
Nashville were integrated.   It is a deeply moving book and
one of the most popular I have ever seen in inner city schools
and on the bookmobile.   Girls who are behind in reading
struggle to read it and it is so universally popular that it is
creating a common background for black girls everywhere.
It is equally a must for white children.

1298   Member of the Gang, by Barbara Rinkoff.   Illus. by
          Harold James.   Crown, c1968. $3.50   (Scholastic
          pb $.60)
          RL: 5   IL: 5-HS   *BSMP
An exciting story of the pressures on a boy in an impoverished neighborhood to join a gang and look cool with his peers
at an age when his family, who are pressuring him to do
well in school, don't seem to understand his problems.   Will
be very popular.

1299   Mr. and Mrs. Bo-Jo Jones, by Ann Head.   Putnam,
          1967. $4.95   (New American Library, Signet, pb
          $.75)
          RL: 5-6   IL: 6-HS   *BSP
An interesting story of a marriage, arrived at hurridly and
of necessity, between two likeable, immature teenagers.   The
characters are credible, the story has surprises and teenagers
will want to read it.   Parents could profit from it also.

1300   My Darling, My Hamburger, by Paul Zindel.   Harper,
          1969. $3.95   (Bantam pb $.75)
          RL: 6   IL: JH-HS   BSP

A good plot holds the reader in this very up-to-date teenage
novel about a love affair, the pill and an illegitimate baby.
The characters are believable and the story is in excellent
taste.   The author writes unusually well and the story has
depth.

1301   North Town, by Lorenz Graham.   Crowell, c1965.
       $4.50
       RL: 6   IL: 6-adult   BSMP
The Williams family, driven from their southern home by the
tensions created by the school desegregation decision and by
their desire to give their son the kind of education the South
won't allow him to have, move to Detroit.   There they run
into the kind of problems any uprooted family would encounter
aggravated by a severe illness of Mr. Williams as a result
of the physical beating he was subjected to in the South.   The
family is a likeable one, their problems are real and not
exaggerated and the reader is filled with admiration and sympathy for the brave way in which they tackle their difficulties.

1302   The Outsiders, by S. E. Hinton.   Viking, c1967.
       (Dell, Laurel-Leaf, pb $.60)
       RL: 5-6   IL: 6-adult   BSP
The outsiders are a defiant group of long-haired leather-
jacket "greasers" (so called by the affluent world across the
tracks), who feel doomed to a world of juvenile delinquency,
reform school and prison by the poverty and lack of family
backing in their environment.   This suspenseful novel, by a
seventeen-year-old author, has an authentic ring and is a
real spellbinder.   It is very popular.

1303   The Pancho Villa Rebels, by Mary W. Sullivan.
       Photographs by Donald Armfield.   Field Educational
       Pub. , Inc. , Happenings Series, c1970. $2.56
       RL: 4   IL: 6-HS   *SM
This book starts with approximately thirty pages of photographs
of Mexican-Americans and their environment in a city.   Then
there is a story about Mexican-American teenagers which revolves around a rock band and a girl who is ashamed of her
Spanish heritage.   The story is simplistic but the book will
certainly be useful since it will surely interest teenage reluctant readers and since it does have a positive attitude
toward dual culture situations.   See comment on Happenings
Series [1288].

1304   Peppermint, edited by David A. Sohn.   Scholastic,
       1966.   pb $.60

RL: 6-7   IL: 6-JH   BS
A collection of stories, poems and articles by junior high
students from all over which have won prizes in contests
run by Scholastic Magazine. A highly motivating book for
junior high students.

1305   Personal Code, edited by Robert E. Shafer and Verlene
       C. Bernd. Illus. by Gabe Keith.   Scholastic Litera-
       ture Anthology, c1961.   pb $1
       RL: 6-7   IL: 6-adult   *SMP
A varied and thought-provoking collection of stories and one
or two poems all of which deal with the subject of integrity.
This is a wonderful collection for a tutoring program in a
junior high or high school.

1306   The Pigman, by Paul Zindel.   Harper, c1968. $3.95
       (Dell, Laurel-Leaf, pb $.60)
       RL: 6-7   IL: 6-adult   BS
This book is enormously popular. From the opening line
"Now, I don't like school" to the end, the reader is spellbound by this story of two alienated youngsters who get involved by accident with a widower and bring him both love
and tragedy. I have never met a teenager who didn't like
this book. Poor readers just skip the difficult words and
get the gist of the story.

1307   Portrait of Deborah, by Florence C. Cohen.   Messner,
       c1961. $3.50   (Grosset, Tempo, pb OP)
       RL: 6   IL: 6-HS   BSMP
A Jewish girl encounters prejudice and friendship when her
family moves East. She also learns how to meet new standards and how to make her own decisions and yet keep her
warm family relationship. Unusually good and popular teenage novel.

1308   Problem Father, by Lou and Zena Shumsky.   Illus. by
       Richard Priest.
       RL: 5   IL: 5-HS   BS
Boy and father's interests clash but a good relationship is
established at the end. This book moves on its title but
model planes and excitement combine to enable it to hold its
readers.

1309   The Questing Heart, by Mildred Lawrence.   Harcourt,
       1959. $3.75   (Berkley pb OP)
       RL: 6   IL: 6-HS   BS
A shy girl, who lives on an island in a thinly populated area,

is drawn by circumstances into new friendships and responsibilities and gains confidence.

1310   Rattrap, by Mary Sullivan.   Photographs by Donald
       Armfield.   Field Educational Pub. Happenings Series,
       c1970. $2.56
       RL: 4   IL: 6-HS   BSMP
Another teenage band story about impoverished youngsters
whose families are having a struggle to find and hang onto
decent housing. One boy's home has been destroyed by an
urban renewal project and his grandfather forced into an old
folks home. One girl, whose family is fighting to hang onto
their home, lives on a street slated to be condemned by the
city. In the rather simplistic story, the kids learn how to
take community action and whom to trust and whom not to.
See comment on Happenings Series [1288].

1311   Ready or Not, by Mary Stolz.   Harper & Row, 1953.
       (Scholastic, 1968, pb $.50)
       RL: 6   IL: 6-HS   B
A high school girl has to shoulder an adult's responsibilities
and succeeds in maturing and finding romance. This author's
books are very popular.

1312   Return to Ramos, by Leo Cardenas.   Illus. by Nilo
       Santiago.   Hill and Wang, Challenger Books, c1970.
       pb $1
       RL: 5-6   IL: 6-adult   *BMP
Juan José Ramos has lived for thirty years in Ramos for
half the year and (since he couldn't find work to support his
family in his home town) gone on the road with his family to
pick crops the rest of the year. His oldest daughter who is
doing very well at school, persuades him to leave her in
Ramos. He returns to find that his dead mother cannot be
buried in the local Catholic cemetery solely because she is
Mexican-American and that his daughter is a leader of a
group of Chicano students who are determined to get decent
treatment. His instinct is not to demonstrate or to protest
but in the end, the determination and courage of the young
move him to speak out against injustice. This brief story
rings with sincerity.

1313   Runaway Teen, by Ann Finlayson.   Doubleday, Signal,
       1963. $3.50 (Semaphore pb $1.45)
       RL: 4   IL: 4-HS   *BS
An immature sixteen year old takes offense at her new stepfather and runs away to Chicago. Not too credible a story

at the start, girls will eat it up as this is a very popular
subject.

1314 Second-Hand Family, by Richard Parker.   Illus. by
       Gareth Floyd.   Bobbs, Merrill, 1965. $3.50
       (Scholastic, 1969, pb $.60)
       RL: 6   IL: 5-9   *BS
A story laid in England of a boy's efforts to fit into
his foster home.   Lots of jazz interest and sympathetic
characters will make this one appealing to both boys and
girls.

1315 Seventeen's Stories, edited by Babette Rosmond.
       Lippincott, 1958.   OP (Pyramid, Willow, 1965,
       $.50)
       RL: 5   IL: 6-HS   BS
Thirteen short stories culled from the best of Seventeen
Magazine's fiction.   The stories all center around young people and the decisions they must make.   Both the backgrounds
and styles of the stories are very varied.   A popular book
with girls.

1316 The Seventeenth Street Gang, by Emily C. Neville.
       Illus. by Emily McCully.   Harper, 1966. $3.50
       RL: 5   IL: 5-JH   SMP
A teenage gang in a New York City setting is involved in accepting a new boy.   The power plays and hostility are of
special interest to girls.

1317 Seventeenth Summer, by Maureen Daly.   Illus. by J.
       Robinson.   Dodd, c1948. $4 (Washington Square
       Press, Archway, 1968, pb $.60)
       RL: 5-6   IL: 6-HS   BS
This old but prize-winning novel of a girl's first romance is
still a fine story for teenage girls.

1318 Snakes, by Al Young.   Holt, Rinehart, c1970. $4.95
       RL: 5   IL: JH-adult   *BS
M C lives with his grandmother in Detroit and lives for his
music and his friends.   He manages to graduate from high
school and to have enough success with his music to feel able
to leave for New York with high hopes for the future.   A
beautiful story of growing up that will be very popular with
black teenagers and young adults.   In its warmth and the
loving relationship between M C and his grandmother, it has
much in common with Bear for the FBI [867], but M C's
experiences are much more deeply affected by his color and

poverty. Much of the conversation in the book is street language which will bother some readers and make the book
more popular with others.

1319   Soul Brothers and Sister Lou, by Kristin Hunter.
        Scribner, c1968. $4.50 (Avon Books, 1970, pb
        $.75)
        RL: 5-6   IL: 5-adult   BSMP
The story of a courageous teenager coping with life in a
Northern ghetto, this is a wonderful book which accurately
mirrors life in the inner city as seen through her eyes.
Although some of the story is tragic (poverty and death)
there are many constructive elements. It is somewhat similar to Soul City Downstairs [1320] but much deeper and more
rewarding. Highly recommended.

1320   Soul City Downstairs, by William Johnston. Pyramid
        Original, 1969. pb $.60
        RL: 5   IL: 5-HS   BMS
An intriguing story of a teenager's rock group trying to break
into the big time. Although the plot at times seems unreal,
the characters are very human. This book will be both popular and inspiring to the many musical teenagers who are
trying to use their talents to break out of the ghetto. See
1319 above.

1321   South Town, by Lorenz Graham. Follett, c1958.
        $4.98 (New American Library, Signet, 1965, pb
        $.60)
        RL: 6   IL: 5-adult   BSMP
The story of a black family in the South which is driven out
of town by the tensions created by the changing atmosphere
which follows the Supreme Court decisions of 1954. This
book has suspense, drama and realistic and attractive characters. It appeals to a wide age range. The hardcover sequel
North Town [1301] tells what happens to the Williams family
in Detroit and is also excellent. See also Whose Town [1329].

1322   The Stars Hang High, by Janet Lambert. Scholastic,
        1960. pb $.75
        RL: 6   IL: 6-HS   BS
A younger sister finally comes into her own in a popular
teenage novel.

1323   Sweet Sixteen, by Ann Emery. Macrae Smith, 1956.
        $3.75 (Pyramid pb $.50)
        RL: 5   IL: 5-HS   BS

A young girl drifts into bad habits with a tough crowd but learns before too late what her priorities really are. A good book by a popular author, the title alone guarantees its popularity with teenage girls.

1324   Too Bad About the Haines Girl, by Zoa Sherburne. Morrow, 1967. $3.95   (pb $1.50)
        RL: 5   IL: 6-HS   *BS
Melinda Haines is seventeen, in her last year of high school and pregnant. A middle-class background and middle-class attitudes but a subject that will vitally interest teens. The book is well written and neither sentimental nor over-dramatic.

1325   Tuned Out, by Maia Wojciechowska.   Harper, 1968.
        $4.50   (Dell, Laurel, pb $.50)
        RL: 5-6   IL: 5-adult   BSP
A real spellbinder, this fictional story of two brothers from a happy middle class home and how one tries to solve his problems with drugs is very much in demand. Although the setting is middle class, the story has insights for all adolescents and their families. So far, no one to whom I have lent it has been able to lay it down.

1326   West Side Story, by Irving Shulman.   Simon and Schuster Pocket Pooks, 1961.   pb $.75
        RL: 6-7   IL: 6-adult   BSMP
Romeo and Juliet on the upper West Side in a novelization of the play and movie of the same name. This is very popular with teenagers. See below.

1327   West Side Story, by Irving Shulman.   Adapted and abridged by Frances Price.   Noble and Noble Falcon, 1970.   pb $.56
        RL: 5-6   IL: 6-adult   BSMP
See above [1326].

1328   Where Love Begins, by Carol Beach York.   Scholastic, c1963.   pb $.50
        RL: 6   IL: 6-HS   BS
A well-written love story in a non-affluent setting. Popular on its merits and also because the title and cover picture are so appealing to girls of this age group.

1329   Whose Town?, by Lorenz Graham.   Crowell, 1969.
        $4.50
        RL: 5-6   IL: 5-adult   *BSMP

This superb book is a sequel to <u>South Town</u> and <u>North Town</u>. The Williams family, around whom all three books revolve, was forced to flee the South at the end of the first book. In the second they lived through some tough times in Detroit but finally seem to be getting on pretty well. In <u>Whose Town</u>, they live through the Detroit riots. David Williams, who has just graduated from school and gotten a scholarship to college, is under great pressure to join a militant black group. He and his friends have to figure out where they stand. This is a very exciting and yet a very thoughtful book and, in my judgment, a must for every high school library in the country. Both this book and its predecessor, <u>North Town</u>, should be in paperback.

9 AUTOBIOGRAPHY, BIOGRAPHY (AND HISTORY)

1330   Abe Lincoln Gets His Chance, by Frances Cavanah.
       Illus. by Paula Hutchison.   Rand, c1959. $3.50
       (Scholastic, Illus. by Don Sibley, 1965, pb $.60)
       RL: 4   IL: 4-adult   BS
A vivid and meaty account of Lincoln's boyhood and young
manhood which ends as he becomes president.   This book
has an excellent beginning which involves the reader right
away.

1331   Abraham Lincoln, by Anne Colver.   Illus. by William
       Moyers.   Dell, c1960.   pb $.65
       RL: 3-4   IL: 3-adult   BS
A useful straightforward biography because it does not write
down to the reader and can therefore be used with any age
group.   It is not very excitingly written but the black and
white illustrations are appealing and whet the reader's curiosity.

1332   The Adventures of George Washington, by Mickie
       Davidson.   Illus. by Seymour Fleishman.   Four
       Winds. $2.50   (Scholastic, 1965, pb $.60)
       RL: 3-4   IL: 4-JH   BS
Colorful, well-written biography;   content of interest to a
wide age range: would be more useful in more adult format.

1333   The Adventures of the Negro Cowboys, by Philip
       Durham and Everett L. Jones.   Bantan, c1966.
       pb $.75
       RL: 5-6   IL: 5-adult   *BS
The history of black cowboys in the West told in straightforward language and illustrated with fascinating contemporary
photographs.

1334   Aleck Bell: Ingenious Boy, by Mabel C. Widdemer.
       Illus. by Charles V. John.   Bobbs Merrill, Child-
       hood of Famous Americans Series, c1947. $2.75
       RL: 4-5   IL: 4-JH   S
Popular biography, simply written;   easy to introduce to a

reader since telephones are popular necessities in every area
of American life.

1335 America and Its Presidents, by Earl Schenck Miers.
        Grosset, Tempo, c1970. pb $.75
        RL: 6   IL: 6-adults   BS
A useful reference book that is much in demand by junior
high school students. It includes President Nixon.

1336 America's First Ladies 1865 to the Present Days, by
        Lillie Chaffin and Miriam Butwin. Lerner Pub.,
        c1969. $3.95
        RL: 5-6   IL: 5-adult   B
Girls will be much interested in the lives of America's first
ladies. This book is up to date and includes Mrs. Nixon.
School children will be fascinated also by the change in educational demands. Lucy Johnson, President Andrew Johnson's
wife, whose biography is the first in the book, taught her
husband writing and arithmetic after their marriage. He had
never gone to school. Contemporary illustrations and photographs.

1337 Amos Fortune-Free Man, by Elizabeth Yates. Illus.
        by Nora Unwin. Dutton, c1950. $3.95 (Dell,
        1971, pb $.95)
        RL: 5   IL: 5-adult   BS
This is the biography of a fine man who was born a prince
in Africa, enslaved and brought to America and who earned
freedom for himself and for many others. It is an inspiring
story that would be much enjoyed by adults if it were in an
adult paperback format. There is nothing childish about his
story.

1338 Anything Can Happen, by George and Helen Papashvily.
        Illus. by Paul Galdone. Harper and Row, c1944.
        $4.95 (Avon, Camelot, 1968, pb $.50)
        RL: 5   IL: HS-adult   BS
A good, easy story for high school students and adults about
and by a beguiling immigrant boy from Armenia. It recounts
his adventures in America with humor and excitement.

1339 Anything Can Happen, by George and Helen Papashvily,
        adapted by Lawrence Swinburne. McGraw-Hill,
        Reading Shelf Series, 1968. pb $1.60
        RL: 4   IL: HS-adult   BS
The same book in an easier to read version.

1340 Answer Book of History, by Mary Elting and Franklin
      Folsom. Illus. by W. K. Plummer. Grosset, 1966.
      $3.95
      RL: 5-6   IL: 4-HS   S
Excellent short passages answering questions of general interest. Can be picked up in odd moments or used for variety to interest a student.

1341 Armed With Courage, by May McNeer. Illus. by Lynd
      Ward. Abingdon, c1957. $3
      RL: 5   IL: 5-adult   BS
Children and young people are looking for heroes and this is
a good collection of biographies. Excellent for reading help
programs, it has to be pushed on the bookmobile because of
the hardcover format.

1342 Arrow Book of Presidents, by Sturges F. Cory. Illus.
      by Leo Summers. Scholastic, c1965. pb $.60
      RL: 5   IL: 4-adult   *BS
A useful reference book with many illustrations, this has
short biographies of all the presidents through President
Johnson. It is easier to read and has better print than
1335 but its younger format works against it in adult reading
programs. Since both are in paperback, we find it worthwhile to carry both. They meet different needs.

1343 Arrow Book of States, by Margaret Ronan. Illus. by
      William Meyerriecks. Scholastic, c1965. pb $.75
      RL: 4   IL: 4-adult   BS
This useful book has a one-page description of each of the
50 states opposite a map of the state and a thought provoking
illustration.

1344 [No entry].

1345 Arthur Ashe: Tennis Champion, by Louie Robinson,
      Jr. Washington Square, c1969. (Archway pb $.60)
      RL: 4   IL: 6-adult   BSM
A straightforward biography of the tennis champion by the
head of the West Coast Bureau of Ebony. TV is making a
wide range of sports popular with city people.

1346 Autobiography of Malcolm X, edited by Alex Haley, ed.
      Grove, c1965. $7.50 (pb $1.25)
      RL: Adult   IL: 5-adult   BSMP
Children are so anxious to read this they will go through it
with a dictionary. It is, of course, popular with all ages

and deservedly so.   Dean Coburn of the Episcopal Theological
School calls it a great religious document.   This autobiography of one of the great Afro-American leaders in this
country who went from the bottom of society to a position
of leadership is already a classic and will always be in demand.

1347 Autobiography of W. E. B. Dubois.   International,
      c1968. $10   (pb $3.25)
         RL: Adult   IL: HS and adult   BSMP
The first section of this book appeared in 1921 when the author was 52;   the second in 1940 when he was 71 and the
present book issued in 1968 was completed in 1960.   The
autobiography of this extraordinary American is hard reading
for many of our clientele but it is a fascinating account of a
unique career which is becoming steadily better known and
more relevant all the time.   There is a small but growing
demand for it among older adults and older students.

1348   The Bannekers of Bannaky Springs, by Deloris D.
       Harrison.   Illus. by David D. Hodges.   Hawthorn,
       c1970. $4.25
          RL: 5   IL: 5-adult   *SMP
By starting her story with Benjamin Banneker's grandparents,
an African prince and an English dairymaid, the author has
given excitement to what is essentially a very quiet story.
The biography of the talented black man who helped to design
Washington and whose scientific ability was admired by Jefferson and Franklin can be an inspiration to many young people.

1349   Bart Starr, by John Devaney.   Scholastic, 1967.   pb
       $.60
          RL: 5   IL: 5-adult   BS
The biography of the famous Green Bay Packer.   Pro football
has become very popular through TV even with boys who never
get a chance to play themselves.

1350   The Baseball Life of Mickey Mantle, by John Devaney.
       Scholastic, c1969.   pb $.60
          RL: 5   IL: 4-adult   BS
Though called the "baseball" life of Mickey Mantle, this book
can be of interest to non-baseball fans.   Mantle, one of the
great ball players of all times has shown great courage in
battling ostiomyletis and other obstacles.

1351   The Baseball Life of Sandy Koufax, by George Vecsey.

Scholastic, c1968. pb

RL: 5 IL: 4-adult BS

The story of another baseball player who has made an extraordinary record in spite of the crippling pain of arthritis. Koufax has just retired to become a sports announcer. A sports biography of wide appeal. Photographs.

1352 The Baseball Life of Willie Mays, by Lee Greene. Scholastic, c1970. pb $.60

RL: 5 IL: 5-adult *BSMP

This book is just what its title says it is, the baseball life of Willie Mays, but his baseball record is so extraordinary and his character and leadership so great both in triumph and defeat that it will interest many who are not ordinarily baseball fans. Photographs.

1353 Before the Mayflower, by Lerone Bennett, Jr. Johnson Pub. Co., 1964. (Penguin, Pelican, 1966, pb $2.45)

RL: Adult IL: HS and adult BSMP

This is a history of the black man in America from 1619-1964, including a brief history of his African past. It includes many fascinating illustrations and many excerpts from original texts of speeches, letters, contemporary accounts, etc. It also has, at the end, an outline of black history. It is by the well known journalist of Ebony Magazine and will be very popular with high school students and adults who are eager to learn the history of their race. It is sad, that, as with many English books, the print is so small that many older people are unable to read a book which would mean a lot to them.

1354 Benjamin Franklin, by Enid LaMonte Meadowcroft. Illus. by Donald McKay, c1961. (Scholastic, 1965, pb $.50)

RL: 5 IL: 5-adult BS

A good life of a great American who seems little known and not very glamorous to today's city children. We carry this but it is not very popular although it is well written and, of course, an interesting and important story.

1355 Bitter Victory, by Florette Henri. Military Consultant Richard Stillman. Illus. by Robert Shore. Doubleday, c1970. $3.75 (Pb $1.75)

RL: 5-6 IL: 5-adult *BSMP

A vivid and depressing account of how black soldiers were treated in World War I and how they handled themselves in

battle and on their return home. A sad chapter in our history. There are moving contemporary photographs as well
as black and white illustrations.

1356 The Black Americans, by C. Eric Lincoln. Bantam,
      c1969. pb $.60
      RL: 6-7   IL: 6-adult   BSMP
This book is a revised and abridged version of The Negro
Pilgrimage in America. Written by the distinguished black
professor of sociology at Union Theological Seminary, it tells
the story of the black American from his African days through
to the present. A good job of telling a lot in a little space,
it has a section of photographs and good print.

1357 Black Bondage--The Life of Slaves in the South, by
      Walter Goodman. Farrar, Straus, c1969. $3.95
      RL: 5-6   IL: 5-adult   *BSMP
Very much like To Be a Slave [1578], this book explains,
with many quotations from slave narratives, how slavery and
slaves came to America and what it was like to be a slave
in the pre-Civil War South. Illustrated with contemporary
woodcuts, etchings and posters, the book has excellent print.

1358 Black Boy, by Richard Wright. Harper, c1937, c1945.
      (New American Library, Signet, 1951. pb $.95)
      RL: 6   IL: 7-adult   BSMP
This autobiography of the famous black author tells the story
of his childhood and youth in Mississippi. It is unfamiliar to
most of the people whom we serve but they are enthusiastic
when they read it. It is very direct. Although most of
Wright's sufferings stemmed from the fact that he was black
(and proud) his writing gives the book a universal quality and
the reader feels as if he were living through the experiences
related.

1359 Black Champion--The Life and Times of Jack Johnson,
      by Finis Farr. Fawcett, 1969. pb $.75
      RL: 7   IL: 6-adult   *BSMP
The story of Jack Johnson, the first black man to become
boxing champion of the world. Exciting and tragic. Photographs. This book is becoming more popular as Johnson's
story becomes known to this generation through plays and
stories.

1360 Black History Lost, Stolen, or Strayed, by Otto Linden-
      meyer. Avon, Discus, c1970. pb $1.25
      RL: 6   IL: 5-adult   BSMP

This unusual book is a must for every school and library in the country.   In the preface, the author quotes from textbooks on American history in current use throughout America, numerous remarks to the effect that slaves were happy, negroes were and are born inferior and should be so treated, etc. He goes on with wit and excitement to prove the opposite by giving short biographies of outstanding black leaders in every field: invention, war, medicine, the arts and so forth.   Illustrated with contemporary drawings and photographs.   A very impressive book which was apparently based on a TV series called Of Black America.

1361   Black Majesty; The Slave Who Became a King, by
       John W. Vandercook.   Harper & Row, 1928.   OP
       (Scholastic, 1956, pb)
       RL: 6   IL: 6-adult   BS
The life of Henri Christophe, the man who won Haitian independence, is growing more popular due to the surge of interest in black history and the increasing number of Haitians in this country.

1362   Black Pilgrimage, by Tom Feelings.   Lothrop, Lee &
       Shepard, c1972. $5.95
       RL: 6   IL: 6-adult   *BSMP
The famous black artist tells his life story, not yet a very long one, and tells, too, why he and his family feel obliged to emigrate to Africa.   There he hopes to find the happiness and fulfillment which he feels are denied to a black artist in America.   The pictures, throughout the book, of people he drew in Brooklyn, the South and West Africa are superb.

1363   Black Pioneers of Science and Invention, by Louis
       Haber.   Harcourt, c1970. $4.50
       RL: Mainly 7-8 IL: 6-adult   *S
A book to stretch for, this contains biographies of fourteen gifted black Americans, the majority of them little known. Many children who are not good readers and who dislike fiction are keen on science and factual material.   Although the reading level of this book is high, it will be an inspiration to black budding scientists and inventors and the stories, dramatic and unfamiliar will appeal to all children.   Illustrated with photographs and facsimiles.

1364   Black Pride--A People's Struggle, by Janet Harris and
       Julius W. Hobson.   Bantam Pathfinder, c1969.   pb $.75
       RL: 5-6   IL: 5-adult   BSMP
In 119 pages, the authors tell the history of the black man

in America. This highly condensed history is vividly told,
mainly in terms of famous people, ranging from Dred Scott
to Stokely Carmichael and the Black Panthers. It is very
popular and poor readers struggle through it with excitement
because it does in fact make them proud.

1365 Black Protest, ed. Joanne Grant. Fawcett, c1968.
      pb $1.25
      RL: Adult   IL: HS-adult   *BSMP
A fascinating and well-arranged collection of documents that
chronicle the history of the black in America starting with
the slave trade and coming down to Ossie Davis' tribute to
Malcolm X and Martin Luther King's Riverside Church speech
Beyond Vietnam. The reading level of many (but not all) of
these documents is high and the print is very small. However, the content is such that it will be popular. Black high
school students have told me how much they are looking for
this kind of book which should also be on the required reading lists of private and suburban schools. See below also
Chronicles of Negro Protest and In Their Own Words.

1366 Black Struggle, by Bryan Fulks. Dell, Laurel Leaf,
      1969. pb $.75
      RL: 5   IL: HS-adult   *BSMP
It is wonderful to see such good books as this one and
numbers 1356, 1360 and 1364 on black history being published.
There is a real demand for this kind of material on the part
of high school students and adults. The books have different
virtues and will reach different audiences but will be eagerly
read and appreciated. This one covers the history of the
black man from early African days through the poor man's
march on Washington. It has larger print than 1356 and
1365 and very simple and direct language. It is a fuller account than 1364. However, it lacks the depth and illustrations
of 1356 and 1383 and the authenticity and excitement of the
original documents of 1450.

1367 Black Think: My Life as a Black Man and a White
      Man, by Jesse Owens and Paul G. Neimark.
      Morrow, c1970. OP (Pocket Books, pb $.95)
      RL: 6   IL: 6-adult   BMP
The story of the famous track star who won at the Olympics
over which Hitler presided. Although some modern black
athletes feel Owens was unfairly exploited and although he
does not minimize the difficulties he encountered, he is
strongly for integration and for the way of life he feels
America offers even to a black man. [1972: I understand

that Owens has now changed and become a militant, a measure of the despair of black Americans as of this date.]

1368   Black Troubadour: Langston Hughes, by Charlemae H.
        Rollins. Rand McNally, c1970. $4.95
        RL: 6-7   IL: 5-adult   *BSMP
This biography of the well-known poet is a beautiful book and
extremely well-written. It will be much enjoyed by high
school students and adults and is the kind of book a non-
reader would stretch for it enough of it were read aloud to
him. Many of Hughes poems and many photographs are interestingly woven into the text. I hope this will soon come
out in paperback.

1369   Blacks in Time, by Douglas Weeks. Illus. by Peggy
        Glanz. New Readers Press, c1969. pb $1.25
        RL: 4-5   IL: 4-adult   *BSMP
A series of short articles on black history from the founding
of the republic through the Civil War, these first appeared
in the weekly newspaper News For You, a newspaper designed
to interest poor readers from fourth grade through Senior
Citizens. The subject, the large print and the fine black and
white drawings will make this book very popular with older
poor readers. It has questions on the text at the end in case
it is used in a classroom situation.

1370   Booker T. Washington, by Lillie G. Patterson. Illus.
        by Anthony d'Adamo. Garrard Discovery series,
        c1962. $2.59
        RL: 3   IL: 3-6   BSMP
This is an easy-to-read biography of a very controversial
black man. For a while, a hero to his people, Washington
is now despised by many for being too accommodating to the
white man's ways. The children who borrow this book enjoy
it, however, and so far no parent has objected.

1371   Born Black, by Gordon Parks. Lippincott, c1971.
        $6.95
        RL: 6   IL: 6-adult   *SMP
This series of articles by the well known black poet and
photographer originally appeared in Look magazine. The articles are biographies of various black Americans whom the
author met at critical moments in their lives. It includes
famous men such as Muhammed Ali and Malcolm X and also
unknown ones such as an impoverished family in Harlem whom
the author befriended. It is very popular in New York City
libraries.

1372   Broken Promises: The Strange History of the Four-
           teenth Amendment, by Richard Stiller.   Random,
           c1972. $4.95
           RL: 5-6   IL: 5-adult   *BSMP
In this book the author tells why black Americans have had
to struggle and still are struggling for the enforcement of
the U.S. Constitution.   He shows that the winning of that
struggle is important for all Americans and explains the vital
part that public opinion plays in deciding issues and the effect of that opinion on the Supreme Court.   With a moving
picture on the cover of a black girl waving an American flag
and with many contemporary illustrations this book will be
very popular in inner city areas and is a "must" elsewhere.

1373   Call It Fate, by William C. McCalip, Jr. with R. E.
           Simon, Jr.   Childrens Press, an Open Door Book,
           c1970. $3.50   (pb $.75)
           RL: 4-5   IL: 6-adult   *BSMP
Mickey McCalip dropped out of school in Washington and
wound up in trouble with the police and with drugs.   After
several unhappy years in and out of prison, a judge sent him
to Daytop Village.   There he learned to understand himself
and to help other people.   Now he is a group social worker
helping to cure addicts of their habit and describes his life
as "happy, exciting and fulfilling."   Photographs.

1374   Call Them Heroes; Books 1, 2, 3, and 4.   Silver
           Burdett Co., 1965.   pb $.59   (Note: These books
           must be ordered direct from the publisher.)
           RL: 5   IL: 4-HS and adult   BSMP
These books are among the most motivating that the School
Volunteers and bookmobile carry.   Unfortunately the outside
format is cheap and the inside is decidedly like a textbook.
In fact, the appearance seems calculated to repel just the
people who most need these books, i.e. able youngsters who
are not succeeding academically because they feel they have
no future.   The contents of the books are superb.   Each consists of a dozen short biographies (2-1/2 pages) of New
Yorkers who have made a success of life against odds.   The
biographies are illustrated with photographs and most of the
subjects are alive and working in New York now.   They are
of every race and creed--united only in that they have achieved
their objectives in spite of hardship and handicaps.   These
books were developed by the New York City Board of Education.   Other cities, I am sure, could do the same with the
lives of their able citizens and would find them an inspiration
for the young.

1375   Captain of the Planter;   The Story of Robert Smalls,
       by Dorothy Sterling.   Illus. by Ernest Critchlow.
       Doubleday, c1958. $3.95   (Washington Square Press,
       Archway, 1968, pb $.50)
       RL: 6   IL: 5-adult   BSMP
The exciting and poignant story of the black Civil War hero
who stole a Confederate boat to bring his family to freedom.
He later fought for the North, became a Congressman and
lived through the bitter Reconstruction days--an authentic
American hero whose name is still unfamiliar to most Americans.

1376   Cassius Clay, by Claude Lewis.   MacFadden, c1971.
       pb $.60
       RL: 5-6   IL: 6-adult   BSM
A well written biography of the black prize fighter by a well
known black newspaper commentator.   Cassius Clay or
Muhammed Ali as he prefers to be called, is a fascinating
and controversial figure.   His story is well worth reading
and is very popular on the bookmobile.

1377   Cesar Chavez, by Ruth Franchere.   Earl Thollander,
       illus.   Crowell, 1970. $3.75
       RL: 3   IL: 2-JH   *BSMP
A fine biography of the Chicano in California who has dedicated his life to improving the living and working conditions
of farm workers, told in a way that will interest even young
children.   See also Mighty Hard Road [1487].

1378   Charles Drew, by Roland Bertol.   Illus. by Jo Polseno.
       Crowell, 1970. $3.75
       RL: 3   IL: 2-JH   *BSMP
A good biography of the blood specialist whose skill and dedi-
cation saved thousands of lives in World War II but in spite
of that fact was a victim of racial prejudice through most of
his life.   He finally bled to death after an automobile accident
because he could not be admitted to a white hospital in the
South.

1379   Childhood of Great American Series.   Bobbs-Merrill.
       $2.75
       RL: 4   IL: 3-JH   BSMP
These biographies of an almost exhaustive list of famous people of the past are sure to offer something appealing to every
reader.   The large print and simple format are still dignified
enough for older readers.   As a rule the story starts off in
the middle of an exciting episode, catching the reader's interest immediately.

1380   The Chinese Helped Build America, by Dorothy and
        Joseph Dowdell.   Messner, c1972. $4.95
        RL: 4-5   IL: 4-adult   *SMP
This is an excellent history of the role of the Chinese in
American history.   It starts with a 16-year-old Chinese boy
emigrating in 1851, the year of the great famine.   He helps
build the transcontinental railroad.   It gives information
about Chinese culture and minces no words about the discrimination they encountered here.   The book brings the
story up to the present day and ends with a list of distinguished Chinese-Americans and short biographies of some
of them: I. M. Pei, Hiram Fong, Dong Kingman, prize-
winning scientists, etc.

1381   A Choice of Weapons, by Gordon Parks.   Harper &
        Row, 1965. $6.95   (Berkley, Medallion, 1967,
        pb $.75)
        RL: 7   IL: 6-adult   BSMP
An inspiring autobiography by a gifted writer and photographer,
which tells of his struggles as a young boy in Minnesota and
Harlem and of his later successes working for Life magazine.
This book is not as well known as Manchild in the Promised
Land to which in some ways it can be compared but every
one who has borrowed it has liked it very much and been
cheered by the success of its author.   See also 1074 and
1371 by the same author.   This book is also available in the
Falcon series [1404].

1382   Christopher Columbus, by Ann McGovern.   Illus. by
        Joe Laskers.   Scholastic, c1962.   pb $.60
        RL: 3   IL: 2-4   BS
A well-written easy-to-read biography of a man all young
Americans have heard of.

1383   Chronicles of Negro Protest, edited by Bradford
        Chambers.   Parents, c1968. $4.50   (available in
        paperback under title Chronicle of Black Protest,
        New American Library, Signet, $.95)
        RL: Adult   IL: JH-adult   *BSMP
This collection of original documents on black history and
black protest is selective and includes documents such as
the famous curse of Noah which I have seen nowhere else.
It has excellent print and many contemporary illustrations
but is still difficult reading.   I include it and Black Protest
on this list because I have personally been requested by black
high school students, some of whom could barely read, to
provide materials on black history and the black heritage.

When I did so, I saw them studying (with the help of a tutor and a dictionary) quite literally with sweat pouring down their faces with the effort involved.   Later, I could hear them in the street or schoolyard passing on their knowledge to fellow students, "Man, you should read about that guy, Prosser," etc. This book should be a powerful motivator for the young.

1384 Clara Barton, by Mary Catherine Rose.   Illus. by
      E. Harper Johnson.   Garrard, Discovery Series,
      1960. $2.39
      RL: 3   IL: 3-JH   BS
Simple biography for younger children of the woman who founded the American Red Cross.   The book involves the reader immediately in Clara's life and is very popular.

1385 Coming of Age in Mississippi: An Autobiography, by
      Anne Moody.   Dial Press, 1968. $5.95 (Dell pb
      $.95)
      RL: 6   IL: 6-adult   BSMP
This moving autobiography of a girl's life in Mississippi is in a class for popularity with Manchild in the Promised Land and Down These Mean Streets.   It is in demand by high school girls and adults.   Anne Moody is an American that other citizens can be proud to meet.   She has shown courage and integrity in her fight to be treated as an equal and has made sacrifices that are heartrending.   A book that will endure.

1386 Cool Cos, The Story of Bill Cosby, by Joel H. Cohen.
      Scholastic, c1969.   pb $.60
      RL: 5-6   IL: 5-adult   BS
The Cinderella story of a black boy who has come from a Philadelphia ghetto to being one of the highest paid men in America.   Bill Cosby is a TV entertainer who is popular with millions of Americans.   He also feels a sense of responsibility to his race and expects to become a teacher of boys such as he was.

1387 Crispus Attucks--Boy of Valor, by Dharathula H.
      Millender.   Illus. by Gray Morrow.   Bobbs-Merrill,
      Childhood of Great American Series, 1965. $2.75
      RL: 4   IL: 3-adult   BSMP
The story of the black sailor who was killed in the Boston Massacre.   His life up until then had not been very exciting but the author's emphasis on his lifelong desire for freedom, first for himself and then for the colonies, gives the book continuity and interest.

1388 The Cruise of Mr. Christopher Columbus, by Sadyebeth
      and Anson Lowitz. Stein and Day, 1932. (Scholas-
      tic, 1967, pb $.60)
      RL: 4   IL: 3-6   BS
Witty, picture biography of Columbus. Its humor is quite
mature and it can be successfully used with older non-readers.

1389 Curse Not the Darkness, by Edison Hoard with Michael
      Reuben.   Childrens Press, an Open Door Book,
      c1970. $3.50 (pb $.75)
      RL: 4-5   IL: 5-adult   *BSMP
Edison Hoard's father died when he was two and a half; his
mother, when he was eleven.   He then lived with a succession of relatives of whom he doesn't have very happy memories.   But some of his teachers inspired him and he somehow put himself through college and law school while support-
ing a family and is now a successful lawyer in Chicago.
Photographs.

1390 Dance; The Story of Katherine Dunham, by Ruth
      Biemiller.   Doubleday, c1969, Signal. $3.50
      (Semaphore pb $1.75)
      RL: 4   IL: 4-adult   *BSMP
This is an excellent life of the famous dancer illustrated with
several pages of photographs of her on her world-wide career.
Dancing comes naturally to most children and many, many
underprivileged children have told me how much they long to
become ballet dancers.   It is a joy to have a book which
documents the fact that it can be done.   Older girls who become really interested in Katherine Dunham might well go on
to her own story of her early life, A Touch of Innocence,
which is fascinating reading but uses a very adult vocabulary.

1391 Dark Companion: The Story of Matthew Henson, by
      Bradley Robinson with Matthew Henson.   Fawcett,
      Premier, 1967. pb $.75
      RL: 6-7   IL: 6-adult   BSMP
This interesting and moving account of the Afro-American who
helped Peary to reach the North Pole and was the only man
to accompany him to his goal is popular with teenagers and
adults.   It is authentic since it was written with Henson's
cooperation.   See also Matthew Henson, Arctic Hero [1483]
and To the Top of the World [1580].

1392 The Death of Lincoln: A Picture History of the Assas-
      sination, by Leroy Hayman. Scholastic, c1968. pb $.60
      RL: 6   IL: 5-adult   BS

Although the subtitle calls this a picture history and the book
does have a great many contemporary photographs and drawings, it has a good deal of text telling the story of Lincoln's
assassination and what happened afterward to those involved.
This is an important book since it shows how quickly rumor
and myth develop after a major event such as this. There
has been recently a bill before Congress to clear the name
of Dr. Mudd who treated Lincoln's assassin's broken leg, not
knowing who he was, and who was then sent to prison for his
humanitarian act.

1393   Diary of a Young Girl, by Anne Frank.   Pocket Books,
       c1952.   pb $.75
       RL: 6   IL: 6-adult   BSMP
The diary of a young Jewish girl who spent years in hiding
with her family from the Nazis in Holland in World War II.
The book would be moving in any case (it is hard to grow up
in a prison) but the fact that she and her family were ulti-
mately captured and killed lends an extraordinary poignancy
to the story.   The book is much liked and admired by those
who read it but should have an appealing picture on the cover.
Young inner city readers have never heard of Anne Frank.

1394   Discovery Series.   Garrard. $2.39
       RL: 3   IL: Read aloud-6 and JH and
       HS slow readers   BS
This series of biographies of famous Americans has good
illustrations, good print and a format designed for young
children.   The books are very popular with young readers
and are liked by older readers when introduced.   Many of
the titles are out in paperback (Dell Yearling) and are even
more popular in that form.

1395   Dr. George Washington Carver, by Shirley Graham
       and George D. Lipscomb.   Messner, c1944. $3.95
       (Washington Square Press, Archway, pb $.60)
       RL: 5-6   IL: 5-adult   BSMP
George Washington Carver was born a slave and orphaned as
a baby.   He managed to educate himself in the face of incredible obstacles and to become a great teacher and a great
scientist.   This well-written biography is a perfect example
of a life of a famous Afro-American which was written especially for young people but in this paperback format is enjoyed and appreciated by all ages--including senior citizens.

1396   Doña Felisa: A Biography of the Mayor of San Juan,
       by Marianna Norris.   Dodd, Mead, c1969. $3.50

RL: 6-7   IL: 6-adult   *BSMP
Doña Felisa shows what a woman can accomplish, even one
who obeys her father and is strictly chaperoned! This book
and her life will be a great source of pride to a Puerto Rican
and anyone who cares about helping other people will find it
a source of inspiration. Photographs.

1397 Don't Stop Me Now, by Dempsey Travis with L.
        Brownlee. Children's Press, An Open Door Book,
        c1970. $3.50 (pb $.75)
        RL: 4-5   IL: 6-adult   *BSMP
Dempsey Travis was a professional musician at sixteen and
thought he had found his career. Then he was drafted and,
as an innocent bystander, shot in an Army race riot. After
he recovered, he was taught typing and made a clerk at a
post exchange. By the time he had finished his Army service, he had learned that his real talent lay in being a pro-
moter whether of music, real estate or civil rights. After
going through college at night, he has wound up with his own
real estate business and his own mortgage company which in
1961 (!) was the first black owned mortgage company to qualify for FHA-VA approval. He has also been president of the
Chicago branch of the NAACP and is on a ten-man task force
appointed by the President to study and make recommenda-
tions on urban renewal and neighborhood redevelopment.
Quite a record!

1398 Down These Mean Streets, by Piri Thomas. Knopf,
        c1967. $6.95 (New American Library, Signet, pb
        $.95)
        RL: 7   IL: 6-adult   BSMP
This is the autobiography of a dark skinned Puerto Rican boy
who grew up discriminated against by his father as well as
the general public because of the color of his skin. In spite
of this, he grew up to be a fine citizen determined to help
his people. This book is very popular with all teenagers and
especially with Puerto Rican teen-agers. It has been banned
in some school systems because of the realistic way he portrays life in East Harlem.

1399 El Rancho de Muchachos, by Arthur Lopez with Kenneth
        Richards. Childrens Press, c1970. $3 (pb $.75)
        RL: 4   IL: 4-adult   BSMP
The true story of a Chicano, son of migrant workers, who
became a social worker and head of a ranch for delinquent
boys. The author clearly gets great satisfaction from his
work. An inspiring book illustrated with photographs.

1400   Eleanor Roosevelt, by Charles P. Graves.   Illus. by
       Polly Bolian.   Dell, Discovery, c1966.   pb $.60
       RL: 3   IL: 2-6 and older non-readers   BS
This biography of Eleanor Roosevelt is exceptionally useful
since it is written so simply and so directly that it can be
enjoyed by people of any age.   Not as full of detail as The
Story of Eleanor Roosevelt [1554], it is still interesting and
the issues she cared about are still relevant.

1401   The Endless Steppe: A Girl in Exile, by Esther Hautzig.
       Crowell, c1968.   (Scholastic, 1970, pb $.75)
       RL: 6-7   IL: 6-adult   BMP
This true story of a Polish girl who was deported with her
family to Siberia in 1941 and survived incredible hardships
will have great appeal to girls and women.   See also I Am
Fifteen--And I Don't Want to Die [1440].

1402   Enterprise, by Joe Williams with Rick E. Simon, Jr.
       Childrens Press, An Open Door Book, c1970. $3.50
       (pb $.75)
       RL: 4-5   IL: 6-adult   *BSMP
Joe Williams had a hard time deciding what he wanted to do.
He tried engineering school and dropped out when he found
he didn't have the aptitude.   After a stint in the Army he
has wound up with his own laundry and dry-cleaning business.
He likes being his own boss and the business has grown to
be five times what it was when he bought it.   Photographs.

1403   Evers, by Charles Evers.   Edited by Grace Halsell.
       World, c1971. $6.95
       RL: 5   IL: 6-adult   BSM
The candid and fascinating autobiography of a complex man,
the black mayor of Fayette, Mississippi.   Mr. Evers is dedi-
cating his life to racial justice and walks with the knowledge
that at any moment he may be gunned down as was his brother
Medgar.   Yet he stands firm against hatred.   See also 105.

1404   Falcon Books.   Noble and Noble.   pb $.56 each
       RL: Mainly 6   IL: 6-adult   BS
A valuable series of interesting titles in an attractive format,
these books have been abridged and adapted for poor readers.
Although the language has been simplified, it is not stilted
and the flavor of the original book has been preserved.   Some
of the titles are: Anne Frank: The Diary of a Young Girl,
A Choice of Weapons, Go Up for Glory, I Always Wanted to
be Somebody and Karen.   These books are only available to
non-profit organizations.

1405   <u>Famous American Negroes</u>, by Langston Hughes.
       Dodd, Mead, c1954.   pb $1.75
       RL: 7   IL: 6-adult   *BSMP
The biographies of seventeen distinguished black Americans,
half of them unfamiliar to most of their fellow citizens.   This
book came out in 1954.   It has now been reissued in paperback and will be very popular.   Illustrated with contemporary
drawings and photographs.

1406   <u>Famous American Negro Poets</u>, by Charlemae Rollins.
       Dodd, Mead, c1965. $3.50   (Apollo pb $1.95)
       RL: 6   IL: 5-adult   BSMP
Short biographies of twelve poets from 1700 to the 20th Century with samples of their poems.   This is very popular with
adults.

1407   <u>Famous Negro Americans</u>, by John T. and Marcet H.
       King.   Steck-Vaughn, c1967.   pb $1.76 retail, $1.32
       wholesale
       RL: 5-6   IL: 5-adult   *BSMP
This book has twenty-three biographies of famous Afro-Americans, each about three or four pages long.   The paperback
format has a long-wearing cover, the print is excellent and
the book is well-designed for looks and lasting qualities.   It
includes the stories of people whom I have not seen celebrated
in other collections such as Matzeliger, inventor of the first
machine for making shoes, Mahalia Jackson, the gospel
singer, and Thurgood Marshall, the Supreme Court Justice.

1408   <u>Famous Negro Athletes</u>, by Arna Bontemps.   Dodd,
       Mead, c1964. $3.50   (Apollo pb $1.95)
       RL: 6   IL: 5-adult   BSMP
It may seem redundant still to carry this book (which was
published in 1964) when so many new ones now celebrate the
black athlete individually and collectively, but I love the way
Bontemps writes and he writes of some heroes who are now
neglected.   Joe Louis, Satchel Paige and Jesse Owens are
almost unknown to a new generation.   Even Jackie Robinson
sometimes isn't recognized.   Yet these men were trailblazers
as was this book.   It was on the bookmobile when we opened
in July 1967 and very popular.   Now most people pass it by
for more up-to-date paperbacks.   It has just been reissued
in paperback which may renew its popularity.   Photographs.

1409   <u>Famous Negro Heroes of America</u>, by Langston Hughes.
       Illus. by Gerald McCannil.   Dodd, Mead, c1958.
       $3.50

RL: 6   IL: 5-adult   BSMP
Sixteen short biographies of heroes from the 16th to the 20th
Century. This book does not duplicate Famous American
Negroes [1405] as only two biographies are repeated and the
language in this volume is simpler. This is another book
which is borrowed on the bookmobile by more adults than
young people but is well liked by junior high and high school
students when introduced to it by a School Volunteer.

1410   Famous Negro Music Makers, by Langston Hughes.
       Dodd, Mead, c1955. $3.50
       RL: 5   IL: 5-adult   BS
Twenty-four short biographies of musicians from the Fisk
Jubilee Singers to Mahalia Jackson. Dated but still very
popular with adults.

1411   First Golden Geography, by Jane Werner Watson.
       Illus. by William Sayles. Golden Press, c1955.
       $1.95
       RL: 4   IL: 2-6   S
An introduction to earth's configurations. Useful for stimulating conversation in Reading Help Programs. Has good
colorful illustrations.

1412   Florence Nightingale, by Anne Colver. Illus. by
       Gerald McCannill. Dell, Yearling, 1961. pb $.50
       RL: 3-4   IL: 4-JH   BS
The biography of the woman who virtually invented the nursing
profession. So many girls are interested in nursing, this is
a very popular book. See also Lady with a Lamp [1463] and
The Story of Florence Nightingale [1555].

1413   A Foot in Two Worlds, by José Martinez with Emmett
       Smith. Childrens Press, An Open Door Book, c1970.
       $3 (pb $.75)
       RL: 4-5   IL: 5-adult   *BSMP
José Martinez came from desperate poverty in Puerto Rico to
a good living in Chicago and a happy marriage in spite of the
many obstacles in his way. But family illnesses and the help
he had been given in crises and emergencies made him feel
that money for his family was not enough to satisfy him. He
wanted a job where he could help people. He is now a police-
man and acts as an interpreter between the Anglo and Spanish-
speaking communities. Photographs.

1414   For Us, The Living, by Mrs. Medgar Evers with
       William Peters. Doubleday, c1967. $6.50

(Ace pb $1.25)
RL: 6-7   IL: 6-adult   BSMP
The unbelievably moving story of the life of the civil rights
leader and his wife. Although Medgar Evers was shot in
1963 and so much has happened since then, the discussion of
violence in this book and the description of violence make it
as timely as tomorrow's headlines. See also 1403.

1415 Four Took Freedom, by Philip Sterling with Rayford
       Logan. Illus. by Charles White. Doubleday, Zenith,
       1967. pb $1.45
       RL: 5   IL: 5-adult   *BSMP
The four who took freedom, i. e. escaped from slavery, are
Harriet Tubman, Frederick Douglass, Robert Smalls and
Blanche K. Bruce. A straight-forward account of the lives
of four great Americans, hopefully this book will send readers
to fuller accounts of the four achievements. The illustrations,
by the well-known black artist, Charles White, are striking.

1416 Franklin Roosevelt, Boy of the Four Freedoms, by
       Ann Weil. Bobbs-Merrill, 1947. $2.75
       RL: 3   IL: 3-7   S
Few of the young seem to have heard of Franklin Roosevelt,
but once this book is introduced it is well liked. Roosevelt's
courage in overcoming his physical handicap is admired and
can inspire others who have handicaps to contend with. Black
and white illustrations by the author.

1417 Frederick Douglass Fights for Freedom, by Margaret
       Davidson. Illus. by Eleanor Mill. Four Winds,
       c1968. $2.95 (Scholastic pb $.60)
       RL: 4-5   IL: 4-adult   BSMP
The story of the man who fought against slavery both before
and after his escape from bondage. His courage and his
talents were equally great and he was not only a leader of
his people but very influential in convincing the North that
slavery was wrong and must be ended. See also 855, 858,
1418 and 1495.

1418 Frederick Douglass: Freedom Fighter, by Lillie
       Patterson. Illus. by Gray Morrow. Garrard
       (Discovery Series), 1965. $2.39 (Dell, Yearling,
       pb $.50)
       RL: 3-4   IL: 3-JH   BSMP
Easy-to-read biography of the famous ex-slave. This is instantly popular due to the good picture on the cover.

1419   Freedom Bound, by Henrietta Buckmaster.   Macmillan
        Collier, 1965. $4.95   (pb $1.25)
        RL: 6   IL: 6-adult   *BSMP
A study of a tragic period in our history--the Reconstruction,
1868 to 1875.   Even poor readers, if they are black, struggle
through this one, it is such a moving part of black history.
This book, combined with Freedom Road [830] gives an in-
delible impression of a shameful era in American history.

1420   Freedom Train, by Dorothy Sterling.   Illus. by Ernest
        Gichlow.   Doubleday, c1954.   (Scholastic, 1969, pb
        $.75)
        RL: 6   IL: 4-adult   BSMP
The thrilling story of Harriet Tubman told by the author of
Mary Jane [1079].   This excellent book has a good format
and is justly popular with a wide age range.

1421   George Carver, Boy Scientist, by Augusta Stevenson.
        Illus. by Clotilda Embree.   Bobbs-Merrill, c1952.
        $2.75
        RL: 4   IL: 3-JH   BSMP
An exciting biography of the great black scientist.   This author makes the reader anxious to know what happens next.
A good biography, slightly harder and in a more grown up
format than number 1422 below but not as full as 1395.

1422   George Washington Carver, by Sam and Beryl Epstein.
        Illus. by William Moyers.   Garrard, c1960.   Dis-
        covery Series. $2.39   (Dell Yearling, pb $.60)
        RL: 3   IL: 3-6   BSMP
A good easy biography of the famous black scientist.

1423   Ghandi--Fighter Without a Sword, by Jeanette Eaton.
        Illus. by R. Ray.   Morrow, c1955.   OP
        RL: 7   IL: 6-adult   SMP
In these days of so much violence and discussion of violence,
knowledge of the life and work of this leader of non-violent
protest is essential for all young people.   This is a very
readable and interesting life of Ghandi and is especially good
at tracing his development from his early years in India
through his time in England and South Africa.   If this book
is introduced by an enthusiast, many people will be fascinated
by it.   He is not well-known in underprivileged areas.

1424   The Gift of Black Folk, by W. E. B. DuBois.   Wash-
        ington Square Press, c1924, c1970.   pb $.95
        RL: 7   IL: 7-adult   *BSMP

This book was first published in 1924 but it is as timely as
today's newspaper. In it Dr. DuBois gives a summarized
history of black folk in America and analyzes their gift to
America. An exciting book which shows that "the American
negro is and has been a distinct asset to this country." The
country shouldn't have to be told, but it does.

1425 Go Up for Glory, by Bill Russell, as told to William
      F. McSweeny. Berkley, c1966 (Medallion). $.60
      RL: 6   IL: 6-adult   BSMP
The autobiography of the great basketball player. This is
also available in a Falcon edition. See Falcon Books
1404.

1426 The Great Escape, by Paul Brickhill. Fawcett,
      c1950. $.95
      RL: 6   IL: 6-adult   BS
This story is so exciting that one tends to think of it as fiction. The fact that the book was made into a movie enhances
that conviction. Actually it is history--the history of the inability of tyrants to imprison free men indefinitely. Because
of the movie and TV programs, this book has been very popular with many young people who know little or nothing about
Hitler and World War II.

1427 Great Negroes Past and Present, by Russell L. Adams.
      Edited by David P. Ross. Illus. by Eugene Winslow.
      Afro-American Publishing Co., c1964. $5.95
      (pb $2.95)
      RL: 6-7   IL: 6-adult   BSMP
One-page biographies of famous black men in every part of
the world starting in 615 A.D. and continuing up through black
history. The value of this book for poor readers is in the
brevity of the articles. The striking illustrations, too, will
lure readers on. The fine print, however, is inhibiting to
senior citizens who otherwise would very much enjoy this
book.

1428 Great Rulers of the African Past, by Lavinia Dobler
      and William A. Brown. Doubleday, Zenith, c1965.
      $3.75 (pb $1.45)
      RL: 6   IL: 6-adult   BSMP
Five short biographies of early African rulers. This series
is intended for junior high students but is mainly borrowed
by adults. This book has fine illustrations and is growing
more popular.

1429   Great Spirit, by A. Cobe with G. Elrick and R. E.
        Simon, Jr.   Childrens Press, An Open Door Book,
        c1970. $3   (pb $.75)
        RL: 4-5   IL: 5-adult   *BSMP
Albert Cobe spent a miserable childhood trying to remain an
Indian while the government seemed determined to turn him
into a second-class white man.   Finally, under his father's
guidance, he decided that the two worlds could be joined. He
buckled down at school, succeeded at every sport and eventually fell in love with golf.   He has been a successful pro
for the last eighteen years and thoroughly enjoys his vocation.
Photographs.

1430   Growing Up Black, edited by Jay David.   Morrow,
        1968. $6.50   (Simon and Schuster, Pocket Books,
        pb $.95)
        RL: Varied but mainly 6-7   IL: JH-adult   BSMP
Nineteen burningly vivid accounts by black Americans of what
it was like for them to grow up black in America.   The autobiographical excerpts range from revolutionary times to the
present.   A superb and moving collection.

1431   A Guide to African History, by Basil Davidson.   Edited
        by Haskel Frankel.   Illus. by Robin Jacques.
        Doubleday, Zenith, c1963. $3.75 (1965, pb $1.45)
        RL: 6   IL: 6-adult   BS
The writing in this short survey of African history is poor
but the cover and the illustrations are exciting and colorful
which probably accounts for the heavy demand.   We have had
many requests for it, mainly on the part of adults.

1432   Helen Keller's Teacher, by Mickie Davidson.   Four
        Winds, c1965.   (Scholastic pb $.60)
        RL: 5   IL: 5-adult   BS
This appealing biography of Anne Sullivan, the girl who taught
Helen Keller how to communicate with the world, has real
excitement and suspense.

1433   Heroes and Heroines of Many Lands, by Jay Strong.
        Illus. by George Garland.   Hart Publishing Company,
        c1965.   OP
        RL: 6   IL: 5-adult   S
An excellent collection of short biographies ranging from
David to Maria Montessori to Ghandi.   Would have great appeal to a wide age range on the bookmobile if it were in an
adult paperback.

1434   Heroes, Heroes, Heroes, selected by Phyllis Fenner.
       Illus. by Bill Lohse.   Franklin Watts, Inc., 1965.
       $2.95
       RL: 6-7   IL: 4-adult   SMP
Fifteen breathtaking stories of heroism include the stories of
two women, Harriet Tubman and Edith Cavell.   If the start
of one of these stories is read aloud, even poor readers will
struggle to finish on their own.

1435   Heroes of the Olympics, by Hal Higdon.   Illus. by
       Paul Frame.   Prentice-Hall, 1965. $3.95
       RL: 5   IL: 6-JH   BSMP
Short biographical sketches of ten Olympic heroes and heroines,
most of whom got their athletic start in school.   Excellent
for junior high school children who are good in sports and
poor in reading and thinking of dropping out.   Would be very
popular in paperback.

1436   His Day Is Marching On, by Shirley Graham DuBois.
       Lippincott, c1971. $6.95
       RL: Adult   IL: Adult   *BSMP
A memoir of W. E. B. DuBois by his wife.   Shirley Graham
first met her famous future husband when she was thirteen
and he was already a well known leader and this book covers
his career as she knew it.   It will be very popular with
adults on the bookmobile when it comes out in paperback and
a knowledge of DuBois's extraordinary career is a must for
anyone who wants to teach black children.   See also his own
autobiography, 1347, and The Gift of Black Folk [1424] and
The Soul of Black Folk [110].

1437   His Eye Is On the Sparrow, by Ethel Waters with
       Charles Samuels.   Doubleday, c1950, 1951.
       (Pyramid, 1967, pb $.75)
       RL: 6   IL: JH-adult   BSMP
Enthralling autobiography of the popular singer.   Today's
teenagers have never heard of Ethel Waters but like the book
when it is brought to their attention.   It is also very popular
with older people.

1438   I Always Wanted to be Somebody, by Althea Gibson.
       Edited by Ed Fitzgerald.   Harper, c1958.   (Peren-
       nial, 1965, pb $.75)
       RL: 6-7   IL: 5-adult   BMP
The story of the famous tennis player from Harlem, this book
is increasingly popular as more and more people watch tennis
on TV.

1439   I Always Wanted to be Somebody, by Althea Gibson.
        Adapted by F. Allen and Stephen M. Joseph.   Noble
        and Noble, Falcon Books, c1967.   pb $.56
        RL: 5   IL: 5-adult   BSMP
This is an abridged and adapted version of 1438.

1440   I Am Fifteen--And I Don't Want to Die, by Christine
        Arnothy.   Dutton, c1956.   OP   (Scholastic, 1966,
        pb $.50)
        RL: 6   IL: 6-HS   BS
This true story of the Hungarian Revolution of 1956 is unrelieved gloom but teenage girls eat it up.   Very popular.

1441   I Am One of These, edited by Kay Kischnick.   New
        Readers Press, c1970.   pb $.50
        RL: 4   IL: 5-adult   BSM
Very like Call Them Heroes [1374], this slender booklet has
fifteen short biographies of people from very varied backgrounds who have one thing in common: they have overcome
poverty and prejudice to stand on their own feet and to make
a contribution to society.   The photographs of the participants
make their stories very real.

1442   I Am Third, by Gale Sayers with Al Silverman.
        Viking, c1970. $6.95   (Bantam, 1972, pb $1.25)
        RL: 5-6   IL: JH-adult   BSMP
Gale Sayers, the well known pro football player, tells the
story of his life and of his friendship with Brian Piccolo,
his white football roommate who died of cancer.   It is an
inspiring story of courage, determination (he started life in
the ghetto) and love.   It is already very popular.

1443   I Know Why the Caged Bird Sings, by Maya Angelou.
        Random, c1969. $5.95   (Bantam, 1971, pb $1.25)
        RL: Adult   IL: HS-adult   *BSM
This is an extraordinary autobiography.   It covers the life of
the author up to the age of eighteen.   She later became an
actress, a dancer and a writer.   This is a moving, spellbinding book which gives a vivid picture of life in a small
rural Southern community.

1444   I Reached for the Sky, by Betty Patterson with Mar-
        garet Friskey and Gene Kinger.   Childrens Press,
        An Open Door Book, c1970. $3   (pb $.75)
        RL: 4-5   IL: 4-adult   *BSMP
The true story of the first Job Corps girl to become an airline stewardess.   Vivid and motivating.   Photographs.

1445 I Was a Black Panther--As Told to Chuck Moore.
          Doubleday, Signal, c1970. $3.50 (Doubleday,
          Semaphore, pb $1.75)
          RL: 4-5   IL: 4-adult   *BSMP
The true story of a New York boy who first joined SNCC and
then became a Black Panther and was at one time quite a
leading one.   He is now enrolled in City College and is waiting trial on a charge of carrying a concealed weapon, a pistol. He has quit the Panthers. I am confident that this book
will be very popular in all areas. There is great curiosity
about the Panthers among the young in every level of society.
Illustrated with dramatic photographs.

1446 If You ... Series.   Scholastic, various dates.   pb
          $.60
          RL: 3   IL: Read aloud-6   BS
Children find these books very appealing and thought-provok-
ing.   They are well liked even by slow readers. All have
good illustrations.   The titles are: If You Grew Up with
Abraham Lincoln, by Ann McGovern, illus. by Benton Turkle;
If You Lived in Colonial Times, by Ann McGovern, illus. by
Benton Turkle; If You Lived in the Days of the Wild Mam-
moth Hunters, by Mary Elting, illus. by S. Folsom Moodie;
If You Sailed on the Mayflower, by Ann McGovern, illus. by
J. B. Handelsman.

1447 I'm Done Crying, by Louanne Ferris as told to Beth
          Day. M. Evans, 1969. $5.95 (New American
          Library, Signet, pb $.95)
          RL: 6-7   IL: JH-adult   *BM
This is an authentic and frank description of life in an urban
ghetto and in a city hospital.   The author fought her way to
becoming a licensed practical nurse in spite of her lack of
education and managed to support and raise her three children
while she did so.   Many women like to read about hospitals--
others hope to become nurses. This should be a popular
book.

1448 In Chains to Louisiana--Solomon Northrup's Story,
          adapted by Michael Knight. Dutton, c1971. $4.50
          RL: 6   IL: 5-adult   *BSMP
In 1841 Solomon Northrup, a free black man from New York
was kidnapped and sent to Louisiana as a slave.   When he
finally regained his freedom, he wrote an account of his experiences and this book is an adaptation of the account.   It
gives a harrowing and authentic picture of slavery and how it
brutalized the masters and the sufferings and endurance of the
blacks.

1449   In the Face of the Sun, by Emmett Stovall with R. E.
       Simon, Jr.   Childrens Press, An Open Door Book,
       c1970. $3   (pb $.75)
       RL: 4-5   IL: 5-adult   *BSMP
Emmett Stovall has his own charter airline company and is
a chartered dealer for Beechcraft.   It took unbelievable determination to achieve his dream of becoming a pilot but he
made the grade.   A heartwarming story.   Photographs.

1450   In Their Own Words--A History of the American Negro
       (Vol. I, II & III), edited by Milton Meltzer.   Crowell,
       c1964, 1965 and 1970.   (Apollo pb $1.65)
       RL: Varied, mainly HS-adult   IL: JH-adult BSMP
A superb collection of authentic documents about the experiences of the Negro in America from 1619 to 1966.   It is illustrated with fascinating contemporary black and white pictures.   This group of books has much better print than Black
Protest.   It is easier to read, on the whole, than Chronicles
of Negro Protest which however, it does not duplicate.   It
will be very popular with people looking for black history
and is a must for private and suburban schools and colleges.

1451   Iron Man, by Billy Williams with Rick Simon.   Chil-
       drens Press, c1970. $3   (An Open Door Book, pb
       $.75)
       RL: 5   IL: 5-adult   *BSMP
Billy Williams grew up in poverty but with a happy united
family.   He went straight from school into pro baseball and
had a lonely time of it as the only black on the team.   He
is now well known and glad he took the road he did.   Will
be very popular.

1452   Island in the Crossroads--The History of Puerto Rico,
       by M. M. Brau.   Illus. by Herbert Steinberg.
       Doubleday, c1968. $3.75   (Zenith pb $1.45)
       RL: 6   IL: 5-adult   *BSMP
At last a good history of Puerto Rico from the time of the
Conquistadores to operation Bootstrap.   Black and white illustrations.   This book has been badly needed and will be
very popular in Puerto Rican areas.   We could use one on
an even easier reading level also.   Excellent format suitable
for any age level.

1453   Jackie Robinson of the Brooklyn Dodgers, by Milton J.
       Shapiro.   Messner, c1957. $3.50   (Washington
       Square Press, Archway, 1967, pb $.50)
       RL: 6   IL: 5-adult   BSMP

The moving story of the first black baseball player in the
white leagues. Engrossing even to those who are not interested in baseball. Photographs.

1454 Jake Gaither--Winning Coach, by Wyatt Blassingame.
      Illustrations and photographs by Raymond Burr.
      Garrard, c1969. (Americans All) $2.79
      RL: 4   IL: 4-HS   *BSM
The biography of Jake Gaither, the well known football coach
at Florida A and M will interest and inspire some boys while
others may find it simplistic and over moral. Gaither is
undoubtedly a very fine man and a very successful coach but
many young militants will feel unhappy that he has spent the
whole of his working life in a segregated world and is the
most successful coach in the National Negro Conference rather
than the truly National Small College League which should
exist.

1455 Jim Ryun, Master of the Mile, by John Lake. Random,
      c1968. $1.95
      RL: 5-6   IL: 6-adult   *BS
The story of Jim Ryun, the amazing track star. The book
brings out to what an extent Ryun's record runs are the product of unremitting work. An interesting story. Many photographs.

1456 Jim Thorpe, by Thomas Fall. Illus. by John Gretzer.
      Crowell, c1970. $3.75
      RL: 3   IL: Read aloud-JH   *BSMP
A good biography of the famous Indian athlete which will interest all would-be football players and also boys who dislike
school. See also below for a more mature biography.

1457 The Jim Thorpe Story, by Gene Schoor. J. Messner,
      1967. $3.50 (Washington Square Press, Archway,
      pb $.60)
      RL: 5   IL: 5-adult   *BMP
The subtitle of this book is America's Greatest Athlete and
the story of Jim Thorpe, the Indian, is in fact an extraordinary one. Will be especially popular with football fans.
Photographs.

1458 John F. Kennedy, by Charles P. Graves. Illus. by
      Paul Frame. Dell, Yearling, 1965. pb $.65
      RL: 4   IL: 4-JH   BS
Good format with large print, black and white sketch illustrations. Uses simple vocabulary to relate JFK's life story.

1459   John Fitzgerald Kennedy: Man of Courage, by Flora
        Strousse.   New American Library, Signet, c1964.
        pb $.50
        RL: 6   IL: 6-adult   BS
A mature biography, illustrated with a few pages of photographs, taking JFK from birth to death.   Very popular with
adults.

1460   Journey Toward Freedom--The Story of Sojourner
        Truth, by Jacqueline Bernard.   Norton, 1967.
        $5.95   (Dell Laurel, pb $.60)
        RL: 7-8   IL: JH-adult   *BMP
The biography of a remarkable woman.   Born in slavery,
she decided at the age of forty-six to walk the roads of the
Northeast telling and singing of the evils of slavery.   Later
she advocated women's rights and prison reform and such
was the power of her personality that she became nationally
known and respected.   Illustrated with contemporary photographs and engravings.

1461   Karen, by Marie Killilea.   Adapted by Floretta Henn.
        Noble and Noble, Falcon Books, c1965. $.56
        RL: 6   IL: 6-adult   *BS
An abridged and adapted version of the inspiring true story
of the girl who overcame her cerebral palsy handicap and
learned to walk and talk and read and write.   Older girls
and women, as well as those with a handicapped child in the
family, will want to read this one.

1462   Lady Sings the Blues, by Billie Holliday with William
        Dufty.   Lancer, 1969.   pb $1.25
        RL: 5   IL: HS-adult   B
A frank and bitter book which tells the story of the famous
blues singer.   It is very popular on the bookmobile partly
because Miss Holliday never lost her sense of humor and
partly because she was so very honest.

1463   The Lady with the Lamp: The Story of Florence
        Nightingale (abr.), by Lee Wyndham.   Illus. by
        Mort Kunstler.   Scholastic, c1969.   pb $.60
        RL: 6   IL: 5-adult   *BS
An inspiring life of the woman who founded the career of
nursing.   Any book about nursing is very much in demand
and this one will be also.   See also Florence Nightingale
[1412] for her biography on an easier reading level.

1464   Langston Hughes: A Biography, by Milton Meltzer.

Crowell, c1968. $4.50
RL: 6   IL: 6-adult   SMP
This simple straight-forward life of the well known author
and poet has been quite popular.   It is gradually being displaced by Black Troubadour [1368], which seems with its
poems and pictures to involve the reader more.   Both books
are excellent.

1465   Lena, by Lena Horne and Richard Schickel.   New
        American Library, Signet, c1965.   pb $.75
RL: Adult   IL: HS-adult   BM
The autobiography of the Brooklyn black singer--her struggles
and accomplishments.   This is a frustrating book as so many
older people want to read it and find the print too small.   It
would be popular in a large print edition.   Photographs.

1466   Life and Words of John F. Kennedy, by James Playsted
        Wood.   Scholastic, c1964.   pb $.75
RL: 6   IL: 5-adult   BS
Well-written biography with many photographs and quotations.
The large picture-book-like appearance of this book and the
one below attracts a wide age range.   Poor readers can be
led from this to 1459.

1467   Life and Words of Martin Luther King, Jr., by Ira
        Peck.   Scholastic, c1968.   pb $.60
RL: Adult   IL: JH-adult   BSMP
This life of Martin Luther King has enough pictures in it to
interest poor readers.   It also has excerpts from several of
his speeches including the "I Have a Dream" speech.   A good
read-aloud to get poorer readers going, it is popular with
adults.

1468   Lift Every Voice: The Lives of W. E. B. DuBois,
        Mary Church Terrell, Booker T. Washington, James
        Weldon Johnson, by Dorothy Sterling and Benjamin
        Quarles.   Doubleday, Zenith, c1965. $3.75 (pb
        $1.75)
RL: 6   IL: 6-adult   BSMP
The contributions of three black men and one black woman to
the struggle for civil rights from the end of the Civil War to
the 1960's is shown in this collective biography.   It is much
in demand by high school students and adults.

1469   The Long Black Schooner, by Emma Gelders Sterne.
        Illus. by David Lockhart.   Scholastic, 1953.   pb
        $.75

RL: 6   IL: 5-adult   BSMP
This excellent book (with a dramatic picture on the cover) is
borrowed by elementary children who cannot read it and ig-
nored, because of its format, by the older students and adults
who would find it fascinating. It is a gripping and authentic
account of the successful mutiny on the slave ship Amistad,
the subsequent trial in New Haven of the mutineers and their
final return to Africa. Very popular with adults who are
persuaded to read it.

1470 A Long Time Growing, by Carmelo Melendez and
     R. E. Simon with Emmett Smith. Childrens Press,
     An Open Door Book, c1970. $3.50 (pb $.75)
     RL: 4-5   IL: 6-adult   *BSMP
Carmelo Melendez, an X-ray technician in Chicago, looks
back to his poverty stricken childhood in Puerto Rico and
tells the reader the story of his life thus far. Photographs.

1471 Look to the Light Side, by Dave Stallworth with R.
     Conrad Stein. Childrens Press, An Open Door Book,
     c1970. $3.50 (pb $.75)
     RL: 4-5   IL: 6-adult   *BSMP
Dave Stallworth, the basketball player for the Knicks had
everything going for him until he had a serious heart attack
and was told he could never play again. This is the story
of his extraordinary recovery and comeback, ending by his
rejoining the Knicks in 1969. Especially valuable for young
people with health problems. Photographs.

1472 The Lord Is My Shepherd, by Truman Gibson with L.
     Brownlee and M. Reuben. Childrens Press, An
     Open Door Book, c1970. $3.50 (pb $.75)
     RL: 4-5   IL: 5-adult   *BSMP
Truman Gibson grew up in poverty and went to a one room
school but managed to earn his own tuition and graduate first
from Atlanta and then from Harvard in the class of 1908. He
has been a leader in the insurance field. Photographs.

1473 Louis Armstrong, by Kenneth Richards. Illus. by
     Bob Brunton. Childrens Press, People of Destiny
     Series, c1967. $4.50
     RL: 6   IL: 5-adult   *SMP
This biography of the great jazz musician is more difficult
reading than Trumpeter's Tale [1582] and less vividly written.
It is worth having for the abundant illustrations which will
whet the appetite of the many non-readers who are interested
in Armstrong. It is also more up-to-date and covers his
later career.

1474   Malcolm X, by Arnold Adoff.   Illus. by J. Wilson.
        Crowell, c1970. $3.75
        RL: 3   IL: 2-JH   *BSM
This straightforward life of Malcolm X for beginning readers
is well done.   It will interest older non-readers and could be
a stepping stone for them to his autobiography.

1475   Malcolm X: The Man and His Times, edited by J. H.
        Clarke.   Macmillan, 1969. $6.95   (Collier Books,
        $1.95)
        RL: Varied-mainly adult   IL: HS-adult   BM
Malcolm X--who he was, what he stood for, where he was
going--given in a series of articles by a number of people
who knew him well and were deeply affected by him.   A fascinating compilation which is too difficult reading for most
of our clientele but is much borrowed just the same.   Anything on or by Malcolm X is popular.

1476   Man Against the Elements: Adolphus W. Greely, by
        Irving Werstein.   Washington Square Press, Archway,
        c1960.   pb $.50
        RL: 5-6   IL: 5-adult   BS
Greely was a very courageous and competent citizen whose
adventures ranged from officering one of the first negro regi-
ments in the Civil War to battles in the Indian Wars, Spanish-
American wars, Arctic expeditions and the creation of the
U. S. Weather Service.

1477   Manchild in the Promised Land, by Claude Brown.
        New American Library, Signet, 1965. $6.95
        (pb $.95)
        RL: 7-adult   IL: 5-adult   BSMP
The absorbing autobiography of a black boy growing up in
Harlem.   Even young children reach for this one.   One of
the most popular books on the bookmobile and in the high
school programs of the School Volunteers.

1478   Marco Polo, by Charles P. Graves.   Illus. by John
        Ferni.   Scholastic, c1963.   pb $.60
        RL: 4-5   IL: 4-adult   BS
This life of Marco Polo is full of excitement and much liked
by junior high and high school students.   In Reading Help programs, it can open doors to reading on a more mature level.
On the bookmobile, it is borrowed by high school students and
adults.

1479   Martin Luther King: Fighter for Freedom, by Edward

Preston.   Doubleday, Semaphore, Signal, c1968.
$3. 50   (pb $1. 45)
     RL: 4   IL: 4-adult   BSMP
A straightforward life of the great leader by a newspaper
correspondent who took an active part in the Civil Rights
movement in the South.   Valuable to have since the easy
reading and the adult format make this biography attractive
to a wide age range.   Illustrated with photographs.

1480   Martin Luther King, Jr. , by Don McKee.   Putnam,
       c1969. $3. 95
     RL: 6-7   IL: 6-adult   BSMP
An interesting life of Martin Luther King by a veteran
news reporter who covered many of the marches and confrontations he describes.   The format is adult.   This has
more content and is more difficult reading than 1479.   It
would have benefited from photographs.

1481   Martin Luther King, Jr. : A Picture Story, by Margaret
       Boone-Jones.   Illus. by R. Scott.   Childrens Press,
       c1968. $2. 75
     RL: 3   IL: Read aloud-4   BSMP
A very simple and simplistic well-illustrated life of Martin
Luther King.   This is very, very popular with children.

1482   Martin Luther King: The Peaceful Warrior, by Ed
       Clayton.   Illus. by David Hodges.   Prentice Hall,
       1964, c1968. $3. 95 (Washington Square Press,
       Archway, c1969, pb $. 50)
     RL: 5   IL: 4-JH   BSMP
This excellent life of Martin Luther King by an old friend of
his, has been recently revised and reissued to bring it up to
date.   As a hardcover book with a young format this did not
do well on the bookmobile.   In its new paperback guise, it
is very popular.   Both this book and number 1479 fill a large
gap between 1481 for young children and the other adult biographies.

1483   Matthew Henson, Arctic Hero, by Sheldon Ripley.
       Illus. by E. Harper Johnson.   Houghton-Mifflin,
       Piper, 1966. $2. 20
     RL: 5   IL: 5-adult   *SMP
An excellent biography of the Arctic explorer in simple language.   Would be very popular with many age groups in paperback.   See also 1391 and 1580.

1484   Meet Abraham Lincoln, by Barbara Cary.   Illus. by

J. Davis.   Random House, Step-Up Books, 1965.
$1.95
RL: 3-4   IL: 3-JH   BS
A straightforward life of Lincoln midway in difficulty between
1330 and 1331.   It has many pictures and is very popular
with elementary school children.   This series is very popular since there is a real demand for easy biography; both
the bookmobile staff and the School Volunteers say, "if only
we could get these books in paperback."

1485   Meet George Washington, by Joan Heilbroner.   Illus.
       by V. Mays.   Random House, Step-Up Books,
       1965. $1.95
       RL: 3-4   IL: 3-JH   BS
A well-written life of our first president.   This books seems
easier than 1332 because of its large print and many pictures
but actually the two books are very similar.   We use this
one with younger children and the former with older slow
readers because its format is less childish.

1486   Meigs Tower, by Joseph Yokley with Michael Reuben
       and Emmett Smith.   Childrens Press, An Open Door
       Book, c1970. $3 (pb $.75)
       RL: 4-5   IL: 4-adult   *BSMP
A real-life account of a young man from the ghetto who is
now an air traffic controller at a field near Chicago.   The
book does not minimize the hurdles that prejudice put in his
way nor the strains and problems of his job.   An honest,
well-balanced and interesting story.   Photographs.

1487   Mighty Hard Road: The Story of Cesar Chavez, by
       James Terzian and Kathryn Cramer.   Doubleday,
       Semaphore, c1970. $3.50 (pb $1.75)
       RL: 5   IL: 5-adult   *BSMP
An unusually fine biography, in direct easy-to-read language
but on an adult level, of the man who is unionizing the migrant workers and is leading their demands for decent treatment.

1488   Mrs. Mike, by Nancy and Benedict Freedman, c1947.
       Berkley, 1968, pb $.75
       RL: 5-6   IL: 5-adult   BS
The true story of a sixteen-year-old girl who went to live in
the wilderness with her husband in 1910.   Very popular with
high school girls and women.

1489   Mission Possible, by Zenolia Leak with George Elrick

and Emmett Smith.   Childrens Press, An Open Door
Book, c1970. $3.50   (pb $.75)
RL: 4-5   IL: 6-adult   *BSMP
Zenolia Leak's mother always encouraged her in her school
work and public speaking but she had a long struggle to get
where she is today--an instructor of reservations at American
Airlines at a good salary.   An unhappy marriage and other
events make this a dramatic book.   Photographs.

1490   Moving On Up: The Mahalia Jackson Story, by Mahalia
       Jackson and Evan M. Wylie.   Hawthorn, c1966.
       $5.95   (Avon pb $.75)
       RL: 6   IL: 6-adult   *BSMP
The autobiography of the great gospel singer who became
known both for her voice and her integrity throughout the
country before her recent death.

1491   My Life with Martin Luther King, Jr., by Coretta
       Scott King.   Holt, Rinehart & Winston, c1970.
       $6.95   (Avon pb $1.50)
       RL: 7   IL: 6-adult   *BSMP
A simply told and deeply moving account of Mr. and Mrs.
King's life together.   Their story is an inspiration to self-
sacrifice.   This book will be very popular with adults, especially women.

1492   My Lord, What a Morning, by Marian Anderson.
       Viking, c1956. $5.95   (Avon Books, 1957, pb $.60)
       RL: 6   IL: JH-adult   BM
The great singer's autobiography;   popular with adult women
who remember her.   Many children have never heard of her.
Her life was a struggle for excellence and success but the
book is not very dramatic.

1493   My Own Back Yard, by Arthur Cavanaugh.   Adapted by
       James Madigan.   Illus. by Norman Nodel.   McGraw-
       Hill, c1970.   Reading Shelf II Series. $1.60
       RL: 4-5   IL: 6-adult   *BS
A curious story (apparently autobiographical) of a boy whose
confidence was shattered in school and who loses his faith as
a result.   Finally, a devout and loving girl gives him back
both faith and confidence.   This book should help many unself-
confident youngsters.   However, it is very closely tied to
Catholicism which may limit its usefulness for those of other
faiths.

1494   My Tribe, by J. C. "Lone Eagle" Vasquez with R. C.

Stein.   Childrens Press, An Open Door Book, c1970.
$3. 50 (pb $. 75)
          RL: 4-5   IL: 6-adult   *BSMP
Joe Vasquez made up his mind to be a pilot when he saw his
first plane at the age of seven.   There were many years of
struggle against poverty and discrimination but in the end he
became a pilot and is now the small business administrator
for the Hughes Aircraft Co.   He is also president of the Los
Angeles Indian Center and helps his fellow Indians to find jobs
and found businesses.   His is a story to be proud of.   Photographs.

1495   Narrative of the Life of Frederick Douglass, written by
          himself.   New American Library, Signet, c1845. (pb
          1968, $. 50)
          RL: 7   IL: 6-adult   BMP
Douglass' own story of his life is still the most moving account of all.   It is difficult reading but many junior high and
high school students will stretch for it after they have read
his story in a simpler version.   See also 1417, 1418 and 855
and There Once Was a Slave [858].

1496   Nat Love, Negro Cowboy, by Harold W. Felton.   Illus.
          by David Hodges.   Dodd, c1969. $3. 95
          RL: 4   IL: 4-JH   *SMP
Cowboys and Westerns are out of favor right now but even
so, most boys will like this exciting true story of Nat Love,
a black cowboy who lived through many adventures.   It is
interestingly written and the illustrations are excellent.

1497   Nat Turner, by Judith Berry Griffin.   Illus. by Leo
          Carty.   Coward, McCann, c1970. $3. 95
          RL: 3-4   IL: 3-adult   *BSMP
An imaginative and convincing biography of the leader of the
famous slave revolt in a young format.   Nat's feeling that
he was chosen by God is handled with sensitivity and great
stress is laid on the fact that he felt an obligation to free
his fellow slaves rather than flee to freedom by himself as
his father had done.   Since Nat felt that killing was justified
in the right cause, it is a frightening book to give young children unless it is balanced with the lives of others who did
not feel that way.   The issue makes for good discussion with
groups of teenagers and young adults.   It is certainly relevant today.

1498   Negro Doctor, by Helen Buckler.   Adapted by Warren
          Halliburton.   Illus. by Norman Nodel.   McGraw-Hill,

Reading Shelf Series II, c1954.   (pb, 1968, $1.60)
RL: 4-5   IL: 4-adult   *BSMP
The inspiring biography of Dr. Daniel Hale Williams who
overcame extraordinary obstacles to become a surgeon and
who was the first man to operate on the human heart.

1499   The Negro Pilgrimage in America, by C. Eric Lincoln.
       Praeger, c1969. $5.95   (Bantam, Pathfinder, pb
       $.75)
       RL: 6-7   IL: 6-adult   BSMP
This history of the black people in America by a noted black
historian is especially noteworthy for the profusion of its illustrations.   Some are drawings, some are photographs;   all
are contemporary to the time described.   The writing is
clear and direct and the price is right.   This book would
sell extremely well in black areas.   It was first published
in 1967 and then reissued in a revised and amplified form
in 1969.   It is brief in its discussion of contemporary affairs
but it covers an incredible amount of history in its 172 pages.
It has a very useful chronology of black history at the end.
The paperback version has been very popular with teenagers
and young adults.   Libraries would be well-advised to carry
the hardcover version as well since the print in paper is very
small.

1500   New Fields, by Chester Thompson with G. C. Skipper
       and R. E. Simon, Jr.   Childrens Press, c1970.
       $3 (pb $.75)
       RL: 4-5   IL: 5-adult   *BSMP
As Chester Thompson says in this book, he's come a long
way from an Arkansas cotton patch.   He is now a systems
engineer with IBM.   Although he was very poor in his boyhood, his family life was so good that he feels he had a happy
childhood which is a pleasant change from many of these
biographies.   Photographs.

1501   Nickels & Dimes (The Story of F. W. Woolworth), by
       Nina Brown Baker.   Illus. by Douglas Gorsline.
       Harcourt, Brace, Voyager, c1954.   pb $.50
       RL, 5   IL: 5-HS   BS
Everyone knows Woolworth's and many find the story of the
man who founded it after many failures as encouraging as the
story of Bruce and the Spider.

1502   Nigger, by Dick Gregory with Robert Lipsyte.   Simon
       and Schuster, Pocket Books, c1964.   pb $.75
       RL: 6   IL: 6-adult   BS

The moving autobiography of the man who is both an outstanding comedian and one of the moral leaders of this country.   This is also available in an abridged and adapted version (see below).

1503   Nigger, by Dick Gregory with Robert Lipsyte.   Adapted
         by B. Dudley.   McGraw Hill, Reading Shelf Series.
         $1.72
         RL: 4-5   IL: 4-adult   BS
An abridged and adapted version of 1502.

1504   No Hablo Inglés, by Betsy Standerford with R. Conrad
         Stein.   Childrens Press, An Open Door Book, c1970.
         $3   (pb $.75)
         RL: 4-5   IL: 5-adult   *BSMP
This book will be especially valuable for Spanish-speaking
students.   Betsy Standerford was a Mexican Indian who had
a very difficult time both learning English and acquiring self-
confidence.   Now she is on top of both problems and as a
personnel worker is helping other people conquer the difficulties she confronted.   Photographs.

1505   Nobody Promised Me, by John Mack with Don Arthur
         Torgerson and Emmett Smith.   Childrens Press,
         An Open Door Book, c1970. $3   (pb $.75)
         RL: 4-5   IL: 6-adult   *BSMP
John Mack and his family have suffered very badly from un-
just treatment at the hands of whites.   However, by dint of
great perseverance and courage he has worked his way
through college, gotten a master's degree and is the head of
the Black Studies Department at Chicago City College.   Photographs.

1506   North Star Shining, by Hildegarde Hoyt Swift.   Illus.
         by Lynd Ward.   Morrow, c1947. $5.95
         RL: 7   IL: JH-adult   *SMP
Subtitled "A Pictorial History of the American Negro," this
book has a picture on one page and a description of some
facet of black history opposite.   It is especially valuable for
its portrayal of the role Afro-Americans have played in all
of the wars America has fought.

1507   On My Own, by Charles Davis with R. E. Simon, Jr.
         Childrens Press, An Open Door Book, c1970. $3.50
         (pb $.75)
         RL: 4-5   IL: 6-adult   *BSMP
Charles Davis was lucky enough to have a devoted father and

mother. He was unlucky enough to lose them both by the
time he was eight and to lose all his older relatives by the
time he graduated from school. However, his family had
given him determination and faith and he has managed, after
working on "The Chicago Defender" to found his own successful public relations firm. This firm serves many black
owned businesses in the Chicago area.

1508   The Open Door Series.   Children's Press, c1970.
           $3. 50 each   (pb $. 75)
This series of thirty titles is composed of autobiographies of
thirty minority group men and women who have achieved a
measure of success in life. When I read where they started
and what they mostly had to overcome to get where they are,
I feel that it is an enormous measure of success. I also
feel the most enormous respect for the authors. That is
one reason I feel that these books should be in private and
suburban schools where the students have so much easier a
life. Another reason is that many students have no idea how
much discrimination there still is in American life. If they
read these true life stories, they will want to fight to see
that justice prevails. Minority group students will be inspired by these life stories and will feel pride in their race.
There are many different occupations represented among the
different stories. At the end of each book there are two or
three pages of career information about the occupation of the
author. In addition to all the other virtues of this series,
most of the books are vivid and dramatic. They are easy
to get into and have a lot of dialogue. The photographs add
a great deal to the authenticity of the stories and the pictures
of the authors as children are often beguiling. The minorities
represented are Puerto Ricans, Blacks, Chicanos, and Indians. I felt proud to be an American after reading these
books.

1509   Out from Under, by James D. Atwater and Ramón E.
           Ruiz. Illus. by Paul Hogarth. Doubleday, Zenith,
           c1969. $3. 75   (pb $1. 45)
           RL: 6   IL: 5-adult   *MP
This book tells the proud story of Benito Juárez and Mexico's
struggle for independence. It is an important book for Mexican-Americans and for the people in the states where many
Mexican-Americans live, some of whom know little about
their neighbors' struggle for freedom.

1510   PT 109, by Robert J. Donovan.   Fawcett Pub. , Crest,
           1961.   pb $. 75

RL: 6-7   IL: 6-adult   BS
This story of John F. Kennedy's adventures in World War II
is still very popular with older boys and adults.

1511 Passage to the Golden Gate, by Daniel and Samuel Chu.
      Doubleday, Zenith, c1967. $3.75 (pb $1.45)
      RL: 6   IL: 6-adult   *BSMP
A clear and simple account of the history of the Chinese in
America to 1910, this book will interest anyone who cares
about American history. It will, of course, have special
appeal to Chinese-Americans. It could well be used as a
sequel to Willie Wong-American [1129] to interest Chinese-
American older non-readers in more difficult books on both
Chinese and American history. See also 1380.

1512 People Are My Profession, by Herbert Hannahs with
      R. Conrad Stein. Children's Press, An Open Door
      Book, c1970. $3.50 (pb $.75)
      RL: 4-5   IL: 6-adult   *BSMP
Herb Hannahs spent five years in a TB hospital when he was
a child and had a lonely time for several years afterward because he was so frail. Perhaps this is why he has always
wanted to help people. He is a case worker in the Cook
County Department of Public Aid specializing in helping ex-
prisoners. Photographs.

1513 People That Walk in Darkness--A History of the Black
      People in America, by J. W. Schulte Nordholt.
      Ballantine Books, Inc. , 1968. $1.65
      RL: Adult   IL: 6-adult   *BSMP
This is a very unusual history of black Americans. It is by
a Dutch scholar who brings out matters not necessarily
stressed in other histories. For example, his discussion
of the economics of slavery and what cotton did to the soil
is an aspect often barely mentioned in some histories.
The book is rich in quotations from source materials, the
writings of contemporary observers and from black literature.
Although the language may be difficult for poor readers in
some sections, it is vivid enough for readers to stretch for
in others and there are many sections which could make exciting reading aloud by a teacher or tutor to a group of students.

1514 Pictorial History of the Negro in America, by Langston
      Hughes and Milton Meltzer. Crown, c1963, c1969.
      $5.95
      RL: 6   IL: Universal   BSMP

In 340 richly illustrated pages, this book covers its subject
including some African history and much American history
and a great deal, of course, about the contributions black
people have made to this country's freedom, prosperity and
the arts. This book has one of the lowest reading levels I
have seen for a book of this kind (in contrast to many of the
paperbacks which cover the same ground) and the many illustrations (often two or three to a page) make its story acces-
sible to people who cannot read the text. This is a highly
motivating book. Many people who would like to do not dare
to borrow it because they feel it is too valuable for them to
risk losing or damaging it. Others who did borrow it would
keep it for weeks, renewing it each week and finally reluc-
tantly returning it. The illustrations for this book come
from prints, engravings and photographs--mainly contemporary,
and took four years to collect. A must for every school and
library in the country. A new edition of this popular book
has just come out. The many illustrations make the history
in this book come alive for all ages.

1515   The Picture Life of Martin Luther King, Jr. , by
        Margaret B. Young. Grolier, Watts, c1968. $3. 50
        RL: 2-3   IL: 2-JH   BSMP
This is the easiest-to-read of all the lives of Martin Luther
King. It is a very well done simple biography of the famous
leader. The photographic illustrations are excellent and the
whole book is a very good job.

1516   The Picture Life of Ralph J. Bunche, by Margaret B.
        Young. Grolier, Watts, c1968. $3. 50
        RL: 2-3   IL: 3-6   BSMP
This picture life of Ralph Bunche, one of America's greatest
peace makers, is a straightforward account of a man America can be proud of. It is illustrated with photographs and
should stimulate interest in the United Nation's peace making
attempts.

1517   Pioneer Germ Fighters, by Navin Sullivan. Illus. by
        Eric Fraser. Atheneum, c1962. $3. 59 (Scholastic,
        1966, pb $. 60)
        RL: 6   IL: 5-adult   BS
Ten biographies of famous germ fighters ranging from Leeu-
wenhoek to Salk. Popular with junior high and high school
students who are interested in science.

1518   Pioneers and Patriots, by Lavinia Dobler and Edgar A.
        Toppin. Illus. by Coleen Browning. Doubleday,

Zenith, c1965. $3.75   (pb $1.45)
RL: 6   IL: 5-adult   BSMP
An interesting collection of six little known but outstanding
black Americans of the Revolutionary era. They are Peter
Salem, Jean Baptiste de Sable, Phyllis Wheatley, Benjamin
Banneker, Paul Cuffe and John Chairs. Many illustrations.
This book was popular immediately with adults and is grow-
ing more popular with high school students because of the
growing interest in black history.

1519   Pioneers in Protest, by Lerone Bennett, Jr. Johnson
         Publishing Co. , c1968. $5.95 (Penguin, Pelican,
         $1.25)
         RL: 7   IL: JH-adult   *BSMP
The story of twenty men and women who pioneered for justice
for black people, this collection has biographies of a number
of people who deserve fame but are not generally well-known:
Prince Hall, Richard Allen, S. E. Cornish, J. B. Russworm,
and others. The author also, of course, includes the famous
characters as well--Harriet Tubman, Sojourner Truth, and
others. I am glad he included whites as well as blacks for
the generation that is now being introduced to black history
are often handed books which omit any mention of men like
Phillips or Coffin or Garrison or Sumner. The writing is
vivid and exciting. It would be great to see this book in
paperback on an easier reading level such as that of the
Semaphore books.

1520   Puerto Rican Patriot--The Life of Luis Muñoz Rivera,
         by Mack Reynolds. Illus. by Arthur Shilstone.
         Macmillan, Crowell-Collier, c1969. $3.95
         RL: 6-7   IL: 6-adult   *BSMP
This life of Luis Muñoz Rivera begins with an excellent brief
history of Puerto Rico from its discovery by Columbus to
1859, the date of the hero's birth. Muñoz fought many years
for Puerto Rican self-government while the island was a
Spanish colony and then had to start all over again when it
was ceded to America after the Spanish-American War. He
died at the age of fifty-seven, having never achieved his goal
but having done so much to clear the way for those who came
after, that he is considered the liberator of Puerto Rico.

1521   The Quality of Courage, by Mickey Mantle. Doubleday,
         c1964. $4.50 (Bantam, Pathfinder, 1964, pb $.60)
         RL: 6   IL: 6-adult   BS
An excellent series of short accounts of people showing bravery, mostly drawn from Mantle's baseball experiences. Very

popular with a wide age range.

1522   The Quiet Rebels, by Philip Sterling and Maria Brau.
       Illus. by Tracy Sugarman.   Doubleday,   Zenith,
       c1968. $3.75   (pb $1.45)
       RL: 6-7   IL: 5-adult   BSMP
This book tells the story of four Puerto Rican leaders: José
Celso Barbosa, Luis Muñoz Rivera, José de Diego and Luis
Muñoz Marín.   It is quite hard reading but is well liked by
Puerto Rican high school students and by adult Puerto Ricans.

1523   R. F. K.   1925-1968, by James F. Hudson.   Scholastic,
       c1969.   pb $.60
       RL: 6-adult   BM
The life of Robert Kennedy told in words and many photos.

1524   R. F. K. : His Life and Death, edited by J. Jacobs
       and R. N. Witker.   Dell, c1968.   pb $.95
       RL: 6-7   IL: 6-adult   BSM
This straightforward biography is a fuller one than the above.
It has 64 pages of photographs and can be and is enjoyed by
people who cannot read the book.   It is also a good conversation piece especially in Bedford-Stuyvesant where his legacy,
the Bedford-Stuyvesant Restoration Corporation is still very
actively at work.

1525   R. F. K. : The Last Knight, by Lawrence Swinburne.
       A Pyramid Hi-Lo Original, c1969.   pb $.60
       RL: 5-6   IL: 5-adult   BSM
The life of Robert Kennedy told by an author who has specialized in simplifying the reading level of many books.   It is
direct and interesting and, in spite of the subtitle, quite objective in presenting the facts.   A valuable book with, however, no pictures.

1526   The Raw Pearl, by Pearl Bailey.   Harcourt, Brace,
       c1968. $5.75   (Pocket Books, 1969, pb $.95)
       RL: 6   IL: JH-adult   BM
Pearl Bailey, the courageous and successful entertainer, is
a heroine to a great many Afro-Americans and her autobiography is very popular.

1527   The Road from West Virginia, by Gail Hardin with
       R. Conrad Stein.   Children's Press, An Open Door
       Book, c1970. $3 (pb $.75)
       RL: 4-5   IL: 5-adult   *BSMP
Gail Hardin grew up in a company town in West Virginia.

Times were hard and she dropped out of school at fourteen.
Now with three small children of her own, she works in a
factory and goes to night school. Her husband encourages
her and both are working to improve their community, a section of Chicago called Uptown. Photographs.

1528 Rocket Genius, by Charles Spain Verral. Illus. by
      Paul Frame. Scholastic, c1963. pb $.50
      RL: 5-6   IL: 5-adult   BS
A not very exciting life of Robert Goddard who invented
rocketry and has been called the father of the Space Age.
We carry it since I have seen no other on this reading level
and he has certainly influenced the course of the world.
Quiet boys of scientific bent borrow it.

1529 Run for Your Life, by Jim Ellis with Don Arthur
      Torgerson and R. E. Simon, Jr. Children's Press,
      An Open Door Book, c1970. $3.50 (pb $.75)
      RL: 4-5   IL: 6-adult   *BSMP
Jim Ellis hated school but his high school football coach persuaded him to stick with it and go on to college. After college and a four year stint in the Army, Jim played pro football and studied at the same time for a master's degree.
After seven years of that he decided his people needed black
teachers more than pro football players and quit to teach
school. He is now a community social worker and assistant
Director of an Urban Progress Center. Photographs.

1530 Runaway Slave, by Ann McGovern. Illus. by R. M.
      Powers. Four Winds, Scholastic, c1965. $2.95
      (pb $.60)
      RL: 3-4   IL: 3-adult   BSMP
This simple account of Harriet Tubman's life is deeply moving. We have had senior citizens read it with excitement.
However, it would do much better in an older format as many
assume its contents would only interest a young child.

1531 Satchmo, by Louis Armstrong. New American Library,
      Signet, c1954. pb $.95
      RL: 5-6   IL: JH-adult   *BM
The great trumpeter tells the story of his early life with
gusto and enthusiasm. The street language and frankness
may bother some people but he clearly was a very good person. The book does not duplicate two other biographies,
1473 and 1582, since it only covers his early years before
he met with success.

1532 Secrets of the Past, by Eva Knox Evans and Dick
      Kohfield. Western Publishing Co., Golden Press,
      c1965. OP
      RL: 6-7   IL: 5-HS   BS
The story of archaeology written in simple vivid language.
The many exciting drawings and photographs in this book appeal to the reader and stimulate an interest in history even
in those for whom the text is too difficult.

1533 Seventeen Black Artists, by Elton C. Fax. Dodd,
      c1971. $7.95
      RL: 6-7   IL: JH-adult   *SMP
After a chapter in which the author gives a brief review of
black art in America up to the present day, he presents
seventeen full biographical sketches. Of the seventeen artists, only three are familiar to me, thus perhaps proving
one of his points, i.e. that black artists have an especially
difficult time in finding chances to display their talent. There
is a center section with photographs of each of the artists
and one or two of their works. An interesting book.

1534 She Wanted to Read: The Story of Mary MacLeod
      Bethune, by Ella Kaiser Carruth. Illus. by Herbert
      McClure. Abingdon, c1966. $2.25 (Washington
      Square Press, Archway, pb $.50)
      RL: 5   IL: 4-adult   BSMP
A well written biography of the great black educator. Born
one of seventeen children of a sharecropper on a cotton
plantation, it was a miracle that Mary MacLeod Bethune got
any education. That she should go on to found a school which
became a college and finally become well enough known so
that President Franklin Roosevelt sought her advice would
seem incredible if the story had been invented. Most people
like happy endings and many students will find her story both
interesting and an inspiration.

1535 Shirley Chisholm, by Susan Brownmiller. Doubleday,
      Signal, c1970. $3.50 (Doubleday, Semaphore, pb
      $1.75)
      RL: 4   IL: 5-adult   *BSMP
A biography of the famous member of Congress from Brooklyn
which is fun to read and will be an inspiration to minority group
members and to girls who hope to make their mark in politics. A good book which cannot compare with Mrs. Chisholm's own book, Unbought and Unbossed [1583], which is,
however, more difficult to read and requires maturity to
appreciate.

1536 Sidney Poitier: The Long Journey, by Carolyn Ewers.
      New American Library, Signet, c1968. pb $.60
      RL: 5-6   IL: 6-adult   BSM
The biography of the famous movie star. He started life in
the Bahamas in such dire poverty that he says he is a com-
pulsive eater, he so often went hungry. A real rags to
riches story of a fine actor. Both he and the book are very
popular.

1537 Singers of the Blues, by Frank Surge. Lerner, c1969.
      $3.95
      RL: 5   IL: 5-adult   *SMP
An excellent account of the lives of seventeen famous blues
singers, most of them unknown to the youngsters of today.
However, there is a growing surge of interest in the early
blues singers perhaps due to the current movie vogue for
nostalgia. Illustrated by photographs.

1538 Six Black Masters of American Art, by Romare
      Bearden and Harry Henderson. Doubleday, Zenith,
      c1972. $3.95 (pb $1.95)
      RL: 5-6   IL: 4-adult   *BSMP
The biographies of Joshua Johnston, Robert S. Duncannon,
Henry O. Tanner, Horace Pippin, Augusta Savage and Jacob
Lawrence range in time from the Revolution to the present
day. Their stories are dramatic and inspiring. In addition
to many black and white reproductions of their work, there
are four pages of colored reproductions. A fine book which
will be very popular. There is a real hunger for art in the
inner cities.

1539 Soledad Brother: The Prison Letters of George Jack-
      son, by George Jackson. Introduction by Jean Geret.
      Coward McCann, Bantam, c1970. pb $1.50
      RL: 6-7   IL: JH-adult   *BM
This is a fascinating human document. It is the brief autobiography and letters from prison of George Jackson, the
California convict in the case where a judge and Jackson's
brother were killed in an attempt to snatch prisoners from
the courtroom. This is also the case which involves Angela
Davis and which has had deep repercussions all across the
country. The letters, starting in June 1964 and continuing
through August 9, 1970 constitute, among other things, an
extraordinary record of self-education and self-discipline.
When I first read this book, much of what Jackson said
seemed wild and fantastic. Now that he has been killed in
prison (whether rightly or wrongly) and now that his fellow

prisoners and Angela Davis have been found innocent by the courts, his charges seem to be more convincing.   This is an extraordinary book that was instantly popular in black neighborhoods and should be read by all who care about justice.

1540   So Many Detours, by Mallory Jones with Rick E.
       Simon, Jr.   Children's Press, An Open Door Book,
       c1970. $3   (pb $.75)
       RL: 4-5   IL: 5-adult   *BSMP
Every time Mallory Jones graduated from a school and thought he was on a straight road to success, something went wrong and he'd have to start over.   Now he is an owner of a MacDonald Food Franchise and seems to be really on his way.   Photographs.

1541   Somebody's Angel Child--The Story of Bessie Smith,
       by Carmen Moore.   Crowell, Women of America
       Series, c1970. $4.50
       RL: 6   IL: 6-adult   BSM
Young people of today have never heard of Bessie Smith, the Empress of the Blues, but her story is extraordinary enough to interest them anyway.   Illustrated with photographs.

1542   Somebody Up There Likes Me, by Rocky Graziano with
       Rowland Barber.   Simon and Schuster, Pocket Books,
       c1955.   pb $.50
       RL: 6-7   IL: 6-adult   BSMP
The moving story of a boy who started out with two left feet and at least two strikes against him but who wound up both famous and a good citizen.   Very popular with boys and adults.

1543   Someday I'm Going to Be Somebody, by John Dunham
       with Gene Klinger.   Children's Press, An Open
       Door Book, c1970. $3   (pb $.75)
       RL: 4-5   IL: 4-adult   *BSMP
John Dunham is now somebody, the Director of Computer Operations for the United States Savings and Loan League. He tells how he got to be somebody in a book which starts with his father's murder and his family's eviction from a three room flat which had neither heat nor electricity.   It's an inspiring story.   Photographs.

1544   Son of This Land, by Jerry Sine with Gene Klinger.
       Children's Press, An Open Door Book, c1970. $3
       (pb $.75)

RL: 4-5   IL: 5-adult   *BSMP
Jerry Sine's other name is White Beaver. His older brother
died in childhood because white hospitals would not take in
an Indian boy. He grew up proud of his Indian heritage and
has managed to blend the Indian and white worlds in his art.
He is a commercial artist in Chicago. Photographs.

1545 Soul On Ice, by Eldridge Cleaver. McGraw, c1968.
      $5.95 (Dell pb $1.95)
      RL: 7   IL: 6-adult   BSM
Autobiographical essays written in prison by one of the
founders of the Black Panther party, reveal his search for
identity and his thoughts about America. This book was instantly and overwhelmingly in demand by junior and senior
high school students and adults as soon as it came out. Even
from exile in Algeria, Cleaver seems to carry a lot of influence among the Panthers and his books still circulate well,
especially this one. However, books by other militants more
in the current public eye, i.e. LeRoi Jones, Bobby Seale and
Rap Brown are more in demand.

1546 Speaking Out, by Ada Deer with Rick E. Simon, Jr.
      Children's Press, An Open Door Book, c1970. $3
      (pb $.75)
      RL: 4-5   IL: 5-adult   *BSMP
Ada Deer is a Menominee Indian. She is also a successful
social worker and once won a beauty contest and a trip to
Hollywood. She is also a fighter for Indian rights and an
American to be proud of. She has a M.A. from Columbia
but is considering law school in order to be better equipped
to fight for her people. Photographs.

1547 A Special Bravery, by Johanna Johnston. Illus. by
      Ann Grifalconi. Dodd, c1967. $3.50 (Apollo
      Junior, pb $1.75)
      RL: 4   IL: 4-JH   BSMP
I include this book on the list because it is the only collection
of biographies of famous black people I have ever seen on
this reading level. It also has the virtue of including among
the fifteen stories, the stories of people whom many students
have never heard of such as James Forten and Box Brown.
However, the text is arranged on the page very confusingly
and it has bothered many children with whom I have used it.

1548 The Spy, the Lady, the Captain and the Colonel, by
      Richard Stiller. Scholastic, c1970. pb $1.65
      RL: 5-6   IL: 5-adult   BSMP

The spy was an ex-slave in the early Civil War days, the
lady was an ex-slave who was Mrs. Lincoln's dressmaker,
the Captain was Robert Smalls and the Colonel was Colonel
Higgenson, the gallant white Colonel of the first black regi-
ment in U.S. history. The book is a chapter out of American history, vividly and excitingly written and illustrated
with drawings and photographs.

1549 Stand Tall: The Lew Alcinder Story, by Phil Pepe.
      Grosset, c1970. $5.95
      RL: 5   IL: 6-adult   SMP
The story of the famous basketball player told by a sports
writer who has known him since the star was thirteen and
just starting his career. For basketball fans.

1550 Step-Up Books. Random House. $1.95 each.
      RL: 3-4   IL: 3-JH   BS
This is an excellent transition series between the reading
level of easy-to-read books and trade books for fourth and
fifth graders and bridges an important step in reading skills.
The print is large and well arranged on the page and there
is just the right amount of space devoted to illustrations.
As in any series, the quality varies. Meet Abraham Lincoln
and Meet George Washington are great favorites and very
well done. I disliked Meet John Kennedy and so did many
children. Most of the books are very popular. Both the
bookmobile staff and the School Volunteers say, "If only we
could get these in paperback!" There are twenty-one titles.

1551 The Storming of Fort Wagner, by Irving Werstein.
      Scholastic, c1970. pb $1.65
      RL: 6   IL: 6-adult   *BSMP
This book is subtitled Black Valor in the Civil War and it is
the story of the black soldiers, their valor and their treatment or unfortunately, sometimes their mistreatment. This
book gives both a sad and a glorious chapter of American
history. It has a great many dramatic contemporary illustrations.

1552 Stories About Abe Lincoln to Read Aloud, by LaVere
      Anderson. Illus. by Tony Tallarico. Grosset Read
      Aloud Wonder Book Series, c1965. $.49
      RL: 3-4   IL: Read aloud-JH   BS
A popular collection of short selections about a president
whom all of the children recognize and revere.

1553 Story of Daniel Boone, by William Cunningham. Illus.

by Wayne Blickenstaff.   Scholastic, c1952.   pb $.60
RL: 5   IL: 4-6   BS
Abridged from The Real Book about Daniel Boone, this is an
adequate biography but not as exciting or well done as the
life of Boone in the Childhood of Famous Americans series.
See 1379 for the same age group.

1554   The Story of Eleanor Roosevelt, by Margaret Davidson.
       Scholastic, c1968.   pb $.60
       RL: 4-5   IL: 5-adult   *BS
This warm, eloquent biography will be chiefly popular on the
bookmobile with adults who still remember what a friend Mrs.
Roosevelt was.   However, I hope the young will also learn
about her.   The appearance of this book is to be highly com-
mended as it will appeal to all ages.   It is illustrated by
photographs.

1555   The Story of Florence Nightingale, by Margaret Leigh-
       ton.   Illus. by Corinne Dillon.   Grosset, Tempo,
       c1952, 1966.   pb OP
       RL: 5   IL: 5-adult   BS
A good easy biography of an interesting character.   This has
larger print than many of the paperbacks which makes for
easier reading.   See also The Lady with the Lamp [1463]
and Florence Nightingale [1412].

1556   The Story of Helen Keller, by Lorena A. Hickok.
       Grosset & Dunlap, Signature, 1958. $2.95
       (Tempo pb $.60)
       RL: 5   IL: 5-adult   BS
The story of Helen Keller's triumph over her handicaps is
very much in demand by girls especially those in fifth grade
through junior high.   Sometimes this book will lead them on
to her autobiography.   See 1558, below.

1557   The Story of John Paul Jones, by Iris Vinton.   Illus.
       by Edward A. Wilson.   Grosset, c1953. $2.95
       (Scholastic, Illus. by David Lockhart, pb $.60)
       RL: 5   IL: 5-HS   BS
This is an excellent book but John Paul Jones seems very
remote to New York City boys, most of whom have never
seen the sea although they live in one of the world's great
seaports.   We carry it for variety and an occasional history
buff.

1558   The Story of My Life, by Helen Keller.   Scholastic,
       c1967.   pb $.50

RL: 6-7   IL: 5-adult   *BS
With a vivid introduction by an author who is also blind
(Robert Russell) this new edition of the autobiography of the
famous girl who was both blind and deaf seems especially appealing. It does not duplicate the biography, 1556 above,
since Miss Keller wrote it in her sophomore year at college
and it therefore covers only her early life.

1559   The Story of Phillis Wheatley, by Shirley Graham.
       Illus. by Robert Burns. J. Messner, c1949. $3.34
       (Washington Square Press, Archway, c1969, pb $.50)
       RL: 6   IL: 6-adult   *BSMP
The story of the black poet who wrote poems in praise of
Washington and the Revolution. Her poetry is unlikely to
appeal to modern students but they will be interested in her
life which ended tragically.

1560   The Story of the Atom, by Mae B. and Ira M. Free-
       man. Random, Gateway Book, c1960. $2.95
       RL: 6   IL: 6-adult   *BSMP
A valuable book by two excellent writers who have a gift for
simple explanations of complicated subjects. The price is
right also.

1561   The Story of the Ice Age, by Rose Wyler and Gerald
       Ames. Harper, c1956. $3.79 (Scholastic pb OP)
       RL: 5   IL: 5-adult   BS
Lunar exploration seems also to have stimulated an interest
in the earth's history. This well told story of the ice age
is very popular.

1562   The Story of the Negro, by Arna Bontemps. Illus. by
       Raymond Lufkin. Knopf, 1958. $3.95
       RL: 6-7   IL: 6-adult   BSMP
Many new books on black history and African history and
slavery have appeared lately but this book which was first
published in 1948 and last revised in 1962, is still very well
worth reading. It tells the story of the black man from the
days of the early Ethiopians to modern times. In simple
language, it traces the story of slavery, the Civil War and
Reconstruction era and brings the tale of the Negro down to
modern times and the Montgomery bus boycott. Although it
is not a long book, it told me facts I hadn't known before in
a field where I have read a good deal. The black and white
illustrations are very dramatic and I found the book a truly
exciting one. I am sure anyone, from sixth grade on
through adult, would find this book interesting and parts of
it truly inspiring.

1563   The Story of Thomas Alva Edison, by Mickie Compere.
       Illus. by Jerome Moriarity.   Scholastic, Four Winds,
       c1964. $2.95 (pb $.60)
       RL, 2-3   IL: 2-6   BS
Subtitled: Inventor, the Wizard of Menlo Park, this is a
good and truly easy-to-read biography of the man who invented
things every family uses. Relevant and popular. There is
also an excellent biography of Edison in the Discovery Series
[1394].

1564   The Story of Winston Churchill, by Alida S. Malkus.
       Illus. by H. B. Vestal.   Grosset, Signature, c1957.
       $2.95 (Tempo pb $.50)
       RL: 5-6   IL: 6-adult   BS
Very well written and exciting biography. One boy in Harlem
said to me of this book (after he had read it), "I want this
book so bad I'd pay $1.50 for it." I couldn't tell him where
in Harlem he could buy it nor could the publisher.

1565   The Strange Case of James Earl Ray, by Clay Blair,
       Jr. Bantam, c1969. pb OP
       RL: Adult   IL: JH-adult   B
The sad and curious story of Martin Luther King's assassin.
Repetitive and hastily written, it nevertheless has a real fascination. The book is very inconclusive as to whether Ray
was a loner. Virtually all the bookmobile patrons regard
him as a tool and almost a victim.

1566   Stride Toward Freedom, by Martin Luther King, Jr.
       Harper Perennial, c1958. $4.95 (pb $.75)
       RL: 6-7   IL: 6-adult   BSMP
This straightforward and simple account of the Montgomery
boycott is an exciting one indeed and should be read by every
American. So many people speak of Malcolm X and Martin
Luther King. How many have actually read what they have
experienced and then written about? I found King's account
of his reactions at being put in jail for the first of many
times deeply moving and so did the people with whom I
worked.

1567   Sugar Ray, by Sugar Ray Robinson with Dave Anderson.
       New American Library, Signet, c1970. pb $.95
       RL: 5-6   IL: 6-adult   BSM
The fascinating story of the boxer who rose from poverty to
make and squander $4,000,000. His story of how he tried
to make a comeback reminds one painfully of the prize-
fighter has-been in Requiem for a Heavyweight [1249]. This

autobiography is a disarming book which has been very popular.

1568 Susie King Taylor: Civil War Nurse, by Simeon Booker.
      McGraw-Hill, Black Legacy Series, 1969. $4.33
      RL: 6   IL: JH & HS   BSMP
It is very exciting to read about a black nurse who was a
real person. Interest in nursing is very great in the junior
high schools in New York. This is the first book I know of
that recounts the story of an historical Afro-American nurse.

1569 Tear Down the Walls: A History of the Black Revolu-
      tion in the United States, by Dorothy Sterling.
      Doubleday, c1968. $5.95 (New American Library,
      Signet, c1970, pb $.95)
      RL: 6   IL: 5-adult   *BSMP
This is a beautifully written history of the black revolution
and black experience in the United States. It is copiously
illustrated and has a stirring quotation usually from a famous
black author, to head each chapter. It is a must for all
schools and libraries. Of the many similar books I have
read in the past few years, I found this the most moving.

1570 That Dunbar Boy, by Jean Gould. Dodd, Mead, c1958.
      $3.95
      RL: 5-6   IL: 6-adult   *SMP
A good biography of the Negro poet, this book will only be
read if it is pushed by someone who has read the book and
likes Dunbar's poetry. Most young people today are put off
by dialect and have never heard of Dunbar. However, there
is much interest in poetry among young people today and
there is much that would interest them in this book if they
were introduced to it with enthusiasm. Until I read the book,
I didn't know Dunbar was a classmate and good friend of the
Wright brothers and Dunbar's experiences as an elevator
operator could give courage to other would-be authors who
are stuck in dead-end jobs.

1571 They Had a Dream, by George Reasons and Sam
      Patrick. New American Library, Signet, c1969.
      pb $.95
      RL: 6-7   IL: 6-adult   *BSMP
Fifty-three one or two page biographies of outstanding black
Americans with a superb pen and ink portrait of each person
described. The subjects covered range from the famous
(George Washington Carver) to the obscure (George W. Bush)
and also cover the whole range of American history. People

418 Read for Your Life

are able to read above their level better in short selections
than in a long essay which disheartens them and I believe
that the striking portraits will make this a very popular book.

1572 **They Had a Dream**, by Eric Broudy, Warren Hallibur-
ton and Lawrence Swinburne. Pyramid Hi-Lo Original, c1969. $.60
RL: 5 IL: 5-adult *BSMP
A quite different book with the same title as 1571 and equally
interesting. This has exciting profiles of eleven distinguished
black Americans ranging from James Brown, the singer, to
Ralph Bunche. The ones on Gordon Parks and Malcolm X
are taken from their autobiographies and the one on Langston
Hughes quotes his poems with telling effect. A must for
every school and library in the country.

1573 **They Showed the Way**, by Charlemae Rollins. Crowell,
c1964. $3.50
RL: 5-6 IL: 5-adult BSM
This excellent book, one of the first in its field, gives forty
short biographies of Afro-American leaders. On the bookmobile it was borrowed chiefly by adults. Now that there
are many books of its kind I would perfer a paperback or,
if a hard cover collection, one with illustrations.

1574 **This Is New York**, by Miroslav Sasek. Macmillan.
$4.95
RL: 3 IL: Read aloud-JH S
A well illustrated tour of New York with enough spark so
that it might well lead a ghetto boy or girl to venture outside
home territory to see some of the sights depicted here. The
author-illustrator has done similar and equally good books on
San Francisco, Texas and Washington, D.C. as well as many
cities abroad.

1575 **Three Lives for Mississippi**, by William B. Huie.
New American Library, Signet, c1968. pb $.75
RL: 6 IL: 6-adult BSMP
The account of the murder of the three civil rights workers
in Mississippi in the summer of 1964, with an introduction
by Martin Luther King, this is a dramatic and harrowing
story of a crime, what caused it and who did it. It is also
the story of youthful courage and self-sacrifice.

1576 **Three Who Dared**, by Tom Cohen. Doubleday, Signal,
c1969. $3.50 (Doubleday, Semaphore, pb $1.75)
RL: 3 IL: 5-adult *BSMP

The account of three young people, two white and one black, who went South as Civil Rights workers. The book tells of their trials, their bravery and their accomplishments, a record to be proud of. The photographs of Civil Rights marches, work and confrontations make the stories real.

1577   Time of Trial, Time of Hope: Negro in America,
        1910-1941, by Milton Meltzer and August Mier.
        Doubleday, Zenith, c1966. $3.75   (pb $1.45)
        RL: 5   IL: 5-adult   BSMP
The struggle for justice and civil rights of the American black man between the end of World War I and the beginning of World War II, this title, again, is mainly borrowed by adults. It was, indeed, a time of hope, unrecognized by the majority. That is one reason why the wide circulation of many of the books on this list could change the point of view of the country. This is again a "time of hope." What is needed is information along the lines of this and many other titles on the list. See especially The Other America [p. 68] by Michael Harrington and other titles on pp. 66-69.

1578   To Be a Slave, by Julius Lester. Illus. by Tom
        Feelings. Dial, c1968. $3.95   (Dell, Laurel, pb
        $.75)
        RL: 5   IL: 5-adult   BSMP
What it feels like to be a black slave in America told in the slaves' own words from the 17th Century to the post Civil War era. This book, beautifully illustrated, should be read by every American. Although in 1969 it was available only in hardcover, it was so instantly popular that we could not keep in on the bookmobile. It went out the minute it came in. It is good now to have it in paperback also.

1579   To Sir, With Love, by E. R. Braithwaite. Prentice-
        Hall. $4.95 (Pyramid pb $.75) c1959.
        RL: 7   IL: 6-adult   BSMP
The autobiography of Braithwaite, a West Indian teacher and leader, covering his years of teaching in a slum school in England. The movie of this book with Sidney Poitier has made the title a very popular one. It is a good book on its own merits and has continued to be popular even though the movie is no longer around.

1580   To the Top of the World: The Story of Peary and
        Henson, by Pauline K. Angell. Rand McNally, c1964.
        $4.95 (Bantam, 1966, pb $.60)
        RL: 6-7   IL: 6-adult   BSMP

420 Read for Your Life

The true story of the white naval officer and the black seaman who became the first men to reach the North Pole, this book is long and somewhat difficult to read. However, the account of the expeditions are very dramatic and the account of how Peary treated Henson is almost incredible. Henson seems to have been a real credit to the human race. This book is unlikely to be generally popular but I can imagine boys and young men whose imagination had been fired getting a great deal out of it. See also 1391 and 1483.

1581 Trail Blazer--Negro Nurse in the American Red Cross, by Jean Maddern Pitrone. Harcourt, Brace, c1969. $4.25
RL: 6   IL: 5-adult   *SMP
Many, many girls are interested in the career of nursing and they will welcome this biography of the orphan girl who fought every obstacle to become the first Red Cross nurse of her race and went on to a distinguished career of public service. After Fanny achieves her goal of becoming a Red Cross nurse, her story will not seem exciting to young people but older people will realize that the second half of her life contained as many joys and sorrows as the first half. I hope this book will be put into paperback with good print. Many adult women would enjoy it.

1582 Trumpeter's Tale--The Story of Young Louis Armstrong, by Jeanette Eaton. Illus. by Elton C. Fox. Morrow, c1955. $4.95
RL: 6   IL: 6-adult   SMP
First published in 1955, this story of young Louis Armstrong is now on its tenth printing. It is a moving story of courage and hardship. Only a boy with extraordinary determination and sweetness of character could have wound up where Louis Armstrong did after the beating the world of New Orleans gave him. See also 1473 and 1531.

1583 Unbought and Unbossed, by Shirley Chisholm. Houghton Mifflin, c1970. $4.95
RL: 6-7   IL: 6-adult   *BSMP
The autobiography (thus far) of the dauntless Congresswoman from Brooklyn who ran for the presidency in 1972, this is a story which will interest a wide range of people. It will have special appeal, however, to the many inner city girls who feel that they are being brought up too strictly. Shirley Chisholm was in college before she was allowed to have a date yet she has managed to wind up happily married and with a great career before her.

1584 The Unfinished March, by Carol F. Drisko and Edgar
      Toppin. Illus. by Tracy Sugarman. Doubleday,
      Zenith, c1967. $3.75 (pb $1.45)
      RL: 6   IL: 6-adult   BSMP
An excellent account of the history of the Afro-American in
the United States from the end of the Civil War to World
War I. It is clearly written and will be in demand by high
school students and adults. It is also a must for private and
suburban schools.

1585 The United States Marines, by Lynn Montross and
      William Miller. Houghton Mifflin, c1967. $2.95
      (Dell, Yearling, pb $.75)
      RL: 5-6   IL: 5-HS   BS
A straightforward and admiring account of the U.S. Marines
and their history.

1586 Up from El Paso, by Paul Diaz with Kenneth Richards
      and Michael Reuben. Children's Press, An Open
      Door Book, c1970. $3 (pb $.75)
      RL: 4-5   IL: 5-adult   *BSMP
Paul Diaz is a building inspector after having tried police
work and given it up because it took him away from his family too much. He likes his work because he is helping other
people and he likes the standard of living which he can provide for his family and which is in contrast to his childhood
as the son of migrant workers. He has pride in his Mexican-
Indian heritage and in the fact that his two cultures make him
trusted in both the Spanish-speaking world and the English-
speaking. Photographs.

1587 Up from Slavery, by Booker T. Washington. Double-
      day, c1901. $5.50 (Dell, Laurel, 1969, pb $.50)
      RL: 6-7   IL: HS-adult   BSMP
The autobiographical story of a famous black American who
is now a controversial and, in many circles, unpopular figure.
The controversy has stirred interest. Many more people ask
for and borrow this book than did a few years ago.

1588 Venture for Freedom, by Ruby Zagoren. World, c1969.
      $4.50 (Dell, Yearling, pb $.75)
      RL: 5-6   IL: 4-adult   BS
Venture Smith was a black man who was captured in Africa
and sold as a slave in America. He published a short autobiography in 1798 when he had earned his freedom. This
book is based on that but expanded with some imaginary scenes
and dialogue. It is a vivid story of bravery and endurance.

This and Amos Fortune--Free Man [1337] are examples of
books which would be much enjoyed by high school students
and adults if published in an adult format. The many authentic accounts we have of kind and highly respected slave owners
who thought it no disgrace to sell a slave's wife or child to
make a profit makes one wonder how future generations, looking back on us, will feel about our attitude toward poor people and our efforts and effect on solving the problems of hunger, poverty and pollution.

1589   Victory Over Myself, by Floyd Patterson and Milton
       Cross. Geis, c1962. OP (Scholastic pb 1965)
       RL: 6   IL: 5-adult   BSMP
This autobiography of the boxing champion is thought provoking
and absorbing even to people who dislike boxing and are un-
interested in sport. It is dedicated to the Wiltwyck School
for problem boys which he feels rescued him from a hopeless
situation and gave him his start to a decent life and an honor-
able career.

1590   We Honor Them, Vols. I, II, and III, by Willie Mae
       Watson. Illus. by Persis Jennings. New Reader's
       Press, c1964, 1965, 1968 and 1969. pb $.40 each
       RL: 3-6   IL: 3-adult   BS
These slender books look more like pamphlets than paperbacks
but they contain much more information than many fatter books.
Each one tells the biographies of twenty distinguished black
Americans accompanied by black and white illustrations. The
first two volumes are on a very low reading level for this
kind of material, starting at third grade and going no higher
than fourth-fifth. The last volume is slightly more difficult.
Some of the biographies are over simplified to too great a
degree but on the whole these books will be very popular and
can fill a real need especially for older boys and girls and
adults who are functionally illiterate. There are word definitions, suggested exercises and a bibliography at the end of
each volume.

1591   West Side Cop, by Williams Sims with G. C. Skipper.
       Children's Press, An Open Door Book, c1970.
       $3.50 (pb $.75)
       RL: 4-5   IL: 6-adult   *BSMP
Bill Sims has found the work he likes as a police cadet in
Chicago. He grew up in poverty and surrounded by gangs
but was "lucky" enough, to quote him, to not get a record
and to be motivated by his family to study and to go on to
college. He finds his job exciting and thinks it will help

him to help other people.   Photographs.

1592 Whatever You Can't Have, by James Coleman with
      Gene Klinger.   Children's Press, An Open Door
      Book, c1970. $3   (pb $.75)
      RL: 5   IL: 5-adult   *BSMP
Jim Coleman made it from a slum in Chicago to a good job
as personnel worker.   The fact that he was a very good basketball player helped but he feels wanting to get somewhere
was what counted most.   He tells his own story and his conviction comes through.   Photographs.

1593 What I'm About Is People, by Chuck Geary with
      Leonard Grossman.   Children's Press, An Open
      Door Book, c1970. $3   (pb $.75)
      RL: 4-5   IL: 5-adult   *BSMP
Charles Geary came to Chicago from Appalachia.   Although
he dropped out of school at fourteen, he has learned a lot
from the world and now has a job with the office of Economic
Opportunity as a group social worker.   Photographs.

1594 What Manner of Man, by Lerone Bennett, Jr.   Johnson
      Pub. Co., c1968. $5.95   (Simon and Schuster,
      Pocket Books, 1968, pb $.95)
      RL: Adult   IL: JH-adult   BMP
An excellent biography of Martin Luther King, Jr., by the
well-known writer from Ebony who knew King from his college
days.

1595 Where There's Smoke, by Emmett Robinson with
      Michael M. Reuben.   Children's Press, An Open
      Door Book, c1970. $3.50   (pb $.75)
      RL: 4-5   IL: 6-adult   *BSMP
Emmett Robinson tells what it's like to be a fireman.   He
has won a medal for bravery and is a fire engineer.   Photographs.

1596 Who Says You Can't, by Beryl and Samuel Epstein.
      Coward-McCann, c1970. $4.50
      RL: 4-5   IL: 6-adult   *SMP
The stories of seven people or groups of people who took on
"The Establishment" and won, this book will be an inspiration
to teenagers.   It ties in well with the idealism of junior high
and high school students.   It makes it clear that one individual
can count and illustrates the fact by recounting the doings of
Nader and others.

1597 Willie Mays, by Arnold Hano. Grosset and Dunlap,
      Tempo, c1966.   pb $.75
      RL: 5   IL: 5-adult   BSM
A well-written biography of the famous ball player. Popular
with all ages.

1598 Wilt Chamberlain, by George Sullivan. Grosset,
      Tempo, c1966.   pb $.60
      RL: 5   IL: 5-adult   BSMP
An exciting biography of the famous basketball player. See
also 1599 below, on an easier reading level.

1599 Wilt Chamberlain, by Kenneth Rudeen. Illus. by
      Frank Mullins.   Crowell, c1970. $3.75 (pb $.95)
      RL: 3   IL: 2-JH   *BSMP
Wilt Chamberlain was born poor and black. He is so tall
that most people would consider him a freak. However, he
is also one of the best basketball players in the world. This
account of his life has enough breadth so that non-basketball
players will enjoy it as well as those who hope to follow in
his shoes.

1600 Women Who Shaped History, by Henrietta Buckmaster.
      Macmillan, Collier, c1966. $3.50 (pb $.95)
      RL: 7   IL: HS-adult   *SMP
So many schools today are concentrating so much on black
history and black studies that I feel a book like this which
tells the story of a number of brave fighters for justice, both
black and white, provides a useful balance and an important
breadth of vision. The women included are Dorothea Dix,
Prudence Crandall, Mary Baker Eddy, Harriet Tubman, Elizabeth Blackwell and Elizabeth Cady Stanton.

1601 A World of Books, by Lillie D. Chaffin with R. Conrad
      Stein.   Children's Press, An Open Door Book, c1970.
      $3 (pb $.75)
      RL: 4-5   IL: 5-adult   *BSMP
The pattern in Brush Creek where Lillie Chaffin grew up was
for a girl to quit school at fourteen and get married. Somehow, with the warm support of her husband, Mrs. Chaffin has
finished school, and become a librarian, teacher and writer.
Photographs.

1602 Worth Fighting For, by Agnes McCarthy and Lawrence
      Reddick. Illus. by Coleen Browning. Doubleday,
      Zenith, c1965. $3.75 (pb $1.45)
      RL: 5-6   IL: 5-adult   BSMP

A well-written history of the Negro in the United States during
the Civil War and Reconstruction. The book has breadth and
is interesting reading. It is mainly borrowed by adults.

1603   The Wright Brothers at Kitty Hawk, by Donald Sobol.
       Illus. by Wayne Blickenstaff. Scholastic, c1966.
       pb $.60
       RL: 5   IL: 4-adult   BS
This story of the three crucial years leading to the first
powered flight ever made by man is a fascinating one but
must be introduced. Most of today's children take flight for
granted and have never even heard of the Wright brothers.

1604   Written on Film, by Peter Sagara with Rick Simon, Jr.
       Children's Press, An Open Door Book, c1970. $3.50
       (pb $.75)
       RL: 4-5   IL: 5-adult   *BSMP
Peter Sagara and his family were sent to a relocation center
in World War II because they were Japanese-Americans.
However, they made a comeback and he is now a photographer
in the advertising field with his own studio. A quiet book
without much excitement but it is good to have success stories
about all the different ethnic groups. Photographs.

1605   Yes I Can, by Sammy Davis, Jr. and Jane and Burt
       Boyar. Farrar, Straus, c1966. $7.95 (Simon and
       Schuster, Pocket Books, pb $.95)
       RL: 5   IL: 5-adult   BSMP
An autobiography of the famous singer, actor and playwright
which is very popular with all ages. This is one of the few
paperbacks whose physical composition does not stand up under
use. It breaks in two very easily.

1606   Young and Black in America, compiled by Rae Pace
       Alexander. Random House, c1970. $3.95
       RL: Varied   IL: 6-adult   *BSMP
This book contains eight accounts of growing up black in America by eight well-known Americans. Each account is an excerpt from an autobiography. Although many of the accounts
are justifiably bitter, the total effect of the book is a positive
one because of the achievements of the writers. Very similar
to Growing Up Black, there is little duplication and both books
will be very popular.

1607   Young Jim: The Early Years of James Weldon Johnson,
       by Ellen Tarry. Dodd, Mead & Co., c1967. $3.95
       RL: 6-7   IL: HS-adult   *SMP

This is an excellent account of James Weldon Johnson's early
years carrying the musician and writer through school and
college and postgraduate work at Harvard. However, most
students have never heard of him and find it dull. I include
it because older students who arc anxious to help underprivileged children do become very much interested in his experiences in teaching both in Georgia and in Jacksonville and they
go on to wanting to know more about him and read and enjoy
the whole book.

1608   Young Olympic Champions, by Steve Gelman.   Grosset,
       c1964. $3.95   (Scholastic pb $.50)
       RL: 5-6   IL: 5-adult   BSMP
Eleven biographies of Olympic champions written with suspense.
Many girls who are not interested in books are thrilled by the
story of Wilma Rudolph, the Olympic track star.

1609   You're On The Air, by Daddy-O-Daylie with Emmett
       Smith.   Children's Press, An Open Door Book,
       c1969. $3   (pb $.75)
       RL: 5   IL: 5-adult   *BSMP
Daddy-O-Daylie has made it from a boyhood of such poverty
that he went to school in rags to being a disc jockey on radio
and having his own show For Black Only on TV.   Here he
tells how it happened.   Photographs.

APPENDIX

A LIST OF NON-BOOK MATERIAL

1) <u>Bookmobile non-book material</u>. Buttercup operated in an area where newspaper stores were few and far between and money for newspapers hard to come by. When we saw people sitting in a public housing playground, on stoops or in the parks, very few of them were reading anything and newspapers were rarely visible. Yet there was an enormous hunger for facts.

The bookmobile tried to meet this need by displaying a number of pamphlets high enough to catch an adult's eye and yet not so low as to tempt children to take material they couldn't read and would only throw away as soon as they left the vehicle. Then, to avoid forcing some one to ask for a pamphlet on a subject that was difficult or embarassing to mention aloud in public, we had several piles of the pamphlets on the table where the books were checked out so the patron could help himself. The two subjects most in demand were also the ones least easy to ask for--facts on drug addiction and on birth control. I list below the material we gave away in the summer of 1969. The leaflets and pamphlets are of an ephemeral nature and are given here merely as examples of the material that is available.

Pamphlet: "Alcoholism--Facts about the Disease and its
                  early warning signs."
Source: Alcoholism Committee
              Community Council of Greater N. Y.
        Simple leaflet describes disease and gives an address in each borough where alcoholics and their families may go for help.

Pamphlet: "Act on Fact"
                  ("Actua de Acuerdo con la Realidad")
Source: Read Your Way Up Booklet

Good Reading Communications, Inc.
505 Eighth Avenue, New York, N. Y. 10018
A top-notch guide to buying on a fifth- or sixth-grade
reading level in English or Spanish, this pamphlet was much
in demand. The humorous illustrations are multi-ethnic and
although we had to pay a small amount for the pamphlets
put out by this company and yet gave them away, we felt that
they were valuable enough to our objective to be well worth
the cost.

Pamphlet: "Better Health for Your Baby and You"
                 ("Mejor Salud para el Bebe y la Madre")
Source: Department of Health, The City of New York
                 125 Worth Street, New York, N. Y. 10013
Excellent pamphlets on child care. Unfortunately, both
these pamphlets, as well as the federal ones and also Dr.
Spock, are on too difficult a reading level (sixth grade) for
many of the parents who need them most.

Pamphlet: "Buying Food Is Big Business--Your Business"
Source: Department of Health, The City of New York
                 125 Worth Street, New York, N. Y. 10013
Excellent pamphlet on food buying and meal planning
in simple language. It also has a helpful list on the back
of the City's health centers and their addresses and urges the
reader to go for further information and help.

Pamphlet: "Cancer of the Lung"
Source: National Cancer Institute
                 National Institutes of Health
                 Bethesda, Md. 20014
A short leaflet on cancer of the lung and the dangers
of smoking, this is on a high reading level with a drab appearance. It would be worth looking further for more eye-
catching and useful material on this important subject.

Pamphlet: "Como Obtener lo Que Desea"
Source: Division de migración
                 Departamento del Trabajo
                 Estado Libre Asociado de Puerto Rico
                 322 West 45th Street, New York, N. Y. 10036
A short leaflet explaining (in Spanish) why it is so important for a citizen to vote and how a citizen can register
and be eligible to vote. This also lists further sources of
information in New York City.

Pamphlet: "For Women of Color"

Source: The Daily News, Box 1375
                 New York, N. Y. 10017
     This excellent guide to grooming and beauty care pub-
lished by the Beauty Department of The Daily News, was enormously in demand. I note that the department also publishes
other useful sounding pamphlets (e. g. , "Diet to Look Younger
and Feel Better") which it gives away free, at least to New
York City residents.

Pamphlet: "Growing Up with Books"
Source: R. R. Bowker Company
                 1180 Avenue of the Americas
                 New York, N. Y. 10036
     An eye-catching annotated book list--33 pages of good,
hardcover books for children from pre-school thru teenagers,
this booklet has excellent advice on how parents can interest
their children in reading and several beguiling black and white
illustrations. Pub. , 1968.

Pamphlet: "Growing Up with Paperbacks"
Source: R. R. Bowker Company
                 1180 Avenue of Americas
                 New York, N. Y. 10036
     A similar booklist of paperbacks, this one was pub-
lished in 1969. Unfortunately, there are virtually no outlets
for books in underprivileged areas. Many parents would
gladly buy paperbacks for their children if they could find
them.

Pamphlet: "The Gold Mine Between Your Ears"
Source: Good Reading Communications, Inc.
     How to think up more and more good ideas. Fairly
high reading level but very motivating and even a poor reader
can get the gist and be inspired. Humorous illustrations.

Pamphlet: "The Home Team"
Source: Good Reading Communications, Inc.
     This pamphlet on family relationships is again on a
fairly high reading level but content is so important that poor
readers stretch to understand the material and the basic concepts are good.

Pamphlet: "How Congress Works"
Source: Good Reading Communications, Inc.
     Not too much in demand but its popularity is growing
with a growing interest in politics among young and old. Ties
in with our voter registration literature.

Pamphlet: "La madre y el bebé"
Source: M & R Dietetic Laboratories
    Excellent pamphlet in Spanish on nutrition and exer-
cise and other health problems for young families.

Pamphlet: "Maturity Vital to Job Success"
Source: Good Reading Communications, Inc.
    There is a tremendous hunger in deprived areas for
the kind of advice and loving counsel one would get from a
wise old uncle or a minister or old-fashioned family doctor
who knew three generations in one family. These pamphlets
don't take the place of such a person but good ones on relevant subjects are really appreciated.

Pamphlet: "Metodo del Ritmo"
Source: Planned Parenthood, World Population
                 515 Madison Avenue, New York, N. Y. 10022
    Rhythm method of birth control in Spanish. Birth con-
trol literature is in demand by the young women, frowned on
by the older women and by many men.

Pamphlet: "Mientras la Bebe Esta en Camino"
Source: U. S. Department of HEW, Children's Bureau
    A well done booklet (in Spanish) on pre- and post-natal
care and care of the baby--much needed and much appreciated.

Pamphlet: "Never Stop Learning"
Source: Good Reading Communications, Inc.
    Quite a low reading level but eye-catching pamphlet on
an important subject. Low-income people are really going to
school. At one point, all but one of our staff were going to
various night schools. If it looks as though studying will
really open doors to new careers, people will study.

Pamphlet: "Preguntas y Respuestas"
Source: Planned Parenthood Federation of America, Inc.
    A good example of a leaflet women wanted and would
not ask for--although it was clearly on a subject they longed
to know about. Made easily available, copies disappeared in
no time.

Pamphlet: "Respect for the Law"
Source: Good Reading Communications, Inc.
    A short pamphlet on a vital subject. Most citizens
are desperate about the amount of crime in their area and
rightly terrified of muggings and robberies. They are also
vague as to their rights. This pamphlet is not all inclusive

but speaks to these problems and give some concept of what
law and justice are intended to be.   I am delighted to see
that there are multi-ethnic pictures of policemen in the book.

Pamphlet: "To Be a Mother--To Be a Father"
Source: Planned Parenthood, World Population
                  515 Madison Avenue, New York, N.Y.   10022
    An excellent, very basic description of why one should
plan a family and how conception occurs.   Also a clear simple
description of alternate methods of birth control.

Pamphlet: "Up the Job Ladder"
Source: Good Reading Communications, Inc.
    Excellent advice on how to look for a job and what to
consider in career opportunities.   Very clear multi-ethnic
illustrations which illumine the text.   This one is really
needed and much appreciated especially by teenagers.   It
stimulates discussion in a group.

Pamphlet: "What is Birth Control?"
Source: Planned Parenthood of Suffolk County
                  48 Elm Street, Huntington, New York
    We carried this little leaflet (although the list of health
centers on the back were not in our area) because its approach
to birth control was so simple, so helpful and so direct.   The
response was a very grateful one from many women.

Pamphlet: "What It Takes to Really Make It"
Source: Good Reading Communications, Inc.
    This one is on an eighth- or ninth-grade reading level
but the content is excellent and the subject, of course, is one
of burning interest to all young men.   Only a few teenagers
could read it but those who did gave it a great deal of thought
and discussed the ideas in it with real excitement with poorer
readers.   This one stretched the mind of several youngsters.

Pamphlet: "Watch Your Weight"
Source: Good Reading Communications, Inc.
    Weight is a real problem in underprivileged neighbor-
hoods and this title plus the picture on the cover, made
this a very popular one.   I always felt a little guilty, however,
since it was so clear that in many instances the cause of over-
weight was poverty (fat people were noticeable in the lines at
the surplus food distribution centers) or unbearable frustration.

Pamphlet: "What You Should Know About Drug Addiction"
Source: Department of Health, New York City

A straightforward and simple description of the problem of
drug addiction; how it happens, how to recognize it and
where to go for help. Our arrangements of this leaflet on
the bookmobile were such that no one noticed who took the
pamphlet but the supply kept diminishing so we knew it was
needed.

Non-Book Material--School Volunteers

       Many of the pamphlets listed above--especially the
career and health ones--were equally appropriate for use by
the School Volunteers with older elementary and junior high
and high school boys and girls. In addition, I list below a
few more aids.

       Negro Americans--The Early Years. A vivid comic
book with biographies of fifteen famous black Americans which
gives a capsule history of black people in the U.S. from colonial days to the days of Peary and Henson. Source: Classics
Illustrated No. 169 ($.25), Classics Illustrated, Department S,
101 Fifth Avenue, New York, N.Y. 10003.

       In addition, there are many other excellent classic
comic books which do indeed inspire the young to go on eventually and read the original. We had on our staff a young
Puerto Rican boy in eighth grade who was reading on the
twelfth-grade level. In fifth grade, in real reading difficulties
due to a language problem and unfriendly teachers, he taught
himself to read one summer with the help of classic comics
and a cheap Spanish-English dictionary.

       Golden Legacy Series. Fitzgerald Publishing Company,
Box 264, St. Albans, New York, N.Y. 10003. This is a
series of comic books which gives the lives of many great
black Americans. Each book is devoted to the life of one
hero or heroine--for example, Harriet Tubman, the Moses
of Her People, Crispus Attucks, etc. These comic books
are sometimes available free, sometimes for $.25 apiece or
less. Write to Fitzgerald Publishing Company.

       Newspapers are an important teaching aid. We used
the New York Times for events of city-wide interest. The
Daily News, ditto, and Amsterdam News for events of more
local interest. In elementary school programs, the cards
that come with bubble gum were an excellent breakthrough on
reading for children who were sure that "books are boring."

The School Volunteers put out at intervals (depending on the amount of money available) a magazine called The Reader's Gazette which was an anthology of the best stories, essays and poems and pictures by the children the School Volunteers were helping. Children loved to look at these Gazettes and were quickly inspired to write or draw something themselves which might prove worthy of inclusion in the next issue. In addition, we used Ebony, Life (R. I. P.), and The National Geographic as supplemental reading materials and conversation pieces.

DIRECTORY OF PUBLISHERS

Abelard-Schuman, Ltd.
257 Park Ave, S.
New York, N. Y. 10010

Abingdon Press
201 Eighth Ave., S.
Nashville, Tenn. 37203

Addison-Wesley Pub. Co., Inc.
Reading, Mass. 01867

Ace Pub. Corp.
1120 Ave. of the Americas
New York, N. Y. 10036

Afro-Am Pub. Co., Inc.
1727 S. Indiana Avenue
Chicago, Ill. 60616

Airmont Publishing Co., Inc.
22 E. 60th Street
New York, N. Y. 10022

American Bible Society
1865 Broadway
New York, N. Y. 10022

Archway Paperbacks
See: Simon & Schuster

Association Press
50 Rockefeller Plaza
New York, N. Y. 10020

Atheneum Publishers
122 E. 42nd St.
New York, N. Y. 10017

Avon Books (Div. of
Hearst Corporation)
959 Eighth Avenue
New York, N. Y. 10019

Award Books
See: Universal

Ballantine Books, Inc.
101 Fifth Avenue
New York, N. Y. 10003

Bantam Books, Inc.
666 Fifth Avenue
New York, N. Y. 10019

Barnes & Noble Books,
Div. Harper & Row
10 East 53rd Street
New York, N. Y. 10022

Baron, Richard W., Pub. Co.
See: Dutton

Beacon Press Inc.
25 Beacon Street
Boston, Mass. 02108

Berkley Publishing Corp.
200 Madison Avenue
New York, N.Y. 10016

Blom, Benjamin, Inc.
2521 Broadway
Bronx, New York 10025

Bobbs-Merrill Co., Inc.
4300 W. 62nd St.
Indianapolis, Ind. 46268

Broadside Press Publications
12651 Old Mill Place
Detroit, Mich. 48238

Childrens Press, Inc.
1224 W. Van Buren Street
Chicago, Ill. 60607

Citizen's Committee
for Children of N.Y.
112 East 19th Street
New York, N.Y. 10003

Collier Books
See: Macmillan

Concordia Publishing House
3558 S. Jefferson Avenue
St. Louis, Mo. 63118

Coward-McCann, Inc.
200 Madison Avenue
New York, N.Y. 10016

Cowles Book Company
See: Henry Regnery Co.

Crest Publishing Co.
See: Fawcett World Library

Crowell, Thomas Y., Co.
666 Fifth Avenue
New York, N.Y. 10019
(Orders: Tyco Shipping Service, 788 Bloomfield Ave.,
Clifton, N.J. 07012)

Crowell Collier & Macmillan
See: Macmillan

Crown Publishers, Inc.
419 Park Avenue, South
New York, N.Y. 10016

Dial Press, Inc.
750 Third Avenue
New York, N.Y. 10017

Dell Publishing Company
750 Third Avenue
New York, N.Y. 10017

Dodd, Mead & Company
79 Madison Avenue
New York, N.Y. 10016

Doubleday & Company, Inc.
277 Park Avenue
New York, N.Y. 10017
(Orders: 501 Franklin Ave.
Garden City, N.Y. 11530)

Dover Publications, Inc.
180 Varick Street
New York, N.Y. 10014

Dutton, E. P., & Co., Inc.
201 Park Avenue, South
New York, N.Y. 10003

Ericksson, Paul S., Inc.
119 West 57th St.
New York, N.Y. 10019

Evans, M. & Co., Inc.
216 East 49th Street
New York, N.Y. 10017
(Orders: J. B. Lippincott Co.)

Farrar, Straus & Giroux, Inc.
19 Union Square, West
New York, N. Y. 10003

Fawcett World Library
(Orders: Fawcett Publica-
tions, Inc. , Fawcett Place,
Greenwich, Conn. 16830)

Follett Publishing Company
1010 W. Washington Blvd.
Chicago, Ill. 60607

Four Winds Press
50 West 44th Street
New York, N. Y. 10036

Friendship Press
475 Riverside Drive
New York, N. Y. 10027

Funk & Wagnalls Co.
(Division of Reader's
Digest Books, Inc.)
666 Fifth Avenue
New York, N. Y. 10016

Garrard Publishing Company
1607 N. Market Street
Champaign, Ill. 61820

Globe Book Company, Inc.
(Subs. of Esquire, Inc.)
175 Fifth Avenue
New York, N. Y. 10010

Golden Gate Junior Books
(Div. of Nourse Pub. Co.)
Box 398
San Carlos, Calif. 94070

Golden Press, Inc. (Div. of
Western Pub. Co. , Inc.)
850 Third Ave.
New York, N. Y. 10022
(Orders: 1220 Mound Avenue
Racine, Wis. 53404)

Grosset & Dunlap, Inc.
51 Madison Avenue
New York, N. Y. 10010

Grove Press, Inc.
53 East 11th Street
New York, N. Y. 10003

Hale, E. M. , & Co. , Inc.
Eau Claire, Wis. 54701

Harcourt Brace Jovanovich, Inc.
757 Third Avenue
New York, N. Y. 10017

Harper & Row Publishers, Inc.
49 East 33rd Street
New York, N. Y. 10016
(Orders:Scranton, Pa. 18512)

Hart Publishing Company
719 Broadway
New York, N. Y. 10003

Hastings House Publishers, Inc.
10 East 40th Street
New York, N. Y. 10016

Hawthorn Books, Inc.
70 Fifth Avenue
New York, N. Y. 10011

Heath, D. C. & Company
(Div. Raytheon Education Co.)
125 Spring Street
Lexington, Mass. 02173
(Orders:2700 N. Richardt Ave.
Indianapolis, Ind. 46219)

Hill & Wang, Inc.
See: Farrar, Straus
& Giroux

Holt, Rinehart & Winston, Inc.
(Subs. of CBS)
383 Madison Avenue
New York, N. Y. 10017

Houghton Mifflin Co.
2 Park Street
Boston, Mass. 02107
(Orders: Wayside Road
Burlington, Mass. 01803)

Indiana University Press
10th & Morton Sts.
Bloomington, Ind. 47401

International Publishers
381 Park Avenue, South
New York, N.Y. 10016

J. Lowell Pratt & Co.
(Dist. by Kable News Co.
777 Third Avenue
New York, N.Y. 10017)

Knopf, Alfred A. Inc.
(School and library orders to
Random House School &
Library Service, Inc.)
201 E. 50th Street
New York, N.Y. 10022

Lancer Books, Inc.
560 Broadway
New York, N.Y. 10036

Lerner Publications Co.
241 First Avenue, North
Minneapolis, Minn. 55401

Lippincott, J. B., Company
E. Washington Square
Philadelphia, Pa. 19105; and
521 Fifth Avenue
New York, N.Y. 10017

Little, Brown & Co.
34 Beacon Street
Boston, Mass. 02106

McGraw-Hill Book Company
(Div. of McGraw-Hill, Inc.)
1221 Ave. of the Americas
New York, N.Y. 10020

McKay, David, Company, Inc.
750 Third Avenue
New York, N.Y. 10017

Macmillan Company
866 Third Avenue
New York, N.Y. 10022

Macrae Smith Co.
225 South 15th Street
Philadelphia, Pa. 19102

Meredith Press
750 Third Avenue
New York, N.Y. 10017
(Orders: 1716 Locust St.
Des Moines, Iowa 50303)

Messner, Julian, Inc.
(Orders: Simon & Schuster
1 West 39th Street
New York, N.Y. 10018)

Moody Press
820 N. La Salle Street
Chicago, Ill. 60610

Morrow, William, & Co., Inc.
105 Madison Avenue
New York, N.Y. 10016

New American Library, Inc.
(Sub. of Times Mirror)
1301 Avenue of the Americas
New York, N.Y. 10019

New Readers Press (Div. of
Laubath Literacy, Inc.)
Box 131, Syracuse, N.Y. 13210

Noble & Noble Publishers, Inc.
750 Third Avenue
New York, N.Y. 10017

Pantheon Books, Inc.
(Div. of Random House, Inc.)
201 East 50th Street
New York, N.Y. 10022

(Orders: Random House, Inc.
Westminster, Md 21157)

Paperback Library, Inc. (Div. of
Coronet Communications, Inc.)
315 Park Avenue, South
New York, N. Y. 10010

Parents' Magazine Press
(Div. of Parents' Magazine
Enterprises, Inc.)
52 Vanderbilt Avenue
New York, N. Y. 10017

Pathfinder Press, Inc.
410 West Street
New York, N. Y. 10014

Penguin Books, Inc.
7110 Ambassador Road
Baltimore, Md.   21207

Pilot Books
347 Fifth Avenue
New York, N. Y. 10016

Platt & Munk Company
(Div. of Child Guidance
Products, Inc.)
1055 Bronx River Avenue
Bronx, New York 10472

Plays, Inc.
8 Arlington Street
Boston, Mass. 12116

Pocket Books, Inc.
(Orders:Simon & Schuster, Inc.
1 West 39th Street
New York, N. Y. 10018)

Popular Library, Inc.
(Subs. of Perfect Film
and Chemical Corp.)
355 Lexington Avenue
New York, N. Y. 10017

Portal Press, Inc.
(Subs. of John Wiley and Sons)
605 Third Avenue
New York, N. Y.

Prentice-Hall, Inc.
70 Fifth Avenue
New York, N. Y. 10011
(Orders: Englewood Cliffs,
N. J. 07632)

Putnam's, G. P. , Sons
200 Madison Avenue
New York, N. Y. 10016

Pyramid Publications, Inc.
919 Third Avenue
New York, N. Y. 10022

Rand McNally & Company
P. O. Box 7600
Chicago, Ill. 60680

Random House
201 East 50th Street
New York, N. Y. 10022

Reader's Digest Services, Inc.
Educational Division
Pleasantville, N. Y. 10570

Reilly & Lee Company
(Orders: Henry Regnery Co.
114 W. Illinois St.
Chicago, Ill. 60610)

Ritchie, Ward, Press
3044 Riverside Drive
Los Angeles, Calif. 90030
(Orders: Golden Gate
Junior Books, Box 398
San Carlos, Calif. 94070)

St. Martin's Press, Inc.
175 Fifth Avenue
New York, N. Y. 10010

Scholastic Book Services
Scholastic Magazines
50 West 44th Street
New York, N.Y. 10036

Scott, William R., Inc.
(Now Young Scott Books,
Imprint of Addison-Wesley
Pub. Co., Inc.)

Scribner's, Charles, Sons
597 Fifth Avenue
New York, N.Y. 10017
(Orders: Shipping & Service
Center, Vreeland Avenue
Totowa, N.J. 07512)

Sheed & Ward, Inc.
64 University Place
New York, N.Y. 10003

Silver Burdett Company
(Division of General
Learning Corporation)
250 James Street
Morristown, N.J. 07960

Simon & Schuster, Inc.
630 Fifth Avenue
New York, N.Y. 10020
(Orders:1 West 39th Street
New York, N.Y. 10018

Steck-Vaughn Company
P.O. Box 2028
Austin, Texas 78767

Universal Pub. & Dist. Corp.
(Award Books Division)
235 E. 45 Street
New York, N.Y. 10017

Vanguard Press, Inc.
424 Madison Avenue
New York, N.Y. 10017

Viking Press, Inc.
625 Madison Avenue
New York, N.Y. 10022

Walck, Henry Z. Inc.
19 Union Square W.
New York, N.Y. 10003

Warne, Frederick, & Co., Inc.
101 Fifth Avenue
New York, N.Y. 10003

Washington Square Press, Inc.
(Orders: Simon & Schuster
1 West 39th Street
New York, N.Y. 10018)

Watts, Franklin, Inc.
(Subs. of Grolier)
845 Third Avenue
New York, N.Y. 10022

Wenkart, Heni
4 Shady Hill Square
Cambridge, Mass. 02138

Western Publishing Co.
1220 Mound Avenue
Racine, Wis. 53404

Westminister Press
Witherspoon Building
Juniper & Walnut Streets
Philadelphia, Pa. 19107

White, David, Company
60 E. 55th Street
New York, N.Y. 10022

Whitman, Albert & Co.
560 W. Lake Street
Chicago, Ill. 60606

World Publishing Company
(Subs. of Times Mirror Co.)

110 East 59th Street
New York, N. Y. 10022
(Also: Dist. for Ameri-
can Library hardcover books)

Young Readers Press, Inc.
1120 Ave. of the Americas
New York, N. Y. 10036

BOOK SUPPLIERS (JOBBERS)

In addition to writing directly to the publishers to order the books on the list, the following jobbers have proved
to be very helpful to the Bedford-Stuyvesant Travelling Library.

For hardcover books only:

Bookazine Co. , Inc
303 West 10th Street
New York, N. Y.

For paperback books:

A & A Distributors Inc.
Mear Road
Holbrook, Mass. 02343
(This company does a large mail order business and
gives quantity orders a larger discount than any one else I
know in the business. However, they are often out of stock
on titles needed especially if the title needed is not a mass
best seller.)

Book Mail Service Inc.
82-87 164th Street
Jamaica, New York 11432
(This company has been extremely helpful and provides very fast and accurate service.)

Scholastic Book Services
904 Sylvan Avenue
Englewood Cliffs, N. J. 07632
(I list Scholastic as a supplier as well as in the
list of publishers since this publisher is in a special category.
The Scholastic books are mainly sold on a book club basis and
are generally available on a retail basis but can be ordered

through the above address. If the reader will write Scholastic
Book Services and ask for their Reader's Choice Catalogue, he
will receive the catalogue and also an order blank explaining
their discount system which makes their already very inexpensive books a very good buy indeed. Over the last ten years,
they have given me pleasant, fast, accurate service both for
book fairs and for the bookmobile.)

> D. Zenilman
> 289 Beach 14th Street
> Far Rockaway, New York
> (This company supplies paperbacks for children and
teenagers and also inexpensive hardcover books such as the
G & D Easy-to-Read Wonder Books. They are unbelievably
painstaking and will supply books by title in cases where the
publisher feels it is not worth his while. Mr. Zenilman also
is pleasant, fast and accurate and Mrs. Zenilman can often
suggest additional titles that are appropriate.)

None of the above book suppliers ever knowingly substitutes a different title from the one you ordered--something
which, alas, all too many companies in the school book fair
market are apt to do.

AUTHOR INDEX
with titles

Cullen, Countee. On These I Stand 502
Cunningham, William. Story of Daniel Boone 1553

Daddy-O-Daylie. You're on the Air 1609
Daly, Maureen. Seventeenth Summer 1317
Darbois, Dominique. Kai Ming, Boy of Hong Kong 68
Daugherty, James. Andy and the Lion 970
David, Jay. Growing Up Black 1430
Davidson, Basil. A Guide to African History 1431
Davidson, Eleanor. The Story of Eleanor Roosevelt 1554
Davidson, Margaret. Frederick Douglass Fights for
    Freedom 1417
Davidson, Mickie. The Adventures of George Washington
    1332, Helen Keller's Teacher 1432
Davis, Angela. If They Come in the Morning 96
Davis, Charles. On My Own 1507
Davis, Charles T. On Being Black: Writings By Afro-
    Americans 1089
Davis, Mac. Baseball's Unforgettables 423, The Greatest
    in Baseball 435
Davis, Sammy Jr. Yes I Can! 1605
Day, Beth. I'm Done Crying 1447
Dean, Leigh. The Looking-Down Game 904
De Angulo, Jaime. Indian Tales 670
De Brunhoff, Laurent. Babar Loses His Crown 973
De Caprio, Annie. One, Two 129
De Carava, Roy. The Sweet Flypaper of Life 112
Decker, Duane. Hit and Run 1236
Deer, Ada. Speaking Out 1546
De Jong, Meindert. The House of Sixty Fathers 831
De La Fontaine, Jean. Fables of Lafontaine 884
De Leeuw, Cateau. One Week of Danger 841
Del Rey, Lester. The Runaway Robot 1197, Tunnel Through
    Time 1203
Dennis, Wesley, Flip 559
Derwent, Lavinia. Joseph and the Coat of Many Colors 34
Devaney, John. Bart Starr 1349, Baseball Life of Mickey
    Mantle 420
Diaz, Paul. Up From El Paso 1586
Di Pierson, Allan. At Your Own Risk 607
Dixon, Lucian W. Chicory--Young Voices From the Black
    Ghetto 89
Dobler, Lavinia. Great Rulers of the African Past 1428,
    Pioneers and Patriots 1518
Dodd, Ed. Mark Trail's Book of Animals 273
Dolch, Edward W. Dolch Pleasure Reading Series 172,

Hill, Frank Ernest. The Kid Who Batted 1000 1244
Hille-Brandts, Lene. Guess What? 404
Hillert, Margaret. Funny Baby 151, I Like to Live in the
     City 491, Three Bears 699, Three Goats 702
Himes, Chester. Cotton Comes to Harlem 1145, The
     Heat's On 1150, Hot Day, Hot Night 1153, Run,
     Man, Run 1167, Third Generation 1116
Hinton, S. E. The Outsiders 1093, That Was Then, This
     Is Now 926
Hitte, Katherine. Mexicali Soup 1080
Hoard, Edison. Curse Not the Darkness 1389
Hoban, Russell. A Bargain for Frances 866, Bread and
     Jam for Frances 874
Hobson, Julius W. Black Pride--A People's Struggle 1364
Hodges, Elizabeth J. Free As a Frog 887
Hoff, Syd. Albert, The Albatross 936, Danny and the
     Dinosaur 989, Grizzwold 564, Jeffrey at Camp 896,
     Who Will Be My Friends? 1125
Hogarth, William. Arrow Book of Jokes and Riddles 365
Holding, James. Mystery of Dolphin Inlet 1162
Holland, John. The Way It Is 117
Holliday, Billie. Lady Sings the Blues 1462
Hoopes, Ned. Ali Baba and the Forty Thieves 642
Hopkins, Lee Bennett. The City Spreads Its Wings 474,
     City Talk 475, Don't You Turn Back--Poems by
     Langston Hughes 478, I Think I Saw a Snail 493,
     This Street's for Me 524
Hopkins, Marjorie. The Three Visitors 703
Horne, Lena. Lena 1465
Hornyansky, Michael. The Golden Phoenix and Other French-
     Canadian Fairy Tales 664, The Magic Tree and
     Other Tales 680
Horton, Mary. ABC and Counting Book 124
Horvath, Betty. Jasper Makes Music 739, Hooray for
     Jasper 736
Hoskins, Lotte. I Have a Dream: The Quotations of Martin
     Luther King Jr. 95
Howard, Elizabeth. North Winds Blow Free 837
Howell, Ruth. Crack in the Pavement 239
Hudson, James F. R. F. K. 1925-1968 1523
Hughes, Langston. The Best of Simple 938, Black Misery
     367, Don't You Turn Back--Poems by Langston Hughes
     478, Dream Keeper and Other Poems 479, Famous
     American Negroes 1405, Famous Negro Heroes of
     America 1409, Famous Negro Music Makers 1410,
     New Negro Poets, U. S. A. 499, Not Without Laughter
     1087, Panther and the Lash 504, Pictorial History

Kinney, Harrison. The Lonesome Bear 572
Kinnick, B. J. I Have a Dream 624, Let Us Be Men 624
Kirk, Elizabeth Mooney. Everyday Reading and Writing 150
Kirn, Ann. Two Pesos for Catalina 800
Kischnick, Kay. I Am One of These 1441
Kissen, Fan. The Bag of Fire 132, Crowded House and
    Other Tales 133, The Straw Fox and Other Plays
    140
Kitt, Tamara. The Adventures of Silly Billy 638, Billy
    Brown, The Baby Sitter 939, The Boy, the Cat and
    the Magic Fiddle 650, Boy Who Fooled the Giant 651,
    Surprising Pets of Billy Brown 964
Kjelgaard, Jim. Fire Hunter 826
Klaperman, Dr. Gilbert. How and Why Wonder Book of the
    Old Testament 32
Klein, Leonore. Arrow Book of Project Fun 326, Brave
    Daniel 144
Klein, Muriel W. From Plays Into Reading 135
Klinger, Gene. Someday I'm Going To Be Somebody 1543,
    Son of This Land 1544, Whatever You Can't Have
    1592
Knight, Clayton. We Were There at the Normandy Invasion
    860
Knight, Eric. Lassie Come Home 569, Lassie Come Home
    (adapt.) 570
Knight, Etheriage. Black Voices From Prison 1035
Knight, Michael. In Chains to Louisiana 1448
Koch, John. Where Did You Come From? 1123
Kohfield, Dick. Secrets of the Past 1532
Komai, Felicia. Cry the Beloved Country 881
Koschnick, Kay. The World of Work 58
Kottmeyer, W. Cases of Sherlock Holmes 1143, The Count
    of Monte Cristo 536
Kramer, Nora. Arrow Book of Ghost Stories 971, Grimm's
    Fairy Tales 665
Krasilovsky, Phyllis. The Man Who Didn't Wash His Dishes
    954
Krauss, Ruth. The Carrot Seed 877, Is This You?
    369
Krieh, Aron M. Facts of Love and Marriage for Young
    People 11
Krumgold, Joseph. And Now Miguel 714
Krusz, Art. Favorite Poems to Read Aloud 480

Lacy, Ed. In Black and Whitey 1154, Moment of Untruth
    1158, Sleep in Thunder 1172

985, Curious George Learns the Alphabet 126,
     Curious George Rides a Bike 987, Curious George
     Takes a Job 988
Rey, Margaret. Curious George Goes to the Hospital 985
Reynolds, Mack. Puerto Rican Patriot--The Life of Luis
     Muñoz Rivera 1520
Richards, Kenneth. El Rancho De Muchachos 1399, Louis
     Armstrong 1473, Up From El Paso 1586
Ridlon, Marci. That Was Summer 523
Rinkoff, Barbara. Elbert, the Mind Reader 991, Headed
     for Trouble 889, Member of the Gang 907
Ripley, Sheldon. Matthew Henson--Arctic Hero 1483
Roberts, Suzanne. Gracie 732
Robinson, Bradley. Dark Companion, the Story of Matthew
     Henson 1391
Robinson, Emmett. Where There's Smoke 1595
Robinson, Louis Jr. Arthur Ashe: Tennis Champion 1345
Robinson, Sugar Ray. Sugar Ray 458
Rockowitz, M. Family 728
Rockwell, Anne. Gypsy Girl's Best Shoes 734, When the
     Drum Sang--An African Folk Tale 710
Rodgers, Bertha. Little Brown Baby--Poems for Young
     People 495
Rollins, Charlemae. Black Troubadour: Langston Hughes
     1368, Christmas Gif' 600, Famous American Negro
     Poets 1406, They Showed the Way 1573
Romano, Louis G. Gertie the Duck 199 & 561
Ronan, Margaret. Arrow Book of States 1343
Rood, Ronald. Bees, Bugs and Beetles 235
Rose, Mary Catherine. Clara Barton 1384
Rosenbaum, Eileen. Ronnie 108
Rosmond, Babette. Seventeen's Stories 1315
Ross, David P. Great Negroes Past and Present 1427
Ross, Marion. The Co-Ed Sewing Book 329
Rowe, Jeanne. City Workers 44
Ruben, Michael. Curse Not the Darkness 1389
Rudeen, Kenneth. Wilt Chamberlain 463
Ruiz, Ramón E. Out From Under 1509
Russell, Bill. Go Up for Glory 432
Russell, Charlie L. A Birthday Present for Katheryn
     Kenyatta 1267
Russell, Patrick. The Tommy Davis Story 460

Sadowsky, Ethel. Francois and the Langouste, a Story of
     Martinique 788
Sagara, Peter. Written on Film 1604

Smiley, Marjorie B.   Coping 605, A Family Is a Way of
      Feeling 605, Stories in Song and Verse 605, Who
      Am I? 605
Smith, Betty.   A Tree Grows in Brooklyn 930
Smith, Emmett.   A Foot in Two Worlds 1413, A Long Time
      Growing 1470, Meigs Tower 1486, Mission Possible
      1489, Nobody Promised Me 1505, You're on the Air 1609
Smith, Hugh.   Reflections on a Gift of Watermelon Pickle and
      Other Modern Verse 516
Smith, Robert.   Small World 618
Snyder, Anne.   Fifty Thousand Names for Jeff 885
Snyder, Zilpha Keatley.   The Egypt Game 883
Sobol, Donald J.   Encyclopedia Brown, Boy Detective 1148,
      Two Minute Mysteries 1176, The Wright Brothers at
      Kitty Hawk 1603
Sohn, David A.   Peppermint 1304
Sokol, Bill.   Lucky-Sew-It-Yourself Book 340
Sokol, Camille.   Lucky-Sew-It-Yourself Book 340
Sonneborn, Ruth A.   Friday Night Is Papa Night 731, The
      Lollipop Party 902, Seven in a Bed 1104
Sorensen, Virginia.   Plain Girl 1097
Speare, Morris E.   The Pocket Book of Verse 505
Spearing, Judith.   The Ghosts Who Went to School 998
Speevack, Yetta.   Spider Plant 772
Spencer, Philip.   Day of Glory 822
Sperry, Armstrong.   Call It Courage 535
Sprague, Jane.   Small World 618
Spyri, Johanna.   Heidi 890, Heidi to Read Aloud 891
Squire, James R.   Survival 621
Srivastava, Jane J.   Weighing and Balancing 310
Stallworth, Dave.   Look to the Light Side 449
Standerford, Betsy.   No Hablo Ingles 1504
Stanek, Muriel.   New in the City 1085, One, Two, Three
      for Fun 130
Stang, Judy.   Read-Aloud Mother Goose 515
Starks, Johneta.   Measure, Cut and Sew 342
Steele, William O.   Flaming Arrows 828, The Perilous
      Road 843
Stefferud, Alfred.   The Wonders of Seeds 318
Stein, R. Conrad.   Look to the Light Side 449, My Tribe
      1494, No Hablo Ingles 1504, People Are My Profes-
      sion 1512, The Road From West Virginia 1527, A
      World of Books 1601
Steinbeck, John.   The Pearl 917, The Red Pony 579
Steptoe, John.   Stevie 922, Train Ride 115, Uptown 55
Sterling, Dorothy.   Captain of the Planter: The Story of
      Robert Smalls 1375, Freedom Train 1420, Lift

Vandercock, John W.   Black Majesty, the Slave Who Became
    a King   1361
Van Peebles, Melvin.   Bear for the FBI   867
Van Zandt, Eleanor.   Hit Parade of Nurse Stories   629
Varga, Judith.   Who Lives Here?   78
Vasquez, J. C.   Lone Eagle, My Tribe   1494
Vavra, Robert.   Felipe the Bullfighter   65
Vecsey, George.   Baseball Life of Sandy Koufax   421, Har-
    lem Globe Trotters   436, Pro Basketball Champions
    453
Verral, Charles S.   Rocket Genius   1528
Victor, Edward.   Machines   341
Vinton, Iris.   Boy on the Mayflower   813, Look Out for
    Pirates   540, The Story of John Paul Jones   1557
Vogel, Ilse-Margret.   Hello Henry   947
Vogel, Ray.   The Other City   103
Vroman, Mary Elizabeth.   Harlem Summer   1280

Waber, Bernard.   The House on East 88th Street   1002,
    Just Like Abraham Lincoln   834, Lorenzo   1007,
    Loveable Lyle   1008, Lyle, Lyle, Crocodile   1009
Waddy, Ruth G.   Black Artists on Art   357
Wadsworth, L. A.   The Bamboo Key   1134, Puzzle of the
    Talking Monkey   1164
Wagner, Jane.   J T   895
Walden, Daniel.   On Being Black: Writings by Afro-
    Americans   1089
Waldman, Frank.   The Challenger   1216
Walker, Barbara.   The Dancing Palm Tree and Other
    Nigerian Folktales   656
Walker, Jerry L.   Favorite Pop-Rock Lyrics   481, Pop-
    Rock Lyrics 2   512, Pop-Rock Lyrics 3   513
Walker, Margaret.   Jubilee   833
Wallace, Lew.   Ben-Hur   807
Wallop, Douglas.   The Year the Yankees Lost the Pennant
    1264
Walter, Mildred Pitts.   Lillie of Watts   747
Walters, Hugh.   The First on the Moon   1182
Warner, Gertrude C.   Schoolhouse Mystery   1169
Washington, Booker T.   Up From Slavery   1587
Waters, Ethel.   His Eye Is on the Sparrow   1437
Watson, Jane Werner.   Dinosaurs   241, First Golden
    Geography   1411, My First Golden Encyclo-
    pedia   4
Watson, Willie Mae.   We Honor Them   1590
Watters, Mrs. Garnette.   Courtis--Watters Golden Illustrated

TITLE INDEX

A few titles are listed in more than one category. In such instances only the first number is cited. Where the title is followed by two numbers, one number will be found in the language category (4) and indicates that title is available in one or more foreign languages. In several instances, there are duplicate titles. For example Poems 506 and Poems 507 are two quite different books.

ABC: An Alphabet Book 123
ABC and Counting Book 124
Abe Lincoln Gets His Chance 1330
About Sex and Growing Up 8
Abraham Lincoln 1331
The Acid Nightmare 1131
Adventure Stories 530
Adventures in Space 225
The Adventures of George Washington 1332
The Adventures of Silly Billy 638
The Adventures of Spider 639
Adventures of the Greek Heroes 640
Adventures of the Negro Cowboys 1333
Aesop's Fables 863
The African 801
African Myths and Legends 641
Afro-American Artists-- New York and Boston 355
Against Time 1132
Air 226
Albert, The Albatross 936

Aleck Bell: Ingenious Boy 1334
Ali Baba and the Forty Thieves 642
Alice in Wonderland 968
Alice in Wonderland to Read Aloud 969
All About Us 227
All Except Sammy 864
All Kinds of Babies 228
All-Of-A-Kind Family 713
All-Scholastic Sports Stories 1207
Amazing Baseball Teams 414
The Amazing Mets 415
America and Its Presidents 1334
The American Heritage Dictionary 1
The American Heritage Dictionary (abbrev.) 2
American Negro Poetry 466
American Negro Short Stories 592
America's First Ladies 1865 to the Present Days 1336
Amos Fortune--Free Man 1337

478

Folk Plays for Puppets
You Can Make 134
The Follett Beginning
Science Series 252
Follow My Leader 886
Follow the Free Wind 829
Foods 332
A Foot in Two Worlds 1413
For Boys Only 1285
For Girls Only 1286
For Us, the Living 1414
The Forgotten Door 1183
Four Took Freedom 1415
François and the Langouste,
a Story of Martinique
788
Franklin Roosevelt, Boy of
the Four Freedoms 1416
Freddy, the Detective 995
Frederick Douglass Fights
for Freedom 1417
Frederick Douglass: Free-
dom Fighter 1418
Free as a Frog 887
Free Throw 1230
Freedom Bound 1419
Freedom Road 830
Freedom Train 1420
Friday Night Is Papa Night
731
From Plays into Reading
135
From the Back of the Bus
368
Fun With Scientific Experi-
ments 253
Funny Baby 151
The Funny Bone 604

Gang Girl 1287
Garbage Can Cat 1054
Gateway Series 605
Gentle Ben 560
George Carver, Boy
Scientist 1421
George Washington

Carver 1422
Georgie 996
Gertie the Duck 199, 561
Get Your Money's Worth
333
Ghandi--Fighter Without a
Sword 1423
A Ghost, a Witch and a
Goblin 663
Ghost Named Fred 997
The Ghosts Who Went to
School 998
The Gift of Black Folk 1424
The Gift of Christmas 606
Gilberto and the Wind 200,
387
Girl From Puerto Rico 1055
Go, Dog, Go 152
Go, Team, Go 1231
Go Tell It on the Mountain
888
Go Up for Glory 432
God Bless the Child 1056
God's Trombones: Seven
Negro Sermons in Verse
29
Going to Meet the Man 1057
The Golden Phoenix and
Other French-Canadian
Fairy Tales 664
Golden Press Paperbacks
254
Golden Shape Books 388
Golden Slippers 483
The Good Bird 153
The Good Drug and the Bad
Drug 350
The Good Earth 789
Good News for Modern Man
30
Gordon the Goat 946
Gracie 732
Graciela: A Mexican-Ameri-
can Child Tells Her Story
93
Grand Prix 1232
Grandpa's Wonderful Glass
255

BIOGRAPHICAL INDEX

There are three reasons why the reader will find many unfamiliar names in this index. First, many of the biographies in this list are of members of minority groups who have had to overcome extraordinary difficulties to survive and to become successful citizens. This makes them an inspiration to others in similar circumstances. It does not necessarily make them famous. The Open Door Series, a collection of thirty autobiographies, typifies this kind of book. Second, many of the people in this index were very famous in their day but are unfamiliar to a younger generation. Jesse Owens, a famous Olympic athlete, and Bessie Smith, a blues singer, typify this situation.

Third, the contribution of minority group members to their country has been omitted for many years from history texts and social studies books. When I find, as I constantly do, well-educated people who have never heard of such distinguished Americans as W. E. B. Dubois ("it seems to me I have heard that name--wasn't he a famous Communist?") and Frederick Douglass, it is inevitable that many other Americans who should be heroes to young people are unknown to them. Harriet Tubman, an escaped slave who had a distinguished career and became known as the "Moses" of her people, and Daniel Hale Williams, a black doctor who pioneered in heart surgery, typify this situation. It is hoped that the books in this bibliography will make these names familiar to many Americans.

An asterisk (*) in the following list denotes a book from the Open Door Series; a dagger (†) indicates a collective biography.

BOOKS OF INTEREST TO BLACKS

13, 17, 20, 27, 29, 39, 55, 56, 80, 81, 82, 83, 84,
85, 86, 87, 88, 89, 90, 91, 92, 95, 96, 97, 98, 99, 100,
101, 102, 103, 104, 105, 106, 108, 109, 110, 112, 113, 114,
115, 116, 117, 119, 120, 121, 135, 170, 171, 299, 303, 315,
325, 330, 339, 355, 357, 358, 361, 366, 367, 368, 373, 374,
378, 381, 382, 392, 397, 409, 422, 426, 427, 428, 430, 431,
432, 436, 440, 441, 442, 443, 444, 449, 451, 456, 458, 460,
461, 462, 463, 464, 465, 466, 470, 472, 478, 479, 483,
484, 488, 495, 498, 499, 502, 504, 508, 510, 519, 520,
521, 525, 568, 571, 577, 578, 580, 590, 592, 595, 596,
597, 598, 600, 605, 607, 610, 616, 623, 624, 625, 626,
627, 630, 631, 639, 641, 643, 648, 649, 654, 656, 661, 669,
672, 685, 715, 717, 718, 727, 730, 736, 739, 740, 746, 747,
754, 756, 757, 760, 762, 764, 767, 769, 773, 775, 780, 782,
783, 784, 785, 787, 788, 790, 794, 797, 801, 802, 803, 806,
810, 811, 814, 816, 817, 830, 833, 837, 838, 840, 846, 855,
858, 865, 867, 870, 871, 873, 875, 876, 878, 880, 883, 885,
888, 889, 894, 895, 897, 900, 903, 904, 906, 907, 911, 916,
920, 921, 922, 923, 924, 925, 931, 932, 934, 935, 938, 961,
1005, 1026, 1028, 1031, 1035, 1037, 1038, 1040, 1043, 1044,
1045, 1046, 1047, 1049, 1052, 1056, 1057, 1059, 1060, 1061,
1062, 1063, 1066, 1068, 1069, 1071, 1072, 1073, 1074, 1075,
1076, 1077, 1078, 1079, 1084, 1086, 1087, 1088, 1089, 1090,
1099, 1105, 1106, 1107, 1109, 1110, 1112, 1113, 1114, 1116,
1119, 1123, 1126, 1133, 1145, 1149, 1150, 1153, 1154, 1155,
1158, 1161, 1165, 1166, 1167, 1168, 1173, 1174, 1202, 1208,
1218, 1221, 1225, 1230, 1231, 1234, 1236, 1239, 1245, 1256,
1258, 1265, 1267, 1269, 1273, 1287, 1289, 1292, 1296, 1298,
1316, 1318, 1320, 1333, 1337, 1345, 1346, 1347, 1348, 1353,
1355, 1356, 1357, 1358, 1359, 1360, 1361, 1362, 1363, 1364,
1365, 1366, 1368, 1369, 1371, 1372, 1374, 1375, 1376, 1378,
1381, 1383, 1385, 1386, 1387, 1389, 1390, 1391, 1395, 1397,
1402, 1403, 1405, 1406, 1407, 1409, 1410, 1414, 1415, 1417,
1418, 1419, 1420, 1421, 1422, 1424, 1427, 1428, 1430, 1431,
1434, 1435, 1436, 1437, 1439, 1441, 1443, 1445, 1447, 1448,
1449, 1450, 1460, 1462, 1464, 1465, 1467, 1468, 1469, 1472,
1473, 1474, 1475, 1477, 1479, 1480, 1481, 1482, 1483, 1486,

1489, 1490, 1491, 1492, 1495, 1496, 1497, 1498, 1499, 1500,
1502, 1503, 1505, 1506, 1507, 1508, 1512, 1513, 1514, 1515,
1516, 1518, 1519, 1526, 1529, 1530, 1531, 1534, 1535, 1536,
1537, 1538, 1539, 1540, 1541, 1543, 1545, 1547, 1548, 1551,
1559, 1562, 1565, 1566, 1568, 1569, 1570, 1571, 1572, 1573,
1576, 1577, 1578, 1579, 1580, 1581, 1582, 1583, 1584, 1587,
1588, 1590, 1591, 1592, 1593, 1594, 1595, 1600, 1602, 1605,
1607, 1609.

BOOKS OF INTEREST TO CHICANOS

65, 93, 111, 200, 387, 484, 610, 625, 714, 759, 786,
793, 857, 869, 915, 917, 1080, 1095, 1100, 1117, 1118, 1124,
1127, 1161, 1215, 1218, 1224, 1252, 1271, 1273, 1399, 1487,
1504, 1508, 1509, 1586.

BOOKS OF INTEREST TO ORIENTALS

68, 69, 477, 484, 492, 573, 652, 655, 662, 674, 679,
691, 696, 753, 755, 771, 774, 781, 789, 791, 796, 831, 872,
879, 883, 1129, 1151, 1377, 1380, 1423, 1508, 1511, 1604.

BOOKS OF INTEREST TO AMERICAN INDIANS

67, 69, 446, 447, 484, 567, 610, 625, 670, 749, 825,
828, 829, 1051, 1091, 1124, 1127, 1429, 1494, 1504, 1508,
1544, 1546, 1586.

BOOKS OF INTEREST TO PUERTO RICANS

36, 65, 70, 91, 94, 118, 170, 171, 200, 213, 219,
220, 315, 385, 392, 430, 450, 484, 610, 623, 625, 673, 684,
706, 730, 731, 741, 743, 752, 759, 761, 765, 768, 770, 772,
777, 783, 865, 878, 902, 908, 929, 931, 933, 999, 1017,
1042, 1048, 1050, 1053, 1054, 1055, 1064, 1065, 1067, 1081,

1082, 1083, 1098, 1103, 1104, 1115, 1117, 1120, 1122, 1172,
1202, 1211, 1219, 1220, 1270, 1277, 1287, 1327, 1374, 1396,
1398, 1413, 1452, 1470, 1508, 1520, 1522.